GLIMPSES IN THE TWILIGHT

TWILIGHT

True-Life Ghost Stories And Modern-Day Urban Legends
From The Haunted Heart Of Merseyside
By Lee Walker

Original Photography: Lee Walker, Tony Barr, Yve Pritchard,
Grant Walker & Stevie Gee
Contributors: Dave Shirley, Billy Butler (*BBC Radio Merseyside*)
Edited by Jonathan DownesTypeset by Jonathan Downes,
Andrea Rider, Jessica Taylor
Cover and Layout by SPiderKaT for CFZ Communications
Using Microsoft Word 2000, Microsoft Publisher 2000, Adobe Photoshop CS.

First published in Great Britain by CFZ Press

CFZ Press
Myrtle Cottage
Woolsery
Bideford
North Devon
EX39 5QR

THE CENTRE FOR FORTEAN ZOOLOGY
www.cfz.org.uk

ISBN: 978-1-909488-34-2

This one's for Mum & Dad. Their love and unstinting support, a beacon in the very darkest of times. For Yvey, the light who shines along the path to fabulous, bright dreams... And for The 96 and the Survivors YNWA

INTRODUCTION:
'THE FINAL HOUR OF THE SUMMER PARTY'

'And now the summer is over,
I close my eyes and pray,
That I'll return on wings of wonder,
To this place some day...'
The Nearest Far Away Place - The Lids

ONE:

The suggestion that I should write this book was first mooted in decidedly less-than auspicious circumstances.

It was the last day of a week-long break in not-so-sunny Devon, and the British weather was suffering from yet another spell of temporary meteorological amnesia, forgetting it was supposed to be summer and substituting the fabled Dog Days of August for the drizzle-laden chill of mid-January. Fortunately, we Merseysiders are well used to glowering skies, cold, stinging rain and madly shrieking gales no matter the season, and when my then-girlfriend, her three children and I had made the decision to drive out to 'The Dinosaur & Wildlife Adventure Park', situated just outside the charmingly picturesque town of Ilfracombe, nothing short of a deluge of Biblical proportions was going to prevent us making the trip.

The glossy, colourful brochure had promised a huge and enticing variety of attractions, and never mind if the majority of these were located outdoors. We were determined to end the holiday on a high, and it beat the alternative of sitting cooped up in the caravan, playing endless games of *Jenga* or murdering classic rock and pop tunes on the portable, tinny-as-hell Karaoke machine, whilst the rain battered ceaselessly at the windows. Well I'd thought it did, anyway. The others had been a little harder to convince.

'Come 'ead, everyone,' I'd said, pumping my fist to drum up enthusiasm. 'Who wants to go and see some dinosaurs?'

If I'd been expecting whoops and cheers, I was sorely disappointed. In fact, the response had been as decidedly underwhelming as if I'd suggested we embark on a five-mile hike through the woods with a healthy packed lunch whilst (gasp!) leaving our mobile phones, iPads and other electronic devices behind.

For the best part of the morning I tried to persuade the three kids, my ex-girlfriend and her dyed-in-the-wool, Mancunian dad, that we really shouldn't waste the opportunity to visit the park, but as noon fast approached, it appeared all my efforts had been in vain, and so I'd been left with very little option than to play my final card...

I resorted to shameless bribery.

'Okay, I tell yer what,' I suddenly announced whilst jumping to my feet, an act which caused the caravan to wobble slightly, and the youngest of the children to start wailing hysterically, 'If yous all agree to go get in the car and 'ead off with me now, it's Macky D Happy Meals all round for tea.' I paused for effect. 'Every single day next week!'

There was a moment of stunned silence. Even the three-year-old's bawling quietened to sobs having digested these miraculous tidings. It took just five minutes for the family to get changed and take their seats in the Renault Megane, (record time for all concerned) and before long we were driving along the slick and puddle-strewn roads towards Ilfracombe, sending sheets of spray whooshing wave-like in our wake.

TWO:

We arrived at the park a little after midday, and actually heard the earth-shaking roar of the 'prehistoric monsters', long before we actually got to see them, in the flesh, so to speak. They were hidden from view by the thick row of swaying tree-tops that lined the entrance, and when they finally did loom into view, we were disappointed to discover the impressive collection of life-sized animatronic creatures were completely motionless. According to the sign on the electrified, *Jurassic Park*-style fence, they were in 'sleep mode', and only dramatically burst into life on the chiming of the hour, and we'd just missed the latest show.

Following a brief family discussion, which in actuality was more of a heated shouting match won, inevitably, by he who yells loudest, which in this case proved to be Tony the Manc, it was decided that we may as well explore the rest of the park, and return later for the 'Resurrection of the Dinosaurs'.

The large, sprawling gardens, though undeniably beautiful, were bathed in a drab, sickly light, and due to the terrible weather, the place was deserted save for ourselves. There was no surprise in that. The incessant rain; the kind of drenching, insidious drizzle that somehow manages to trickle down the back of your neck and soak your entire body, despite the all-weather clothing manufacturer's confident claim that their garments were 'totally precipitation proof', was enough to put most people off walking anywhere out of doors. Least of all, a wildlife park, where most of the animals seemed to be as every bit as low-spiritedly miserable as the dank and dismal conditions.

We stubbornly tried to make the best of it, but I think each of us knew in our heart of hearts that all we were really doing was fighting a rain-sodden, losing battle against the elements. There was something utterly dispiriting about traipsing past saturated cages and muddy enclosures, filled with assorted bedraggled-looking lemurs and monkeys, wolves and meerkats, wallabies and kangaroos. Even the resident lions appeared doe-eyed and forlorn, as desperate as a platoon of British Tommy's about to go over the top amidst the muddy hell of the Somme.

The overwhelming temptation, I have to admit, was to head back to the comparative warmth of the car, attempt to dry off, and then maybe head for the nearest pub for a couple of revivifying drinks and a hot meal, (not a Macky D's yet, though – that 'gastronomic delight' awaited later in the evening), and I'm sure we would have done just that if it hadn't been for the dinosaurs. Those reassuringly familiar companions from the halcyon days of childhood, their names and appearance as well-known to me as any species of modern-day domesticated animal, had, not for the first time in my life, come charging to the rescue, fiercely intent upon tearing the cloak of disillusionment asunder.

And so here we were at last, right back where we'd started. Standing in the midst of a virtual monsoon before the impressively towering Tyrannosaurus, an equally convincing Triceratops, a couple of mean-looking Velociraptors and a strange creature, considerably smaller than the others, that I couldn't readily identify and which looked to me to be as out of place as the waddling armadillo, mooching around (for no particular reason), the crypt of Universal's 1931 version of *Castle Dracula*, poised at the edge of the 'electrified fence'. They each took turns to slowly twitch and jerk into bellowing, shrieking life, and whilst they didn't actually move around too much, they at least gave the impression they were more than capable of breaking free from the compound at any given moment.

Strangely though, it was that relatively diminutive dinosaur, the one I strongly suspected might well have been nothing but the product of its creator's imagination, that quickly proved to be the star of the show. And this it did by virtue of exhibiting its secret weapon:

Without warning its jaw suddenly dropped open to emit jets of ice-cold water all over our already thoroughly saturated bodies. You could be forgiven for thinking that this sounds very much like the crowning absurdity at the end of a seemingly endless, deluge-stricken day, and yet I found the experience to be oddly exhilarating, and I was unable to suppress a grin, and when I turned to look at the kids I saw they were grinning too, and I felt my spirits soar like I'd just caught the briefest glimpse of the sun slipping below the rain-clouded horizon.

*****

'I'm feeling...
In a shaky frame of mind,
The look on my face...
This is like a new beginning...'

Colourless Dream – Sad Lovers And Giants

(Photo credit: Tony Barr)

CHAPTER ONE
BENEATH THE LAST SLICE OF AN AUGUST RAINBOW

An Encounter With Jon Downes of the CFZ

Later that same evening, Tony and I arrived in the tiny village of Woolfardisworthy, searching for the home address of the estimable Jon Downes, head of the Centre for Fortean Zoology, renowned author, publisher, researcher, bass guitarist, and self-confessed anarchist-hippie.

Oh, and he also happens to be one of the nicest people you could ever hope to meet. And this is not just my admittedly, slightly biased, opinion.

When I called in at the village post office and general store, to ask the lovely, forty-something woman stood behind the counter, whether she happened to know where Mr Jon Downes lived, her face instantly lit up with a big, beaming smile and she insisted upon not only giving me directions to his house, but accompanying me the couple of hundred yards or so down the road to the very entrance of Jon's front garden.

'Myrtle Cottage' the sign on the tiny wooden gate announced, and having offered my sincere thanks to the post office lady, she smiled again and told me I was 'very welcome'. I lifted the latch, and with Tony following close behind, began making my way up the garden path.

As we did so, for a wonder, the rain finally ceased cascading down and the early evening sun was shining in golden lances between the gaps in the trees and the borders of thick hedgerow. Where its bright rays caressed the lawn, the grass sparkled like glistening jewels, and the air smelled of newness and the pungent aroma of sweet, late summer flowers.

And almost immediately, there was Jon sat at a desk in his office, all but buried beneath stacks of jumbled paperwork, his heavily-bearded face the only part of him that was visible, though still instantly recognisable from the first time I'd made his acquaintance three years earlier, illuminated by the pale glow of a computer screen.

'Come on in, come on in!' he yelled excitedly, the second he set eyes upon us.

'The door's not locked.'

We entered Jon's 'study', and were immediately confronted with a senses-assaulting mass of paraphernalia; there were several well-maintained fish tanks containing various species of tropical fish and giant sea snails, a large selection of suitably obscure cask ales, the vast majority of which had been completely drained, huge piles of newspaper cuttings, some of which were yellowed with age, and haphazardly assembled stacks of CDs featuring the likes of Crass, David Bowie, and Big in Japan.

Meanwhile, every available inch of wall space was lined with shelves that literally groaned under the combined weight of assorted books and magazines. They were arranged in no particular order, but even the briefest of glances revealed that the collection was mostly made up of journals and volumes about natural history and cryptozoology.

'It's lovely to see you both,' Jon exclaimed with a theatrical flourish as he spun round in his swivel chair.

'The bona fide word-smith Mr Walker, and his even more venerable companion, Mr Tony Barr esquire, as I live and breathe. Welcome to you both. Corinna, dear,' he said to his wife via an intercom device. 'Could we possibly rustle up some liquid refreshment for our two esteemed guests, Lee and Tony?'

He paused for a second and asked us out of the side of his mouth; 'What's it to be, gents? Tea, coffee, or something a tad stronger?'

'Actually, Jon, it's very kind of you,' I replied, 'but can you tell Corinna we can't stay long. We've just come to say a quick goodbye. The missus and the kids are waiting for us back at the caravan.' I rolled my eyes in an exaggerated 'well-really-what-can-you-do?' gesture.

'It's the last night of our holiday, yer see, and they wanna go out for a meal and a couple of farewell to Devon drinks.'

'Oh, now that is truly a great pity,' Jon replied, and I could see in his eyes that he was being completely sincere.

'I was hoping you could bring the whole family round for supper. I'd love to meet the kids. I've always found the wonder-filled worlds of children to be so much more interesting than the hard-headed, material realms of adulthood.'

'Is right, Jon,' I said. 'I totally agree with yer. It's like that old Robert R. McCammon, line about how, as soon as we leave our childhood behind we get the magic educated right out of our souls, or that famous Sid Vicious quote about 'you can be ninety-nine and still be a kid!''

'Which definitely applies to Peter Pan, here,' Tony sniggered, pointing at me, and shaking his head wonderingly, 'I've got a seven-year-old grandson who acts with more maturity than him, at times!'

Jon laughed loud and long at that one, and I turned to Tony, intent on thinking up some witty response, but couldn't think of anything remotely amusing, and decided I was better off simply agreeing with him. It was the God's honest truth, after all. I mean, how many other grown men do you know who still shed a tear or two when Kong falls from the top of the Empire State Building? Or who whoops with barely restrained joy just because his nieces bought him a Jack Skellington model for Christmas, last year? Or who can truly consider the highlight of his summer holiday to be the standing face to face with a collection of plastic-coated dinosaurs.

As if reading my mind, Tony, purveyor of the killer put-down, chose that moment to deliver another of his kick-in-the-plods insults; 'Yer know what, Jon. I caught soft lad, here, standing there in the pissing rain today, grinning from ear to ear, like a prize gob-a-loon, all because a tiny, robotic prehistoric monster spat water smack in his face! Can you friggin' believe that?'

That got Jon going again, and this time he laughed so hard he very nearly fell from his swivelly chair to collapse in a giggling heap on the floor of his study. Unable to drum up a half-way amusing response once more, I just stood there shrugging my shoulders, with a wry smile on my face, waiting patiently until they were all laughed out, which seemed to me to take an unreasonably long time.

In fact, it was only when I made a big show of checking the clock on my mobile, and muttered that we'd better start making a move, that they managed to regain enough of their self-control to continue the conversation.

'Oh, I'm so sorry, Lee,' Jon said dabbing at the corners of his eyes with a hankie, 'I don't mean to be cruel. I'm sure Tony doesn't, either.'

'Oh aye,' Tony said. 'It's a back-handed compliment.' He considered this for a second, and then added; 'Well, *kind* of.'

'There you go,' said Jon, as if some great and immutable truth had been imparted. 'And anyway, I think you should actually thank, Tony, for two things.'

'And what are they, Jon?' I asked.

'Well, firstly, as I can state from experience, being a father-in-law myself, it's our prerogative to keep our daughter's boyfriend's on their toes. We don't want them getting complacent or too big for their boots. Am I right, Mr Barr?'

'Spot on, Mr Downes,' Tony snapped back smartly.

'There you go. You see, Lee. He's actually doing you a favour!'

'Nice one,' I replied, derisively. 'And what's the second thing I should be *thankful* for?'

"The second thing is, by mentioning dinosaurs, Tony has inadvertently served to remind me that there was a question I wanted to ask you."

'What's that, Jon?' I sighed. 'Do I wanna embark on an expedition to deepest, darkest Africa, in search of the "Water-Spitting Monster of The Congo?" At the height of the rainy season? Yer know, just for added chuckles, like. Or maybe, would I enjoy presenting a Power-Point lecture describing the countless, saturated, drizzle-filled joys to be found at "Devon's Dinosaur & Wildlife Adventure Park"?'

'Not *quite,*' Jon said. 'I was wondering, having recently read your article on the "Giant Crabs of West Kirby", in one of your old and crumpled back issues of *Dead of Night* magazine, whether you would you be interested in writing a follow-up to your first published book, but perhaps with a more cryptozoological slant, this time around?'

'Oh, right,' I said, swallowing a sudden click in my throat. 'Well, er, of course, that would be totally boss. I mean, if you're really sure you want me to, like.'

'Don't be so immodest, Walker,' he said, sounding for all the world like my old school headmaster. 'You are a writer blessed with at least a *semblance* of talent. Of course I would like you to write it, you silly sod!'

As much as I think of Jon, (and it's fair to say I think a great deal of him), if I were a medical man, it's highly unlikely I would ever have cause to diagnose him as suffering from extreme distension of the hyperbole gland. Nevertheless, I felt honoured by the 'praise', not least, of course, because I am currently an entire solar system away from anything resembling household-name status as an author.

'One more thing, before you go,' Jon said, catching Tony sneakily glancing at his watch. 'I want you to write it in your own, usual highly irreverent style. There's nothing wrong with most of our other author's penning meticulously researched, highly literate, fully cross-referenced case studies. There'll always be a market for that type of book. And at the risk of sounding like an extra in some cheesy, 1950s, science fiction epic, may it always be so!'

He paused, and as he did so, a single ray of gilt-edged sunlight slanted through the dusty windows, as a blackbird's plaintive song; "a symphony for the day's expectant dawn, and the evening's weary, but contented unwinding," as my beloved Auntie Anne used to say, back when we were kids, floated melodically on the late summer air.

'I know how it is with certain writers, Walker,' he said, and now his voice had turned a shade more sympathetic.

'Writers who are either blessed or cursed with the ability to dream. They're the type who find that simple anecdotes, no matter how fascinating, aren't enough, in and of themselves. They have to dig a little deeper. Elaborate. Expound. And whilst they strive, like all true, open-minded Forteans, to stick to the bare facts, adhere to the hard proofs, still they find that all too often, despite, or maybe *because* of, the ephemeral nature of the reports of what we term, for want of a better phrase: 'The Paranormal,' the stories have an alarming propensity to tumble out of stories, like an uncontrollable flood of Russian dolls.'

Jon looked me in the eye, 'Write me that type of book, Lee, and you never know, we might just have a half-decent little read on our hands.'

He smiled, and I saw, just for the briefest of moments, how Jon had looked as a young man, barely out of his teens, the decades falling away, like a filmic representation of the years flying backwards, the flimsy pages of a calendar caught in the grip of a wild, time-eroding gale. And after we'd shook hands and said our goodbyes, and stepped out into the sweet, rain-washed summer light, I found myself offering up a silent thanks to the dinosaurs once more, my prehistoric saviours and the source of eternal inspiration...

> Lee Walker,
> Toxteth,
> Liverpool 8

CAVEAT EMPTOR....
Or What This book is Most Avowedly NOT

Just before we get started, may I please crave your indulgence for a just a little while longer?

I feel, given this book's controversial subject matter, and the inevitable criticisms that will come flying my way like a hail of fire-tipped arrows launched from the ramparts of some Tolkien-esque fortification - Helm's Deep, say - it's necessary to point out that this work is not intended to be an academic treatise on the reality or otherwise, of 'The Paranormal,' a scientific study of 'The Unknown,' a cold, clinical catalogue of strange occurrences, or an overly-sceptical laugh-riot at the naive gullibility of people who claim to have experienced something they can't rationally explain.

Nor, I might add, is it intended to be any sort of "shove-my-beliefs-down-yer-throat Gospel According to Lee Walker".

I don't claim to be any sort of 'expert' on 'The Unexplained.' I don't subscribe to any particular belief system, and I'm not a paranormal investigator, per se, though I enjoy a good 'ghost hunt' as much for the camaraderie, and a few cold beers in the alehouse afterwards, to be honest.

This book is simply a collection of modern-day examples of urban folklore, supposedly true-life ghost stories and encounters with all manner of types of 'Fortean Phenomena,' related to me by apparently sincere witnesses, including in some cases, the experiences of my own family members and several close friends.

There is very little in the way of hard evidence for the objective reality of the majority of the experiences recounted in these pages. Much of what follows is purely anecdotal, and the same applies to the sources of the information acquired, although where possible, I have made reference to any relevant newspaper or magazine articles, radio stations, etc.

It seems to me, though, that the real reason Jon Downes asked me to write this book, and the reason I readily agreed, is because I am as fascinated with the often ordinary lives of the people who claim to have encountered the strange and the seemingly inexplicable, and the honest verve with which they relate their stories, as I am by the phenomena they describe.

Someone once said; 'It's the teller, not the tale'. And within these pages, I would humbly contend, you'll find ample proof of that.

Oh, and one more thing. There will be people out there, not all of them cold-hearted cynics, who will cast doubt on the veracity of some or all of these stories. That's fine, That's their prerogative. I would merely like to remind the justifiably sceptical (extraordinary claims require extraordinary proof, and all that), that my sole intention here is to record the unusual experiences of a handful of witnesses, and hopefully entertain in the process. I make no excuses then for quoting that famous line from John Ford's classic Western, Who Shot Liberty Valance?

'When you have to choose between truth and the legend, print the legend.'

Here then is a collection of printed (urban) legends....

CHAPTER TWO:
THE GREAT WHISTLING EMPTINESS IN THE ABSENCE OF WONDER

'One cold, damp evening, the world stood still...
I watched as I held my breath....'

***Second Skin* - The Chameleons**

Photo Credit: Stevie Gee

Here's a classic paradox for you.

Whenever I find myself struck by the dreaded curse of Writer's Block, I draw upon an experience that left me speechless and heart-sick, and suffering from a veritable crisis of faith, for wordy inspiration.

Last summer, for very probably the first time in my life, my faith in that oft-quoted Shakespearean maxim; *There are more things in heaven and earth, Horatio, than are dreamt of in your philosophy*, had been not so much shaken, as pummelled out of me by a lunatic, hooked on PCP, and armed with a jack-hammer.

Or a fiercely intelligent man, with a degree in biology who also happens to be one of my very best friends.

ONE

I had somehow gotten myself involved in one of those intensely deep, philosophical debates, (the sort I only ever seem to find remotely appealing during a long walk home from the alehouse in the early hours of a midsummer morning, after having sunk the equivalent of an entire barrel of 'Oak Wobbly Bob'*), w*ith Mikey, or *Doctor* Michael Ward, PhD, to give him his full and richly deserved title.

After having succeeded in putting the North Korean nuclear crisis to rights, jointly solving the myriad problems of The Middle East, and dreaming up a foolproof plan aimed at getting the scum-bag Tory party out of power, the good Doctor and I, turned to the comparatively simple theory of Darwinian Evolution.

As you do.

In truth, this actually wasn't much of a debate.

Mikey, who had graduated from St Andrew's University in Aberdeen, with a PhD in marine biology, back in the late 1990s, plainly knew his stuff, whilst my sole qualification regarding the subject amounted to little more than reading the blurb on the inside cover of *On The Origin of Species.* Besides, and rather fortunately for me, I'd found myself agreeing with nearly everything my friend had to say on the subject.

I'd never really been much of a fan of Creationism, not even during my long-ago schooldays, when it was considered perfectly okay to believe in everything and anything. It's fair to say though, that I've always found it hard to shake the notion that there may well be some kind of benign force, somewhere 'out there' in 'The Great Beyond', (and by definition, a horribly malignant counterpart, too: something born with the blank, emotionless face of a mass serial killer, or the flinty-eyed vileness of a politician or authority figure, the kind who quite happily besmirches the innocent to save their own skin, if the occasion arises), but we're getting a little ahead of ourselves, here.

To return to that mid-summer, three-quarters drunk discussion, Mikey, in a slightly slurry voice, was busy educating me about how Mr Darwin had theorised that mankind, after having descended from the apes, thereby *losing their special status as beings created by an omnipotent God,* had developed intelligence by means of 'natural selection', and somewhere along the way, mankind had become cognizant of its own mortality, the thoroughly demoralising realisation that death was the ultimate fate of each and every member of the species.

And hot on the heels of that less than cheery consequence of our unique sense of awareness, a need to believe in the soul's survival, probably because, as Mikey put it, 'It would have been such a harsh truth to face; the sure and certain knowledge that our days here on Earth are strictly numbered, whilst every other species, so far as we know, anyway, blithely goes around eating, drinking, and shagging, like there was no tomorrow, because they have no concept of the passing of time, or the relentless ticking of the body clock.'

'Well, that sounds like a totally boss way to live your life, to me' I'd said, rubbing my chin thoughtfully, in what I'd hoped was a rough approximation of a learned college tutor, though, in all likelihood, I'd probably looked more like what I actually was: a gormless, drunken idiot, idly scratching his itchy jaw-stubble, for want of a half-way decent shave.

'But if that's really the case,' I'd added, 'it still doesn't explain why we developed the capacity to wonder. To actively consider our place in the grand scheme of things, and acquire a sense of er, watchamacallit call it, "spirituality"?'

'I wasn't aware that *you* had acquired those highly commendable attributes,' Mikey sniggered, and seeing the hurt expression on my face, added quickly: 'I thought I'd already explained all that clearly, like, but I suppose it is kind of complex.'

'Well, yeah,' I'd agreed, struggling to stifle a beer-induced burp. 'I'm half-shot, lad, and you are talking to someone who hasn't got a PhD. Well, not unless those initials stand for "Pathetically Hopeless Dimwit"!'

Mikey chuckled again before stroking his own chin, and I guess all those years spent studying at various universities not only provided the insufferably brainy with a fancy qualification, they also taught you how to appear every bit as professorial as Albus Dumblemore, even without the elaborate robes, wispy white hair and bushy beard. 'I suppose what I'm trying to say is this,' Mikey said, and I could see, even in my tipsy state that he was choosing his words carefully. 'We humans developed a whole stack of beliefs in things that perhaps don't truly exist, for two reasons:

'Firstly, our creative faculties have provided us with the inspiration to look up at the stars, gaze across the wide expanse of oceans, consider the summit of the tallest, mist-shrouded mountains or the depths of tropical rainforests, and allow our limitless imaginations to run wild. And without the retention of our child-like sense of wonder, that inherent ability to dream, we would never have been blessed with any of the world's great writers, composers, song-writers, film-makers or philosophers. No Hitchcock or Beethoven, Dickens or Camus, no Lennon or McCartney. Not even another of Lee Walker's, everwafflin' paranormal books, if you can imagine *that*!

'And secondly, that sense of "spirituality", you referred to earlier? It's just my opinion like, but I honestly think we humans developed the sensation of ethereal otherness, because it provides us with a strict moral code, a set of rules that clearly denotes right from wrong, good from evil, and a belief in a higher authority than man, to ensure we lived these set-in-stone "Commandments," if you like, without which, civilised society would almost certainly collapse like the proverbial deck of cards, assuming it had ever gotten started in the first place.'

'Okay, okay, well done, mate. I've got the picture!' I said. And I truly *had*. This made perfect logical sense, even to a non-college educated, wannabe writer like me.

But nevertheless, as we lapsed into something resembling thoughtful silence for a moment, I desperately tried to come up with something, *anything*, to punch a fist-sized hole in his well-constructed hypothesis.

And you can call me Mr Unimaginative, (though yer can form an orderly queue behind Dr Mikey, if you feel compelled to do so. He's at least *earned* the right) but I couldn't think of a single thing that would inflict the merest scratch in the structure of his theory. Let alone anything resembling a gaping fissure.

'The thing is, Lee,' Mike continued, as if determined to twist the knife in, 'all that stuff you waffle on about on the Radio Merseyside, can be dismissed with a contemptuous wave of the hand...

'Ghosts? A shit-scared refusal to accept that death is the end.

'Monsters? An inherited trait to create magic out of the mind-numbingly mundane.

'UFOs and Aliens? An evolutionary need to believe in superior beings.

'The same with Angels, Faeries, Demons.

'And yes,' he finished with an arm-raising flourish, 'Even the Great God Almighty, Himself!'

I glanced briefly at my friend, feeling thoroughly deflated and wishing like hell we'd never broached the subject. The thing is, I'm not saying for one single minute, Mikey *(Doctor Mikey, if yer please)*, had *all* the answers. To be fair, I'm sure he would never be so conceited as to even attempt to make such outrageous a claim.

But it seemed he had drummed up a fair few of them. Answers, that is...

I've got to be honest, along with delivering several faith-bothering dagger blows deep into the very kernel of cherished belief, the good doctor's, "reality check", put a complete and utter dampener on what had been, up to that point, a fairly decent night out. When I finally got home, I slammed the front door shut behind me, went straight upstairs, turned on the bedroom lights, and greeted my eternally grinning "Garfield" stuffed toy, a supposedly 'good luck mascot', sat on the edge of the bed, with a British Lions-style rugby drop kick.

Sometimes, having the harsh, bitter "truths" spelled out in seemingly inarguable terms can have that effect on me…

TWO

Remember what I said earlier about paradoxes, though?

Only a few short days after I'd been subjected to my friend's road from the alehouse conversion to the ranks of the "Hard Headed Realist Brigade", I nonetheless made the conscious decision to subject myself to the often thankless task of whiling away hours sat at the computer, incurring spates of acute backache, severe eye-strain and the not inconsiderable wrath of my girlfriend as I burned the midnight oil, armed with nothing more than a stack of handwritten notes, printed-off emails, USB sticks crammed with digital photographs, and a head filled with stories related by seemingly genuine, perfectly ordinary people, who claimed to have undergone decidedly *extra-ordinary* experiences…

We live in increasingly cynical times, it seems. But sometimes, just when it appears as though my "faith", in the what is loosely termed as "The Supernatural", is being sorely tested by logic and rationale, along comes something that makes me think that perhaps science doesn't have all the answers just yet. Consider the following, for example….

CHAPTER THREE
THE SILENT, SMILING
WATCHERS:
A New Liverpool Urban Legend

ONE

It was Dave Shirley, an experienced paranormal investigator, with an admirable sense of humour and a healthy dose of scepticism, who first told me about the horrors that have since haunted my dreams like the dark, prancing silhouettes that hover on the periphery of morning memory.

They've been "with me" ever since, the Silent, Smiling Watchers.

Though I wish to God they weren't.

Let me tell you how they came, unbidden, into my life.

And pray hard they never come into yours.

A humid, sultry evening in late September.

A Sunday.

A mere three weeks after my fascinating, if ultimately depressing conversation with Dr Mikey, I was standing in the twilit beer garden of *The Bromborough Hotel,* a large pub over on the Wirral, beneath heavy, overcast skies. I'd made the relatively short journey from Liverpool, to meet up with Richie White, an old friend I hadn't seen for nearly 15 years, and the aforementioned Mr Shirley, (and before any wannabe comedian pipes up, rest assured, he's heard all the tired old *Airplane* jokes related to his surname, thanks all the same), whose acquaintance I was making for the first time, having only ever corresponded with him via e-mails prior to this occasion.

The weather was that weird, curious juxtaposition of seasons, peculiar to these islands. It was unbearably close and late summer-hot, and yet at the same time, strangely autumnal. There was the faintest whiff of wood-smoke drifting from a bonfire, hidden behind the thick screen of trees; oaks and sycamores, mostly, that lined the right-hand side of the beer garden, where bats flitted and small, night creatures rustled invisibly. The bells of the St Barnabas Church clock tower chimed sweetly in the dead, oppressive air, and there was an indefinable sense of wanderlust, the unspoken compulsion that bids you to don your totally unflattering but thoroughly essential waterproofs, before determinedly stomping along the road *that leads forever on and on.*

We three were the only ones standing outside this evening, nursing our drinks, whilst gathered around one of the multiple wooden benches, although the bar itself was fairly busy with the usual crew of last-day-of-the-weekend drinkers, desperately trying to hold the grim inevitability of Monday morning at bay with a frothing pint of ale, or a Bacardi and Coke, and a defiantly wide-eyed stare at the sixty-inch plasma TV screens showing the darts or the highlights of the afternoon's footy, whilst the most recent Kings Of Leon album played on endless repeat on the pub's bass-heavy sound system.

It was so humid I could almost visualise the beer squirting out of my pores faster than I could drink it in, like Bugs Bunny downing a glass of water after he's just been peppered full of holes by a direct hit from Yosemite Sam's still-smoking twelve-bore. Nevertheless, we engaged in a passionate three-way chat about everything and anything, from Liverpool and Everton's prospects for the new season to the current state of horror cinema, and to the wonders and horrors of Internet Dating, and somewhere amidst the incessant, back and forth conversation, the sort that flows freely like a burbling brook swollen by a heavy summer shower, the subject of local urban legends came up…

TWO

'Okay, now here's something!' Dave had suddenly announced with a flourish, and it was easy to imagine those four simple words being delivered in the sensationalistic tones of a carnival huckster. The sort who sets about beseeching the passers-by at a travelling funfair to "Roll up, Roll Up! Come and see the unique attractions! This is a once in a lifetime opportunity, ladies and gentlemen! Once seen, never forgotten. They will haunt the winding corridors of your memory, forever! I apple-solutely guarantee it!"

I'd only met Dave a couple of hours earlier, but I think I knew in my heart already that he was no mere sideshow pedlar, no desperate purveyor of the grotesque, simply for the sheer, "You cross my palm with silver (or crumpled bank notes, preferably), and I'll tell you some scary stories, that I just know will render you sleepless!" He was genuine. The type of open-minded agnostic who simply enjoyed sharing tales of the apparently inexplicable.

'Have either of you ever heard of "The Watchers?" he asked, and before I could drum up an answer, in my mind's eye I was struck by a vivid image of 'The Watchers' of Biblical lore. The Grigori, the stony-faced sentinels who looked down from on high and witnessed the affairs of ordinary mortals and reported back to their superior, the vengeful and unforgiving God of the Old Testament: like the school prefects snitching on the miscreants who were caught smoking in the toilets or copping a feel of a teenage girl's breasts behind the bike sheds.

And hot on the heels of that charming little vignette, came another: A spray-painted line of graffiti spelling out the hugely pertinent question, in these "Big Brother", twenty-four-hour CCTV surveillance obsessed times: ***Who Watches The Watchers?***

But thankfully, before I could ponder that great imponderable, Dave was telling Richie and me about his days as a Special Constable four or five years earlier, and I was all ears again.

'I was based at Bromborough Police Station, back then,' he began, and I noticed there was that glazed, faraway look in his eyes, the kind people get when they're lost in reminiscence about some memorable, past series of events. 'During my time there, honestly lads, believe me, I saw more than my fair share of strange things. Things that the general public seldom, if ever, have the opportunity to see. And I heard stories too. Tales from reliable sources that, excuse the language, scared the living shite out of me.'

He'd paused, and I couldn't help but see that his hands were shaking, just a tiny bit like, but enough for me to notice. He caught me looking and grinned nervously, before continuing.

'I mean, just to give you a few examples, right off the top of me head: There was the Frankby Horror, supposedly a white, shapeless gibbering form that, according to various eyewitnesses, sometimes manifested itself at the far end of a tiny, winding village road called The Nook, and terrified locals and visitors alike, and where hardened police officers were sometimes afraid to tread...

'Especially after midnight.

'There was also this block of flats in Wallasey, where a suspected, paedophile once lived, and who one night wound up being tortured to death by a couple of young, smack-head burglars, who'd broken into the premises, found a stack of dodgy video cassettes and caught sight of the glut of CCTV cameras visible in every room, and decided to mete out their own version of justice upon this middle-aged "paedo".

'They took him into his bathroom, tied him up, and armed with a collection of brown-handled kitchen knives, slowly subjected him to "The Death Of A Thousand Cuts". They began their work slowly and only gradually increased the ferocity of the attacks. And the whole thing was caught on video. We had to sit and watch the footage as part of the ongoing murder investigation, and the weird thing was that because there was no audio, no sound whatsoever, after a quarter of an hour or so of watching, it became monotonous. Boring almost, if you can believe that. It sounds mad, but I quickly grew immune to the scenes of horror. I dunno, it just didn't seem real, probably because you couldn't hear the screams, the cries for help.

'But other residents in that apartment block, did.

'Not on *that* night, though.

'The screams were only heard several weeks later, long after the murder victim had been laid to rest beneath the cold, dark earth of Landican Cemetery.

'I remember we received a number of phone calls from various people who lived in the same block of flats, scared out of their wits by the terrible sound of someone shrieking and pleading for their life, coming from the dead man's empty apartment, and I was sent round to investigate with several of my brother officers.

'One resident, an attractive young woman in her mid-20's, with the tell-tale signs of several sleepless nights clearly visible in the dark semi-circles beneath her eyes, told me she'd been awoken on three consecutive nights by the sound of loud banging noises, what sounded like the smashing of glass and a series of high-pitched screams.

'I'll never forget the expression on her face when she took me to one side and spoke in a voice that was barely a whisper: 'Officer, can I tell you something?' she'd asked, and although I'd had to lower my head to make out exactly what she was saying, I readily did so .

'And was immediately sorry that I had.

'Do you know officer, there is nothing in life more chilling, than hearing a man of older years, a *dead* man, mind, screaming; screaming frantically for his mother.'

'Of course, as soon as we'd arrived on the scene, we checked out the flat, and there was absolutely no one there. The rooms had been unoccupied ever since the murder. No one would live there. Not even with the country in the grip of a housing shortage, and quite honestly, who could blame them? I mean, would either of you wanna live in that flat?'

Dave never paused to allow us to answer what was clearly a rhetorical question. He was on a roll, caught up in the telling of his stories.

'Not long after that unsettling incident, I became involved in the case of the so-called "Scally Family", an unemployed mother and father, and two kids, who were virtually begging the local council to re-house them, because they claimed they were being systematically attacked by an invisible assailant. Both the parents and their children suffered frequent injuries, including heavy bruising and multiple deep scratches that didn't appear to be self-inflicted, and there was no evidence that any human agency had been involved.

'It goes without saying though, that with kids involved, Social Services were pretty quickly on the scene, but despite their best efforts, they too were at a loss to find an explanation for the various injuries, though equally obviously, no one wanted to openly admit that supernatural forces were possibly at work. The victims though were adamant that their attacker was some kind of invisible entity and that they were living in constant fear of further attacks by what they honestly believed was some kind of demonic force.

'Of course, the cynics will say they were just making the whole thing up, so they could get themselves on the re-housing list, because to be fair, the house was, and please excuse my language once again, a total shit-tip.

'But still, there were those unexplained injuries….

'And there's something else, too. I have it on good authority that a local vicar, who went round to bless the house and attempt to rid of its unwelcome visitor, later stated that he'd felt a presence so intrinsically evil it had proven far too powerful to be exorcised by a simple ritual of "bell, book and candle".

'But the most frightening thing I've ever heard, either before, during or since my time as a Special Constable, concerns an incident which was alleged to have taken place on Bidston Hill, a year or so ago.

'Do you mind if we head back inside the bar before I tell you about it, though. It's getting dark out here, and I'd really rather tell this story surrounded by people and bright lights.'

I raised my eyebrows at this, but he likely didn't see the quizzical expression in the rapidly gathering gloom, though perhaps he read my mind, because he added, almost apologetically, 'I know it sounds soft, but just because I don't completely believe in the supernatural, doesn't mean I don't get scared by the subject, now and again. Especially of an evening,' he added, with a glance over his shoulder at the wall of trees, scarcely visible in the near-full dark. He mumbled something else, under his breath, and I couldn't be sure but it had sounded like he'd said, 'I don't like it when the shadows start lengthening.'

THREE

Almost as soon as we were back inside the cheerfully-lit bar-room, Dave's mood brightened considerably, and after we'd ordered a fresh round of drinks, and grabbed ourselves a couple of chairs, he immediately launched into the tale that had so obviously spooked him out in the beer garden.

'I first met John, the sole witness in this case, first-hand as part of an assault allegation, and found him to be a badly frightened man in his late forties, who's always insisted on partial anonymity, and I'm sure you'll soon understand why.

'John claims he was up on the hill one warm, clear-skied April evening, not long after dusk, to take the rare opportunity to walk beneath the stars. He insists he wasn't remotely troubled by anything. On the contrary, he was content with his lot in life. He hadn't been drinking and he had never taken drugs. He was single, had been all his life in fact, but was happy in his own company.

'As he was he walking past the windmill, that along with the old Observatory, dominates the Bidston skyline, he paused to glance up at the heavenly firmament; *The sky all hung with jewels* to quote Ian Mac of "The Bunnymen".

'There's very little in the way of light pollution up there at the summit, as I'm sure you'll know if you've ever been up there after dark. Not that I'd advise it. Not on your own, anyway.

'Anyway, John claims that as he was glancing skywards, he suddenly felt several "people" standing directly behind him, but before he could turn round to confront them, he was violently assaulted by assailants he later described as "aliens", although he couldn't make out their precise forms, as they seemed to shift and change the harder he tried to make them out.

'John swore that they weren't human, despite my suspicions that his highly visible injuries, bruising, scratches and a suspected fractured skull, were likely caused by a gang of robbers. John insists nothing was taken from him, however, and that "The Tree People", as he later referred to them, were malignant extra-terrestrials, (who he now claims to have seen on several subsequent occasions), who jealously guard their territory on the hill, and don't take kindly to the intrusions of humans, especially after sundown.

'You've probably heard that Bidston Hill has long been rumoured to have associations with witchcraft, UFO sightings and ghostly phenomena, and John's account, as bizarre as it undoubtedly is, is just one of hundreds of similar encounters I have on record featuring otherworldly entities, and I could go on and...'

'Well, yeah,' Richie and I both replied in unison. And there was a brief moment of awkward silence. I eventually broke it.

'That's really fascinating, Dave,' I interrupted. 'But I thought you were gonna tell us about, er, what did yer call 'em?

"The Watchers?"

'I was just coming to that,' Dave smiled humourlessly, and I could see that although he wanted to affect an air of calm, casual indifference, just at that moment, he was actually reluctant to continue with this part of the story. When it had come right down to it, he no more wanted to talk about "The Watchers", than he wanted to discuss the intimate details of his previous internet dating disasters, but he was locked into it now, and I think he knew there was no going back.

And so, as the barmaid called last orders, the televised dart's match drew to a close, and The Killers' first album took over on the pub's sound system, Dave paused to take a huge gulp from his glass, and finally continued. 'Okay,' he sighed. 'Many's the time since that alleged incident on "The Hill", that I've struggled to find a rational explanation for what John claims took place that night.

'Yeah, he may well have been delusional, a self-harmer, suffering from mental health problems, or he might have been jumped by local scallies who left him in a heap after they'd sussed out he had no money. I've gotta say, that makes perfect logical sense, don't yer think?' 'Well, yeah,' Richie and I both replied in unison. And there was a brief moment of awkward silence. I eventually broke it.

'But you don't really believe that, do yer?' I asked.

'I don't know exactly what I believe,' Dave responded. 'I just know that John claims to have been attacked, and that part at least, I happen to think wasn't imaginary. I'm not a doctor, but I don't think there's any way he could have inflicted those injuries upon himself. I'm as sure as I can be that would have been physically impossible. But that isn't what I'm trying to get around to telling you about. The thing I've so far omitted, and not just for dramatic effect, is the thing that has given me constant nightmares ever since…'

'Well, do you wanna share it anyway?' Richie piped up. 'I mean, you've come this far.'

Dave sighed, and after the briefest of hesitations, he said: 'It was "The Watchers" he saw at the height of the assault, of course. I'm guessing you knew, or at least suspected, that already. "The Couple". "The Man and The Woman". Adults of indeterminate age.

'They didn't *gradually* emerge from the trees at the edge of the high-grassed field to gaze at the spectacle.

'They were just *there*. "The Watchers".

'Standing at the edge of the woods beneath the largely leafless boughs, illuminated in a single shaft of moonlight. Their clothes funeral black. Their faces the pallid, sickly-white colour of blind, squirming creatures, roiling horrors that exist deep within the bowels of the earth, and shun the light of day. Nevertheless, the man who was being attacked looked to them for assistance, the way someone caught in desperate circumstances will cling to the smallest crumb of hope when salvation seems an increasingly unlikely prospect. John told me he actually yelled at the top of his voice for them to help, and for a blessed moment, they seemed to respond to his pleas. They edged closer. Almost imperceptibly, perhaps, but undeniably closer, and John almost raised a hand to thank his potential rescuers.

'But then they took a step nearer still, and as the attack continued unabated, he could clearly see that they were smiling.

"And the only reason they were making their slow, methodical way towards him, was not to offer assistance, but to afford themselves a better view, and just before he slumped into unconsciousness, he was aware of their narrow, vulpine teeth, glinting in the lunar light like porcelain tombstones.

'And the last thing he remembered was their looming over him like silent, gloating sentinels, as awareness slipped mercifully away from him.'

FOUR

'If that had been the only sighting of "The Watchers", I may have simply put it down to John's over-active imagination. After all, he honestly thought he was assaulted by aliens, or "Tree People", if you'd prefer. Logic dictates he was suffering from a trauma-related delusion, brought upon by what was, undeniably, a particularly vicious assault.

'But not long after I heard John's story, I started hearing strikingly similar accounts from work colleagues, associates, and yes, even that old, essentially fact-less source, the friend of a friend.

'These urban legends varied slightly, depending on the source, but one thing remained constant; the description of the phantoms, ghosts, call them what you will, were always identical. A couple, a male and a female, are seen standing, immobile on roadside pavements, or on the corners of city streets, dressed in curiously old-fashioned clothes, with unnaturally pale-faces and jet black eyes that stare intently at some invisible point in the middle distance, as if waiting for something to hove into view.

'Ordinary people walking or driving past seem largely oblivious to them, almost as though they don't really see them, and certainly, no one thinks to stop and ask them who they are or what they're doing. Older people, though, or very young children, seem to be more aware of their presence. In fact, the majority of the stories I've heard largely feature both of these age groups, and it's from them that I have learned the thing that frightens me most.

'Whenever "The Watchers" appear, something terrible always happens soon after. A fatal car crash. A hit and run. A suicide. A murder.

'And instead of hanging their heads in sorrow at the victim's demise, these entities simply smile the sly, malevolent grin of those who take great delight in the awful misfortunes of others.' Dave paused suddenly, and tried, and failed, to suppress a shudder. I opened my mouth to tell him not to worry. I knew exactly how he was feeling: The shivers were running madly up and down my spine (and likely Richie's, too) but before I could say anything the bell rang again for last orders, and I had to throw my hand over my mouth to stifle a scream.

The expressions on my friends' faces told me they'd both been on the verge of shrieking out loud, too.

'Er, maybe we'd better call it a night?' Richie suggested, and the three of us laughed nervously, although clearly there was nothing remotely funny about that remark.

We all agreed that it was getting late though, and there was work tomorrow, and there are few worse prospects than having to start the week with a king-size hangover.

We quickly finished our drinks and headed out into the still-sultry night with a haste which seemed, in retrospect, entirely unnecessary. There was no need to rush, but we did so anyway, as though there was somewhere else we desperately needed to be, despite the fact that we'd all enjoyed the evening and each other's company.

'We'll have to do this again sometime,' I said as we prepared to go our separate ways.

'Yeah,' Richie agreed, slapping me on the shoulder. 'Let's just make sure this time we don't leave it for another fifteen years!'

'No way,' I replied, my mind still a-whirl at this scarcely believable fact; that fifteen years had slipped by with such unobtrusive ease.

And I meant it, too. Genuine friendship is as rare and precious as finding a gleaming nugget of truth amidst the bric-a-brac of our daily lives.

FIVE

I can't speak for the others, but I had trouble sleeping that night.

I lay awake until well into the early hours, endlessly replaying the 'highlights' of the evening's conversations, and at some point, just as the ash-grey light of a false, four am dawn began poking through the curtains, a truly horrible thought suddenly leapt up from out of some dark place, like a malign Jack-in-the-box, with coal-black eyes, and madly-grinning mouth.

What if those silent, smiling watchers are not, (if they truly exist) simply harbingers of doom? Maybe they appear just prior to the scene of some dreadful accident, not merely to gloat at impending tragedy.

Maybe their sly, knowing grins are worn for reasons other than gleeful anticipation.

Maybe they're really the carnivorous smiles of a pair of feral beasts, that having cornered their prey, are now preparing to feed.

And maybe, just maybe, mind, *"The Watchers"* don't always just simply *watch...*

THE ALBERT DOCK
Photo Credit: Grant Walker

CHAPTER FOUR
THE HEART OF ALL SORROWS:
John Peel, Probe Records And The Death-Predicting Hound
of 'Ye Hole In Ye Wall'

'And like cold breath on a mirror, your hopes can fade,
With nothing left to believe in,
Faith in the future is wearing thin... '
The Happening – **The Lids**

ONE
A chilly Sunday afternoon on the very last day of October.

It was fast approaching noon but a hush has descended upon Liverpool City Centre like a weighty, velvet curtain, the kind that falls with grim finality at the end of a captivating but dimly-recollected stage show; a thickly-billowing accompaniment to the nursing of collective hangovers, regretful musings and the heart-sinking realisation that there's a very real possibility lives are about to be irrevocably changed. For the worse...

Always it seems, for the worse.

Christ, even the shrieks of the Mersey seagulls seemed half-hearted, muffled; the sound of a man with a woollen scarf wrapped tightly round his face, coughing fitfully into a gloved hand as a dense, impenetrable fog-bank drifts in from the invisible river.

It's an unarguably dead time.

And Liverpool resembles a ghost town.

The sort that Terry Hall once sang so evocatively about back in the era of the riot-torn early 1980s. (At least until Craggy Island's "Spin Meister" contrived to reduce that plaintive, soulful lament for the sad decline of England's inner cities, to bursts of unconstrained hilarity * - a *Father Ted* reference, trivia fans).

I'm walking alone along an all but deserted Dale Street, with no one but a shark-eyed traffic warden and a hopelessly optimistic *Big Issue* seller sat in the shuttered entrance of Tait's Health Store, looking every bit as forlorn as the solitary bird lady in *Mary Poppins* (in fact, I could see what looked suspiciously like dried pigeon-shit stains splattering the shoulders of his crumpled navy-blue coat), as he mechanically croaked out his pleas for someone, *anyone*, to purchase the publication.

I only had enough on me for a few drinks, and I had a whole welter of sorrows to drown, so I guiltily averted my gaze as I walked past him, staring at the pavement as though there was something of immense interest there amongst the squashed chewing gum, discarded cigarette butts and crumpled remains of "lucky dip" cards. I then turned left into Hackins Hey, an alleyway or "jigger," in the most literal, Liverpudlian sense of the word, and entered *Ye Hole In Ye Wall*, widely considered to be the city's oldest alehouse.

Built way back in the impossibly distant-seeming year of 1726, and reputedly erected on a Quaker burial site, the former coaching house is said to be haunted by at least two ghosts. The spectre of a Spanish sailor who, according to legend, was stabbed to death for having the temerity to refuse to take the "King's shilling", and a black-cowled figure that is apparently so solid-seeming it is often mistaken for a real flesh and blood regular (although quite how anyone would consider a man dressed in a hooded, monkish robe propping up the bar, or sat in the shadowy corners, on any occasion other than some local fancy dress fund-raiser, to be a perfectly *ordinary* customer, perhaps says something about the potency of the pub's vast array of real ales – unless assorted priests frequently elect to pop in for a swift half during a break from taking confession, of course).

I wasn't looking for phantoms, real or imagined, on this particular Sunday afternoon, however. Although I have to admit I *was* planning on raising a glass or two to the cherished memory of the recently departed.

And the second that I stepped across the threshold, and smelled the familiar odours of traditional pub food, cask-conditioned beer and the wispy smoke from a roaring fire, I knew I'd come to the most appropriate venue imaginable in my attempt to soothe the heart of all sorrows. Or at the very least immerse that most fragile of bodily organs in sense-numbing alcohol.

This was a place where visions and images of the past shimmered in the move-less air with all the sepia-toned vividness of the numerous framed photographs of the City Centre, and its glorious yesteryear, that lined the oak-panelled walls.

And as for *me*...

I was only recalling the events of a few days earlier, and the loss of someone who'd I'd regrettably never got to meet, but who I nevertheless missed with all the desperate, aching sadness that trawls forlornly in the wake of a loved one's absence.

HOLE IN THE WALL PUB

Photo Credit: Tony Barr

I ordered a frothing pint of Hobgoblin and a single malt whisky chaser before taking a seat in one of the two cosy, oakwood panelled booths (the one nearest the real coal fire – that pervasive autumnal chill had seeped into my bones with all the grim and steely determination of a persistent gate-crasher at a house party). The bar was fairly busy, even at this relatively early hour, with the usual Sunday crowd of older people, all dressed up in their weekend finest; the men, proud and distinguished in immaculate freshly-ironed three-piece suits, the women in extravagant hats and party frocks. Most of them were gathered in the opposite snug, and as I watched, a couple of acoustic guitars, a banjo, and a "gob-iron" or two magically appeared seemingly from out of nowhere and within seconds, and amidst much cheering, and ear-piercing 'Wuh-yells!' of encouragement, an impromptu 'band' began belting out highly passable renditions of *Your Cheating Heart, I Walk The Line,* and *The Leaving Of Liverpool.*

I watched transfixed as prior to me taking my first eager step along the road to beery, pseudo-consolation, my eyes were drawn to an elderly woman who was sat amongst the group. At least in a *physical* sense. One glance at the dreamy expression playing upon her perfectly-made up features as she absent-mindedly twisted her plain gold wedding ring around and around her finger was enough to indicate that spiritually, she was about a billion light years removed from any of her companions.

That, and the fact that she was staring intently at a slant of late October light that spilled greyly through the pub's windows, and where dust motes danced in madly swirling eddies. It was obvious to me that her rheumy eyes were focused on some distant, cherished memory, momentarily brought back to life by the strains of a well-loved song, drifting in the smoky air like a symphony for the remorseless passing of time.

And that brought me back to the sole reason for my being here.

I was here to remember, too.

It was October 31st, 2004.

Halloween.

A mere five days since news broke of the untimely death of one of the greatest musical (or indeed otherwise) influences on my life.....

TWO

The afternoon when I first heard John Peel had tragically passed away, (although it turned out he'd died the previous day, during a working vacation in Peru) I was sat at my office desk at the solicitor's firm where I used to work, *supposedly* poring over that afternoon's stack of paperwork and mindlessly dictating our criminal client's details onto our computer database. In actual fact I was busily engaged in arguing the toss with one or two of my colleagues over the pros and cons of Liverpool FC fielding what amounted to a reserve side in that night's League Cup tie at Millwall. The increasingly heated conversation had suddenly been interrupted by the shrill, insistent ringing of the telephone.

It was a friend calling to relay a slice of truly awful news. And immediately, everything else had ceased to matter. As with the equally unexpected death of the late, great Joe Strummer, of The Clash, (and in company with an endless cast of taken-before-their-time luminaries, including Ian Curtis, Bob Marley, Malcolm Owen, Kurt Cobain, Bill Shankly and John Lennon; a cluster of eternal stars that eternally "lend light to the Vaults Of Heaven") I was totally overcome by a powerful combination of both shock and bitter-sweet nostalgia. It's one of life's harshest lessons to learn after all, that the heroic, untouchable icons of our youth are every bit as fallible and ultimately *killable* as the rest of us mere mortals.

I replaced the receiver and excused myself on the pretext that I needed some fresh air. And was that really so far from the truth? Certainly, I'd suddenly found it difficult to catch my breath in the overbearingly stuffy confines of the office, and I'd stumbled, gasping and misty-eyed, into the firm's car park, ignoring the concerned glances of my workmates and their half-formed enquiries as to whether I was feeling all right. My head was too busy reeling with the implications of irreplaceable loss and the recollections of the very first time I'd heard John Peel's iconic programme two and a half decades earlier.

THREE

I'd been a few months shy of my fifteenth birthday, and about to enter my final year at quite possibly the worst school on Merseyside, on just about every conceivable level. Inter-school discipline? Inspiration to realise even a tiny portion of your potential? Encouragement to pursue career opportunities? These were all about as alien a series of concepts to our so-called teachers and governing heads as educational excellence was to Pol Pot and the laughing boys of the Khmer Rouge.

There were the occasional glimmers of joy to be found amidst the soul-destroying drudgery of my school-days, however.

For instance during our one hour dinner break, my friends and I would gather under the corrugated iron roof of the bike sheds, on even the brightest and warmest of days, and there, out of sight of the teachers and their arse-kissing prefects, we'd act out the rituals of stereotypical teenagers; smoke a surreptitious ciggie or two, play cards for a massive big stake of 10 pence a hand, make increasingly outlandish boasts about our alleged sexual conquests, and listen to music on the cheap radio-cassette player provided by the resident "sweat" in our gang, its unbearably tinny speakers blaring out an endless procession of heavy metal songs.

I can't say I cared much for that particular genre. Those 15-minute guitar solos and the cheesy lyrics about getting it on with *Satan's Horny Sex Slaves,* just didn't do it for me. But we put up with it, just the same, and at some point those dirty, sleazy power chords and over-top-vocals faded to a hardly noticeable background noise, like the lazy drone of an aeroplane passing high and invisibly overhead.

And then one day, El Sweato announced he had to go down to London with his parents to attend his auntie's funeral, but he would very kindly leave the tape recorder for us in his locker. This news was greeted with a silent chorus of euphoric cheering, because it meant we could now play whatever music we liked, and a big mad scramble for tapes ensued. I don't know whether you'd call it chance, fate or blind luck, but one of the few *bona fide* Punks in our class, a tall, gangly boy with jet-black spiky hair who we christened (with a quite deplorable lack of imagination) "Sid", got his tape in there first. I'd disappointedly thrust my Top Forty recorded-off-the-radio Memorex cassette back in my trouser pocket and prepared to relegate the anticipated tuneless dirge to an infinitely more tolerable 'background hum.'

And thirty-odd minutes later I found my life had been magically transformed.

The tape proved to be a compilation of wonderfully exciting bands, some whose names were vaguely-familiar: (The Clash, The Damned and The Teardrop Explodes), others I'd never heard of before (The Notsensibles, Peter & The Test Tube Babies, The Fatal Microbes), and by the time the bell sounded for the dreaded resumption of lessons, my entire body was tingling with a fully-blown adrenaline rush.

Not wanting to appear un-cool in front of the rest of the gang, I took "Sid" to one side and whispered quietly; 'That's one smart tape that, kidder. What did yer record it off?'

He looked me up and down and smirked disdainfully; 'Friggin hell, lad, haven't you ever heard of John Peel?'

'Nah, I haven't, yer know,' I mumbled, feeling a little like the way I did when one of the maths tutors asked me a tricky question about algebra or one of those fiddly-fuck equations. And then I was struck with what I thought at the time was a sudden spark of brilliant inspiration: 'Oh, hang on, isn't he the fella who invented the bizzies?'

'That's *Robert* Peel, ya bell-end,' "Sid" replied, and from the look in his eyes, he plainly thought he was dealing with someone who considered the likes of Brotherhood Of Man and Boney M to be the epitome of "teen-dream hipster" music, back in the sun-kissed days of the Summer of '78. I was about to put him in his place by telling him I was the proud owner of a Darts cassette, so he needn't bother launching into a lecture about cutting edge, modern-day rock and roll, when, mercifully, he placed his right hand on my shoulder and leaned close to me in the manner of someone about to impart a piece of worldly advice:

'Honestly, lad,' he said, 'do yerself a favour. Grab hold of a radio tonight, and fill yer lug-holes with a dollop of Peelie's show. I'm telling yer, you won't regret it. He plays some of the bossest tunes, ever!'

When I got home that evening, I hastily scanned the programme guide in the *Daily Mirror,* and there it was. Stark and simple, and totally bereft of any clues as to the nature of the programme's contents.

Radio One. 10pm. John Peel

I only owned a crappy, portable transistor back then, the kind of hopelessly screechy plastic affair that rendered even the very heaviest of reggae dub-bass tracks tinnier than a Mikey Dredd gig being held inside a giant-size tin of Golden Virginia, but it just about did the job.

I remember it was a Thursday night. There was school the next day, and my mum and dad had imposed a strict "Lights Out, Music Off By Ten" policy during the week, so shortly before the curfew, I'd gotten into bed, placed the radio on my pillow, leaned my ear against the speaker and switched on a couple of minutes before the show was due to start. I thought at first I must have tuned to the wrong frequency when I was greeted by an innocuous-sounding, old-time rhythm and blues intro. I was just reaching for the dial when the tune suddenly faded and the DJ began speaking in a laid-back, faintly Scouse twang laced with a ready wit and a self-deprecating sense of humour. I knew immediately, even at that relatively tender age, that here was someone who was the complete antithesis of every phoney radio presenter I'd heard before, or indeed since. And when at last he'd fallen silent, there followed a welter of unbelievably eclectic music, a heady mix of punk, new wave, reggae, ska, and totally unclassifiable alternative music that held me enraptured for the next two hours.

Oh, and to cap it all, he made it abundantly clear during the show that he was, like myself, a massive fan of Liverpool Football Club, and almost refused, on one memorable occasion in 1980, to play *A Forest* by The Cure, for no other reason than the song's title bore a resemblance to the name of the team from Nottingham, Liverpool's greatest rivals at the time (Lordy, how times *do* change).

I mean, honestly, could it *get* any better.

I also quickly learned to love the fact that the usual array of cheesy jingles and horribly inane advertisement breaks were noticeable only by their absence, that he sometimes played records at the wrong speed, and upon realising his mistake, simply lifted the needle (sometimes with that ear-piercing, stylus-scratching *schweewchhwwupp* sound pouring from the speakers), and started them all over again, with the accompaniment of an embarrassed chuckle.

It was more than apparent that he held a great and genuine affection for the music he was playing, despite his apparent tongue-in-cheek irreverence (at one point he re-christened, for reasons best known to himself, Ian McCulloch's iconic Liverpool band as "Echo & The Knights Of The Bun") and he actively encouraged his listeners to write to him so he could provide them with details of how to obtain a particularly obscure record released on some defiantly independent label, a billion light years distant from the familiar majors: Le Disque du Crepescule, Factory or

Creeping Bent, say.

These were tunes John loved so much he wanted you yourself to personally own a copy. He was once asked by some faceless interviewer from one of the music paper weeklies, 'What is your greatest talent?' John replied, with a typical display of drier than a Death-Valley-puddle wit, 'Well, I can make a noise like a dolphin and I'm really good at parallel parking.

'I keep hoping I can find some way to combine these two talents for commercial gain.'

It's true, too, that like the legendary Joe Strummer, lead singer with the aforementioned Clash, that whenever John Peel spoke, it felt like he was talking to *you* personally, his eternally benign tones drifting from the radio's speaker in a quiet and gentle torrent. It's little wonder then that the likes of the XFM presenter, and former singer with the band Kenickie, Lauren Laverne, called him a surrogate father, and bands like Stiff Little Fingers, The Cockney Rejects and The Undertones, referred to him warmly as "Uncle John".

It might sound like a sentimental cliché, the kind the hordes of heartless cynics, the smug, crisp white, open-necked shirt wearing zealots writing in middle-age-pandering publications, and the faceless nobodies who prowl the grim backwaters of Internet forums, would sneeringly dismiss as being a "typical example of Merseyside mawkishness," but deep within the innermost core of my heart, the place where all truth lies constant and immutable, I felt like I actually *knew* John Peel, be he Father or Uncle, or just plain close friend.

And that blessed familiarity was instrumental in bringing me closer to all these wonderful new bands, the do-it-yourself Punk mentality and, ultimately, the inspiration to write.

And I only wish I'd had the opportunity to thank him in person. And tell him that I completely disagreed with his assertion that *Teenage Kicks,* classic though it is, is the greatest, most impossible-to-improve-upon song ever.

I've got an old Darts cassette that says *Daddy Cool* knocks spots of that greasy-haired, snorkel-wearing, warbler, any day.

FOUR

In the days and weeks that followed that hugely rewarding experience, listening to "Peelies" show became more than just a habit. It became a kind of nightly ritual. Here was a DJ, whose voice was so rich, oddly-soothing and laced with a surreal sense of humour, I actively sought to keep his introductions to any given track on tape, though Mr Peel himself made no secret of the fact that he hated the way other radio presenters talked over *any* part of the song. On the rare occasions that he mistakenly did so, he'd quickly mumble apologetically: 'Sorry, that's me talking over the end of the track ruining it for anyone recording!'

But, the strange fact was, nothing could have been further from the truth. I remember my friends and I would walk along the streets of our home town with a massive tape recorder, a real ghetto blaster, long before I was aware the term had even been invented, belonging to a close friend by the name of Jason Barnes, playing back the previous night's show in its entirety, and later re-recording all the songs we especially liked, complete with John's frequently amusing intros, onto compilation tapes, just like our class-mate, "Sid".

Peelie was also responsible for initiating a love of live music and for our gang taking the logical step of attending gigs at the likes of Brady's (formerly Eric's) on Liverpool's famous ley-line riddled, Mathew Street, to see bands I would likely never even have heard of otherwise, and for my picking up the latest vinyl releases from Probe Records, (see the rather lengthy footnote, in truth it's more the size of a novelette, included below) then situated on the corner of Whitechapel, on Button Street, by artists so wilfully obscure they often disbanded the moment they'd achieved their sole ambition of having their track played on national radio.

The show was also responsible for unleashing within me a whole host of musical inspirations, foremost amongst them, a love of dub reggae music and leftfield electronica, as well as Punk, Indie and New Wave, and giving me the incentive to become lead vocalist in a couple of mildly successful local bands (Last Night At The Fair and The Lids, for all you completists out there), and eventually, to take up DJ-ing virtually every weekend, playing the usual array of weddings, birthday parties, anniversaries, retirement dos, witch dunkings and the like, but with more than a handful of old and new "alternative anthems" thrown in, *striking a blow for the good guys,* as I like to call it in my more hubristic moments.

It is to my eternal regret that I had seldom listened to Uncle John's programme in the four years or so prior to his death, not I hope, because I'd grown inured to the auditory magic or begun to take it for granted, but rather with the advent of MTV 2 and the rise of the internet, the sources of hearing vital new music had grown exponentially, and listening to the radio late at night was no longer the nocturnal delight it once was. But still, as the highly respected music writer Charles Shaar Murray noted at the time; *it was a comfort to know that both he and the magical hours between ten and midnight, were still there.*

And now that sense of comfort had well and truly gone.

I was finding it difficult to imagine how anyone could ever hope to replace John Peel.

Perhaps, I thought, sat in the snug surroundings of *Ye Hole In Ye Wall,* as the last few hours of autumn were swept away on a chill wind that carried with it the steel-cold promise of impending November and the true birth of the year's dying season, no one should even try.

I guess I can only speak for myself, but those "magical hours between 10pm and midnight...?"

They'd just become as devoid of meaning as the tuneless nonsense that fills the waves between stations.

Pictured at the top of this page, in all its former glory, is the original, highly-venerated premises of Probe Records, situated at the far end of Mathew Street, home to both The Cavern, and later, during the glory years of Punk, New Wave, "Two Tone," Mod, etc, the ever fabulous venue named Eric's.

These two hugely iconic venues were said to have been built upon a Ley Line, *giving energy to all it meets,* in the words of Ian Prowse, a genius singer-song-writer who formed the excellent local bands, Pele, and latterly, Amsterdam).

On alternate Saturday afternoons, when Liverpool were playing away, and we couldn't afford to go, my friends and I would pretty much spend the entire day hanging around the store and its immediate environs. There was something indefinably magical about the combination of garishly-designed band T-shirts hanging from the ceiling like the captured banners of some defeated army, the posters for upcoming festivals and local gigs and the sea of iconic singles covers lining the walls in plastic sleeves: The Comsat Angels, The Fall, The Pop Group, Joy Division, and a thousand more.

On one memorable, for all the wrong reasons, occasion, I decided on a whim, to buy

Duran Duran's really rather excellent Planet Earth *single from the store. Needless to say, the Hierarchy of the New Wave/Post Punk Police considered this "glorified boy band" to be charged (and subsequently convicted) with the heinous crime of being tragically un-hip. And so I tried guiltily to conceal the record amongst the Aztec Camera and Orange Juice singles I'd selected from the racks (both of which were released on the highly revered Scottish label, Postcard), and made my way up to the counter. I have to admit it was a pretty pathetic tactic, the sort that I'd previously employed as a child during Sunday afternoon roast dinners, with a thoroughly dispiriting lack of success. Back then, I'd hated sprouts, more than any other food, with a passion, despite my parent's insistence that they were wholesome and good for me. The moment my mum and dad's backs were turned, I used to flatten the dark green balls into a barely recognisable mush with my fork and then try and conceal the mess beneath a stack of mashed potatoes or Yorkshire puds. It never worked then. And surprise, surprise, it didn't work on this occasion, either.*

✳✳✳✳✳

It was well-known around Merseyside that the staff's policy at Probe was to pass judgement on the records that you bought, and woe betide you if you selected something that was considered to be uncool, Plazzy or just plain shite.

God knows, I'd seen hard-core Punks and vicious-looking skinheads reduced to blubbering wrecks by the withering putdowns of Geoff or Bernie, or the beautiful, but permanently sardonic Lyn, in response to a dodgy purchase.

Pete Burns was by far the worst, though.

Soon to become famous as the lead singer of Dead or Alive, and rather less gloriously, as a voluntary inmate in Channel Four's Big Brother *house, he had been cursed with the terrible misfortune of attending the very same crappy school as me, though being a little older, he was two or three years above me during the time that I was there. He was expelled from The Esteemed Institution Of Virtually Un-expellables, due to "psychological" reasons. At least that was the official line. I'm not so sure that the education authorities had the slightest semblance of a clue as to how to deal with him. In life it seems there are those characters who were simply born to buck the trend of convention, and affront the easily-offended. And if so, Pete Burns was certainly a classic case in point.*

(I often imagined a lonely, late-middle-aged teacher dressed in a hideous brown cardigan, creased checked shirt and ill-fitting slippers, puffing on his pipe before the flickering TV screen on a cold, wet Thursday evening. He has had a typically stressful day at school, but he silently congratulates himself on maintaining a semblance of order and still salutes the day he was instrumental in the removal of that lunatic Peter Burns, potentially the biggest threat to the school's existence since the German Luftwaffe launched its raids either side of the River Mersey.

He chuckles at the memory, and the sound of anything approaching humour or a degree of happiness in this soul-less living room, falls flat and thin, like mid-winter shadows in the bitter glare of watery sunlight. He doesn't notice its cheerless, hollow quality, though. He's far too busy reminiscing about 'the good old days' and the little vital victories that made life worth living.

And then the pipe drops from his suddenly wide open mouth to the carpeted floor. And he coughs and splutters at the sight of his former "hopeless, good-for-nothing pupil" cavorting across a stage on Top Of The Pops *in 1985, looking camper than John Inman and Larry Grayson mincing around in a tent shop, as Mr Burns proclaims that some anonymous person of indeterminate sex, causes him to gyrate at the speed of a slice of vinyl spinning on a turntable!).*

Pete was the first 'punk' I had ever seen, although in truth, he probably hated that term, the very second it was coined. It's been said before, but it bears repeating; from both a cultural and social perspective, Britain, in the mid-1970s, was the colour of the sun-blasted Mojave Desert, or "The Brown Times", as the writer Jonathan Coe once memorably termed them in his excellent book, The Rotter's Club.

So, seeing Pete Burns parading around town like a preening peacock amidst the crowds of baggy-flares and platform sole-wearing men and women, was, I guess, akin to the reaction of the people of New York's initial sight of the incandescent, neon lights that lit up Times Square, and turned the former, all-enveloping darkness into what was later christened The Rainbow Ravine.

As I approached the counter, there appeared to be no sign of Mr Burns, but just as I was about to hand the records over however, he suddenly popped up from beneath the counter from where he'd been retrieving some singles that had fallen out of their picture sleeves. I almost panicked and ran, to be honest, but before I could so much as turn away, the pallid, black lipsticked figure with the long, raven-coloured crimped hair, was reaching out to take the records from me. He sniffed dismissively at the Postcard selections, (which I knew from experience was just about the closest to a nod of approval I was ever likely to get). I got the impression too, that he was desperately disappointed that he had been denied the opportunity to berate me for my taste in music. But then his mascara-lined eyes lit up like a pair of bright, shining halogen lamps when he caught sight of the Duran Duran single.

And oh, how he played to the gallery.

'Buh-loody hell,' he said scathingly, in a voice so camp it made Lily Savage sound like Conan The Barbarian, after three solid hours of gargling with razor blades, and chunks of jagged broken glass. 'Duran Duran? Yer big gaybod!' he uttered disbelievingly. 'Who's this for then, lar, yer boyfriend?'

There's something distinctly disconcerting about having the nature of your sexuality scornfully called into question by a man dressed in a one-piece PVC body-suit. I felt my face flush and turn as crimson-red as a December sunset, and I tried to drum up some witty response, but the only thing that emerged was an unintelligible stream of mumbled nonsense, which of course only made Pete laugh all the more. The rest of the staff members laughed right along with him, as did the group of gorgeous-looking, young punkettes gathered in the far corner of the shop, clutching a Slits album, and really, who could blame them?

Especially when Pete announced in tones of mock seriousness: 'I hear "Extremes", the alternative clothes shop just over the road there, are doing an absolutely rooooaaaring trade in frilly blouses and big baggy leather kecks, hun. And I have it on good authority that they're offering a massive discount to tight-bunned little Duranies, like yerself.'

Cue waves of laughter so overwhelmingly powerful they threatened to sweep me out onto the choppy waters of the Mersey, if the hole I prayed would suddenly open up below my feet, didn't swallow me first.

It was a while before I went back to Probe.

When I eventually did, I made sure I bought only obscure, John Peel-endorsed records or those championed by the welter of small press fanzines whose combined readership very probably didn't exceed that of the editor's circle of immediate family and friends.

Even if (though on admittedly rare occasions) I didn't actually like them that much.

But, and here's the thing, did I once catch "The King Of Cool", Mr Ian McCulloch, of the aforementioned "Bunnymen", glancing intently at the track listing of Duran Duran's first album? And did it briefly cross my mind to race across to the counter and yell loudly, in a nah, nah, dee nah, nah voice, so everyone in the store could hear; 'Hey, Pete, that big gay-bod, McCulloch, is a secret New Romantic! Why don't yer have a go at him?'

Did I?

Well, with all due deference to the respect I have for Norris Green's finest, and for fear of being sued for libel or defamation of character, I couldn't possibly comment further.

FIVE

But to return to that morose, late October afternoon…

As I raised my glass one more time, in a silent toast to the irreplaceable, and drained the last remaining dregs, I rattled the loose change in my pockets, summoning up just enough shrapnel to pay for another couple of pints. I rose wearily to my feet and walked across to the bar, almost colliding as I did so with an old man who had just emerged from the toilets.

'Sorry, lad,' he mumbled, placing his hand on my shoulder in much the same way young "Sid" had once done beneath the shelter of the school bike-sheds, all those long years ago. 'I didn't see yer there. These new glasses are bloody useless.'

'No problem, mate,' I replied, and flashed that crinkly, half-embarrassed little smile again. 'I was in world of me own there. I should've been looking where I was going.'

'Ahhh, you've probably got loads on yer mind, son,' he said pleasantly. 'You young ones always have.' He paused, thought for a moment, and then added; 'Life slows down a bit when you get to my age, though.'

'Is that right?' I replied, with a distinct lack of enthusiasm, taking a step backwards, as I did so. I like to think I'm a fairly sociable person most of the time, but today I wasn't in the mood for a conversation with anyone, least of all some cracker-barrel-wisdom-spouting stranger, old enough to be my granddad.

But whatever his skills in bar-room philosophy, arl Albert Camus here, was plainly useless when it came to analysing less-than-subtle inflections of speech. Because instead of dropping his hand from my shoulder and stepping to one side to let me go on my not-so-merry way, his fingers gripped my collarbone with surprising strength and it was all I could do to keep myself from grimacing in pain.

'Oh, aye, lad,' the old man continued, as though we were a pair of trusty companions, enjoying a nice cosy chat over a beer in the familiar surroundings of our favourite watering hole. 'Let me tell you a little somethin' about gettin' old.'

He smiled, and I could smell brandy on his breath mixed with extra strong mints and the remnants of pork scratchings, and I saw he'd made a bad job of shaving that morning. His skin looked red and irritated, and there was a tiny piece of blood speckled tissue paper stuck to his chin that flapped, almost hypnotically when he spoke.

'Sometimes, I feel like I've spent a lot longer than was remotely sensible, sprinting on one of those exercise treadmills, working up a sweat like I was in a big mad hurry to get somewhere terribly important. Only to have someone, God maybe, or some other kindly deity whose job it is to look out for arl farts like me, knock the machine's speed down to a slow walking pace, and suddenly I realise that actually, I'm running nowhere fast, and as a consequence, there seems to be a whole lot less for me to worry about.'

He chuckled, and rubbed his cheeks gingerly; 'Except maybe rememberin' to buy new razor blades once in a while.'

He finally dropped his hand, took a step back from me, and I noticed for the first time that he was dressed immaculately in a jacket, shirt and tie. There were a set of a brightly polished medals positioned just above his top pocket, doubtless awarded for service in some half-forgotten war; Burma maybe, or Malaysia, and as I regarded him with new-found respect, he said just about the very last thing I would have expected him to say. 'Ahh, I'm sorry for botherin' yer, lad. I can tell you've suffered a terrible loss. I should have got on to that one straight away. You could blame it on approaching senility, I suppose, but God knows, I've seen that hang-dog demeanour more than enough times in my life to be able recognise it for exactly what it is.'

He took off his thick glasses and began polishing the lenses with a spotless, white handkerchief, and struggling to keep his voice steady, added, 'I told yer, these glasses are a total waste-of-space. Friggin' stupid things keep on steamin' up.'

I saw, with no real surprise, that there were a couple of tears pooling on his cheeks like tiny glass globes, and my heart went out to him at that moment and I was momentarily lost for words.

'Nah, it's *me* that's sorry,' I eventually blurted out, without being entirely sure what it was I was apologising for, before uttering that timeless Merseyside remedy for all the world's hurts and wrongs and perceived injustices, 'Listen lad, do yer wanna bevvy?'

Aye, go 'ead, why not?' he replied, and with a visible effort, pulled himself together, stood up straight, and shook my hand. 'My name's Harry, by the way.'

'Nice to meet yer. I'm Lee,' What yer havin? Another brandy?'

'Christ, is the smell of arl Napoleon still *that* powerful?' Harry said, reaching into his pocket for the pack of mints and popping one into his mouth. 'Doris, me missus hates me drinking shorts. She says it makes me all depressed and melancholy and yer know what, I think it's fair to say she might have a point there. But, what the hell, eh?'

I didn't respond to that, but instead ordered a pint of bitter for myself and a double brandy for my new friend and placed it on the bar before him.

'Cheers,' we both said simultaneously, and clinked our glasses to a combination of the present, the deep well of memory, and the undeniable hurting chill of absence.

SIX

I think we were on our fourth of fifth drink (certainly the dull light had rapidly begun to leak from the day, the way it did in all those classic vampire movies, just as the heroes are frantically searching for the leader of the undead, armed with sharpened wooden stakes and silver crucifixes) when Harry began launching into the story of his best friend, Billy Myers, and his incredibly loyal dog, Luke.

I'm not entirely sure how we got onto the subject, but I can recall that I thought the recounting of this tale, a modern day version of the famous Legend Of Greyfriars Bobby,

*** (a hugely heart-warming tale that has recently and rather sadly been dismissed by some cynical spoilsports as being nothing more than the entrepreneurial invention of a couple of local businessmen in an effort to boost their trade), was entirely appropriate, given the sombre circumstances.

We'd plonked ourselves down on a couple of tall, but comfortable stools at the far end of the bar, so we didn't have to shout to make ourselves heard above the tuneful renditions of *The Leaving of Liverpool,* a couples of Beatles standards and a varied selection of sea shanties, wafting melodiously from the snug, when Harry began telling me about how, eight years earlier, he and his closest friend, Bill (they'd fought together side by side at the Battle of Inchon during the 1950-53 Korean War) used to drink regularly here at this very pub.

'He had a half-decent voice, did Bill, and he could certainly hold a tune. He was top-notch on the arl acoustic guitar, too, so he was hugely popular with the sing-a-long crew over there. I couldn't play the bleedin *spoons,* never mind anything resembling a real musical instrument, and me singing voice had all the tunefulness of a tramp fartin' into his wellies, but I used to join in, all the same. I loved it back then, and I suppose I still do. But you know, it seems like there are less and less of us with the passing of each and every month these days, and that's one hell of a harsh reality to have to face.'

Harry sniffed and removed his glasses once again, but this time he made no pretence of cleaning them, and instead dabbed at the corners of his eyes, moist and sparkling like the glisten of raindrops in the wake of a summer shower.

He cleared his throat and wiped a trembling hand across his face before continuing.

*** FOOTNOTE RE: THE LEGEND OF GREYFRIARS BOBBY:

One of the most moving stories of how "Man's Best Friend," remained loyal to its owner, even after death, was apparently nothing more than a cynical publicity stunt created to encourage custom in a particular section of the haunted heart of Edinburgh, it was "revealed" in the press, back in August, 2011.

According to certain miserable, spoil-sport historians, (who seems to be the type of people who gleefully announce to their kids that Santa Claus and the Easter Bunny were nothing but made-up fairy stories when they are only about three-years old, and still infused with wonder), the 140-year-old story of a dog, whose alleged vigil at the grave of its departed master, that subsequently inspired a couple of movies and several books, and has even been commemorated with a bronze statue, was actually an ordinary stray hound kept at Greyfriars Cemetery with bribes of regular food.

But researchers based at Cardiff University now maintain that the moving tale was fabricated by James Brown, the cemetery's curator and John Traill, a local restaurant owner, and when word spread, as rumours good and bad are wont to do, visitors to the churchyard increased a hundred-fold. Many people were conned into donating money to Brown for having the 'Christian charity' to look after the well-being of the dog, and almost all felt compelled to then dine in Traill's restaurant, afterwards.

Historians now insist that portraits of the dog, as well as contemporary accounts, suggest that the original 'Bobby' died in May or June of 1867. And they further state that the pair of snides then substituted the original hound with a similar dog and passed him off as the immensely loyal terrier, for their own greedy, commercial purposes….

'Another thing about Bill, who'd lost his wife to cancer ten years before this story takes place, and had never remarried, was that he used to love bringing his dog in here with him. A lovely-natured black Labrador he called Luke, the alter-ego of Hank Williams, the famous Country & Western singer. Yer know, *Luke The Drifter,* and all that?

'Well, anyway, Luke was just about the most faithful and downright intelligent dog I have ever known. Bill never had to tie him on a lead. He never had to shout at him to "sit" or "lie down". He'd trot into the pub alongside Bill and me, with all the quiet obedience of a fully-trained guide dog, and once we'd ordered our drinks and were sat in our usual specs, he'd immediately lie flat, as happy as a bee in a bunch of begonias, at my friend's feet and behave himself impeccably. Luke would never resort to begging from any of the customers for scraps of food, not even those amongst our inner circle, and who quite honestly loved that dog almost as much as me and Bill did.

'It's fair to say Luke would gladly accept any offerings placed before him, though. Crisps or salted peanuts or a handful of fat, tomato sauce-covered chips were his favourites. Or pork scratchings. I remember he *absolutely* loved pork scratchings. He used to wolf them down as though he hadn't been fed in weeks, I can still hear him crunching away like the boots of a well-drilled army marching up and down some gravelly parade ground. He also reacted to the music we played and the varying moods of the songs, and I truly believe that if he'd been capable, he would have grabbed a guitar or a bongo, or a gob-iron and joined right in, giving it beans with the rest of the "Sunday Afternoon Jigger-Thon Brigade".

'I think what impressed me most about him though was that whenever Luke farted in our company, especially if it was during one of those quiet interludes between songs, when we were having a chat about something that seemed important back then, or more likely deciding which song we should attempt next, the dog managed to look deeply, deeply ashamed, not in the way most dogs seem to do, but *genuinely, sincerely* embarrassed.

'I had a Jack Russell once, and I totally loved that hound to bits, but I was never particularly fussed with the way he used to race up to greet me the moment I stepped through the front door after a hard day's graft at the Tate & Lyle factory. He'd jump up into me arms and wait till I was scratching behind his ears and tellin' him what a good doggy he was, before, without fail, letting off an almighty rip-snorter so rank I could almost see the noxious gases rising from his arse in a stinkin' green cloud.

'Not Luke, though. He'd whimper softly and place his front paws firmly over his nose to block out the smell, as though by denying its meaty aroma, he could rob it of its power to affect the rest of us. A remarkably brainy, if ultimately futile, action.

'He smiled, too, whenever anyone stroked him or when he had his tummy rubbed. He'd roll over on his back and grin that doggy grin, with his tongue lolling out of one side of his mouth and his bright, intelligent eyes sparkling like diamond-chip stars.

'But the most curious thing that Luke did, didn't endear him to anybody, though it certainly mystified them big time. It did me and Bill, too.

'Basically, what would happen is this. Luke would be lying in his usual position, right under Bill's legs, probably hoping that someone would order a massive plate of chips, and not go easy on the arl ketchup. And then without warning, or any obvious cause, Luke would suddenly haul himself up onto his feet, and with his head low, his ears flat and his tail firmly between his legs, he'd slowly saunter over to that ornate fireplace, irrespective of whether it had been lit or not, and then sit down smartly as though he'd been ordered to do so by his master with the promise of some lipsmackin' treat.

'Luke would then stare intently at some undetectable point a few feet above his jet-black, shiny-wet nose, something only he could see, hovering invisibly in the smoke-filled, bar-room air. I remember he'd make these very soft whining noises at the back of his throat. And whenever he started making those sounds, I swear the whole pub went so deathly quiet, you could have heard the proverbial pin drop. There was just something undeniably human-like about that dreadful crying, and God knows I've heard more than my fair share of that kind of hopeless, inconsolable grief during the course of my life. It brought to mind memories of the desperate cries of mortally wounded soldiers in field hospitals set up at the edge of some foreign battlefield, their agonised screams testament to the fact that, despite being pumped so full of morphine it was practically spilling out of their ears, still some conscious part of them ensured they remained acutely aware that they were beyond all hope of salvation.

'This would go on for a minute or so, and no amount of gentle cajoling or angry shouting could persuade that ordinarily most obedient of animals to cease its strange, deeply unsettling actions, even when several of us attempted to physically drag Luke away.

'I remember we often joked nervously on these occasions that Luke must have encountered one of the two ghosts that are said to haunt this pub. I'm guessing you've heard the stories - The Spanish sailor who back-heeled the British King's "request" that he join up for some vainglorious crusade in the name of Empire, and was beaten to death for stubbornly, if you'll forgive the rather inappropriate analogy, sticking to his guns, or the wandering Ghostly Monk, whose origins no one seems certain of, except that this alehouse was reputedly built on a burial ground for the rotting victims of some incurable plague or other.

'Of course, I've heard it said that certain animals, like very young children, have a kind of sixth sense, an uncanny ability to see spirits, phantoms, apparitions, and the like. But I'm not sure any of us really considered the possibility that Luke was holding one-way canine conversations with some totally invisible-to-us ghost, *seriously*. I mean, come on. I've been drinking here for the best part of thirty years, and I've never seen anything remotely out of the ordinary.

'Well, okay, granted nothin' that would pass as being considered half-way unusual for a pub smack

(Opposite): The wonderful, old-fashioned fireplace at the far end of the bar of *Ye Hole in Ye Wall*, in Liverpool city centre: The focus of Luke, the 'Death-Predicting' hound's "spirit walks".
Photo Credit: Tony Barr

in the middle of Liverpool City Centre, at least!'

'But I found Luke's behaviour very disturbing, just the same, although I never admitted this to any of me friends, especially not Bill. What we soon started to refer to as "Luke's Spirit Walks," played heavily on me mind. It sent some serious shivers up and down me spine, like a monkey on a stick if you wanna know the truth. I suppose it's similar to how you sometimes find yourself being creeped out by something as innocuous as the sound of your bedroom door creaking slowly open on a still, windless night, or the way in which a gibbering shadow, with no obvious source, plays across a plain white wall.

'Anyway my unformed fears were given a potential focus, of sorts, when one of our mutual friends, Jimmy Doyle, a tall, thin fella with a Brylcreemed flat-top, blessed, or cursed, with a voice higher than a castrated hyena on helium, suddenly announced, as we were busy tuning up one day, that it had just occurred to him that whenever Luke embarked on his strange ritual, someone in our crowd passed away not long after.

'Of course, we laughingly dismissed this too, as being complete and utter nonsense. Actually, we called it great big steamin' pile of coincidental shite, but of course, looking back, that shrug-of-the-shoulder, fixed-grin denial was nothing more than a collective whistling in the dark. I mean, I can't speak for the others, but there were many occasions, usually, though not always, during those unspeakably soul-draining, dark hours before dawn, when I'd lie awake and wonder:

'Was there a single grain of truth in what Jimmy had half-jokingly said?'

'Well, like I said earlier, none of us were getting any younger, and it was inevitable that as the weeks and months passed, fewer and fewer of our circle of friends would be able to turn up for our Sunday afternoon shindigs.

And besides, it wasn't as though anyone had immediately keeled over and died the very second Luke began his weird antics.

No one instantly succumbed to a fatal heart attack whilst getting the ale in (which you've gotta admit, can sometimes be a highly stressful business, especially when you find yerself faced with the unenviable task of getting the "lasties" in when it's packed to the rafters on a busy night) or collapsed with a brain aneurysm as they struggled to reach that incredibly difficult high note at the end of *I Will Always Love You!*

'Nah, all of those who passed away did so several days, or even whole weeks, later and so it was relatively easy to dismiss Luke's occasionally bizarre behaviour, as bein' just that: the mad-arse antics of a "wonder dog." 'And besides, as I say, these incidents happened so infrequently, it was all-too-easy to consign their occurrence to the purple bin of discarded memory.

'However, one stiflingly hot August night, a couple of years back, when Luke performed his dreaded "Spirit Walk" for what was to prove to be the second-to-last time, one of our best mates died, just forty eight hours later, and even though news of his passing was hardly a shock, 'cos he'd been seriously ill for some time, still something noticeably changed between our friends, and Bill and I. The atmosphere soured, became tense and filled with excruciatingly awkward silences, the second we set foot in the pub. I mean, nothing was ever said out loud. No ultimatums were issued by anyone. But just the same, I felt we were no longer welcome in our favourite alehouse, and I know Bill felt it too. We both knew the problem lay with Luke, and not ourselves, but there was no way on God's earth Bill was ever gonna consider leaving the dog at home whilst we went out drinking. We eventually decided, by unspoken consent, to start spending our Sunday afternoons visiting various other watering holes in and around the City Centre, like *The Grapes, The Cornmarket,* and *The Ship & Mitre.*

'We missed our circle of friends terribly. Of course we did. Even though, thankfully, one or two of them chose to break with tradition every now and again, to meet us for a drink in one or other of these other pubs. To be honest though, they always seemed to spend more time casting nervous glances at Luke, and checking their watches, as though they had somewhere else they urgently needed to be, than gluggin' a bevvy and engaging in carefree banter.

'It was a major consolation to me though that the dog behaved impeccably, and never once left Bill's side, and before too long, the bad feelings associated with Luke's "Spirit-Walking" antics dissipated like a summer morning mist burned off by the heat of the sun.

'The best part of a year passed, and, things carried on pretty much that way, right up until Christmas, when on a whim, Bill rang me to suggest it might not be such a bad idea to pop in to *Ye Hole In Ye Wall* for a quick pint; a flying visit, to wish our old mates all the best (and yeah, of course, a couple of them *had* since died, without any "precognitive input" from Luke, whatsoever), and yer know wha,' and I didn't take much persuading.

'And so we returned to the pub on a freezing cold December afternoon, the middle of that melancholy, week-long period that stretches between Christmas Day and New Year's Eve. I remember a fierce wind was sweepin' in from the Irish Sea, blasting cold sheets of sleety rain along the length of Dale Street and directly into our faces as we stepped from the blessed warmth of my wife's car. The second I stepped from the front passenger seat, the first doubts regarding the wisdom of our returning to the pub after so long began to surface. It had only been a little before three in the afternoon, but the day was so murky and gloomy the street-lights were already switched on, and for some reason, their misted artificial glare conjured up images of the jagged, knife-slit orange eyes of October Jack O' Lanterns.

'Predictably, Luke was the only one of us to able to summon up a degree of enthusiasm for this arl arse's reunion. He was positively straining at the leash, or at least he would have been if he'd been wearin' one. On the other hand, I suppose I felt a little like a teenager on his first date, nervous to the point of almost-regret, as he prepares to knock at the door of the girl of his dreams.

'The loud cheer that greeted us the moment we stepped inside, however, soon served to raise our spirits and sent any qualms flying out the door faster than I've seen drunken head-the-balls get ejected by City Centre bouncers.

'I was moved to see that our old friends quickly rearranged their positions so they could make room for us to sit in our usual specs, as though we had never truly been away. They even made a genuine fuss of Luke, who of course, revelled in the attention and played to the gallery, like the seasoned pro he was.

'Like I say, we had only intended staying for an hour or two, but somehow, time had sneakily slipped by, the way it sometimes does when times are good and the drinks are flowin' and the conversation is mixed with that mad, carouselspinnin' whirl of jokes, songs and laughter.

'I think, looking back though, some inner part of me knew that The Bad Thing was gonna happen again, a few seconds before it actually did.

'I'd turned to Bill, intending to tell him that we'd best be getting a move on or we'd miss the last bus and Doris would have me guts for garters, when I saw Luke pause in his frantic sniffing of various people's shoes, and with a terrible sinking feeling in the pit of my stomach, I watched as his ears suddenly pricked up and with that all-too familiar pitiful whine, he began slowly making his way over to the fireplace.

'When he got there, the entire pub fell silent, and he sat back on his hind quarters, gazed up at that imperceptible point of grim fascination with his soft brown eyes, and cried more mournfully than I'd ever heard him cry before. Just as I was about to jump from my seat and race across the bar to forcibly drag him back by his collar, the dog abruptly turned his back, as though he'd been dismissed and padded slowly towards us, and before Bill could reach out his hand to attempt to soothe him, Luke placed his head on his master's lap and regarded him with an expression of such desperate sadness, I can't find the adequate words to describe it. The only thing that comes to mind is a line I once heard in some vaguely recalled song by a half-forgotten Liverpool band; some desperately lovelorn singer croonin' about *The Heart Of All Sorrows...*

'I suddenly felt like I was intruding on some intensely private moment: the shared grief of a couple of bereaved relatives, for instance, and I turned away and looked out through the windows and the murkiness beyond, gazed at the soles of my shoes, the manky dregs of my almost-empty beer glass, *anywhere* but at the sight of that frighteningly intense sadness radiating from the dog in virtual waves.

'After what seemed like the longest time, Bill, his face chalk-white with shock and looking as though he'd suddenly aged by about twenty-odd years, rose to his feet and swayed unsteadily, like a man struggling to keep his balance on the decks of a ship in the midst of a full-blown typhoon, and for a horrible moment I was sure he was going to keel over and fall flat on his face, right there and then. Luckily, before that could happen, several people in our party, and others who were stood over by the bar, ran over to support him. They got him to sit back down and someone suggested calling an ambulance, but the moment he was seated, Bill wouldn't hear of it.'

"I'm not goin' to no stinkin' hospital!" he shouted in a voice that brooked no argument. "There's nothing wrong with me that a good, stiff, single malt won't put right."

'I saw with relief that some of the colour had returned to his cheeks, though he still looked more than a little dazed, even after he'd thrown back the double whisky the head bar-maid had handed him after telling him it was "on the house", and it was clear someone would have to arrange for transport to get him safely home. Good old Jimmy Doyle phoned his missus, Janice, to come and pick the three of us up and by the time she arrived, mercifully, Bill was in far better spirits and thankfully, Luke seemed to have perked up a little, too, although he still wasn't on top form.

'Neither of us spoke much during the short drive home to Otterspool. Bill was sat on the back seat, with his dog lying face down alongside him, whilst I sat up front trying to make small-talk with Janice.

'It's funny the things you most vividly remember about the occasions that you know will later serve as bitter landmarks; those defining milestones situated at various points along the winding path of your life.

'I recall the way the warm air blasted in waves from the heater.

The used, luckless lottery ticket, crumpled in the foot-well.

The pungent odour of the dangling Scots pine air-freshener.

The city's roads, shiny with black sheet ice.

And on the radio, Greg Lake cynically pronouncing that *The Christmas We Get We Deserve.*

'Those things…

'And the way I never even got to shake my best friend's hand when it came time to say goodbye at the end of our last night out.'

SEVEN

'I couldn't sleep at all that night. I just knew instinctively, that something was dreadfully wrong.

'My wife, Doris, bless her, who could read my moods with an almost eerie precision, did her best to reassure me that everything was gonna be all right, and tried to hug me to sleep the way she used to do back when we were young lovers, and all the troubles of the world could be banished by something as simple, but life-affirming as a cuddle beneath a fold of warm blankets.

'It never worked on this occasion, though, and after lying awake for most of the night tossing and turning and listening to the sound of my wife's gentle snoring, I quietly sneaked out of bed and made my way down the stairs to the kitchen to make myself a pot of piping hot coffee. I peered blearily at the clock over on the far wall and saw that it was 4:30am, and then found my eyes drawn to the house phone, one of those imitation 1950s models that one of our friends had bought us for our Silver Wedding Anniversary. In truth, I'd never liked the ugly friggin' thing, and I found I liked it even less at that moment, sitting there all black and silent and squat, at least three long empty hours before the dawn.

'The time dragged by with agonising slowness, the way it will when you're sat in a hospital waiting room for the final test results to come back, or for news, good or bad, to filter through regarding the well-being of a loved one in the wake of some terrible disaster.

'When the call finally came, at a little after seven, with a madly, shrilling, insistent tone I'd never noticed before, I wasn't a bit surprised to find the voice at the other end of the line was Bill's neighbour, John Harrison.

'He was my friend's unofficial carer, the one who checked up on him on a daily basis, and even before he spoke the first words, in halting, sombre tones, I knew he'd rung to tell me that Bill had died.

'I listened with tears streaming down my face as John told me he'd been awoken at two in the morning by the sound of a terrible howling noise coming from next door. He'd quickly thrown on a set of clothes and legged it round there. He had his own set of keys and let himself in, but for some reason he'd felt compelled to pause the moment he stepped into the hallway. The howling was coming from one of the upstairs bedrooms, a sound that spoke of such utter misery and abject desolation, it was all John could do to stop himself from turning and bolting out of the house without investigating any further.

"I really, really didn't want to go up there, Harry," he told me a little sheepishly. "I mean, I knew it must surely be Luke making that dreadful noise, but to tell you the God's honest truth, it just didn't sound remotely like any dog that *I've* ever heard. It reminded me more of the hysterical wailing of one of those arl Middle Eastern women you sometimes see on the news, mourning her relatives following another one of those "collateral damage" inflicting Western airstrikes!"

"I just stood there, for how long I couldn't say, and I felt every bit as arse-twitchingly terrified as I had when I was a little kid, and I'd sneaked into that supposedly haunted warehouse in the middle of Seel Street, after dark, on a Hallowe'en dare.

"Then, suddenly, that awful baying stopped, cut off in mid-yowl, like somebody lifted the needle from the world's worst slice of vinyl, and it turned deathly quiet. And somehow, that was worse.

"I got moving, then, though. I ran up the stairs two at a time, actually, and stepped into what I knew to be Bill's bedroom.

"I switched the light on, and there was Bill and his dog, sleeping contentedly, on top of the bedclothes, side by side.

"Except of course, they weren't *really* sleeping. I'm no doctor, but even I could see, as I stepped a little closer, that they were both dead.

"They both looked peaceful enough, though, Harry. Neither of them appeared to have suffered at all. And I suppose that's at least some kind of bitter-sweet consolation."

'I had to agree with John, it kind of was.

'It just didn't feel like much of one at the time.

'And it still doesn't now."

EIGHT

'Billy was seventy-five years old when he passed away. Not a bad innings, as they say. I'm just twelve months shy of reaching that milestone myself, God willing.

'As far I know, my best friend had been in fairly good shape for a man his age, but death has a way of sneaking up on even the seemingly healthiest of people, and taking them to wherever it is we go when the final velvet curtain falls, and here was yet more proof of that unpalatable fact.

'As for Luke, well, he was of indeterminate age and the vet who examined him stated that the dog had died due to a stress-related illness, doubtless brought on by its owner's sudden death.

'The veterinarians can say what they want, though, They've got the qualifications, and I'm just a old soldier, from a war that's been consigned to an all but discarded footnote, so who am I to argue with their findings?

'But me, I've got my own theory as to what truly killed Luke.

'I think that dog died of a broken heart.'

NINE

'When you're feeling a bit messed up,
So gone...
When you're feeling your heart go slipping away
May all the Earth's space surround you'
The Guillemots

'There was to be no burial service for Billy Myers. No church funeral. He had long ago stipulated that he be cremated at the end of a deliberately low-key ceremony (it was common knowledge amongst his family and friends that he had a morbid fear of being buried alive, which was hardly surprising seeing as how he'd personally witnessed the carnage of a Chinese trench collapse at the height of the Korean War) and so of course, his final wishes were respected.

'Only a handful close friends and family members gathered on Otterspool Promenade, near to where Bill had lived all his life, to witness the spraying of his ashes on the River Mersey on a bitingly cold, but gloriously sunny February day.

'I watched his younger sister, Sheila, slowly lift the lid off the dark-grey urn and let the weightless dust-like flakes drift slowly across the choppy, shifting waters. As she muttered her last farewells, a personal eulogy to the memory of her dear departed brother, I happened to glance across to the tangled clumps of dead-brown bushes that lined the shoreline, and for just the briefest second, I saw, or thought I saw, a darker shadow lurking amongst the leafless branches.

'I couldn't be sure. Not even when I shielded my eyes to protect them from the dazzling glare of the late-winter sun. But, just for a second, the shadow took on the appearance of an achingly familiar outline, etched against the drab, lifeless, pre-spring undergrowth.

'A silhouetted form that resembled, for just one moment, a canine form.

'A black Labrador.

'Present and correct to witness his beloved master's final journey.'

TEN

Of course, I can't vouch for the truth of Harry's tale, any more than I could openly accuse him of telling outright lies, for some reason best known to himself, on that memorable autumn afternoon; the very afternoon I chose to embark on a solitary stint of remembrance for the passing of someone not personally known to me, but whose absence had left a giant-sized hole in my life.

Whether through choice or circumstance, several years were to pass before I again set foot in *Ye Hole In Ye Wall,* after that impromptu meeting with Harry. And when I finally did, there was no sign of the man, and a few discreet enquiries from the locals and the bar-staff revealed that they knew of a couple of older men named Harry, but neither of them came close to matching the description I'd provided.

No one remembers a black Labrador called Luke, either, but again, that could also be due to the relentless passing of time and the notorious fallibility of memory.

I can only add that for my part, I believed arl Harry on the day I toasted the memory of John Peel, and that his story gave me some degree of comfort on what had been, up until that point, a thoroughly depressing day.

There are those times, infrequent, but no less insistent for all that, that I find myself wondering if Harry is still doing the rounds in Liverpool's pubs, other than *Ye Hole In Ye Wall.*

If so, I hope he happens by lucky chance to read what is after all, *his* story.

And if he does, perhaps he'll consider dropping in to his former local, and we'll have pint or a double brandy or two, and talk and swap stories as though we were a pair of old and trusty companions, enjoying a beer in the familiar surroundings of our favourite watering hole.

CHAPTER FIVE
'UNCLE NORMAN'S LAST FAREWELL'
& THE PHANTOM DOG OF EASTHAM

And speaking of decidedly unusual canine-related phenomena, back in the late 1990s, when I was still spending an inordinate amount of my life sat at the office computer long after everyone else had gone home for the evening, furiously typing away for the (ahem), "vast legions of avid readers" of my self-produced, small-press magazine, I came across a couple of letters very kindly sent to me by a couple of fellow Merseysiders; a man named Richard Thompson, and a woman with the rather lovely name of Debbie Fair.

The accounts they related concerned two very different examples of doggy weirdness, which may or may not, have a bearing on the veracity of the previous tale.

To begin with, Richard's well-written missive.

"Dear Lee,

I wish to make it clear at the outset that I have never been a religious person. At least not in the conventional sense, (although I do hold the greatest of respect for those who have faith in a power greater than mortal man). Somewhat paradoxically though, I do have a deep interest in various aspects of "The supernatural."

I think it's important that I make you aware of this state of relative open-mindedness, if not outright gullibility, before I get to my story.

In the mid-winter of 1993, my wife's Uncle Norman died suddenly from a massive coronary. News of his death had come as something of a shock as we'd always considered him to be an exceptionally fit man, who was only in his mid fifties. Norman enjoyed virtually all forms of exercise, including running, playing football, tennis, and going swimming.

It could therefore be considered more than a trifle ironic that he met his death after collapsing at the local swimming baths whilst striving manfully to beat his personal record.

Norman, a life-long bachelor, was a kind and considerate man who was what you'd call these, everyone-needs-to-be pigeon-holed and compartmentalised days, a "dog-person," and really enjoyed taking our bitch Sadye, for long walks along Moreton Shore, (a largely unspoiled beach stretching along a goodly-sized part of the western coast-line of the Wirral peninsular), together with his mother's dog, also female. It had been plainly obvious to everyone that Sadye very much enjoyed these expeditions, and treated the older dog as her "step-mother."

Immediately prior to his funeral, Norman's body was placed in a Chapel of Rest in the centre of Upton Village. This was then, and for all I know still is, the premises of 'Alex Taylor Undertakers', and the family duly attended for the sad ceremony of paying their last respects to Norman, at the Chapel.

I feel it's only right that I should mention at this stage, that whilst Norman frequently took Sadye for these leisurely shore-line walks, he didn't take her on a daily basis. This task fell to myself, and I have to say that I took a deal of pleasure in carrying it out. It was also something of a standing joke amongst our family that Sadye, actually took me *for walks, and not the other way round! Although quite a relatively small dog, of indeterminate breed, she always pulled like a bleedin traction engine, and had a fiercely independent nature. I have to admit, much to my regret, this can very probably be put down to extremely poor training by yours truly.*

In the wake of Norman's death, the whole family immediately realised that Sadye would terribly miss her regular walks down to Moreton Shore, and I made a mental note to take her there in the not too distant future, as soon as the latter stages of the funeral arrangements had been completed.

*During the interim period, I continued to take Sadye on her two daily walks from our Beechwood Estate home, and I used to enjoy trying to guess in advance which of her four favourite routes she would literally drag me along. It might sound a little childish, but I had these routes numbered in my head; one through to four; and as occasionally there were slight variations from her chosen paths, I would add a letter to the number – rather like bus routes. I know. **I know.** You doubtless think me a trifle sad. But I'm trying to be truthful, here. Warts and all, as they say....*

Anyway, these four main routes were as follows: One ran straight into the centre of the Beechwood Estate, (the posh name substituted by the local council for the apparently more vulgar, Ford Estate – though it seems, no amount of name-changing could deter from the fact that the area was still largely populated by "druggies, burglar's good-for-nothing dole scroungers and other undesirables." At least according to those journalistic stalwarts in the local press.
But I digress..

The other three routes took us up the steep, sweat-inducing incline of the nearby Ford Hill, the second led directly along Manor Drive, heading towards our family's previous home, whilst the third was straight through the middle of a large green field opposite a set traffic lights, in between the first two destinations.

Two days prior to Norman's funeral, Sadye headed towards her regular Manor Drive Walk, but suddenly, she unexpectedly hesitated by the set of traffic lights at the top of this road. After pausing to give it 'some thought,' Sadye took me to the beginning of the road leading into Upton Village, where she once again hesitated, looking in the direction of Upton. It might sound a bit soft, but she seemed strangely unsure of herself, which was highly unusual for this particularly decisive dog, After a few moments though, she turned and resumed her usual route. We returned home soon after, and I thought no more of it.

The very next day, though, the same thing happened. However, on this occasion, Sadye seemed rather more determined to carry on with this new journey, and we took the road into Upton Village itself. 'I was rather surprised because this was very much off the beaten track for Sadye. It's long been my experience that dogs, and Sadye, in particular, only go where they recognise those tempting smells that are immediately familiar to them, but this proved to be a notable exception to that widely-accepted "Doggy Tradition".

With a resigned shrug I told her "Okay, girl. You seem to know where you're going, even if I haven't got the slightest clue. Lead on!" She took at me at my word, and continued at her usual sprightly pace and despite my previous words of encouragement, with each step I began to grow a little concerned as to just how far she was planning on taking me. I had some important things to do when we eventually got back home, so I was more than a little pushed for time.

Granted, I could, and perhaps should, have simply done an about-turn, and forcibly dragged Sadye back the way we'd come, but the truth is I liked her to do her own thing, and I felt mean even thinking of depriving her of the opportunity to "fill her boots", so to speak. And so we continued on right through the heart of the village, and we walked past the rows of local shops and beauty salons and butty bars and I was half-hoping that she would turn down a side road so that we could have taken a circular route back home. But she seemed resolutely determined to carry on, as though she were on a mission entirely of her own choosing. We eventually came to another set of traffic lights, and at this stage it was slowly dawning on me that things were beginning to take a decidedly odd twist:

I remembered (and how had I ever truly forgotten), Norman was still lying in the Chapel of Rest.

Just a little ways up the road, now.

"Surely not," I thought. "No way is Sadye hell-bent on heading there, of all places..?"

But yes....It was indeed to be.

Sadye crossed over by the lights and trotted straight up towards the aforementioned undertaker's premises, and I'm not ashamed to say, I began to feel distinctly uneasy.

Sadye chose to stop directly outside the Chapel of Rest.

She sat her haunches, glanced intently towards it, and refused to take a single step further.

The blood did freeze in my veins, though when she raised her head, glanced to the heavens and *began to whimper – the most mournful sound I've ever had the misfortune to hear in my life.*

I stood there, clapping my hands over my ears in a forlorn attempt to block out that desolate, anguished whining, whilst a highly pertinent question skittered across the surface of my mind. How could Sadye have possibly known, as seemed all too apparent by her otherwise inexplicable behaviour, that Norman's body was at rest inside this very chapel?

I'm not at all sure how long we two remained there, immobile, oblivious to the passing of strangers and the constant hum of traffic.

Time itself ceased to have any meaning. It could have been minutes or the best of an hour, but eventually, Sadye gave a last, lingering howl, and the notion struck me that it sounded very much like a final goodbye, before slowly getting back to her feet and without pausing, or once looking back, led me home by exactly the same route we'd taken earlier.

Now though, she seemed to have an added bounce in her step – almost as though she had achieved something worthwhile. 'And perhaps she had. In her own delightfully doggy way, she had dutifully paid her last respects to someone she'd miss for the rest of her lifetime.

Sometimes, it seems supposedly dumb animals are gifted with abilities we humans would give anything to possess. "

Oh, and there was an interesting postscript to Mr Thompson's letter.

"I wish to add, Lee, that at no time prior to this occasion had Sadye ever walked through any part of Upton Village, never mind approached anywhere near The Chapel of Rest. Not even when we'd gone shopping with her sat on the back seat of the car. It was all completely new territory to her. And as far as I know, she has never been back since. 'Even now, when I think about it, I get cold shivers. Though not necessarily inspired by fear.

Whether you, or anyone else believes me or not, I will always maintain that it was Sadye who took me directly there that day, just two days shy of her master's funeral. I swear that I never encouraged or egged her on in any way. That was the last thing I would have done. Thus, I find it hard, if not impossible, to shake the belief that there was some sort of spiritual communication between Sadye and the dearly departed Norman, and that he was determined to call her to his side for a last, final farewell. "

The second letter dealing with a similar theme, this time concerned an actual spectral hound, one of those calamity predicting Black Dogs that populate the annals of British folklore. Back in 1999, the aforementioned author of the account, Debbie Fair, a former resident of Merseyside, was working on the editorial staff at the *Paranormal-online* web site, and in her letter to me, she related the following experience....

"Back in the late 1980s, I used to regularly drive around the dark, winding back roads of the Wirral side of the Mersey.

My parents lived in Bebington, back then, and I also had several friends who lived in the nearby town of Eastham.

I was living in Chester, at the time, and rather than constantly take the boring, monotonous route along the A41 motorway, as I drove too and fro visiting my friends or relatives, I often chose to take the more scenic countryside route.

Sometime during the spring of 1999, whilst I was driving home late at night, I would often spot a large black dog sitting calmly by the roadside near to Eastham Village. The animal looked real and solid enough and was very dark in colour. I would describe it as looking a great deal like an adult Irish Wolfhound.

I always naturally assumed it belonged to one of the people who lived nearby and that its owner was somewhere nearby, so I'd simply drive past affording the dog only the briefest of glances.

One night, however, as I was travelling home, I spotted the dog, initially sitting on its haunches in its usual spot, but no sooner had I had opportunity to acknowledge its presence than to my surprise and horror, the animal suddenly darted right out, directly in front of the car. I was totally convinced that I must have run the dog over because it didn't reappear anywhere before me.

I can't recall now whether I noticed any kind of impact, but I immediately jerked the car to a halt and got out to look for the dog, which I felt sure, with a sickening knot in my stomach, must be badly injured, if not dead. I was already dreading telling the owners.

However, not long after stepping from the car it quickly became apparent that there was absolutely no trace of the dog whatsoever. I checked under the vehicle and on both sides of the road. I even called out to the animal, once or twice...

But there was nothing...

Suddenly, I grew frightened, and I quickly jumped back into my car and drove home as hastily as the law would allow. 'You may not be surprised to learn that I subsequently stopped using that route, and indeed have never chosen to use it again, to this very day.

I do wonder now, though, whether the appearance of the black dog was some sort of warning to me. 'I'll tell you why. Very shortly after my last sighting of the animal, I was involved in a rather nasty car accident which happened at the exact point that I would normally have joined the A41 from the back roads of Eastham.

I wonder if I had gone by the old route, the dog would have been waiting to stop me again, and the accident would never have happened?

Certainly, I've always regarded the area in and around the Village, to be possessed of some indefinable strangeness..."

And Debbie, it seems, is not the only one to be struck by the peculiar, almost otherworldly aura that permeates the locale. When the American author, Nathaniel Hawthorne, was acting as the United States consul to Liverpool, he paid a visit to Eastham Village, and wrote of how he found it *quite the finest old village I have seen, with many unique houses, and altogether a rural and picturesque aspect, unlike anything in America, and yet possessing a familiar look, as if it was something I had dreamed about...*

EASTHAM VILLAGE
(Above): One of the oldest hamlets on the Wirral Peninsula, Eastham Village has been inhabited since Saxon times, and from the wooded banks of which, a ferry service used to exist, transporting passengers across the River Mersey, to and from Liverpool. It's hard to believe, walking through this tiny collection of quaint, white-walled cottages, village pub and the beautiful St Mary's Church, replete with its ancient yew tree, that you're scarcely a few hundred feet away from modern, terraced housing, shops and the constantly traffic-heavy, A41 motorway
Photo Credit: Dave Shirley

CHAPTER SIX
Follow Your Dreams,
Never Regret The Unrealised

'Now there comes a darker day,
Abandoned in a lonely place
Where only broken hopes remain...
And black is the cross silhouetted by rain...'
In Dark Dreams - The Lids

ONE

We *all* of us seek to follow our dreams....
To a greater or lesser extent, we do.

We chase them, these long-held fantasies and cherished ambitions, along endlessly twisting paths, like we're pursuing some undiscovered species of butterfly deep amidst the vibrant green jungles of the Amazon, or along the banks of Mokele Mbembe-haunted Lake Tele in the depths of the Congo.

And during the long-ago days of childhood, soon after I'd been forced, by cruel reality, to abandon my dreams of transforming my skinny, curly-headed, pre-teenage self, into the incredibly cool Fonz, from *Happy Days,* my biggest aspiration was to somehow persuade my parents to allow me to own a dog, any dog, I didn't care what breed. I just longed for a loyal and constant companion, a faithful hound to accompany me on all kinds of exciting adventures and acts of derring-do (which, at various times ranged from my planning to stow away on a merchant ship bound for some exotic land, to solving the age-old mystery of Spring-Heeled Jack, and defeating the evil, school-kid-terrorising members of the local Harvey Gang).

This might not sound like much of a dream, to you, Dear Reader, but the truth is, when I was growing up, nearly all of my favourite novels, comics, films and TV programmes seemed to feature a host of heroic, smartly resourceful, canines. The selfless actions of Rebel, for me, the *real* star of *Champion, The Wonder Horse.* Pongo, the paternal founder of "The Twilight Barking", the post-sunset network of doggy communication, in Dodie Smith's *One Hundred And One Dalmatians.* The tear-jerking antics of the dogs featured in the likes of *Old Yeller, Lassie Come Home,* and *The Incredible Journey.*

It seemed though that despite my impassioned pleas to my parent's that what I really wanted for my 'main prezzy,' every time Christmas or the occasion of my birthday came rolling round, was a real-life dog, I may as well have been asking them for a one-man submersible so that I could single-handedly explore the murky depths of Loch Ness, for all the good it did.

I remember one particularly heart-breaking incident when my mum and dad promised to buy me "something special" as a reward for my making "good progress" in English class. I'd spent several sleepless nights, consumed with barely contained excitement, sure that I'd be called downstairs for breakfast one morning, and there'd be a tail-wagging puppy, scampering clumsily across the polished kitchen floor in its eagerness to greet me.

A day or so later, though, I was forced to hide my soul-crushing sense of disappointment when my "something special" turned out to be a bicycle – one of those ubiquitous, 1970s, red-painted, black-seated Choppers, that I promptly wrote off later that very same day, making my debut ride around the block with a face every bit as miserable as the drizzly, February weather. I'd momentarily lost control and wound up crashing head-long into the metal base of a lamp-post. I was physically okay, aside from a few bruises, but the

Chopper was so horribly twisted and bent out of shape it was scarcely recognisable as having once been a bike.

My dad had always insisted that owning a dog was simply too demanding and time consuming, whilst my mum was a confirmed cat lover, and though I've always admired felines for their fierce sense of independence and their sleepy, curled-in-yer-lap, purring-ness (is that last a real word? If it isn't, it certainly *should* be) as well as their cool indifference when confronted with impending danger, I've never considered them to be an adequate substitute for a dog. And so the years of pre-teen adolescence slipped by, and it seemed as though I had about as much chance of ever owning a dog, as I had of acquiring a live Mongolian Death Worm

Or, for that matter, ever being mistaken for Henry Winkler, by the beautiful young girls I'd increasingly begun to notice as being something other than complete and utter nuisances when it came to building dens, organising apple scrumping expeditions, or breaking into empty houses to hunt for any resident ghosts.

'Looks like I'm destined to be forever Fonz-less and dog-less!' I told myself out loud, one late August night, a week or so before my final year at Junior School began. 'Some things just aren't meant to be! The old *Happy Days* dream is *never* gonna happen, I understand that now, and it doesn't matter how many PVC jackets, plain white T-shirts, and jars of Brylcreem I buy with me pocket money. I'll probably be really old, like, 21 or somethin,' before I finally get to own a dog! But it turned out I was wrong about that last bit. *Partly,* at least.

TWO

I first encountered "Wolf", a filth-covered Border Collie, cowering between the rows of oily-black pipes and metal containers that lined the Mersey dock-side, one beautiful October afternoon, at the start of the half-term school break, when I was eleven years old.

I'd been in the company of my brother, Grant, and three of my best friends: Philly Bennett, Gary Appleton, and the wonderfully-named Peter Penny, busy foraging around for planks of wood or sheets of tarpaulin to help repair the roof of our den which had been all but torn off by the gales that had caused extensive structural damage across the county the previous weekend. The focus of our search had been amongst the waste-strewn plot of land at the back of an old abandoned building that, judging from the stacks of broken chairs and long, narrow tables piled up outside in bonfire-like heaps, had once been a dockers' canteen.

It was an eerily lonely place, silent save for the sigh of the wind and the lonely cry of the occasional seagull, but even those notorious scavengers seemed to steer clear most of the time, almost as though they were consciously avoiding the place. It was odd, too, that despite the fact that most of the building's large window panes were broken, and the front door was always stood slightly ajar, there was very little sign that anyone; no local tramps seeking overnight shelter, gangs of bored teenagers armed with a litre bottle or two of

Merrydown, nor horny courting couples, desperate for some privacy, had ever set foot in there. There was no graffiti on the cracked and paint-peeling walls, either. No declarations of undying love or pledges of allegiance to a particular football club. Even the local ubiquitous proclamation:

"SCOUSERS RULE AND DON'T YOU FORGET IT!" was noticeable only by its absence.

To be honest, it was only with extreme reluctance that I ever paused to stop and glance inside the building, but whenever I did, I couldn't help but be struck by the notion that there was something not quite right with the place. It was nothing you could see, exactly Nothing you could quite put you finger on. But nevertheless, the mere sight of the canteen never failed to unsettle me. The sickly pale quality of light that permeated the building, even on the very sunniest of days, did nothing to afford the place some cheer, but there were other things, too.

There was a garish 1952, calendar, posted like an afterthought, slap in the centre of the far wall featuring some scantily clad female model or film-star that I didn't recognise, her too-bright-red lipstick turning her supposedly sexy smile into a silent, bloody scream; a former employee's donkey jacket was slung haphazardly on a coat hook like a flag of defeat; the serving hatch, its wooden door hanging drunkenly on a single rusted hinge (the slightest breeze causing it to sway gently, its awful screeching sound echoing around the empty hall bringing to mind the terrible noises I'd once heard coming from a cattle truck filled with frantically squealing pigs on a one way trip to the local slaughterhouse).

Many years later, whilst carrying out some research for an article on the subject of Fallen Angels within the magnificent surroundings of Liverpool's Picton Reading Library, I came across a reference to an ancient Greek demon named, Erebus.

And the following sentence had all but leapt off the page of a musty old tome:

Erebus is the manifestation of humanity's grief and negative emotion. He represented the personification of darkness and shadow, which filled in all the corners and crannies of the world.

Immediately upon reading this, a vivid image of that derelict canteen from the distant days of childhood had suddenly popped into my mind, and I remember thinking at that moment that if there truly were such things as portals leading from the very depths of the infernal regions up into our modern-day world, then that godforsaken shell of a building on the banks of the River Mersey, was a potential dimensional gateway. Something through which, a shapeless, slithering horror, the demon, Erebus, for instance, might slink into our world on occasion.

Or as I was later to learn, something far more human, deceptively ordinary in appearance, but terrifyingly, infinitely, worse.

THREE

Perhaps then, I really shouldn't have been too surprised, that this was the place where we first set eyes upon what seemed, to my friends and I at the time, to be a living, breathing symbol of desperation and despair.

Well, a barely living, breathing one, anyway.

Actually, we heard it before we saw it.

I was rummaging through a pile of assorted rubbish, and a sheet of corrugated iron that might serve as a roof for our wind-battered den had caught my eye, when I suddenly froze, and all those old horror story clichés about the hairs standing up on the back of your neck, and your spine tingling like someone had dropped an Ice Pop down the back of your T-shirt, proved to be all too true.

An ear-piercing howling rent the still October air, like a note of long-lost hope, and it appeared to be coming from a clump of vile, diseased-looking bushes a couple of hundred yards from where my friends and I were stood, stunned into silence by that eerily melancholic sound.

I think it was Peter Penny, the tall, thin, heedlessly curious one amongst us, who finally broke the spell. 'What the hell's making that noise?' he shouted to no one in particular. Before adding, in his best Roger McGough-Scouse drawl: 'There's a howlin' in the bushes...In the bushes, there's a howl!'

'Knock it off, lad!' Gary said, pointing a finger in warning, but he may as well have been busy yelling his encouragement for all the good it did.

'Come on, men,' Pete said, charging towards the tangle of wilted scrub. 'Let's go an' have a look and see what's making that friggin' racket!'

Shrugging our shoulders we followed his skinny-as-a-bean-pole frame, though, it has to be said, at a far slower pace, and it was only when our brave or foolhardy friend peered into the midst of the thicket, parted the dry, crackling stalks and then turned back towards us with an expression of shocked surprise on his face, that we quickly forgot our fears and raced up alongside him.

The source of that terrible, lonely howling was lying slumped, tied with a length of rope to the thick, twisted trunk of a shrub in the centre of a small, muddy clearing surrounded by dead or dying plants.

It was an adult dog, a male Border Collie, by the looks of it, though it was difficult to be sure due to the fact that its horribly matted fur was completely covered in a slimy coating of jet-black oil, and layers of foul-smelling waste; a viscous, chemical substance, the identity of which I didn't know, and honestly didn't want to, but which conjured up images of the poisoned earth of Tolkien's Mordor.

He looked absolutely terrified and rent the air once more with another of those blood-curdling howls, but upon catching sight of us standing there, our mouths wide open on a perfect series of O's, that might have appeared comical in happier circumstances, his obviously parched tongue lolled out and he began wagging his tail weakly as we approached, murmuring words of comfort. His soft brown eyes stared up at us hopefully, and when he next made a sound it was less a howl, more a pitiful whimper that broke my heart to hear.

'Oh God, we've gotta help him!' I heard myself saying, my voice choked with emotion. 'It looks like some cruel shit-bag's just tied him up and left him here to die.'

'God, how could anybody do that?' my brother said, wonderingly, and nobody answered, but I couldn't help cast a nervous glance over my shoulder, just for a second, feeling my skin begin to crawl at the sight of that long-derelict canteen.

And was there, just for the merest second, a vague outline of a darker shadow, shifting silently in the black emptiness behind one of the cracked windows?

Of course not. That was just my over-active imagination.

Surely...

'Lee, are you all right, lad?' Philly Bennett asked, shaking me from my less-than delightful reverie. 'You look like you've seen a ghost.'

'Yeah, I'm fine,' I said, summoning up a smile that felt for all the world like it was ironed on. 'I think I just lost me arl happy thoughts there, for a minute.'

'Well, it's good to have yer back in the land of the living,' he said with a nod, 'cos we've got a bit of a dilemma, here. And, I'm sorry to be pain, like, but we need to concentrate and get our heads together if we're gonna solve this problem.'

'All right, what is it, mate?' I asked.

'Well,' he said, 'basically, it's this. You wanna help get the dog the hell out of this shitty place, and I do too, but I can't see how we're gonna actually be able to set about shifting him.' He paused, and looked at each member of our little gang individually, and smiled what he liked to call his "Philly-Sophical" smile, before adding, 'I mean, I'm not tryin' to be awkward or anythin', but I don't think the dog's anywhere near strong enough to be able to walk by himself, and I mean, even though he looks half-starved, he still far too big and heavy for us to carry him very far. Even between the five of us.'

He paused again, and now the smile was gone, replaced with a nose-wrinkling grimace. 'And besides,' he said, 'I don't know about yous, but as much as I feel sorry for arl howlin' boy here, I don't fancy getting any of that poisonous lookin' chemical crap on me clothes, thanks all the same. Me ma will kick me arse all the way to the Pier Head and back, I'm tellin' yer.'

'I reckon one of us should go home and phone the RSPCA,' Grant suggested. 'Let them sort it out.'

Looking back now, that proposal should have met with unanimous approval amongst the members of our gang. After all, it made perfect sense on just about every level. It would have solved, in a matter of half an hour or so at most, the undoubted logistical problem we were faced with here, and more importantly, it would have ensured the plainly distressed, seemingly abandoned dog, received some much-needed professional care and assistance.

We didn't take that sensible course of action, though, due to our typically juvenile mistrust of adults in general, and of authority figures in particular, and we all, my brother included, immediately agreed with Pete's exclamation of 'Nah, that idea totally stinks. If anyone's gonna help "Wolf", then it's gotta be us. We found him. It's our duty to get him to a place of safety. Not some uniformed, head-patting adults with their "Well done, chaps, but we'll take it from here!!" attitudes.'

'Pete's right,' I said. 'It's up to us to save, er....' I hesitated for a second, before adding, "Wolf".

'Wolf? Is that what we're callin' him?' Philly asked.

'Sounds about right to me,' Grant piped up. 'He certainly howls like something outta one of them arl, black and white, horror films me mum and dad sometimes let us stay up and watch if we've been behaving ourselves'.

'Okay, Wolf, it is then,' I said, and even though he looked about as much like a vicious, feral prowler of the snowy wastes and night-time forests as an under-developed Chihuahua, dressed in one of those ridiculous pink tartan, strap-on coats, the name stuck.

And then I suddenly had one of those cartoon light-bulb-ping-into-life-above-your-head moments.

'Hang on,' I said. 'What about if a couple of us nip round to Andy Parr's dad's house, and borrow his dad's camping trailer from the front garden? We could lift Wolf into that and wheel him round to our house. Me mum and dad are both at work, there's just that cute babysitter, Georgina, there lookin' after our Kearry and Dale.' I shrugged my shoulders before adding; 'Well, Georgie and me younger brother and sister aren't gonna bother us. We can clean up Wolf, and then work out a plan as to what we're gonna do with him after that. Unless anyone's got any better ideas?'

'Yeah, that's a totally ace idea!' the members of our little gang chorused as one, and I afforded myself a smile, moved by their obvious enthusiasm and unconditional support. Andy Parr was a kid roughly our age, who sometimes hung around with us, most often when we were trying to organise an eleven-a-side footy match and we were short of numbers. Andy lived no more than a fifteen-minute walk away, and, more importantly considering the situation at hand, his dad had always kept a fairly small, and usually empty metal trailer, in his front garden. It was easily light enough to lift and pull along, even with a couple of kids sat in the back, and Andy had in the past allowed us to mess around in it, taking turns to drag each other down the street like a makeshift go-kart, but only when his dad was at work, of course.

'Right,' I said, encouraged by the positive response, 'I reckon me and our Grant should go and get the trailer. We'll pick up a hack saw from me dad's tool shed to cut that manky rope, too. The rest of yous wait here and look after the dog. Wolf, I mean. We'll be back as fast as we can.'

No one argued. No one said a word. They just gave us a thumbs-up.

So we got going.

FOUR

So great was our confidence of success that it didn't once occur to us, running up Dock Road North bathed in that unusually warm Indian summer sunlight, that the trailer wouldn't be there, or that Andy's dad would have decided to take the day off work. We were embarking on a vital mission, a literal life or death assignment, and nothing was going to stop us carrying it out. And with this in mind, we ran along the street, singing (or gasping, between breaths), the inspiring lyrics of the theme tune to *The Flashing Blade, (It's right to fight for what you want. For all that you believe)* convinced that God, or Fate, or King Aslan of Narnia was on our side.

'There it is!' I shouted, as we reached the Parr's home address, and indeed, the trailer was there, like it was just waiting for our arrival sat in its usual place, and there was no one around and the house seemed slumber-silent and empty.

Without pausing for a second, we grabbed hold of either side of the trailer's handle, and began dragging it back down the road towards the docks and our waiting friends. I remember feeling a sense of wild exultation as we all but flew past the seemingly deserted houses, pausing only to grab a decidedly blunt-looking hacksaw from my dad's metal toolbox. I glanced across at our kid and saw he was grinning from ear to ear as he punched his fist towards the deep blue October skies, like he'd just scored the winner in the last minute of the FA Cup Final.

Almost before we knew it, we'd reached the docks, and directly up ahead were our friends, waving excitedly as we yelled triumphantly: 'Okay....Stand by boys! Here come the lads of the 7th Cavalry, to the rescue!'

FIVE

Getting Wolf into the back of the trailer, though, proved to be slightly more difficult than it had first seemed. Firstly, we had to tread warily across the boggy ground, directly into the centre of the diseased-looking clumps of wiry, yellow-leaved plants, before we could even begin to take turns to hack away at the coil of rope, tied in a knot of near-Gordian proportions, with the rusted saw, and we were sweating cobs and swearing like troopers by the time we eventually succeeded in severing the bonds.

But if that was difficult, it was sheer bliss compared with actually heaving the dog into the trailer.

Our efforts were hampered by the fact that at one point, Wolf had totally misunderstood our intentions as we tried to lift him up between us, and his sudden panic had caused him to whimper and struggle with surprising strength, considering the awful state he was in. He shook his coat wildly, spraying us all with flecks of mud and oil and God only knew what other type of filth, and poor old Philly Bennett, seemed to get the worst of it, ("Looks like there's gonna be a serious bout of arse-kicking administered in the Bennett household tonight!" I remember thinking to myself), but eventually, through a combination of soothing words and grim determination, we managed to get Wolf to flop in an admittedly undignified heap, in the middle of the trailer.

'Right, let's get him the hell out of here!' Peter gasped, struggling for breath, and we all nodded our heads in agreement. We were all, I think, more than a little anxious to get away from that wretched place, and so we quickly began dragging the trailer through one of the many large holes in the wire fence that had been erected to keep people, especially kids like us, out.

By the time we'd gotten Wolf safely on to the tarmac and began the short journey to my parent's house (Grant and I again holding either side of the handle; Gary, Peter and Phil, taking turns to try and calm the still badly-frightened dog) it was a little after 2:30 in the afternoon. Thankfully, the road was fairly quiet at that time on a Friday, a good ninety minutes or so before what amounted to a rush hour, in those quieter, long-ago days. We only encountered a couple of cars and a single lorry, its wagon stacked high with rusty scrap metal, headed down towards the docks. One or two of the drivers honked their horns and gave us a "how's-it-goin', lads?" thumbs-up as they drove by, and we responded in kind, grinning cheesily, thankful that none of them thought to slow down to take a closer look. If any of them had have done they'd very probably have asked us what the hell we thought we were doing transporting a clearly distressed dog in the back of a camper trailer, caked in at least ten different shades of effluence.

We didn't bump into anyone walking along the road, either. There was no one out washing their cars, or pottering about in their front gardens, or sat on their doorsteps reading the papers. There was no sign either of the usual groups of kids playing games, riding their bikes or scooters, or just generally hanging around, and I considered this to be some sort of minor miracle, especially seeing as how this was half-term, and the weather was as perfect as it ever gets here in the fair county of Merseyside, this late in the year.

We were literally just a couple of hundred feet short of my mum and dad's house, when a sudden movement, slight, but eye-catching nonetheless, caught my attention. I had to look twice, but there was no denying the jerky, almost guilty flicker of heavy, purple-coloured curtains that adorned the windows of number 168.

And on that second glance, I thought I caught sight of the woman who lived there, a fifty-something, life-long spinster named Helga, who my parents had told me had been born in Northern Germany back in the mid-1920s, and just for a second I was convinced I'd glimpsed her face, a featureless white oval framed by iron-grey hair, clipped in a screamingly tight, permanent bun, as she peered from the black spaces that pooled in between the drapes.

I tried to tell myself I was just being paranoid, but my fears were hardly without foundation. Helga had a less-than savoury reputation amongst the locals, not least because (and this was something I'd only ever heard around the corner of adult conversations) she had been seen on many occasions being overly friendly with the local dockers and foreign sailors who regularly called into port back then. It was alleged that a near-constant stream of men, of all ages, a number of them distinctly "swarthy and foreign-looking", were seen to enter Helga's house, late of an evening, only to re-emerge during the early, pre-dawn hours, bleary-eyed, their hair visibly tousled, their shirts and trousers creased and like they hadn't seen a hot iron in a month or two. Just last Christmas, in fact, I'd overheard my mum talking on the phone to my Auntie June, discussing how when she and my dad been returning home from a Boxing Night party in the early hours, they'd seen Helga with three young men making their obviously drunken way to her house, a couple of them linking arms with the *"shameless arl slapper"*, singing some *"German Drinking Song"*, whilst the third made *"these sort of horribly obscene, pelvis thrusting gestures, directly behind her!"*

Far more pertinently though, at least as far as our gang was concerned, Helga was also well-renowned for being an interfering busy-body (although we called her something far less diplomatic - "a pain in the arse curtain twitcher") and she seemed to loathe kids, with a burning passion. My friends and I had experienced this irrational hatred first-hand the previous spring, when I'd accidentally kicked my brand new, bright orange, black-lined Wembley Trophy regulation weight football into her garden whilst playing headers & volleys on the road, using the chain link fence of the John Beech Storage Company warehouses as a makeshift goal.

I swear Helga must have been standing in the hallway, waiting for just such an opportunity, because no sooner had the ball landed smack in the middle of the branches of a well-maintained rhododendron bush, than the front door had been wrenched open. Helga had raced out, plucked the ball from the centre of the plant, and, with a self-satisfied grin, produced a sharp-bladed kitchen knife from behind her back. She'd then proceeded to stab the ball repeatedly, with a maniacal fury that had, quite frankly, terrified us all into open-mouthed silence.

When Helga had finished, all traces of anger had simply dropped from her face, and what had replaced it was something approaching pity, if you can believe that.

"Don't you know you should not be playing football in the street!" she'd said, in her soft, almost camp-sounding German accent. "You may think it is an innocent enough pastime, but please allow me inform you that for a lady, like myself, who prefers peace and quiet and moments of blessed tranquillity, your actions are entirely unacceptable. And I can guarantee, your parents, who seem to be extremely nice people, will completely understand my actions."

Helga had grinned then, but there was no absolutely no trace of mirth in it. No degree of warmth. (It had put me in mind of the false mechanical smile worn by the "Jolly Jack Tar Sailor" puppet I'd regularly encounter when on our annual family summer holiday in North Wales, a virtually life-size mannequin, jauntily-capped and rosy-cheeked, that stood in a glass case in the centre of one of the many amusement arcades that line that section of the Welsh coastline.

The mere sight of it, leering at me from over the tops of the rows of one armed bandits, shooting galleries, primitive video games, and the copper-coin-pushing, strangely addictive, slot machines, used to terrify me, especially when, every five minutes or so, the puppet suddenly burst into 'life,' and began dancing in an unnervingly jerky fashion, all the while, laughing like a literal lunatic, cackling in the milky light of a full moon....)

"Soooo, chillll-dren," Helga had said, drawing out the words for extra emphasis, "I think maybe you should go on now. Go on and play nicely, somewhere else. Somewhere far from my sight. Don't you agree?"

None of us, not even Peter Penny, king of the snappy one-liners, dared raise their voice in argument, and we'd begun backing off, with heads bowed, shoulders slumped.

"Oh, and please remember," Helga had added, dropping the ruined, crumpled football like the hideously torn-out bladder of some poor dead animal. "Be sure to be good boys from now on. Because, rest assured, I will be watching you. Making certain you are not, *any* of you, in any way *baaaad!"*

So saying, and still clutching that lethal-looking kitchen knife, she'd turned, slammed the door behind her, and we'd immediately turned away and backed on up the road, with no clear idea of exactly where we were headed.

Little wonder then, that I held my breath as we made our way past her house, with what seemed agonizing slowness, my heart hammering in my chest, as I fully expected at any moment the front door would burst open to reveal Helga, kitchen knife in hand, smiling that dead-as-a-carnival-puppet smile, as she raced towards us screaming; 'I told you'd I'd be watching!' I warned you to make certain you were not to be in any way....baaaaddd!'

An eternity passed, but Helga's front door remained firmly closed, and suddenly, the house was lost to sight behind her next-door neighbour's privet hedge, and I heaved a massive sigh of relief, though I didn't feel completely safe until we'd reached the sanctuary of my parents' front garden. I told myself I must have imagined that twitching of the curtains, and the sight of Helga's pale face peering out of the immaculately clean windows, and I turned my attentions fully to the task at hand. We had to clean-up Wolf, and then give him something to eat and drink as quickly as possible. One glance at his emaciated form was evidence enough of that.

I helped kick open the garden gates, and we pulled the trailer into the centre of the concrete driveway.

SIX

In the end, we'd had no choice but to take my younger brother, Dale, my sister, Kearry, and the lovely Georgina, of course, into our confidence. They were playing out in the back garden, and the minute we set down the trailer, Wolf had raised his head and let out a howl as ear-piercingly loud as it was unbearably mournful. That had served to bring the three of them running, and the sight of their faces, at once shocked and surprised, but ultimately so concerned as they issued a combined chorus of sympathetic *aaahhhs*, was enough to convince us that we could probably trust them to keep our secret.

'Okay, listen, there's no time to explain everything now,' I said in my most authoritative voice. 'We just found this poor dog here abandoned down the docks, and as you can see for yerselves, he needs our help.'

Obviously, my authoritative tones carried all the weight of ash flakes drifting from a distant bonfire, because the trio simply stood there making those increasingly irritable, and entirely unhelpful, *aaahhh* noises, whilst giving not the slightest indication that they'd heard a single word I'd said.

'Er, like, he means, like, RIGHT NOW! Philly Bennett suddenly roared, and maybe his formerly balls-haven't-dropped-yet voice had chosen that precise moment to break because it suddenly boomed incredibly deep and bassy and yeah, I've got to concede, wholly authoritative. Certainly, it got them all moving, and for that I was thankful. Along with Peter, they quickly formed a chain-gang starting from the sink in the back kitchen to provide several bowls of piping hot water laced with a couple of bottles of lemon-scented washing-up liquid and my dad's Head and Shoulders shampoo. I wasn't entirely sure that the combination was entirely dog-friendly, but each bowl was filled with satisfyingly frothy, sudsy water, and the accumulated filth came off Wolf in thick, gelatinous gloops that floated on the surface like they had some weird science-fiction life of their own. It took twelve whole bowls and some arm-achingly vigorous bouts of scrubbing to clean him up properly. But when we'd finished, Wolf looked like a completely different dog. Healthy, and sweet-smelling, and impossibly resplendent, his newly-washed fur blowing like rows of silken corn in the gentle autumn breeze.

However, there remained the disconcerting fact that he was so pitifully thin you could clearly see the bones of his ribcage poking through his skin like the bony keys of a xylophone. Looking at them, though it reduced me to tears to do so, I was reminded of the army of sword-wielding skeletons out to defeat Jason and his crew of intrepid Argonauts, in a wonderful film I'd watched just a few weeks earlier.

And another, far darker image also leapt into my mind. Of a line of hundreds of desperate-looking people crowded together in what appeared to be some sort of compound. They were all dressed in identical clothing; tattered and filthy rags that resembled stripy pyjamas, with most of the buttons missing, revealing sections of pale, almost translucent skin stretched thinly over their all-too prominent bones.

I'd once seen a dreadful photograph depicting crowds of Nazi Concentration Camp prisoners in a book my beloved Granddad Smith had given me the year before as a present for my 11th birthday. It was called *History of the Second World War,* and I never did get the chance to read it properly as a child. I always used to tell myself that the sole reason for this was because I'd had a whole stack of Marvel comics, *Famous Monsters* magazines and *Shoot* footy periodicals, along with several Mary Danbury Ghost Story collections I needed to get through first, but the honest truth was, I simply couldn't stand to look at that picture. It had unnerved me greatly, of course. It made me feel sick to the pit of my stomach. But it wasn't entirely due to the sight of the awful expressions of uniform hopelessness, etched on the faces of those half-starved men, women and children, trapped on the other side of a barbed wire fence. As undeniably horrible as that was.

There'd been something else, too.

For some reason, the very second I laid eyes on the picture, I'd found myself being struck with the same wave of nauseating fear and revulsion as when I'd first caught sight of that eerily empty canteen building down by the dock-side, and I'd quickly slammed the book shut with an audible thud. I'd then placed it (although perhaps *buried it* would have been a more accurate description), at the bottom of the wardrobe beneath a pile of old scrap-books, personal diaries and photo albums.

The only reason I didn't immediately throw the book away was because it had been a present given to me by my Granddad, who I loved very much. Not only that, but he had taken the time and trouble to write a message inside, the words of which have stayed with me:

"Happy birthday, son.

"I sincerely hope you will find this work to be of great and lasting interest. Remember, the past is important, for it shapes both who we are now, and all that we aspire to become in the future. For good or for evil.

"It has always been my most earnest wish that if only we as a species could pause now and then, to take time out from our frantically busy lives, to consider the harsh and frequently bloody lessons of history, it may help prevent us from repeating the same terrible mistakes that our forefathers made, in the days that hopefully, lie ahead.

"I appreciate that you may not understand these words at your tender age, or the heartfelt sentiment contained therein.

"But I know how much you enjoy reading, and in time, I trust, they will make perfect sense to you.

"Love, now and always,

"Granddad. X"

I couldn't have known it then, of course, but another 15 years or so would slide by before I began to understand the true meaning of my Granddad's words.

And even then, it took a quite shocking discovery, a terrible revelation, for them to make *perfect* sense to me.

SEVEN

We had just about finished the mammoth task of cleaning Wolf, and Georgina had taken my younger brother and sister inside to watch one of their favourite TV programmes, *Scooby Doo* most likely, when a shadow fell over us, as though a black rain-cloud had suddenly obscured the sun. I looked up and I felt my stomach sink as I saw Helga standing there. She was smiling that familiar chilly smile, the one that conjured up images of bitter, white Antarctic wastes or the desolate surface of some long-dead planet.

'Well now,' she exclaimed in that faintly Teutonic accent. 'That is certainly a most handsome looking beast you children have there. Tell me, what is his name?'

No one answered her. We just cast sidelong glances at each other, but our collective, squinty-eyed silence only served to pique her curiosity further.

'Oh, come now,' she said. 'Lord knows, I've watched you all do such a meticulous job of cleansing this apparently anonymous dog's beautiful fur, and restoring him to his former glory. Surely, at least one amongst you must know his name?' She paused, as if she needed to think for a second, and then added slyly, 'That is, of course, if he *truly* belongs to one of you?'

Helga let the words hang in the still, October air for a single, endless moment, before adding; 'I think perhaps your wall of stubborn quietness speaks volumes, children. It speaks of deception and secrets and bare-faced lies.'

A thin-lipped grin, devoid of humour, slit her pancaked features.

'You can all of you, rest assured, I will make it my business, my *mission*, to discover the truth here, and believe me, when I do, I shall...'

'Actually love, his name's Wolf, if yer really must know!' Peter 'motor-mouth' Penny, suddenly blurted out, before I could stop him. 'And yer know what, he's defo ours now, if he wasn't before, 'cos we found him abandoned down the docks, half-starved and covered in tons of shite, and so we rescued him and cleaned him up, his name's Wolf, like I said, and he is defo ours!'

'Oh, I see,' Helga exclaimed in a high, reedy voice, as she clapped her hands together delightedly, her pinched smile stretched wider still, to reveal twins sets of pale yellow teeth, that looked at that moment, to be almost, *wolfish,* if that doesn't sound dreadfully inappropriate.

'My dear, dear boy,' she continued, 'I am extremely grateful to you for your display of honesty. Your open sincerity flatters me. And, really, the awful things one hears about the youth of today.' She tutted and shook her head at the injustice of contemporary adult perceptions.

Then she fixed each of us with a stony gaze, Medusa-like in its intensity. 'Now, please allow me to tell you something,' Helga cried, pointing a single, blood-red fingernail in the air for added emphasis. 'It could well be that I know who that dog, pardon me, I'm so sorry, *Wolf,* truly belongs to.'

She paused, to let these portentous words sink in.

'And not only that,' she added, her perfectly manicured nails still pointing towards the peerless, blue skies, 'but I am more than willing to take Wolf off your hands and return him to the gentleman in question, this very moment. I will, of course, inform him of your great kindness, and I am sure he will be extremely grateful to you. There might even be a reward. Sweets. Chocolate bars. Who knows, perhaps even a sum of money?' Helga licked her lips, as though anticipating the confectionery delights that could be ours if we only agreed to play ball. 'Now tell me children, what do you have to say to that?'

'We say, you'd best give us the scumbag's name, and we'll call the RSPCA and report him for animal cruelty,' I snapped, angered at her presumption that we'd give up Wolf for a glorified "Lucky Bag", a Curly Wurly, and maybe enough cash to pay for a for a cheap water pistol or the latest *Planet of the Apes* comic. 'Maybe we should give the police a ring too, while we're at it. That twisted psycho, whoever he is, doesn't need his dog back. He needs locking up!'

My companions, initially shocked by my outburst, quickly recovered to yell a chorus of approval, and one of them, I think perhaps it was Gary, actually slapped me on the back in a 'hail-fellow-well-said' type of gesture.

But our display of solidarity cut no ice with Helga. Identifying me as the ring-leader, she summarily dismissed the others, and glared at me with eyes that seemed to radiate pure malice.

'You're a very obstinate young man, Mr Walker,' she said, her voice low, and dangerously composed. 'And I must say, I am somewhat surprised, and not a little disappointed by your, how shall I put it, "contrary" attitude. I know your parents well, and I am sure that Charles and Margaret have brought you up to always be respectful to your elders and your peers. I am also certain that they will be rather shocked, and not a little hurt, when I inform them of your rudeness, as believe me, I most assuredly will.'

Ordinarily, the threat to tell my parents that I'd misbehaved would have been more than enough to have me gushing apologies as though my life depended on Helga's forgiveness, but something inside me had snapped. Something about the total unfairness of the situation in which we found ourselves, combined with the sense of loyalty and affection I felt for a dog that we'd liberated just a few short hours earlier, and I was damned if I was going to cower before this evil arl boot, who might be German, but who speaks like she's swallowed a whole stack of Oxford Dictionaries.

'Actually, missus,' I said, 'me mum and dad have taught me if you wanna gain respect, first you've gotta earn it. I don't think anyone who sides with a fella who tortures his pet dog, then leaves him to starve to death, deserves anythin' but a two-fingered salute and a great big boot up their fat arse cheeks.' So saying, I amazed both myself and her by flashing a V-sign before adding, 'Now go 'ead an' do one, yer ugly arl trout!'

I've never seen a human face turn such a deep, flame-grilled shade of crimson, as I did on that day. Helga's already-less-than-pleasant features became so hideously contorted they became almost demonic-looking, and it was easy to imagine little puffs of white smoke coming out of her ears and nostrils, like a bull about to charge in a Loony Toons animated short.

'Why you insolent little brat!' she hissed. 'Oh, mark my words, you will have cause to regret your vile and abusive language. *Nobody* dares speak to me like that. Absolutely *nobody*, do you hear me!'

She took a deep breath, in a bid to compose herself, and then moved to push open the three-foot high metal gate. 'But in the meantime, I think it will wound you all deeply enough if I simply take the dog, with or without your permission, right now!'

'And *I* think you should stop right there, right *now*!' Georgina yelled, suddenly throwing open the front door, and bounding down the steps to confront Helga. 'Unless you want me to call the police, you'd best take your hand off that gate, yer miserable, crinkle-faced blert!'

I gave a silent cheer, and if possible, I loved our gorgeous babysitter even more at that moment, though, it appeared at first as though Helga wasn't about to back down. She remained standing at the gate, with her white-knuckled hands clutching the iron handle, plainly undecided as to what she should do next.

'Grant, go back inside and check on your brother and sister,' Georgina said, never taking her eyes from Helga's still visibly-smouldering face. 'And Lee, you go and ring the police. Tell them some madwoman is threatening to trespass on your mum and dad's property, and that there are young children present. That should get their arses into gear pretty sharpish.'

I was reluctant to leave my friends, even for an instant, but I could see the logic and urgency of her request, and I spun smartly on my heels, and as I did so, I saw a truly wondrous thing. My brother and three of my closest childhood friends had formed a steady line of support directly alongside me, backing me to the hilt, and I was deeply moved by this display of loyalty, and although there'd be several other occasions later in life when I'd have cause to be grateful for the unquestioning faithfulness of those dearest to me, there'd be few so memorable.

I caught one last glimpse of Helga, too, still standing there, hovering between impending defeat and barely restrained fury, and I had a vision of the time I'd accidentally left the immersion heater on for most of the day, whilst I was home alone and I'd been confronted with the sight of the hot water tank hissing and bubbling away in its grey, padded, insulation jacket, seemingly on the very brink of exploding.

I honestly don't know whether she would have stayed right there at the gates, locked in a battle of wills with Georgina right up until the moment the police arrived, if just then the wailing of a distant siren, an ambulance or a fire engine perhaps, on its way to some local emergency, hadn't drifted on the autumn breeze, and served to bring Helga to her senses.

Her eyes widened, as awareness gradually dawned on her and she opened her guppy-like mouth to speak, and a vein pulsed visibly in her neck, but no words came out. Instead her face suddenly deflated like that orange and black Wembley Trophy football she'd once frantically stabbed with a kitchen knife, a year or so earlier.

'Yeah, that's right!' Georgina said, nodding in the general direction of that far-off wailing. 'And I think you'll soon be hearing those sirens one hell of a lot closer if you don't fuck off right now, and leave us all in peace!'

Helga didn't summon up an answer, and to be honest, I don't think she could think of a single thing to say. She knew she was beaten, for now at least. And silence, it seemed, was her best, if only, option. She slowly lifted her hand from the black and yellow painted gates, and without so much as a sideways glance, she sloped slowly away along Dock Road North, and gradually out of sight.

After all the drama that had led to this tense, Mexican-style stand-off, the final showdown, when it came, seemed almost anti-climatic.

But we all breathed a big sigh of relief, just the same.

'Come on, gang,' Georgina said with a smile. 'Let's take Wolf into the back garden. I think you'd all agree we've had more than enough excitement for one day.'

We unanimously agreed that we had.

EIGHT

We whiled away the remainder of that afternoon messing about on the still-green lawn, the air sweet with the smell of the last flowers of the season. I remember we were all of us wearing these great big dazzling grins, still buzzing from our victory over Helga, and though we were old enough to know there would likely be serious repercussions for our actions in the days to come, still we revelled in the moment, frequently giving each other high-fives and playful claps on the back and shoulders, and making a massive big fuss of a now well-fed, Wolf.

The hours slid by quickly, as hours are wont to do when life seems good, and you're lost in the glorious, carefree joy of the moment. All too soon, it seemed, the shadows had lengthened, and the sun was starting to sink below the roofs of the houses opposite, but it was really only when I noticed the goosebumps rising on my bare arms as the temperature dropped appreciably, that I realised it was getting late, and that my parents would soon be home from their respective shifts.

We still needed to return the portable trailer in which we'd transported Wolf, back to Andy Parr's house, and come up with a half-way workable plan as to what we were going to do with 'our dog,' from here on in. It was quickly established that Peter, Gary and Philly would not be able to look after him overnight, (Pete's mum hated dogs with a passion, Gary's dad was allergic to them, and Phil's family were in the process of moving house) and so in the end it was down to me and our Grant, and although I made a big show of playing the role of a wounded martyr, inwardly I was delighted, because in truth I would have hated to have had to give up Wolf, for a single night, even to a close and trusted friend.

'Well, the way I see it, we've got two options,' I said, as the air grew chillier still. 'Firstly, we could just come clean, and admit the whole thing to my mum and dad. Tell them how we found Wolf, and hope like hell they'll be sympathetic and understanding, and allow us to keep him.'

'Aww, lad, I hate to tell you this, like, but that idea sucks more than one of them black hole thingys doing the hoovering,' Peter said, shaking his head gravely. 'I know yer ma will fall in love with him instantly, like, but yer dad, God love him, he'll just start waffling on about Hank, and how it broke his heart into pieces when his beloved hound died, and how he couldn't bear to own another dog, *any* dog, after Hank passed away.'

I knew immediately what Peter meant.

My dad had loved that jet-black Labrador, *the most loyal and faithful hound in the entire history of canines,* who'd died in his sleep at the ripe old age of 13, back in the early 1960s, several years before I was even born. I'd seen the old pictures though, carefully pasted in a hard-backed photie album. That series of polaroids.

Oh yeah, and of course Hank's silver dog lead and plain leather collar that my dad kept in the top drawer of a bureau at the back of his tool shed. The one packed with yellowing holiday postcards (those typically 'saucy ones,' that made me giggle self-consciously, the way I sniggered at the antics of Sid James and Hattie Jacques in the endless series of *Carry On* films), along with moulding stacks of Ian Fleming and Raymond Chandler paperbacks, and still-sealed packets of sunflower seeds.

This brought me to Option Two:

'Okay,' I said. 'How's about we swear me younger sister and brother, and Georgina, of course, to keep their gobs firmly shut about Wolf. I think we can trust them not to say anything about him. Meanwhile, the five of us can take him out with us during the day-time. We can walk him using Hank's old lead and collar, until we can afford to get Wolf a brand new one. We can even sneak him off to school with us, when we have to go back after the hols, next week. Maybe hide him in that old store-room at the far end of the playground during lessons. It's toasty warm in there, even on the coldest of days. And we can let him out on the playing fields during dinner-break. All the other kids will love him, I'm sure. We might have a problem keeping him out of sight of the teachers and the dinner-ladies, like, but we'll worry about that nearer the time. Meanwhile, overnight, we can keep Wolf in our club-house, down the bottom of the garden.' I shrugged my shoulders, and paused for breath. 'Unless anyone's got any better ideas?'

There was a momentary silence, as my companions pondered the pros and cons of this admittedly-thrown-together strategy, with a seriousness that was almost disconcertingly adult, and I had a brief vision of how each of them would look ten, maybe even fifteen years or so down the paths of their lives.

'It sounds like as good a plan as any,' Philly said eventually, 'But you know, Lee, don't you, even if by some miracle it does work, and even supposing the likes of Helga, or that fella she reckons owns Wolf, doesn't call round to spill the beans to yer mam and dad, it's only a matter of time before we get sussed out.'

I nodded, and swallowed a nervous click in my throat. Of course I knew the truth of that only too well. This was, at best, the type of improbable hare-brained scheme dreamed up by the scriptwriter's of "hey, that's so crazy it might just work" 1950s B-movies, and at worst, merely a way of delaying the inevitable unhappy ending. But it was marginally better than having no strategy at all.

So we did what we always did when our gang reached an agreement or made a decision. We stood in a circle and piled the palms of our hands atop each other in a solemn gesture of solidarity.

And set about implementing "The Plan".

NINE

Unbelievably, despite several close calls, and being constantly on the look-out for the re-appearance of our dreaded nemesis, our luck held for just under a week.

For six days and nearly as many nights, to be precise.

I treasured every precious moment with an intensity exclusive to youths who are too old to cling to childhood innocence, but still too young to have completely forsaken the rich promise of boy's own adventure. The sense that we were breaking the law a little, to achieve a greater good, of keeping a secret hidden from the adults (including our parents) who imposed the endless rules and regulations that reined us in for better or for worse, ensured the time spent with our newly-acquired pet took on a magical, almost dream-like quality.

As I'd suggested, Wolf slept in the wooden club-house my dad had built for us the previous summer. It was a sturdy building, replete with glass windows, a carpeted floor and a tarpaulin-covered, rain-resistant roof, and was fairly well furnished, from an 11-year-old lad's point of view anyway. The single room contained a couple of stools, a rickety picnic table and several threadbare, seam-split cushions from an old settee our next door neighbours had left out for the rag and bone man to collect, and when I added a couple of spare blankets and a pillow or two from the airing cupboard, Wolf had a nice warm bed upon which to sleep.

There was a lock on the front door too, and as much as I loathed the idea of incarcerating him again after the terrible ordeal he'd been through, it just wouldn't do to have him wandering around the gardens after midnight, drawing the attentions of bleary-eyed, but incurably nosey neighbours.

Some nights, as I lay in my own bed unable to sleep, I'd be sure I could hear Wolf whimpering with loneliness, and I'd panic, worried that he'd start that howling the way he had the day that we'd found him, and wake my mum and dad, and on those occasions, I'd had no choice but to get up, throw on my slippers and dressing gown, and sneak out the back door to go and keep him company till dawn. I'd fall asleep with my arms around him, the musty air thick with his rich doggy aroma.

Luckily, Grant and I have always been early risers, and we were always up and about well before the alarm clock went off at 6:00am, especially at weekends and during the school holidays. We hated wasting time lazing around in bed when the day seemed filled with endless possibilities. Even on the very foulest of mornings, when ice-cold rain sheeted down, stinging our hands and faces like tiny pin-pricks, and it was still pitch-black outside, we'd scribble a note to our parents telling them we'd just nipped out for a bit, change out of our pyjamas, throw down our bowls of cereal, and race out of the house a good hour or so before any of our family members had even thought of throwing back the bed-covers. There was something eerie, but undeniably exciting, about walking the deserted streets when it seemed all the world was still fast asleep. We used to joke it was a little like starring in a scene from some science fiction film about the end of time, in which all of the people had been beamed up aboard a fleet of giant, invisible, alien mother-ships, or were perhaps lying comatose in their greenhouses or garden sheds, whilst intelligent green vegetables from outer space were busy snatching their slumbering bodies.

We'd always be back home just as our parents, and my younger brother and sister, were sitting down to breakfast. We'd wish them all a good morning, maybe grab a slice of buttered toast, and then we'd be back off out again, this time for the entire remainder of the day, though with stern orders to be "back no later than six o'clock for your tea!" ringing in our ears.

Of course, this penchant for early morning strolls around our home town provided a perfect cover story for us now being able to take Wolf out for an hour or so, with no one around to catch sight of us, save for the milkman, and people making their weary way home after an another endless stint on the night shift. And it very quickly developed into something of a routine. On the way back, Grant would walk ahead to check the coast was clear, and then, all being well, we'd sneak Wolf back to our den, before returning to the house to say our cheery good mornings to our family, as though it were just another regular day in the Walker household.

We'd then head back down to the club-house to feed the dog as soon as Georgina had arrived to continue with her childminding duties, and my parents had left for work, (my dad spent his days slaving away at The British Leather Company, in Birkenhead, a truly awful place, with an intensely evil reputation, whilst my mum worked in the slightly more hospitable surroundings of the Viota Cake factory).

The days passed by so quickly they seemed at times to stretch into one. Each morning dawned with thick autumn mists that obscured the landscape, rendered the familiar strange, and muffled sound like a thick, grey cloak, but by eleven, the sun would emerge, raising steam from the tarmac and glistening the dew-laden lawns and hedges. I remember, too, there was this crisp, wonderful aroma, that conjured up images of early spring, and the air felt fresh and sweet like a new beginning, and I fantasized about sharing all of the year's seasonal events in the loyal company of Wolf, and about all the adventures we'd have, and how, whenever I found myself beset by life's crushing disappointments, he'd be there for me, his mere presence a source of heart-warming consolation.

It's hard to believe, let alone describe in mere words, how quickly, and how strongly I became attached to Wolf. Partly, I suppose, it was due to the fact that he seemed to be the answer to all of those unrealised hopes and dreams I referred to at the outset. And partly, it was the disconcerting, but unavoidable fact, that I knew that like the glorious spell of Indian summer weather we'd been blessed with during the last school break before Christmas, these halcyon days couldn't possibly last for very much longer. And I was determined to make the absolute most of our time together.

I'd like to think I did.

I followed my dreams without regret.

Even the hopelessly unrealised.

TEN

I'll always remember the very last time I ever laid eyes on the dog I'd grown to love every bit as much as if I'd raised him from a pup.

It was a little before seven pm, on Thursday, October, 26th 1976.

Three nights before the clocks went back, heralding the true end of the hottest summer in living memory. It was full dark, and I'd been sat at the table in our den, re-reading one of my all-time favourites, *Great Expectations'* by torch-light, whilst Wolf dozed contentedly upon the pile of cushions and fur-covered blankets that lay at my feet. We were otherwise alone, my friends having long since gone home, and Grant, who had returned from a late afternoon five-a-side kick-about on the patch of waste-ground we used as a football pitch, with his legs absolutely caked in mud had been ordered to take a long hot bath, and to get changed straight into his night-clothes the second my mum, just home from her day-shift, had laid eyes on him.

I had my head buried in the faintly musty-smelling pages of the classic Dickens novel, and was so engrossed in the story that I only became aware that my dad was calling me from the top end of the garden, when Wolf suddenly raised his head, and with his ears pinned back, began making that soft, almost child-like whimpering sound in the back of his throat. I jumped out of my seat, knocking the book to the floor, and almost dropping my torch in my haste to calm the dog before he started barking, alerting my dad to his presence, and leaving me facing a whole stack of incredibly awkward questions.

My dad called out again, and this time I could just make out what he was saying; 'Lee, Lee. *Top of the Pops*, is about to start. Are you coming in or what?'

It may sound ridiculous if not entirely laughable today, but back then, in those far off, impossibly distant pre-internet days, the weekly chart round-up, complete with badly-mimed renditions of the nation's favourite, *topper-most, popper-most tunes,* along with groups of scantily-clad, madly cavorting women who possessed all the rhythmic elegance of a bunch of orange-tanned slappers, sloping round their imitation Burberry handbags in *The Grafton,* was simply must-watch TV.

In common with most kids my age, growing up in the mid-1970s, I was hugely addicted to *Top of the Pops*. It was right up there with *Dr Who, Fawlty Towers* and *Monty Python,* as far as I was concerned, and I never willingly missed an episode, unless I was left with little choice, like the time

I was confined to bed suffering from a frighteningly acute dose of glandular fever, or during the scary, but equally kind of exciting, blackouts during the seemingly endless winter of two years before.

My dad shouted again. Actually, it was more of a brink of getting pissed off-type of yell, and worse, he sounded like he was getting closer. I was scared he would soon come stomping down the garden path to find out why I hadn't answered him, and that was the last thing I needed. I gave Wolf a final stroke of reassurance, mouthed a silent prayer that I'd calmed him enough to ensure his silence, and quickly stepped through the door, bolting it firmly shut behind me.

It was as well that I emerged from the club-house right then, because I saw his silhouette, framed by the lights spilling from the back kitchen windows, marching purposefully down the garden path. Trying to keep my voice steady, I shouted, 'I'm coming now, Dad. I just fell asleep reading in the den.'

'You and them bleedin' books,' he said as I approached him, and though he was shaking his head, I saw to my relief that he was smiling, too. 'Right, yer best get yer arse into gear, lad, or yer gonna miss the first song. And, guess what...I've heard Queen might be on again, tonight!'

Even though I was never a big fan of the band, I knew immediately what my dad meant by this remark. It had become kind of a running joke in our family, ever since we'd seen Queen's epic video for *Bohemian Rhapsody,* some months earlier. At the sight of Freddie Mercury, leaping from the grand piano during the epic rock-out section of the song, dressed in skin-tight, white satin trousers, to prance around the stage with a microphone stand, my dad was moved to point out: 'Yer know what, that big-lipped, long-haired tart's kecks are so arse-munchingly tight, if he let's loose a fart, they'll split like a piece of soggy bog-roll in a force-ten gale!'

The memory of that comment, every time Freddie and the Boys appeared on screen would always surface and have us rolling round the floor, until I'd wind up losing control, and laugh so hard I'd end up letting loose a series of shiny pyjama threatening rip-snorters, myself.

Queen weren't actually on the bill that evening, as it turned out although it wouldn't have made much difference to my mood, even if they had been. From the moment I flopped onto the settee, next to our Grant, I was plagued with vague feelings of unease, and that indefinable sense that something was terribly wrong grew with each passing moment. For once, the show seemed to drag by with agonising slowness, and I breathed an audible sigh of relief when, at long last, the Number One Song, a Country and Western tune by some Dutch band called Pussycat, had mercifully finished.

I felt compelled to go and check on the dog, but I forced myself to wait until my mum was busy escorting my younger brother and sister upstairs to bed, before leaping to my feet and telling my dad I'd just remembered I'd left one of my favourite bed-time reading books in the den, and he just rolled his eyes, picked up his newspaper, and began reading the sports pages.

I raced down to the bottom of the garden with my heart thudding like it was trying to beat its way out of my chest. Though it stilled and sank like a stone when I saw in the thin but powerful beam of my pencil torch, the front door of the club-house was standing slightly ajar.

'Oh, no!' I sobbed, as I threw the door wide open, 'Wolf, come on boy, please still be here. *Please...*'

But though I shone the torch into every shadow-darkened corner of the single room, there was no trace of him whatsoever. Just Hank's "borrowed" lead and collar lying atop the cushions, and the vaguely dog-shaped indentation where I'd left Wolf dozing, thirty minutes earlier.

I stood there for a moment, staring into that rough, uncaring, *empty* darkness, my eyes blurry with un-shed tears, and a wave of helplessness and utter despair washed over me. Someone had obviously found out where we were keeping Wolf, and had waited patiently until he'd been left all alone, before seizing their opportunity to take him. There really was no other explanation. There was only way out of the den. It was a calm, windless night so the door couldn't have simply blown open, and anyway, I'd made sure that the thick bolt had been firmly slotted into place when I'd left him, despite my being in a rush to placate my dad.

I had no idea who had gone to the considerable trouble of sneaking into our back garden under cover of darkness to snatch Wolf, or where they might have taken him. Except, I think perhaps maybe I did, though I could scarcely bring myself to believe it.

But then suddenly, I caught the faint whiff of a sickly-sweet aroma drifting in the evening air, and with a shiver of revulsion I realised that I recognised that nose-wrinkling odour.

I'd smelled it before.

The day Helga had stood at our front garden gates, threatening to take Wolf back down the docks, to return him to his original, sadistic owner.

ELEVEN

With no clear plan of action in mind, and without even pausing to tell my parents where I was going, I headed straight for the ominous, semi-lit darkness that marked the end of the street and the beginning of the docks.

I wasn't sure what I expected to find, as I ran, breathlessly, towards one of the holes in the fence beside the locked, chain-linked gates, ducking out of sight of the uniformed guard at his security post, but I was filled with some inner certainty, an almost psychic intuition that I had to hurry to prevent something truly awful from happening.

Once through the jagged gap, I felt myself drawn to the lines of hulking ships moored at the quayside, and to one merchant vessel in particular. Back in the mid 1970s, there were dozens of vessels gathered in the docks, the decks of each of them blazing with white and yellow light beneath the cold, indifferent, diamond-chip stars, and I can't honestly say what it was that compelled me to head straight for the unremarkable-looking ship bearing the name *Harlequin*.

I noticed the vessel was flying Nigerian colours from its stern, (I recognised the flag straight away, because I collected the *National Flags of the World* cards lying at the bottom of fabulously-scented boxes of PG Tips tea bags*)* and that it appeared to be the only boat with its gang-plank fully extended to the wharf.

As I watched, I saw large groups of men scurrying about frantically making preparations for the ship to disembark from the dock-side, and in stark contrast to this hive of activity, a pair of silhouettes were etched against the white-walled cabins, a man and a woman, locked in a passionate embrace.

I can't say I was really that surprised when the female eventually broke off the kiss and slowly turned to make her way back down the gang-plank, and I saw it was Helga, her garishly made-up face bathed in the cruel glare of a halogen light. I think, rather, there was an air of dreadful inevitability about it, like I was living out the events of some eerily prophetic dream, the ending to which I couldn't quite see the shape of as yet.

I decided I really didn't want Helga to see me, so as she approached I quickly dodged behind a twenty-foot tall collection of hollow metal pipes and sealed crates, stacked neatly near the water's edge. And as she passed close by, I could almost see a misty cloud of horribly familiar perfume so thick, I nearly gave myself away by choking on the fumes.

I also had to strongly resist the urge to jump out and confront her, and threaten again to inform the police if she didn't tell me what she'd done with the dog, but I remained where I was until she was well out of sight, before getting to my feet, and slowly making my way over to the *Harlequin*. The crew were clearly making their final preparations to set sail and I felt sure that something more than just a simple farewell had taken place between Helga and her lover. I was suddenly anxious to check out the identity of her latest "flame". As I stood at the edge of the dockside, where the huge, thick stretches of rope were in the process of being loosened, I raised my gaze to the upper deck and saw immediately the dark form of the man I was seeking. He stared right back at me, and I could see, even from a distance, that his face was deeply tanned and weather-beaten, that he bore a single, jagged scar on his right cheek, and that his eyes resembled twin pools of impenetrable blackness.

I'd never met him before.

And yet I felt the spark of instant recognition, nevertheless .

I knew him, you see.

Of course I did.

He may have been wearing a mask of relative ordinariness, a bland façade that helped him fit right in with his fellow sailors, and those who counted themselves amongst his (likely) small circle of friends, but at times of his choosing he allowed the mask to slide from his weather-beaten features, like melted wax in the heat of a burning flame.

And now, such a moment had arrived.

I saw him revealed as the gibbering horror that lurks amidst the shadowed corners of the bedroom.

The silent, patient figure who stands concealed in the clothes racks at the back of the wardrobe or who slithers, impossibly paper-thin, in the tight space between the mattress and the carpeted floor.

The Terror That Comes By Night.

The Bogey Man.

As we exchanged glances across the flood-lit gap between the dockside and the ship, he winked conspiratorially, and as a chill crept into my bones, I knew he'd recognised me, too. I took a step backwards, fear momentarily overcoming my concern for Wolf, and as I did so, the anchor was raised, and *Harlequin* began slowly pulling away from its moorings.

And then I heard it. A faint noise, echoing from somewhere deep within the bowels of the ship. It sounded like a keening howl – a desperately lonesome sound, that was likely nothing more than the grinding of the ship's mighty engines, but which nevertheless brought to mind vivid images of the day we'd first stumbled upon Wolf, in his abject state of abandonment.

Too late, I began trying to push my way through the small crowd of dockers, shouting at them to stop the ship from sailing, but they just ignored me, or looked at me with expressions of mild bemusement, until one of them, a huge bearded man in a thick woollen hat and a buttoned-up donkey jacket, shoved me none-too-gently in the chest, and told me to "sod off home!"

I tried to explain to him what I strongly suspected had just taken place, but he wasn't having any of it. Besides, the ship by this stage had already pulled out of the dock itself and out onto the still, wave less waters of the Mersey, and I was forced to watch as it drifted inexorably, down the river's evening hush.

It gradually faded from view, until it was no more than a flickering glow on the horizon.

Before winking out of existence, like the dying light of a falling star…

TWELVE

God, I honestly wish this was a wholly made-up story. The sort where the good guys win all the time. But it's all true, I'm sorry to say, and as we know, real life seldom conforms to the clichés of happy ever after endings, perfect sunsets and swelling strings. More's the pity.

I can't say for certain that Helga took Wolf from our back garden that night, and handed him back to "his rightful owner", a cruel-hearted sailor on board the *Harlequin,* bound for West African shores.

I only know I never saw Wolf again. And that whenever I laid eyes on Helga, in the years that followed, she never once spoke to me, but always wore this permanent, dreamy-kind of smile, and an expression that spoke of satisfaction at having completed a job well-done. I never confronted her with my suspicions, not least because I couldn't see what good it would have done. She took the truth of the matter with her to the grave when she passed away, a decade or so after the events I've related took place.

I've never forgotten Helga, though. Not least because of something that happened many years after her death.

One cold, sleety February afternoon, when I was still living at my parents home, I was clearing out the stacks of books and magazines piled at the bottom of my wardrobe, when I came across that old *History of the Second World War* book my granddad had given me as a present for my 11th birthday.

I'd picked it up and briefly flicked through the pages with little real interest, but then I'd happened upon that hideous black and white photograph I remembered from childhood; the stark illustration of unimaginable suffering and horror that had caused me to bury the book out of sight, (although never truly out of mind) at the bottom of a heap of dog-eared comics and old scrap-books.

Now, as an adult however, I'd felt strangely compelled to peer closely at the picture of what the single sentence printed in italics running below it, informed the reader was **Dachau Concentration Camp, 11th September, 1943.**

It showed this awful place bathed in swathes of sunlight on a deceptively idyllic, summer's day. Behind the rows of concrete posts and barbed wire fencing, stood the lines of pyjama-clad prisoners, their true ages impossible to determine given their dreadfully emaciated state. Their faces bereft of hope. Their eyes sunken, like dried-up slurry pits.

I'd noticed other things, too. Things I either hadn't understood as a child, or else hadn't wanted to. There were three things, actually.

Firstly, the chapter bore the headline:

THE BANALITY OF EVIL
(Evil acts can be committed by people who consider their actions to be perfectly normal, in the manner of individuals, simply following orders – Hannah Arendt)

As I pondered those words, nodding my head in silent agreement, my eyes were drawn to that which stood in the background of the photograph. There was a long wooden hut with a low roof, and black, reflection-less windows, and I felt fear slither into my skin as I saw at once that the building bore an unnerving similarity to that redundant dock-side canteen, the outwardly ordinary-looking building that had been demolished, but which had continually haunted the days of my youth with something akin to ... well, yes ... *THE BANALITY OF EVIL*

I'd wanted to cast the book aside, as though it were infected with some virulent disease, and perhaps that's really not so far from the truth, but before I'd been able to do so, the second thing had occurred. I'd suddenly caught sight of a small band of wildly laughing men and women gathered on the left-hand side of the crowd of wretched prisoners.

Wearing grey German army uniforms, adorned with Swastika armbands, they'd appeared less like genuine soldiers than a bunch of drunken party-goers, all done up in macabre fancy dress. One of the officers was kneeling on the seat of a chair, his fingers placed upon the keys of an open accordion, whilst his companions pumped their fists or raised their arms towards the cloudless skies as they belted out some silent anthem.

And there ...

Right there... In the very centre of the group of care-free revellers, their arms around each other's waists, stood a man and a woman, resplendent in their immaculately cut uniforms, the collars of which were emblazoned with the unmistakable insignia that marked them both as clearly belonging to the *Waffen SS.*

The man was rugged-looking, though clean-shaven, and sported a recent scar, an angry red line that wound down from his cheek, almost to his jawline, where it split off into two, like a fork in a crooked road, and whose jet-black eyes bore no trace of warmth or humour, for all his beaming smile, and air of wild celebration.

His partner was a mildly attractive young lady, little more than a girl really, barely out of her teens, and her uniform, an open grey jacket, crisp white blouse and knee-length skirt, seemed to hang somewhat on her skinny frame. Her blonde hair was swept back from her forehead in the style of the day, and her heavily made-up face seemed on the verge of cracking as she grinned manically into the camera lens.

They were both complete strangers to me, of course.

They were both instantly recognisable.

With a chill that had had nothing to do with the freezing winter weather, I'd slammed the book shut, as the wise words of my dear old granddad echoed round and round my head in an endless loop: *Remember son, the past is important, for it shapes both who we are now, and all that we aspire to become in the future.*

For good or for evil.

CHAPTER SEVEN
'RUN, CRIED THE CRAWLING DARK'

'Time slips away,
And the light begins to fade..
And everything's quiet now ... '
Seventeen Seconds - The Cure

I received the following story via an e-mail in response to my request for stories about
the paranormal, on one of my regular appearances on Billy Butler's programme on
BBC Radio Merseyside. At the risk of sounding horribly immodest, one assumes
my stints on the show must mildly entertain a moderate amount of people, or else I wouldn't
have been asked back so frequently, or indeed, have inspired people to waste half an hour
or so of their lives, composing an e-mail or calling me up to regale me with stories of their
encounters with the 'supernatural'

One such post was sent to me by "John Maddison", a father of three,
who hails from Aigbuth, South Liverpool, and concerns the strange events that a friend of
his claims took place during the late summer/early autumn of 2012

ONE

One week after the strange and nightmarish events that apparently overtook my good friend Harry Watson, we were sat in the beer garden of Otterpool's *Britannia Inn,* nursing a pint. Harry had a lump the size of a duck egg protruding from the left-hand side of his head and with dark semi-circles under both of his squinting, blood-shot eyes, and he looked like he'd aged ten years in the space of a mere seven days.

I didn't tell him that, of course. Instead, I summoned up a hearty smile, raised my ice-cold lager to his then sat back to listen to what he had to tell me, just as I'd promised him I would when I'd gone to visit him in the hospital the previous Monday morning.

'Okay, mate, you've got my undivided attention,' I told him. 'Start from the beginning, H, and don't miss nuthin' out.'

So he did.

And he *didn't*....

If yer know what I mean.

He began by stating, in massively eloquent terms with a posh southern accent, that it was "the soft strains of half-familiar music drifting across the vibrant summer meadows, that first drew me to the old Otterspool Café".

'It was the music first, John. And then the tantalising glimpse of the pristine white walls, dazzlingly bright against the azure skies and the verdant green of the rolling lawns and the lines of trees beyond. The twin assault on my senses, and the tempting promise of blessed shade and a brief respite from the blistering heat, combined to entrance me, Siren-like, and had me striding across the fields without so much as a second thought.'

My madly poetic friend paused to take another large swig of his ale, and I'd noticed his hands were shaking slightly, and if I were to believe even half of what he claimed had happened to him, that was entirely understandable.

I'd known straight away which old café he was on about. I'd been born and raised in Aigburth, a proverbial stone's throw away from the Prom, so to me the place was like an honest to God monument of memory. It was, and still is, a lovely looking building, just about visible from the main road that stretches along the Prom, poking through the trees that loom over the circular structure.

I used to love going there with me mam and dad, of a weekend, back when I was a kid.

But, and here was the thing ...

The café had stood empty and derelict since the late 1980s.

It had long been closed for business, and, despite its desirable location, appeared very likely to remain that way; its once white walls, dirty and graffiti-strewn, the windows shuttered with metal plates, and its doorways sealed and bolted.

Dead to the world in every sense of the phrase.

TWO

Before we get to Harry's story proper, though, I think it's important that I point out that though it sometimes felt like I'd known him all my life, I had in fact only met him for the first time a month or so earlier, at the 2012 London Olympics. The Games that had proved the undisputed highlight of a never-to-be-forgotten summer. Me and the wife, Eleanor, had been lucky enough to get a couple of tickets for that glorious magical night at the

Olympic Stadium, when Team GB won a trio of gold medals. We were supposed to be sat in our plazzy seats high up in the gods in the packed stadium, but of course, no one was sitting down. Instead, 80,000 people stood as one, lost in wild celebration, as Mo and Greg and Jessica achieved sporting immortality, and I swear I saw grown men, some of them big and ugly and built like Scotty Road dockers, hugging complete strangers with tears streaming down their granite-like faces.

Harry, though, had been a relatively slight fella, only a little taller than me, but when Mo had crossed the finish line and shaped his hands above his head into that now famously iconic 'M,' shape, this middle-aged chap, dressed in a pair of ripped jeans and what appeared to be an original Clash 'White Riot Tour' T-shirt, grabbed me by the waist and lifted me off me feet like I weighed less than Kate Moss on a month-long, broccoli-only diet.

And we got talkin, and though he spoke like he had a gob full of plums and was given to spoutin' flowery metaphors, still it turned out that we had loads in common, and not just a love of all-time classic punk bands.

Mary, Harry's missus, who was stood with him, was great company too, and later, when we walked out of the stadium and out onto the buzzing streets of the "arl smoke" together, the four of us headed for the nearest alehouse to drink and chat the night away. The atmosphere was electric in the packed pub, and as we sat around a table lit by candle-light, and quite literally groaning under the weight of wine and beer bottles, life-long friendships were forged.

Me and Eleanor spent the remainder of our fortnight's break in London, enjoying Harry and Mary's company, and at the end of our holidays we exchanged numbers and addresses. As neither of them had ever visited Liverpool before, although they said they'd both wanted to for many years, we arranged for them to come and visit us as soon as they could get some time off work. That turned out to be the second week in September. They booked into *The Blackburne Arms*, a quaint old Georgian pub in the heart of Liverpool 8, on a Friday evening, and whilst Eleanor made plans with Harry's missus to embark on an all-day shopping spree in the City Centre, I arranged to meet up with H at the car-park on Otterspool Promenade, at about half two in the afternoon after I'd finished my shift at the printing firm where I worked, and had time to shower and change.

'I'd love to show yer the area where I was brought up,' I said to Harry on the phone. 'It's a lovely place, with some cracking woodland walks, a large park, lots of local history, and best of all, there's a boss pub with a beer garden with fantastic views across the Mersey.'

'That sounds like an excellent idea to me,' Harry replied. 'I've got a highly-reliable sat-nav in my car, so I'm sure I won't experience any problems finding the place.'

'Look forwards to it then, mate,' I said, and prepared to hang up, but then an idea occurred to me. 'Tell you what, Harry. There's a really nice café just over the road from the car park. You can't miss it. It's the only one along the whole stretch of The Prom. We'd be better off meeting in there, cos I'll be walking up from that direction anyway.'

'The café, it is, then,' my friend agreed. 'See you at two-thirty.'

THREE

I think it's best if I let Harry take up the story from here on in.

It's far too strange and totally way-out for me to even attempt to get me head around, never mind try and put it into coherent sentences.

And after all, the voice of experience always rings far truer than the words of someone who simply wasn't there.

As so many of us in this wonderful, but sometimes tragedy-ridden city, know all to well..

FOUR

'It was getting on for two o' clock, and heading towards the hottest part of the day when I pulled up in the car park at the edge of the sparkling, white-capped river. It was a perfect mid-September day, at the end of yet another heartily depressing, rain-sodden summer.

'I'd spent the morning in the thriving hub of Liverpool City Centre, being dragged around the shops by your Eleanor, and my own, shoe-obsessed wife, and I was tired, hungry and throat-parched, and thankfully, The Promenade had proven to be a straight-forward fifteen minute drive or so from our hotel.

'I stepped from the air-conditioned coolness of the car into late-summer heat, and I saw immediately that the area was packed with groups of people of all ages, picnicking at the wooden tables, or sat around on the grass, cooking up barbecues, their mouth-watering smell wafting on the light, slightly-cooling breeze, along with the heady aromas of alcohol and melting strawberry ice-cream and cheap, coconut sun-tan lotion.

'Elsewhere, children, and not a few adults, were playing football, or were engaged in semi-serious games of cricket or rounders, or flying kites with the flags of various nations attached to their tails as they flew impossibly high up into the clear and flawless blue.

'I took a little time out to wonder at the sheer, unadulterated joy of life's simple pleasures. The uncomplicated things that yet serve to make us deliriously happy; a cloudless sky, a drowsy warmth that brings out freckles and helps the ice cold cans of beer or chilled wine slide down dry and dusty throats, the blessed shade afforded by the leaves of an oak tree, and a packed lunch laid out resplendent on a tartan blanket.

'I smiled to myself as I locked the door behind me, and was just about to ask someone if they knew where the 'Otterspool Café' was, when I heard music drifting on the briny air and I looked across the road towards the rolling fields of a park. As I did so I caught a glimpse of bright white amongst the shrubs and trees, and raising the small but powerful binoculars I'd brought with me, I saw there was a building with the single word '**CAFE**' painted in plain black lettering down the left-hand side of its upper floors. I could clearly make out too, the members of a smartly-dressed string quartet gathered on a raised area just in front of the building, and I realised I recognised the tune they were playing. It was one of my dear departed grandmother's favourite old crackly 78's. I even remembered the strangely evocative title: *Song d'Automne,* and I dimly recalled having read somewhere about it being part of the *White Star Line's Songbook,* back in the early part of the 20th century.

'Hearing that dreamily yearning sound, all those years later, sparked a bitter-sweet nostalgia in me; the sort that stings the most vulnerable parts of one's soul, and yet sends parts of it soaring with the joy of precious memory. Almost without being aware of it, I found myself striding purposefully over the fields, and along the edge of the natural hollow that was dotted here and there with sunbathers and family picnickers, until I reached the path that led up to the café and its paved concourse. As well as the sweating, red-cheeked, band members, I saw there were crowds of mostly elderly men and women sat in rows of deckchairs, some fanning their faces with newspapers or drinks coasters, in a bid to ward off the heat, as they watched the musicians playing the golden-oldie hits of yesteryear. I paused to watch for a moment, musing on the sheer timelessness of this quintessentially British scene, and if it hadn't have been so blasted hot, I might have remained there a while longer. As it was, I soon grew anxious to get in out of the sun, and mopping my brow with a pocket handkerchief, I entered the café, the welcome coolness of the air enhanced by the whirring of the overhead fans.

'It took a few moments for my eyes to adjust to the relative gloom, but when they had I glanced around the sparsely populated dining area and was pleasantly surprised by the decidedly 1950s décor. Adorning the walls, alongside the retro-style adverts for the likes of Lyon's Maid Ice Cream, Coca Cola and Lipton's Tea, were a series of posters for a clutch of classic films from the era: *The Day The Earth Stood Still, All About Eve,* and *Rebel Without A Cause,* to name but three, and as I peered closer, I saw they must have been either high-quality re-prints or immaculately preserved originals, because they appeared as fresh as they though they were promoting films on current release in the cinemas of Liverpool.

'I've long been something of a film buff, with a particular affection for the films of the 1950's and '60's, not least because this was the magical period when I first began frequenting the picture houses of West London, and I was fascinated by this gallery of cinematic greats. It's a good job Mary wasn't with me at that moment, though. She would doubtless have tutted loudly, raised her eyes to the ceiling and begun tugging impatiently at my sleeves. I regret to say that the wife, God love her, doesn't understand my obsession with anything she considers long past its sell-by date.

"Revelling in the relics of long-lost youth," she calls, it. "Digging up golden nuggets of memory," say I. It's long been a bone of contention between us, but Mary's absence meant I could indulge myself for as long as I liked. Or at least until you turned up, John.

"I was wearing a great big grin as I slowly made my way across the shiny, polished floor, and I was further delighted to discover that sharing the wall space with the old movie posters were equally mint-condition advertisements for live performances by a host of legendary bands and artists, including Louis Armstrong and Gene Vincent at The Liverpool Stadium, and Little Richard and Bill Hayley at The Empire.

"I was checking out the details on a poster featuring The Quarrymen, (later to become *slightly* better-known as The Beatles, of course), when the unmistakable strains of Elvis Presley, during his Rock n Roll heyday, began blasting from the far corner of the room, and I turned to see a wonderful, retro-style jukebox, blue and silver in colour, and with a large letter 'W' near its base, the glow of the display console illuminating millions of dust motes that danced wildly to the beat of the music.

"I quickly forgot all about the posters. I felt my mouth snap open with an audible click (and in my mind's eye, I saw an image of Jacob Marley's ghost, its jaw suddenly untethered from the filthy bandages that had long held it shut). I could see, even from where I was stood, twenty-odd feet away, that the jukebox was the real deal. A genuine Wurlitzer that must have been imported directly from America. I knew because I'd badly wanted one of my own, and had spent countless hours scouring the internet for a decent deal on an original 1950's jukebox just like this one. I doubt very much whether Mary would agree, but I've often voiced the opinion that there is nothing more rewarding, from a musical perspective at least, than the sight of a stylus dropping onto a seven-inch slice of vinyl, the second or two of preliminary crackle, followed by the deep, resonant sound of the music itself; something I've always considered to be sadly lacking in its tinny, processed compact disc equivalent. Another glaring example that modern-day technology doesn't always change things for the better.

"This was a view the proprietors of this wondrous place very obviously shared, as evidenced by the loving recreation of a long-vanished era, and so what if it was a highly idealised slice of 50's Americana in the centre of a British city? I loved it, and I intended to thank you John, when you arrived, for suggesting we meet at a such a fantastic venue. As the thought crossed my mind, I reached into my pocket for my mobile phone to check whether you had messaged me or whether I had any missed calls, and as so often happens, the second I glanced at it the phone burst into life, its shrill, insistent ring tone, the one I hated and kept promising myself to change for something rather less jarring, but had somehow never gotten round to, causing me to jump out of my skin and nearly drop the phone on the café floor. I caught it just in time, and saw the screen light up, displaying your caller ID, John."

"Hi mate, I'll have to be quick," I heard you speak breathlessly, "I'm in me car just about to go back through the Tunnel, and I won't be able to get a signal once I'm under there.

"Sorry, I'm running a bit late. I had to drop a work colleague off, over the water. I should be there in abar fifteen minutes."

"That's no problem, John. I'm already here. But there's no need to apolo…"

"Sound, you said, cutting me short. "Listen, do us a favour, will yer, Harry? Try and grab a table if there's any available, 'cos it gets mad busy of a weekend. I'll have to go. See yer soon."

'You hung up before I had a chance to tell you that this must be an unusually slow Sunday afternoon, because glancing around the room I saw it was virtually deserted. Aside from myself, the only other people present were a group of young men stood at the counter, entering into the spirit of things what with their greased-quiff hairstyles, white T-shirts and leather jackets, and a far more conservatively dressed older couple sat sipping coffee over in the far corner. It looked to me like most of the café's regular customers were sat outside, listening to the quartet's soothing strings and soaking up the sunshine, and who could honestly blame them for that? From the not-so-merry-month of May, this year, and right on through to mid-August, it seemed it had never stopped raining, so the price of winding up with painfully burned skin the colour of a boiled lobster was one they considered well worth paying.

'I was content to remain indoors though enjoying the coolness of the café's interior. I took a seat at a red and white chequered window table from where I could gaze out at the view across the fields towards to the river, glistening in the distance.

'I began to text you, John, to reassure you that I'd acquired "the best seats in the house", when a pretty waitress in a cream-white blouse and tight pencil skirt and with her hair tied back in a pony-tail, approached to take my order.

"Good afternoon, sir," she said in a soft Irish accent. "Welcome to Otterspool Café. Are you planning on dining with us today?" She flashed a brilliant smile that caused my heart to flutter a little, and though, God knows she was young enough to be my daughter, there was no denying her fresh-faced beauty, and as she stood there waiting patiently, pen and note-pad in hand, my eyes were drawn to the name tag pinned just above her left breast, informing me her name was Keela.

And I then I felt my tongue suddenly cleave to the roof of my mouth as a memory surfaced, like the recollection of some half-forgotten dream, sparked by a slant of sunlight piercing the dusty corner of an attic room.

Keela....

'The name of a girl I'd once met, and who bore more than a passing similarity to the young waitress standing before me, whilst on a family holiday in Dublin, when I was just seventeen years old, and though I hadn't thought about her in years, decades even, as the world's romantics never tire of saying "you never forget your first true love", and here was proof that that well-worn adage, had at least a degree of truth.

Keela.

'I remembered admiring her from across the space of a crowded bar-room for the space of an entire evening, throwing back the whisky and coke my dad, who never missed a trick, had placed before me with a wink and a conspiratorial whisper; "Get this down you before you go over to chat her up. I promise it will quell your nerves."

'I remembered the way her smile lit up her face when I asked her to dance.

'I remembered the glorious way it had felt to hold her close, the peppermint scent of her breath, the sight of the tiny rows of freckles dotting her cheeks that somehow made me want to cry a little, and the DJ playing that old, classic Bobby Darin song, *Dream Lover.*

'I remembered walking the city streets on the way back from Keela's parents' house, at a little after midnight, and the way in which the fluorescent late-night bar signs shimmered dream-like in the oily puddles that formed in the gutters of the rain-slicked pavements.

'I remembered the way we said our goodbyes at the end of the two-week vacation, and the promises we made to stay in touch, and the heartfelt vows that nothing would ever keep us apart.

'And the scented photograph I kept for years at the bottom of my travelling trunk, as a form of bitter consolation when she'd suddenly stopped writing or returning my calls. It was a picture of the two of us together, holding hands near the banks of the River Liffey. And printed on the back, in a graceful, curling script, were the words:

"To my darling Harry. My father once told me that my name, Keela, can be translated from the old Gaelic to mean 'a beauty that only poetry can capture.' I'd beg to differ. My "beauty", such as it is, has been captured, not by mere verse, or rhyming words on paper, but by YOU, the love of my life."

'I *remembered....*

'And I almost jumped out of my seat when the strains of that familiar song, the one Keela and I had called "our special tune", that long-ago summer began playing on the café's jukebox, in the here and now.

'Instead, I quickly took out my pocket-handkerchief, and dabbed at my face, clammy with sweat despite the swirling of the overheads fans.

"Forgive me for asking, sir, but are you feeling quite alright?" the waitress asked, and I was touched by the genuine look of concern that clouded her features. "You look *terribly* pale."

'Oh, I'm dreadfully sorry,' I replied, submitting to that infuriatingly English habit of apologizing for something that is clearly not remotely anyone's fault, least of all your own. 'I'm perfectly fine, thank you, just a little tired I guess. I find this hot weather drains my energy.'

'I tried to summon up a smile, to show her just how 'perfectly fine' I really was, but in truth, my grin felt face-achingly false, and I suddenly felt duty-bound to explain why I was sitting here, sweating like a stuck pig whilst my deep tan faded to a ghostly shade of white.

'Well, okay, perhaps I am not being entirely truthful,' I said a little sheepishly. 'I think it has more to do with the song currently playing on that old Wurlitzer, over there.'

'I pointed in the general direction of the machine, as if the waitress could be in any doubt as to the source of the music filling the dining area. 'I haven't heard it in ages,' I added. 'The song, I mean. It never fails to have a powerful effect on me, a melancholic one, more often than not, and I must admit, I was rather startled when it began playing on the jukebox at the very moment that I'd begun thinking about that haunting melody, and it began running through my head, another of those bizarre coincidences that sometimes occur in life, and make us question the nature of reality, or whatever passes for it, and....' I trailed off, knowing I was babbling nonsense to a complete stranger who was probably growing increasingly worried about the fragility of my mental state, or worse, that I might keel over and die before she even had a chance to take my order.

'Oh, listen to me, rabbiting on like some Lambeth market trader,' I said, clapping my hand over my mouth, and lowering my gaze, as if something of immense scientific interest had suddenly emerged from between the bottles of brown sauce and tomato ketchup. 'Please take no notice, miss. I'm just being overly sentimental. ' "Hokey Harry", my good lady wife often calls me. It's a nickname I've earned, as you'll doubtless agree.'

'I looked up, fully expecting to see the young lady beating a hasty retreat, establishing a safe distance before dialling the number of the local mental institution, and the proverbial men in white coats, but instead I was astonished to see that she was still stood there at the right-hand side of the table, smiling as she slowly shook her head, and Dear Lord, she'd suddenly looked to be the absolute mirror image of the young Irish girl I'd fallen for, and who had subsequently broken my heart all those years before.

'I don't think you're "Hokey" in the slightest, Harry,' she said, and something about the way she'd referred to me by my first name, convinced me she wasn't merely being polite or condescending. 'I've always loved that song, too. It's by some feller named Bobby something or other, isn't it?'

'Yes, yes. Bobby Darin it is,' I replied wonderingly. 'My father bought the record the morning of the day I was born. March, 1959, that was. He's held a great, unwavering affection for the song, ever since. Dad's in his mid-eighties now, and you know what, he's even requested it to be played at his funeral.'

'Well, I knew it was from way back before my time, of course,' the waitress said, absent-mindedly twisting the plastic pen between her slim fingers. 'But my parents played it endlessly when I was growing up. Me ma, especially had a fondness for it. She told me it was her favourite record because it reminded her of me dad.'

She paused for a second, before adding. 'I wasn't so sure about that, though. Something in her eyes told me she wasn't being completely honest with me. She'd been spinning kind of a white lie. The tune definitely did remind her of someone, of that I'm certain, but I'm convinced it wasn't me dad. It was someone she'd met long before him. A childhood sweetheart, or a holiday romance, perhaps. Someone me ma had fallen for when she was a mere teenager living in Dublin.' She shrugged her shoulders and sighed. 'Don't ask me how I know that. I just do.'

'For a moment I couldn't speak, but I felt tears prick at the corners of my eyes, and I was scared to blink in case they came cascading down my cheeks in a veritable flood. The sort that won't stop until you resemble one of those gibbering, drunken wrecks, the kind you sometimes see sat slumped in the corner of an alehouse, too afraid to stagger home.

'The coincidences, (if that's what they truly were), were piling up by the second, and I began to feel increasingly like Alice, sliding down the rabbit hole into a realm of surreality, but still, there was something I simply had to ask, even though I was sure I already knew the answer, and having it confirmed would likely only add to my sense that I was being made the butt of some slyly grinning god's idea of a joke.

'Mentally steeling myself, I looked the waitress squarely in the eye. 'Please, miss, I don't mean to be rude, but your mother's name. Was it the same as yours? Was it Keela?'

'Aye, so it was,' she replied, 'She blessed me, her youngest, with her Christian name, and I'm immensely proud of that fact. And do you know something else, I think the feller me ma still carried a torch for was named Har....'

'Keela!' an unmistakably Scouse female voice thundered across the room, and the waitress jumped like she'd been struck in the nether regions with an electric cattle prod. I glanced across the room and saw a huge battle-axe of a woman stood behind the counter, her pale-as-the-moon face twisted into an ugly grimace, her eyes bulging with barely constrained rage.

'What the 'ell do yer think yer playin' at, motor-mouth? I don't pay yer to stand around chattin' nonsense when there's customers need servin'. Take that feller's order and then come and see me and we'll have a good arl chin-wag about yer chatter-box behaviour, just the two of us. In me office. Do yer get me drift girl?'

'Yes, ruh-right away, muh-muh Miss Flynn!' Keela stammered, and my heart went out to her at that moment, and I was filled with righteous anger on her behalf, too. I've never been able to abide bullies of any sort, and I went to get to my feet to remonstrate with this vile woman, who was clearly the café's manageress, concerning her distinct lack of manners, and her grossly unprofessional conduct, but before I could move a muscle, Keela shot me a pleading look that spoke of the terrible consequences that might befall her if I were to try and intervene. Reluctantly, I remained in my seat, and locked my hands together at the back of my head, an old habit of mine whenever I feel especially frustrated.

'It's quite alright, Keela,' I told her. 'I'm waiting for a friend. He'll be along presently. I'll order some food and drinks when he finally deigns to turn up. Thank you so much for taking the time to talk to me.'

'She smiled gratefully, bowed her head, and for a mad second or so, I honestly thought she was going to favour me with a full-on, maid-style curtsy. Instead, without another word, she turned and headed towards the counter, the unseen office beyond, and the anticipated wrath of her tyrannical boss.

'I watched her disappear from view, and I was offering up a silent prayer for her well-being when my mobile rang again, and for some reason I jumped as though a cold hand had reached out from some abyssal darkness, and gently caressed my cheek.

'And this time, I did drop my phone.'

'It slipped from between my fingers, hit the floor and slid across the polished, recently swept linoleum and came to rest right under the chair opposite me. I reached down to retrieve it and as I did so, I cracked my head on the wooden edge of the table with such force that I didn't just see stars, I saw entire constellations. I rubbed the area just above my right eye and whilst there was no blood, I could feel a large lump had already formed there, and it hurt like hell. Cursing under my breath, I grabbed my phone, just as it stopped ringing.

Flopping back in my chair, with the beginnings of a pounding headache, I saw I had a voicemail message from you, John, probably apologising for running even later than you'd predicted, and struggling to keep my temper in check, I pressed the receiver to my ear to hear whatever excuse you were about to give me.

"Alright, Harry, lad!" you shouted down the phone, and I could hear what sounded like a large group of people, along with the unmistakable pounding beat of modern music blaring away in the background.

"Where are yer, mate?" You all but yelled. "Yer said yer were here, lad, but I've looked all around this friggin' café, and I can't find yer anywhere." You paused momentarily. "Mind you, it is chocka, like. Tell yer what, why don't we jib it and go straight down the alehouse instead. *The Britannia* pub is only abar a fifteen minute walk away. Meet me at the café's entrance and we'll head over there."

You paused again, and I could hear a woman screaming at someone, maybe her daughter; "Eh, girl, shut that whingeing gob of yours! I told yer, yer gettin' no ice cream if yer don't eat all yer greens! I seen yer flickin' those sprouts under the table, sly arse!"

There was an answering high-pitched wailing, that sounded like the tortured yell of an inhabitant of the Tower of Babel, and then you were speaking, or rather shouting, again. "Christ, Harry, I don't know abar you, but I really fancy a nice cold pint of suds. I'm sweatin' cobs here, lad! See yer in a bit.''

The line went dead, and it hit me then that for some reason you had sent me on a bum steer, and that there was more than one café in the area, despite your assurances to the contrary, and for all its obvious charms: the 1950s vibe, the pretty, memory-stirring young waitress, the old Wurlitzer jukebox, I was hungry and thirsty, and still not fully recovered from that morning's interminable shopping expedition. Suddenly I was so bloody angry that I almost launched my phone from the end of my ridiculously expensive brothel creepers right across the room.

But instead, I emitted a world-weary sigh, got to my feet, and headed for the exit.

'As I did so, I saw Keela standing with her back to me, framed in the doorway: a pony-tailed silhouette. Her shoulders were hunched, and she was smoking a cigarette. I stopped to tell her I was sorry if I'd gotten her into trouble with her boss, and I reached out a hand to gently touch her arm. At that moment she wheeled round, and I saw with a degree of shock, that it wasn't Keela, at all. It was a woman in her mid-fifties, wearing an identical waitress uniform and with the exact same hairstyle, but her hard, almost masculine features were quite literally caked in thick layers of bright orange make up, powdered blusher and glossy red lipstick. She regarded me with an expression of withering contempt, and I had the ridiculous notion she was going to slap me hard across the face. But then Chantelle, as her name-tag proclaimed her to be, leaned forward to peer more closely, and I saw her panda-like eyes gradually widen, and a smile spread slowly across her face. I could lie and say that smile knocked years off her, but as I'm trying my best to stick to the facts here, I'd have to be honest and say all it achieved was to cause the pancake foundation around her mouth and upper cheeks to crack and split open like a stretch of sun-baked mud-flats.

'And then my stomach sank as I saw the look of recognition sparking in her eyes....

'To my disgust, I felt the first stirrings of familiarity too, and gradually it dawned on me that I knew her, as she knew me, loathe as I was to admit it, even to myself.

'For the second time on that seemingly endless September day, I found myself remembering....

'I'd been in my mid-twenties, and employed by a well-known firm of London solicitors, and at the drunken end of a staff night out, I'd found myself slumped, semi-conscious, on a velvet couch in some dimly-lit dive bar being chatted up by some strange woman, (in every sense of the term), who I gauged to be at least fifteen years my senior. She was wearing an indecently low-cut, skin-tight,

dress, and seemed to be floating in a sea of perfume. I didn't find her in any way attractive, not even in my hopelessly inebriated state, but somehow I wound up back at her dingy flat, somewhere near Finsbury Park. I vaguely recall her telling me her name was Chantelle, as she poured me a large glass of red wine, which I later suspected may well have been spiked, and subsequently being pushed fully-clothed, onto the double bed, with the room spinning wildly, and the sound of a baby wailing from over in the far corner like an air raid siren, and then Chantelle was loosening the belt of my trousers and unbuttoning my shirt, and I could no more have resisted than if I'd been bound hand and foot to the bed posts...

'My next conscious memory had been of waking in the early hours, with my groin throbbing painfully, specks of dried blood on the sheets, and Chantelle fast asleep beside me, her face, shorn of make-up, deadly pale and drawn in the admittedly cruel light of a false dawn.

'In the grip of the worst hangover I've ever known, before or since, feeling nauseous, and wincing from the deep scratches that criss-crossed my back, I'd somehow managed to crawl from the bedroom, my clothes in hands that shook like those of the homeless alcoholics I sometimes saw sat near the entrance of King's Cross Station.

'I prayed I hadn't given Chantelle my phone number, nor told her my home address whilst lost in my drunken state, and in the days and weeks that followed, I lived in constant terror of bumping into her. I even took to purchasing a baseball cap, the bill of which I pulled as low as possible to obscure my face whenever I left the house, and I stopped visiting the local pubs and bars for the best part of a couple of months.

It might sound ridiculously cowardly of me, going to such extremes simply to avoid encountering the woman who was likely just a sad and lonely individual, caught in the depths of a mid-life crisis, but the truth is, she scared me. Terrified, me actually. There was something creepy and disturbing about her, (and not just her vampish, virtual date-rape seduction technique), that gave me no end of nightmares.

'I never did see her again.

'And I'd been eternally thankful for that.

'But then she'd seemingly appeared in the entrance to the café. Standing before me, looking as though she hadn't aged a day since that awful night at her flat in Finsbury Park, thirty-odd years ago.

"Hey, hun," Chantelle said, smiling widely . 'Don't even think about leaving just yet! At least not till you've tried today's special. It's raspberry ripple ice cream with extra chocolate chips! Just the thing for a devilishly hot, sultry day like this one, wouldn't you say?''

'She picked up a laminated menu card from a nearby table, and began fanning herself with it, and I saw that she'd unbuttoned her blouse to the point where it revealed the swell of her not inconsiderable cleavage.

'My stomach roiled, and I began backing away towards the exit with my hands raised, as if to ward off the approach of some dangerous, stalking animal.

"Oh, come on now, handsome" she said licking her lips, "You *know* you want to try a taste. Don't deny yourself a guilty pleasure. I promise you, it's absolutely *delicious!"*

'So saying, she reached behind her and produced a cracked and multi-stained dessert bowl and shoved it towards me. I baulked as I saw it was overflowing with a colourless, half-melted morass that looked more like freshly spewed vomit than any type of ice cream. The waitress leered at me, revealing her yellow and nicotine-stained teeth, and I noticed too, the way her once carefully coiffured hair-style suddenly seemed horribly dead and matted, and for a hideous moment, I thought I saw something black and shiny scuttle in and out of her long, greasy fringe.

'I think I screamed out loud, then, but if I did, no one present paid me the slightest attention.

'The café did though, if that doesn't sound like the crowning insanity on a day already replete with examples of outright lunacy.

'It began to reveal its true face to me, and I was struck with the horrid realisation that the place I had initially thought filled with an abundance of charm and the magical glow of 1950s nostalgia, turned out to be akin to the unfurling of some outwardly attractive flower that proves, upon closer inspection, to be blighted and diseased, and home to some vile species of parasite.

'I felt a subtle shifting in the air, and a faint vibration beneath my feet, almost as if something were stirring, coming fully awake deep within the bowels of the earth. Something huge and incredibly ancient.

'Something *evil*.

'The scene before me began to dissolve and grow wavily indistinct, as though I was viewing things through a shimmering heat haze. Though my body trembled with the impossibility of it all, and my head ached abominably, still I stood absolutely transfixed, unable to move a single muscle.

'I watched as the changes wrought themselves upon the building, and the small band of people gathered there, as still and unmoving as shop-window dummies. The pristine film and concert posters on the walls I'd so admired earlier, slowly drained of colour and started to tear and curl at the edges; the thick clouds of dust descending from a ceiling suddenly festooned with hideously sagging cobwebs.

'Elvis began crooning the line "Love Me Tender", over and over on the Wurlitzer, the needle stuck in a groove, "The King's" voice slowing to a demonic-sounding growl before the record mercifully, ground to a halt.

'And finally, the light leeched from the room, bathing everyone present, the foul, ice-cream-proffering waitress included, in pools of dark shadow, despite the fact that I could clearly see through the increasingly grimy windows, it was still full daylight outside.

'It was only when this flood of encroaching blackness began to seep across the room towards me, bringing with it the inarguable certainty that if it were to touch even the smallest part of me, I'd be lost, trapped forever in this terrible place, that I managed to will myself to move. I turned and fled through the open doorway, out into the bright afternoon sunlight, only pausing once to glance back over my shoulder, and saw with horror that the whole inside of the building was now encased in a thick, gelatinous slab of darkness so opaque, you couldn't see a single thing beyond the doorway.

'Worse, a vast collection of inky tendrils began to emerge from the building, spreading across the raised terrace at a frightening speed towards the assorted crowds of sun worshippers and members of the string quartet were gathered, seemingly ignorant of the approaching danger. I raced towards the crowd of men and women, gesticulating wildly and shouting warnings, but they appeared to be completely unaware of my presence, no matter how loudly I screamed in their faces. They just continued to sit there in silence, their gaze fixed intently upon the members of the string quartet, who I now noticed had begun to sound increasingly out of tune.

'The audience didn't appear to care, though. They simply sat and stared with uniform mechanical smiles, as a combination of sweat and sun-tan lotion oozed down their cheeks in greasy rivulets, their ice creams melted, and a large swarm of fat, bloated bluebottles buzzed madly around their heads.

'As the unnatural blackness pooled at their feet, and quickly made its way up the rest of their pink-fleshed bodies however, the people began to slowly dissolve as though eaten away by relentless waves of acid. The darkness took everything else along with it, too. The ranks of deck-chairs and empty drinks cans. The flat cokes and half-glasses of lemonade. Handbags and rucksacks, the newspapers and their Sunday supplements...

'An unpleasant odour suddenly assailed my nostrils, like spoiled meat and dead fish, and flowers rotting in a charnel house. The notion that the crawling, all-enveloping darkness was acting on behalf of the cafe, to reclaim this parade of the damned for Its own was crazy, but impossible to dismiss.

'The musicians were the last to go, still playing, albeit with a jarring succession of bum notes, as the darkness engulfed them, and I was struck with a vivid image of the band who nobly continued to provide the consoling soundtrack, when all was hopeless and lost amidst the tragic death throes of RMS *Titanic*.

'As the last of them disappeared from view, I finally found the strength to turn and vault over the metal fence at the edge of the café's terrace in a single bound, and tore across the field, still bathed in eye-wateringly bright September sunshine. I had no clear idea where I was headed. I just had to get away. To put as much distance between that truly godforsaken building as quickly as possible, and oh, God, my head had been splitting, and purple flowers bloomed and the world had spun out of focus, and I'd half-glimpsed a group of people sat around a woollen blanket laden with food and drink.

'One of the men present, shouted "Are you alright, mate?" and I opened my mouth to answer, but before I could utter a single word, those dark violet blooms burst into showers of minuscule stars, and I fell to my knees like I'd been shot, and I knew no more.'

SIX

'I regained consciousness in the back of an ambulance, speeding towards what I subsequently learned, was The Royal Liverpool University Hospital.

'I don't remember much about the journey. Only that I babbled semi-coherently to a pair of sympathetic paramedics about avaricious walls of darkness, buildings possessed of some malignant form of intelligence and the seemingly-solid apparitions who resided there.

'Some time later, a doctor, with neatly trimmed facial hair and a pair of piercing blue eyes, reassured both me, and my wife, Mary, who was standing, smiling nervously at my bedside, her arms filled with a collection of paperbacks, a copy of *The Guardian,* 'and my favourite pair of pyjamas, that I had suffered a relatively minor concussion, and undergone an excessive degree of shock brought upon by the vivid, but nonetheless purely imaginary delusions I'd experienced as a result of my head injury.

'I had to remain in "The Royal", overnight, "purely for observational reasons, you understand, " the doctor had said with a nod and a wink, as though the three of us were sharing some all-pals-together, conspiratorial secret.

'After he'd wandered off, clipboard in hand, Mary had placed an arm on my shoulder and all but begged me to cut short our holiday, and return to London as soon as I was well enough. I have to be honest, I'm not normally one to turn tail and scarper home at the first sign of trouble, but these were definitely no ordinary circumstances. My wife may not have believed a single thing I claimed had taken place prior to me blacking out in the middle of a field earlier that day, but she understood implicitly that *something* unpleasant had happened to me, purely illusory or otherwise, whilst she and Eleanor had been engaged upon a "Marathon Shoe-Shopping Expedition."

'I think, in the end, it was only you and your wife's undeservedly shame-faced appearance at the hospital, early the following morning, John, just as I was preparing to leave the ward, that inspired a dramatic change of heart, and persuaded me that actually, there was very little to be gained by returning to London immediately. If I were to take it easy for the next few days, relaxing and recuperating, and made sure to steer clear of any and all cafés situated in the Otterspool area, I'd likely be just fine.

'So, for better or for worse, that's precisely what I did.'

SEVEN

'And here I am today at *The Britannia Inn,* exactly one week later, enjoying a cold pint of beer, on another gorgeous September day, recounting to you an experience that a sizeable part of me still believes to have had at least some basis in reality.

'Thanks for lending me a sympathetic ear, my friend, and for not judging me in any way. I feel a great sense of relief at having finally gotten things off my chest. At peace, almost. And who knows? Maybe I'll be able to enjoy a restful sleep untroubled by bad dreams for the first time in what seems like an age?

'I do love it here, John. This part of The Prom, I mean. Watching the tankers and the ferry boats sailing by, the view of The Wirral coastline and the Welsh mountains beyond. I even like the string multi-coloured fairy lights lining the pub's roof. They give the place a holiday-resort-type feel...'

'It's hard to believe, that just over my shoulder, a mere fifteen minute's or so walk from here, stands a long-closed-down café that, according to you, hasn't seen a paying customer since 1987. A building that though it might possess a grandiose facade, is in reality, nothing more than an empty shell within.

'Empty, that is, except for its multiple array of ghosts, real or imagined, of bitter regrets and sullied memories of things I'd much sooner forget.

'I know its precise location and distance from here, because whilst nothing could persuade me to re-visit that awful place in person, I spent most of yesterday carrying out some research on the internet and scrolling through the archives over at Toxteth Library, and I made several unsettling discoveries. Chief amongst them were the two colour photographs that immediately popped up the moment I typed Otterspool Café, into Google.

'The first depicted "The New Otters Café", and was very obviously the place where I should have met you John, situated on the opposite side of the rolling green fields from where I'd parked up last Sunday. It was easy to see why it had escaped my notice when I'd first arrived at The Promenade. The building looked more like an elongated log cabin or one of those stores that sells hiking and camping equipment, and whilst it looked inviting enough, it certainly lacked the elegant charm, outwardly at least, of the old one.

'I very nearly fainted dead away, for the second time that week, when I set eyes on the second photograph, though.

It showed the exact same café where I'd spent part of that nightmarish afternoon, right enough. There was no mistaking that. But, featured under the banner headline *Old Derelict Cafe In Otterspool Park,* was a picture taken on 11th August, 2012, of a decrepit, boarded-up structure, that looked like it hadn't been open to the public in decades. It was immediately apparent that it would require months, if not a year or so of hard work to renovate the building to anything approaching the standards of the one I'd entered, just a few short weeks after this photograph had been taken.

'This is absolutely impossible, it just can't be,' I muttered to myself, causing a stereotypical female librarian to peer at me reproachfully from over the top of her spectacles. I shook my head, trying desperately to deny the dreadful reality of that which was staring me fully in the face: I'd either experienced some sort of terrifyingly vivid hallucination, which deeply disturbs me regarding the state of my mental health, to say the least. Or worse, I'd encountered a form of malign time-slip, or a tear in the fabric of what passes for everyday reality.

'Much as I value my sanity, it's the latter prospect that frightens me most. The possibility that what took place at the café was entirely real, fills me with an innate sense of dread, too afraid to glance behind me, like that accursed sailor in Coleridge's *Rime of the Ancient Mariner.*

'I scrolled through the small collection of other photographs of the old café posted up on Flickr, a succession of pictures taken at all four seasons of the year over the course of the last decade or so, and from wildly different angles and perspectives, but all of them depicting the building in its current dilapidated state.

'I read the short comments posted beneath the snaps by various people, the majority of which went along the lines of "Wow! What a beautiful building!!! So sad to see it closed down. Why doesn't someone set about re-opening it?"

'There were several responses to this question, the most popular being "maybe it's set too far back from the road to be prominent to visitors," and "There's a new cafe opened just up the road, near to the Adventure Playground, so I doubt it would be commercially viable."

'There was one comment that held particular resonance for me, though. It said simply...

"Sometimes, there is a good reason for closing things down!"

'It could have meant anything, of course, but a chill went running up and down my spine, just the same.

'I decided to search the net for details of the history of Otterspool Promenade and of the café in particular, and I came across a brief, but well-written article by a local historian named Mike Royden, who had been born and raised the proverbial stone's throw away from the Park.

'After informing the reader that Otterspool was originally the name of a small creek or pool at a point where the Oskelesbrook, as it was quaintly known in the days of King John, flowed directly into the River Mersey, Mike wrote:

"My childhood fascination with the place never waned and even from an early age I felt there was a history to the Park that did not readily reveal itself to visitors; something was missing. Strange footpaths, tunnels, dried up pools and river beds, and a cafe I always felt did not belong on the raised terrace, the steps and walls of which I was sure once surrounded something a little more grand."

'It turns out that this was indeed the case. The café had been built upon the site of a typically grand 18th century mansion called, imaginatively enough, Otterspool House. It was once owned by a man named John Moss, a former slave trader, it seems, and the entire edifice was demolished in 1931.

Nowadays, only the wide terrace and the set of stone steps leading up to the café remain. I found it a little strange that no one, be they historians, visiting tourists or local residents seemed to know exactly when the café had been erected on the site, nor precisely when it was finally closed down, although it was generally agreed to have shut its doors for good some time in the late 1980s, as you said, John.

'I also searched in vain for any photographs of the interior of the café during its heyday, but despite the glowing reviews the place received from those who did recall paying it a visit, I couldn't find a single picture.

'There was no mention of it being haunted, either, though a couple of apparitions are reputed to haunt the area. A phantom Stuka shot down over the Mersey sometime during the Blitz, has reportedly been sighted by various witnesses over the years of so-called peace that have since elapsed, as has the wandering spirit of a signalman in full uniform, carrying a red flag near to the arching darkness of the nearby railway bridge, the eyewitness statements describing an entity not dissimilar to the titular spectral character of that old classic Dickens story.

'This lack of corroborative evidence for the reality of my experience was perversely disappointing, but it didn't necessarily mean there hadn't been any incidences similar to mine. And if there had, it was hardly surprising the percipients were reluctant to record their experience, even on one of the many paranormal sites on the internet.

'I remember reading somewhere, probably amongst the pages of some dusty theological volume or other left open on the desk of my father's study, something along the lines of *"The face of Evil craves to remain hidden behind an outwardly attractive façade, the better to lure and trap the unwary."*

'And there's one more thing I feel worthy of mention before we talk of other, brighter things. It concerns that initial, and most recent, on-line photograph that had flashed up the moment I began my Google search.

'The off-white walls of the café were covered in various forms of graffiti, and there was nothing unusual about that. Abandoned buildings act as a magnet for wannabe artists, after all.

'But it was the three figures, spray-painted by someone with at least a modicum of talent, and which dominated the Promenade-facing wall, that greatly unnerved me.

'A bright green cartoon clown cavorted there, its hideous form piled, traffic light style, on top of another two, slightly more traditional but entirely bodiless, clown faces. They were doubtless meant to be a vague source of amusement to the viewer, but to me, in my current frame of mind at least, their presence was a mocking verification that I truly didn't imagine the events I contend took place within that accursed building.

'I agree that might sound dangerously paranoid sitting here on yet another miraculously sun-bright September day, when all seems right with the world.

OTTERSPOOL CAFE

(Above): The sadly neglected, long-closed-down café, at the edge of the wide expanse of fields on Otterspool Promenade. Today, it peers from amidst the rows of ancient trees and surrounding woodland like a white-walled epitaph. A monument to time's relentless march. For most, at least...

For others, the gifted or the cursed, it's a place where The Old Ghosts of Yesteryear sometimes gather

Photo Credit: Tony Barr

But try dismissing it as such when you're lying awake, caught in the heart-pounding aftermath of a terrible dream.

'The one that seems so unbearably *real.*

'The one where pale white, half-familiar faces, suddenly loom up out of the roiling blackness, wide-eyed and grinning.

'In the dark, silent watches of the night....'

EIGHT
John's account of his friend, Harry's bizarre experience, entirely illusory or otherwise, contained the following intriguing postscript:

'I suppose, Lee, I should make it clear, that I don't believe anything remotely paranormal had actually happened to Harry, in September, 2012.

'I agreed totally with his original theory that he'd somehow slipped and whacked his head big time on his way over to the wrong café, at the wrong moment, at the entirely wrong time, and it's to my eternal regret that I hadn't simply arranged to meet him at the edge of the car park or somewhere on the Prom front!

'Harry, God bless him, stayed in Liverpool, along with his missus, for the best part of a couple of weeks, and he left amidst reassuringly firm handshakes, manly bear-hugs, and heart-felt promises to stay in touch.

'He was as good as his word, as well, although a part of me secretly knew that the moment me and Eleanor watched his jet-black Mercedes disappear amidst the yawning mouth of the Mersey Tunnel, we'd likely never see either of them again. And so it proved. We exchanged Christmas cards and seasonal greetings later that year, but I instinctively knew the promises we made to meet up in the future were empty ones. It's sad, like, but it happens sometimes.

'Anyway, last Boxing Day, I took a bike ride out along the trail that leads from my home on Jericho Lane, through the Park and out to *The Britannia*. This is something I do every year in an ultimately futile attempt to burn off the excess weight caused by chomping on all that Chrimbo food and guzzling down huge amounts of ale.

'I'm only telling you this because of what happened on that cold and frosty late December afternoon, as I neared the end of the path that leads through the thick woods towards the Promenade. It was one of those gloomy, windless days, and I noticed there were very few fellow bike riders, joggers or dog walkers about. I supposed most people were warm and snug indoors, spending quality time with their friends and family, or sat with their feet up watching the box, and I actually felt a stab of jealousy as I cycled alone through the silent winter woods.

'The path was fairly slippery with a thin covering of black ice, and I kept my eyes peeled for potholes and fallen branches, whilst occasionally casting glances at the boss scenery all around me, making my exertions seem more than worthwhile. I'd reached the edge of the woods when a blur of reddish-brown streaked across the pathway directly in front of me, and I slammed on the brakes and skidded to a halt, narrowly avoiding collision with what I saw was a large male fox, diving into a clump of rhododendron bushes away to me right. I was so startled, it took me half a minute to recover me composure. As I did so, my gaze fell upon the old café, just up ahead, sitting in the middle of its frozen terrace, shrouded in a late afternoon mist.

'I can't say why exactly, but I began to feel vaguely uneasy, and I told meself "Come on, soft lad, get yer act together."

'I put me feet on the pedals, sorted me balance out, and began riding towards the Park exit. I got about thirty feet, before I whacked on the brakes again, and sucked in a lungful of freezing air.

'I saw the fox emerge from another cluster of dead-looking bushes and slowly saunter towards the rear of the café, cool as yer like, and once it got there, it turned, sat on its haunches, and grinned its sly, feral grin.

'At that precise moment, I thought I heard the distant strains of slightly off-key music emanating from somewhere deep within the suddenly sinister-seeming building, all misted and somehow *waiting*....

'I must have trod or rode along this path a thousand times over the years, but for the first time ever, I really didn't want to be there. I admit I was frightened, and I was scared to turn me face from the building in case, as ridiculous as it sounds, someone or *something* sneaked up on me. I got off me bike and started wheeling it back the way I'd come, and as I did so, me feet slipped on something and I almost lost me balance. I tore my gaze from the café and the strangely motionless fox and glanced down for a second to see what I'd stepped on.

'It was a glossy magazine, a Sunday supplement most likely, its ice-encrusted pages lying open to reveal a brightly coloured picture, startlingly vivid against the gloomy greyness of the deserted woods and surrounding fields. I saw it featured an article entitled *Fabulously Festive Fifties Nostalgia,* and there was an artist's rendition of a crowded café or American-themed diner at Halloween time. There were groups of smiling people in various types of fancy dress dancing around an old-fashioned juke-box in a room festooned with orange streamers and glowing Jack O' Lanterns. I could see straight away that the venue bore an uncanny resemblance to the one Harry had described to me, that day in late September....

'But that wasn't what chilled me the most, and had me scrambling on to the bike and speeding away from there as fast as my legs could pump the pedals, my mouth wide open in a silent scream.

'It was the sight of the simple, yet horribly apt-seeming words that made up the picture's tag-line:

There's A Witchery to Wurlitzer Music

There's a Witchery to WURLITZER MUSIC

Musical Fun for Everyone

Call it magic, witchery or what you will... Wurlitzer Music has a way of making dull moments a bygone memory. More fun. More life. More laughter. Remember it the next time you're out for your enjoyment, it's where they have Wurlitzer Music. Music so alluring, it breaks in and has the nearest point of America is a most language. The Rudolph Wurlitzer Company, North Tonawanda, New York, 101 for Phonograph Section of Chamber Employee. Watch for some of Wurlitzer Dealers.

CHAPTER EIGHT
LIKE SPECTRES RISING FROM DARK WATERS
The Giant Crabs Of West Kirkby

ONE
The long golden summer of 1976.

That glorious sun-baked sequence of cloudless skies and dreamy heat-waves.

Of horizons that seemed to melt into a never-ending series of Saharan mirages.

Of white-sailed boats prancing like snowy-white horses on the bright blue waters of the bay.

Of beach trips and family days out and the mouth-watering smells of fish and chips, (replete with vinegar-soaked, cheap wooden forks) and peering into the bottom of a perfectly clear rock pool; the gob-smacked fascination of witnessing a micro-marine world illuminated by jagged shafts of sunlight spearing down to illuminate the mini-depths.

The way the music from a pub jukebox or a car radio, drifted on the heat-stilled air like the sweetest melody you ever heard. The way your skin felt pleasantly tight when you pulled on your going-out clothes and the freckles that erupted onto your cheeks like a benign form of acne (that brown-speckled rash me Ma used to call with a beautiful sense of throwaway whimsy: "An outbreak of Sun Kisses").

Or, on the other (badly sunburned) hand....
The totally *shitty* long hot summer of 1976.

For these whose sense of romance was every bit as redundant as a prog rock super-group in the wake of the incendiary, three-chord, blast of punk, that never-ending heat-wave was a grim prospect indeed.

The incredible hot spell that lasted from June to late September, that year, was a totally horrendous ordeal as far as they were concerned; a seemingly endless sequence of sweaty Mediterranean-like weather that quickly parched the farmer's fields, dried up the rivers and caused hose-pipe bans to be implemented across the vast majority of Britain.

I guess some people take delight in being so perennially gloomy they make the manky dregs of winter positively sparkle by comparison.

TWO

For those too young to have actually experienced that record-breaking summer, it must seem like some dimly recalled fable of "ladybird invasions and street vendors charging a pound for a can of Coke in the park!"

As for me, I can remember being sat on the base of a rock surrounded by miles and miles of pristine sand on a July day so idyllic it resembled the slick, scenic reproductions on one of those cheap, mass-produced postcards – the kind you send to your absent family and friends in an attempt to mask the grim reality of your fortnight's break, which often turns out to be a miserable, argument-ridden washout, where the nearest you've managed to get to a break from the nine to five treadmill is to gaze mournfully out the caravan windows to study the ever-present storm skies looming above.

And grimly wonder how perfectly they mirror the chaotic, turbulent, path of your life.

However, the summer of '76 was one of those rare occasions when all of the pre-holiday expectations were realised, encapsulated in the shape of a general store, situated at the entrance to Presthaven Sands Holiday Park, on the North Wales coastline.

From the outside, this typical slate-coloured building with a *Wall's* ice cream sign and a sandwich board advertising freshly-made sarnies near to its front door, appeared depressingly ordinary. The only thing that marked it out as being different in fact, was the wonderfully-colourful Welsh flag flying in the permanent sea breeze.

Once you stepped within however, everything changed. From a 12-year-old boy's perspective, at least.

You were immediately confronted with an Aladdin's Cave of Wondrous Delights: A vast collection of buckets and spades, bamboo-poled fishing nets, glossy sea shells and kid-sized ship's captain's caps, with transparent, bright green brims, that turned the sunlight an alien shade of verdant when you pulled them low over your brow; something I instantly felt compelled to do the moment my parent's handed one to me. There were assorted cheap, rubber monster toys, (including terrible, but still somehow wonderful, King Kong and Frankenstein Monster rip-offs), dinosaurs, comic book super-heroes and assorted creepy crawlies. There were ceramic models of thatched cottages, seaside pubs and cosy little harbours, huge sticks of rock and bird-shaped kites that looked capable of soaring into the upper reaches of the stratosphere if you were to let them go flying free from your hands.

My absolute favourite things in the entire shop though were the three or four spinning metal book racks situated in the centre of the store. These stuffed-to-overflowing stands contained a wide selection of publications; short story anthologies, fantasy adventures, crime novels, fictional historical dramas, and the obligatory *Mills & Boon* romances. But what always served to grab my attention were the unusually large number of horror novels and supposedly true-life, supernatural books stacked amongst them. It wasn't unusual back in the mid-1970s, but I know from recent experience that in these overly PC-times, there's more chance of finding a nugget of truth in a politician's pre-election pledge than stumble upon a *single* horror title in today's, "family-friendly", holiday stores.

On the first day of our vacation, my Dad, who was in charge of my holiday funds, (which I think, if memory serves me, was a whopping great total of £7:50, a veritable fortune in 1976!), told me I was allowed to purchase three items, and I therefore knew I had to choose carefully. Twenty minutes later, and with my Dad's patience wearing dangerously thin, I eventually decided on a magazine called *House of Hammer,* a non-fiction book entitled *The Dark World Of Witches,* by Eric Maple, and the sole reason why we're taking this trip down a summer-dappled Memory Lane in the first place:

Night Of The Crabs.

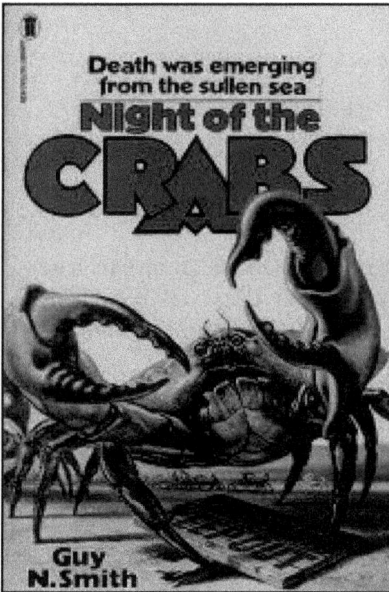

Even the most casual of glances at the book's contents revealed that the plot was about as far from anything approaching a genuine slice of originality as a male, middle-aged karaoke singer with a desperately thinning-on-top straggly mullet, a shirt button-straining ale-gut, and a voice so flat it was like Barry White had parked his arse on it.

The author's name was hardly inspiring either:

Plain old Guy N Smith.

But it was the suitably lurid cover that grabbed my attention: A numberless army of giant, grey, crustaceans with beady, obsidian eyes, gaping mouths, and fearsome sets of pincers that looked well capable of cutting through thick layers of sheet metal, never mind tender human flesh, marching along a moon-lit beach, clearly intent on wreaking bloody mayhem amongst the local populace. The flattened "Danger Keep Out" sign, its post apparently snapped by those lethal-looking claws, provided more than enough evidence of their intention to avenge their sea-food platter brethren.

It seemed an entirely appropriate choice of novel, given that my family and I were about to spend the week at the seaside. One glance out of the store's windows revealed a glimpse of the miles of shoreline, currently bathed in the rays of that remorseless summer sun, but which, a few short hours from now, would be illuminated by beams of silver moonlight.

And who knew what horrors might emerge from the inky waters, to slither or scuttle along that flawless stretch of sand on the wrong side of midnight, when the cheery lights of the holiday homes and mobile tourers, the pitched tents and the static caravans, the resident's night club and junior disco, the amusements arcade and the mini-fairground had all long since been extinguished?

A prehistoric, lighthouse-smashing Rhedosaur, rudely awakened from its 65 million year period of hibernation by the testing of a newly developed nuclear weapon?

A glistening, black, sinuous sea monster, a creature that variously resembles a basking shark, a seal, a whale or a dolphin, but is in reality a shape-shifter; a Lovecraftian terror from the uncharted depths of a bottomless ocean?

Or a merciless platoon of gigantic, man-eating crabs, striding relentlessly towards the people sleeping unawares...?

'Northern lights are fading,
Still people dance in these haunted times...'

In Dark Dreams - **The Lids**

THREE

And so when I heard, thirty-odd years down the path of my life, about the urban legend (in reality, more a series of whispered half-rumours) of the Giant Crabs Of West Kirby, the picturesque town, situated on the far north western side of the Wirral peninsular, I experienced a curious sense of déjà vu.

West Kirby is a Victorian holiday resort that has never truly fallen from favour, like so many others. Its attractions to both locals and visiting tourists alike are as obvious as they are timeless. There's a large artificial marine lake, a haven for windsurfers and sailing enthusiasts, (the footpath perimeters of which I'd walked one mild October evening, long after sunset, with my former brother-in-law, in the wake of the sudden collapse of my marriage. The light pollution out there, at the edge of the River Dee, is virtually non-existent, and the stars were laid out above us like some vast, sparkling canopy, and I remember feeling tiny and insignificant beneath their heavenly majesty. Just writing of it now, brings to mind Coleridge's wonderfully grim line about finding one-self being brushed by the "dusky wings of melancholy").

The West Kirby Sailing Club stands at the far end of town, its boatyard permanently filled with yachts, catamarans and rubber dinghies, the sight of which always fills me with an almost overpowering sense of wanderlust: an intense yearning to drag one of those boats down to the water's edge, clamber aboard and just sail off to some foreign clime.

The town centre itself is flanked by streets of large, imposing red-bricked houses, some of which are former hotels and bed & breakfasts, whilst others are still very much open for business. There are numerous bars and restaurants, too, and on warm summer evenings people, young and old, will gather on the verandas of the numerous blocks of flats or on the rooftop bars, sipping ice-cold pints of lager or exotic cocktails and watching the summer people drifting by, or the silhouettes of horses galloping along the shoreline, the lines of kids lining up outside the ice cream shop, whilst others played football, or threw Frisbees or took turns to bury each other in the sand. *

One of the most popular activities, indeed something you almost feel compelled to do, at least once, whenever you paid a visit to West Kirby, is to take a low tide walk across to Hilbre Island, the largest of a three island chain that includes Little Eye and Middle Eye.

Hilbre, (named after St Hildeburgh, a 7th century hermit who lived alone on the island), is famous, locally at least, for its large seal population, and magnificent views of North Wales, the lines of frequently snow-capped mountains that stretch away to the Point Of Ayr, and nestling between them, there's good arl' Presthaven Sands, where I spent more than one magically, enchanted holiday, and had my first 'encounter' with giant crustaceans.

FOUR

In May, 2009, on an unseasonably chilly, though sun-bright afternoon, I went merrily hiking over to Hilbre Island together with my brother, Grant, and close friend, Stevie Gee, each of us wearing our best going out clothes, to shoot a scenic, suitably majestic home-made video for our band, The Lids.

Anyone watching us, and there must have been hundreds, (not, I hasten to add, due to in any measure to our group's 'enduring fame and local renown', but for the rather more prosaic reason that we'd chosen to embark upon our self-promotional expedition on the day of "The Great Wirral Run" – a hugely popular event held for various charitable causes), must have shaken their heads incredulously at the sight of the trio of village idiots, very obviously heading for a "Knob-Head's Day Out Convention". And the truth is, they wouldn't have been a million miles wide of the mark with that supposition, because not only were we traipsing across the warm, wet sand in shoes that were likely to be ruined beyond repair before we'd gone a mere hundred yards, but there was also the

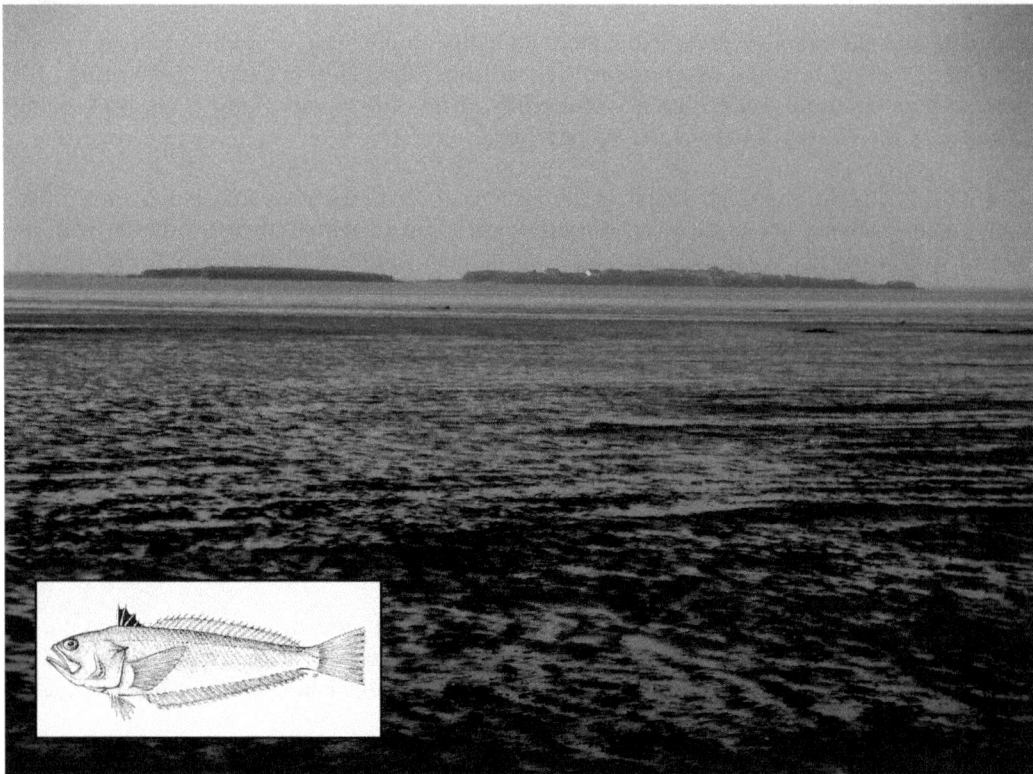

(Above): The two miles of sand that stretch across to the islands of Hilbre at low tide, a haven for all kinds of marine wildlife, including real-life mini monsters, the barbed and poisonous, bare feet-bothering, weever fish. Whatever the reality or otherwise of its semi-mythical creatures, this section of shoreline has more than its fair share of these sneaky, camouflage experts which lurk just below the surface of the wet sand, as evidenced by the collection of ominous warning signs posted at the various entries to the beach, announcing their less-than-welcome presence. The fish have sharp spines laced with venom running along their dorsal fins, capable of inflicting agony on any unsuspecting, shoe-less, beachcomber, should they be unlucky enough to tread on one. The excruciating pain caused by the fishes' poison can last for several hours, and can even cause limbs to swell or cause temporary paralysis, though thankfully, their sting rarely proves lethal.

Photo Credit: Stevie Gee

glaringly obvious fact, to the more experienced amongst them at least, that none of us had considered it might have been wise to have checked out the times of the notoriously treacherous tides before setting off.

The notion hadn't occurred to any of us until we were over three quarters of the way to the island when my companions and I had simultaneously paused for a second to exchange puzzled glances to wonder just why it was everyone else on the beach not involved in the charity event, seemed to be walking *back* towards the Promenade, (although perhaps, it might have been more accurate to say they were *jogging* at quite a fair pace, as though they were suddenly eager to join the ranks of runners, wending their way in endless bobbing lines like a column of soldier ants determinedly marching towards some strange, "insectoid" destiny).

Stevie Gee was the first to give voice to the potential for catastrophe when he suddenly exclaimed, "Oh, shit, lads! I don't wanna worry yous like, but I think there's a good chance the tide's gonna start comin' in soon and it's gonna cut us off from the prom!"

This remark inspired a hastily gabbled phone call to Steve's wife, Melanie, who confirmed, after checking on the internet, that we had at most half an hour until that grim eventuality occurred. A hurried, heated debate then took place regarding the most sensible course of action we should take, a slightly-panicked, three-way conversation given added impetus by the fact that the beachcombers were no longer jogging but had adopted something akin to a lolloping run; the sort of awkward, almost-sprint people make when they see their bus preparing to pull away from their stop, not quite willing to go flat out in case they don't quite make it and are left standing embarrassed as the people on the back seat crane their necks to point and laugh at the sweating, unfit loser left belching in the exhaust fumes of the "Arriva" double-decker.

I remember my argument being coloured by the fact that I'd arranged to meet a seemingly, (judging by her photographs, at least), attractive-looking woman, I'd "met" on some dating site, later that evening, and I'd gone and left my phone at home, so I wouldn't be able to ring her to cancel. I was struck by the all-too vivid mental image of me calling her the next day, begging in vain for forgiveness, that I honestly hadn't meant to stand her up. I'd been marooned overnight on Hilbre Island!

So yeah, obviously, whichever way you looked at it, we all agreed it made *perfect* sense to turn around right now, before it was too late.

Equally obviously, we did no such thing.

We just kept right on walking (in those already ruined, sand-encrusted shoes) towards the island and a night spent cut off from the mainland by three miles of deep seawater, like a crappy, low-budget production of *Robinson Crusoe*.

Well, we hadn't wanted to be late for the "Knob-head's Day Out Convention".

We had a well-earned reputation to maintain, after all.

FIVE

As it turned out, (and somewhat anti-climatically, you might feel), we managed to shoot the band video, briefly explore at least part of the island, and make it back to the, by then, all but deserted Promenade, having suffered nothing worse than three sets of soaking wet clothes, one saturated, and therefore useless, mobile phone, and the glowering faces of the uniformed coastguards, as the price for having undergone our "ordeal".

My memories of our brief time on Hilbre are of the lonely-looking lighthouse, the rows of clothes-filled washing lines in the centre of the gardens of the few inhabited houses, drying in the sea breeze. The weird, sea-eroded rock formations and dark caverns, including Lady's Cave (about which we'll be hearing a great deal more, in due course) and of course, the stunning views from the highest summit of the island.

I'd known before we'd set out that that Hilbre was rumoured to have once been a place of holy pilgrimage; "a shrine dedicated to Our Lady of Hilbre", according to the local historian, Mike Royden, and as we (somewhat hurriedly) traversed the isle, I saw in my mind's eye a host of cloaked, 12th century, Benedictine monks, gathered there to worship in silent contemplation. It made sense to me that those imbued with a strong sense of spirituality, of devout reverence, would, when faced with a vista so peaceful and so heart-stoppingly beautiful, come to believe it could only have been created by a benevolent deity.

These days, of course, the only form of pilgrimage most people make to Hilbre, is to try find a good spot to sit off with a six pack of lukewarm, super lager, to get high on clouds of wacky backy or to top up their bronzy's and idly watch the resident colony of seals gambolling on the sun-dried rocks.

Or of course, to shoot videos for local, Joy Division-influenced bands, like ourselves..

But that's okay, I guess.

Better that than it be declared off-limits to the public, or for it to become a virtual dumping ground for humanities' detritus; a dismal collection of bike frames and wheel tyres and used rubber johnnies.

I enjoyed our mini-day out on Hilbre, even if it amounted to little more than a necessarily brief, whistle-stop tour.

Oh, and I made the date later, too.

Although for reasons that I won't go into here, I later found I had good cause to rather wish I'd wound up temporarily stranded on the island.

Perhaps I shouldn't joke about such things, however.

It's certainly no exaggeration to state that when the tide comes in at West Kirby, it does so unbelievably quickly, as my friends and I can now readily attest.

One minute there are only a series of tiny, crystal clear, rock pools and shallow rivulets that serve to pleasantly cool the burning soles of your feet on hot, sun-baked days. The next (whilst you're maybe marvelling at the way in which the horizon, the curved line that marks the blue-hazed end of the beach and the beginning of the Irish Sea, seems remarkably like the very edge of the world, and that if you chose to sail out there, your craft would simply fall over the rim into a void of cobalt nothingness) the sea water comes rushing in faster than you can ever hope to sprint, be it for a charity fun day or your continued survival. And those virtual puddles and refreshing little creeks have suddenly transformed themselves into a series of viciously swirling lakes. They rapidly surround you, cutting you off from both the island and the Promenade, in snake-like tendrils, and you're left with a stark and simple choice, that's really no sort of choice at all. You either attempt to brave those dangerously swift currents and risk swimming back to shore, or else jump up and down, frantically waving your arms in the air like you're performing a particularly powerful drug-fuelled series of star-jumps, whilst yelling for help at the top of your lungs, and hoping the coastguard can be bothered rescuing "the biggest bunch of balloon-heads since those two young girls reckoned they were attacked by a giant crab on Hilbre Island, back in the 1950s!"

Ah, the Legend of the Giant Crabs!

Here, at last, we arrive, at the kernel of our story, somewhat bedraggled, and shame-faced, it's true, but better late than never, and all that.

SIX

The legend, or rather a thick, stodgy slice of over-baked urban folklore, was usually spouted by groups of grizzled old men sat in the shadow-filled corners of *The Dee Inn* or *The Black Horse,* or else excitedly narrated by groups of giggling, half-drunken teenagers taking turns to scare each other senseless by indulging in the age-old tradition of swapping a series of "true-life" horror stories whilst gathered round the roaring fire of a midnight beach barbecue, as the sun sank slowly behind the rows of tiny silhouetted islands, that blood-red orb gradually immersing itself in a fiery, crimson sea.

The version I heard (courtesy of a friend of a friend, of course), goes something like this:

Back in the winter of 1954, on a grey, overcast afternoon, a couple of teenagers named Susan Rogers (13), and her cousin, Tina Jones (18), decided to make the trip out to Hilbre Island on foot. As I stated earlier, it's a fair hike, and although I've never thought to record the actual length of time it takes to make the journey on a stopwatch (well really, why the hell would I?) I reckon it takes the best part of an hour or so to stroll across the sands and reach the island.

It's a hugely rewarding experience, even in the depths of winter. During the months that stretch from November to late February, wispy smoke from the chimneys of idyllic cottages dotted along the banks of the Dee estuary curls lazily towards the bruised, snow-pregnant skies like delicate threads of white lace, and banks of river fog often descends, drifting by like the ghosts of last summer's flowers.

The beauty however was lost on Tina and Susan as they stepped safely on to the rock-strewn shoreline. A raw wind whipped their faces and blew through the thin, wiry grass, causing it to emit a curiously susurrating sound that for some reason brought to mind the soft desperate whispering of the lovelorn and damned.

Maybe too, it was the eeriness of the place; the peculiar sense of misery that seemed to hang in the air, or the fact that Hilbre seemed unusually deserted, devoid of life, but Susan and Tina soon found themselves arguing with each other, the kind of pig-headed dispute that is seemingly the sole preserve of teenage girls, and which inevitably results in one or the other storming off in a po-faced strop. On this occasion it was Susan who marched off on her own, shouting "see yer later, yer blert, I'm off and don't bother comin' tryin to find me!" (whilst of course, casting sly, surreptitious glances over her shoulder, just to check whether Tina was in fact bothering to follow). She raced across the stony beach, looking for a place to hide in a bid to guilt trip Tina into raising her hands to the sky and shake her head in consternation at the choice before her; either begin the long walk back to the mainland on her own, or swallow her pride and go searching for her companion to tell her she was sorry.

After a few minutes had passed, Tina, being the eldest, and one would assume, the more mature of the two girls, and perhaps also because she was worried about the vagaries of that swiftly, insidious tide, chose the latter option, and began shouting, calmly at first, but with an increasing sense of urgency, for her cousin to come out of hiding. "We need to start making our way home."

Susan, though, had too much of a king-size cob on to pay any attention to Tina, and in the stubborn manner of schoolgirls the whole world over, decided to sit and sulk with a self-satisfied smile on her face, deep within the depths of what is known locally as Lady's Cave, where, according to local folklore, the drowned body of a young woman had washed up after she'd decided to throw herself into the sea from the decks of a ship rather than succumb to the horrors of an arranged marriage, many years before.

The fact that it had suddenly started raining heavily, a thoroughly dispiriting downpour that soaked the semi-frosted sand and dripped from the cavern entrance like rapidly melting stalactites, more than likely contributed to her desire to stay put, too. So she sat in a quiet, dark corner, listening to the oddly comforting sound of raindrops pattering on the roof of the cave, feeling curiously safe and snug, peering out at the late afternoon gloom, oddly hypnotised by the way the impossibly distant-seeming lights of the Promenade were softened by the misted, drizzled haze. She drifted into a kind of trance, and fantasised about Tina growing increasingly desperate as she searched frantically for her younger cousin. "That'll teach her not to talk down to me," she sniggered. "I bet she's sorry she crossed me, now!"

After a while though, when Tina didn't appear at the cave mouth and she could no longer hear her calling out her name, Susan began to grow uncomfortable as she considered the disconcerting possibility that Tina had given up looking for her, and had left her there alone on the island. She tried to reassure herself that her cousin would never abandon her, but she made her way to the cave's entrance just the same, and gazed longingly at the all-but obscured shoreline, cursing herself for a fool and for being so childishly stubborn.

The young girl had just about decided she had best start walking, never mind the teeming rain, when she heard a weird scuttling sound coming from somewhere just behind her. Puzzled rather than frightened, she whirled around to locate the source of the noise, and as she did so, she felt something touch her bare ankle. Susan looked down and saw what, according to contemporary accounts, her confused mind at first perceived as *"a dark brown length of cane covered with bristles, quivering between the toes of her sandaled feet"*.

This strange, almost surreal sight was accompanied by a musty, rich, rotten smell, like a shoal of dead fish, dark, foetid and rank.

Suddenly, Susan's stomach felt squeezed by a powerful hand, and for a moment, panic blurred her vision as she spun completely around to be confronted with the horrific sight of an impossibly huge crustacean, *"four feet high and six feet wide. It was standing on four or maybe even six jointed legs, whilst its body was a sickly-grey colour and clad in a series of segmented shells.'*

As undeniably terrifying as that nightmarish visage was though, Susan found it was the huge pair of saucer-like eyes that frightened her most. They were glowing bright red (a commonly reported feature of all kinds of "zoo-form" phenomena, as even the most cursory of glances through the annals of cryptozoology will confirm) and confronted with such a blatant, nigh on Demonic absurdity, Susan almost fainted away with sheer terror. The "bristled cane" tentatively prodded at her skirt, and it was then that she realised it was actually one of the crab's two antennae, attached to the head of the creature, jabbing with arthropod insistence, intent upon announcing its awful presence in what passes for everyday reality, on a small island off the coast of West Kirby.

The creature's mouth then "opened and closed with a dreadful rattling sound", and its spindly legs clicked like dry old bones rattling in a velvet pouch as it lunged forward.

Susan, giving way to blind panic, leaped from the cave mouth only to land on the jagged rocks below, suffering a badly sprained ankle as she did so. Though white-hot agony tore through every fibre of her being, still she was unable to summon up a scream for help or as a form of primal release from the grip of an all-consuming fear, and instead she almost blacked out on a couple of occasions as she desperately scrambled across the stony beach.

Despite the fact that her movements were severely restricted by her injured ankle, still Susan knew she had to keep moving because she could clearly hear that awful rattling noise in the near distance, and felt sure that it was only a matter of time before that crab-like monstrosity came scuttling after her.

She was unable later to say how long she spent crawling across the rocks and pebbles towards the beach on all fours, but at some point, just as the last of the light went leaking from the day, she saw to her blessed relief Tina, running towards her, her face a mask of concern and not a little guilt at having allowed things to get this far.

Tina later described her cousin as appearing "disconcertingly adult", but also vulnerable and child-like, almost as though she had just awoken from a bad dream. And when she finally told me what had apparently happened, whilst she was hiding in Lady's Cave, perhaps that wasn't so very far from the truth.

Tina dismissed Susan's story about the thing she claimed to have encountered in the cave, but she was honest enough to admit she wasn't too keen to go and check it out for herself, *"you know, just in case".*

After a long and arduous struggle, the two girls eventually managed to cross the wide expanse of sand and reach the safety of the Promenade, as a raw wind whipped across the shore and buffeted around the brightly-lit windows of the beach-front houses and hotels.

And Tina says she glanced back only briefly towards the island, nothing but a dusky outline against a starry sky now that full dark had descended.

But just for the briefest of moments, so fleeting it could easily have been her imagination or some form of optical illusion, she could have sworn she saw two twin pin-pricks of light near to the cave's entrance. The burning tips of a pair of lit cigarettes. A couple of out-of-season Roman candle fireworks. The winking tail-lights of a parking vehicle.

Or some quivering, chitinous horror, a creature with bright red, glowing eyes, washed up from the black depths of the ocean.

SEVEN

Whatever your opinion of this, admittedly far-fetched urban legend, there have, allegedly, been sightings of the same, or a similar "crab monster", on or near Hilbre Island.

These frustratingly sketchy reports originate from sometime in the 1960s, and despite extensive enquiries via the pages of the local press, radio and the internet, I have been unable to glean even the tiniest sliver of further information or additional detail in respect of these accounts, so all we can do for the moment is record that they were *meant* to have taken place, and hope someone out there reading this will be able to supply me with the specifics in due course.

In the meantime, there is a *slightly* more detailed account on record from a little further up the coast, at another of those former ports and sea-side resorts, the 18th century village of Parkgate.

It seems hard to believe nowadays, but the 100sq kilometres of salt marshland that are a veritable haven for wildlife, were once a stretch of pure, golden sands and crystal clear waters that were thought at the time to have potent curative powers, increasing Parkgate's popularity to the point where visitors flocked to the resort from far and wide.

Unfortunately, the Dee estuary silted up, the beaches deteriorated rapidly, becoming over-run by a hardy species of marsh grass and the resort's fortunes suffered accordingly. However, it still attracts large crowds of day-trippers during the summer holidays and at weekends due to the charming row of olde-worlde pubs, restaurants, and a couple of shops selling the most fantastic array of different flavoured, home-made ice creams imaginable, that stretch along the sea-walled banks of the Promenade.

Apparently, sometime in the late 1940s, "*a huge crab-like creature*" was washed up on the quayside, following one of the terrifyingly fierce winter storms that can sometimes whip in from the Irish Sea, often resulting in structural damage to the exposed buildings on the river front, and causing waves to crash over the sea defences, resulting in disastrous floods that sends thousands of rats streaming from the suddenly submerged marshes.

The unnamed witnesses of this giant crustacean were made up of a group of men delivering beer to *The Boathouse,* an idyllic, mock Tudor pub situated at the far end of the Promenade, at the start of the Wirral Way coastal footpath, and with a breath-taking view of the wild marshes, the mouth of the Dee estuary, and the tempest-bearing waters beyond. Braving the ferocity of the elements (these fine upstanding gentlemen were clearly firm adherents of the edict that states that '*Nothing – Not Hell Or High Water – Can Prevent the Provision Of Ale To a Pub's Eternally Thirsty Customers*') the delivery men said they first spotted the strange creature as they were struggling to roll the heavy barrels from the back of their wagon, as sheets of icy-rain lashed their faces, and a shrieking gale sent debris whizzing into the air like ugly confetti.

They described how the giant crab, some seven feet in length, was kicking frantically on its back in the middle of the road, unable to right itself, like a beetle that's been over-turned for the cruel amusement of giggling school-children, until eventually, a particularly huge wave crashed over the Promenade and righted it. The creature then quickly crawled back into the sea and was soon lost to sight.

I am forced to readily concede that this legend may appear to have been built on the very lightest of foundations, and very probably stands up to the slightest degree of scrutiny about as well as a hastily-written message inscribed by a leaky ink pen on a soggy paper towel in the midst of a full-blown hurricane.

But that the story has since passed into the annals of urban folklore is undeniable, and in common with all the tales recounted in this book, I leave it to the reader to make their own minds up regarding its authenticity.

CHAPTER NINE
ON THE DAY THE 'BLACK SUN' CAME

Incidentally, sightings of things that look like they have no business existing in this quaint, picturesque corner of the Wirral Peninsular, are not solely confined to cryptozoological phenomena.

One Sunday afternoon, during the autumn of 2004, I'd travelled with an ex-girlfriend, named Gill Gabriel, over to *The Boathouse,* for a meal and a couple of drinks, (the pub's excellent selection of real ales had always acted as a clarion call to yours truly, whenever we'd decided to spend some quality time together, prior to the dreaded Monday return to the nine to five treadmill).

At some point, not long after our arrival, whilst we were sat at a candle-lit table near to the window, Gill and I got talking to the pub's licensee, a large, rotund, inherently cheerful individual; the archetypal "jolly landlord".

Rather disappointingly, given the Dickensian-style literary build up, the pub manager had introduced himself as being plain arl, Dave, and after a smattering of small talk, I happened to mention the fact that I edited a local magazine dealing with all types of Fortean phenomena. Instead of quickly walking away whistling the theme tune to *The X Files,* or *The Twilight Zone,* Dave promptly pulled up a chair, and with a quick glance over his shoulder to check his wife wasn't watching ("she'll have me guts for garters, if she catches me skivving!") leaned forwards conspiratorially and told us about something that had apparently occurred the previous weekend.

'You should have been here this time last Sunday, mate,' Dave began. 'We were fairly busy, but I wasn't exactly rushed off me feet or anything ("a bit like now, then," I was tempted to say, but Gill, who was doubtless thinking the same thing, kicked my ankle, under the table, and none too gently, I might add).

'Anyway,' Dave continued. 'I was stood at this very table, pouring a party of six a large glass of our finest house red.

'You really should try it by the way, if you get a chance, before you go. It's a crackin' vintage, and although I'm no connoisseur, it knocks spots off anything offered up by any of the other pubs and restaurants around here and…er, I'm sorry, where was I?'

'Pouring someone a glass of expensive el plonko,' I replied, a wry smile playing across my face.

'Oh, aye,' Dave grinned. 'Anyway, like I was saying, I'd just finished topping up the glasses, when I caught sight of something out of the corner of my eye. I turned to look properly and through the windows overlooking the marsh I saw there was this strange, dark black circular object hanging fairly low in the sky, just above that large pool of water over there.'

He pointed through the large, plate glass window out towards the centre of the marsh where a silver expanse of water, almost completely surrounded by swaying reeds, rippled in the afternoon breeze.

'It was freezing cold, but there wasn't a single cloud in the sky, and I remember thinking at first that the object looked a bit like the sun does during a total eclipse. It was also completely silent, and it crossed me mind that it might well be some sort of inflatable object, like a helium balloon, for example. The thing was, though, it was completely motionless, even though there was a fairly strong north-easterly breeze blowing. You could see the marsh grasses swaying, and this object, whatever it was, didn't move an inch. It didn't reflect any trace of light, either. In fact, it seemed to *absorb* it somehow, and it gave me a strange sensation just looking at it. Have yous ever heard of David Lynch? That mad arse movie director? Well, the sight of this thing freaked me out a lot like the first time I saw *Eraserhead,* that surreal nightmare of a film of his.'

Dave had paused for a moment and I'd noticed his eyes had taken on a glazed and far-away look as though the memory of what he claimed to have seen still had the power to mesmerise.

'Er, did anyone else in the pub see this object?' I asked, keen to shake the landlord from his trance and break the dragging, uncomfortable silence that had descended.

'I'm sorry,' Dave had said, shaking his head bemusedly. 'I kind of drifted away a bit, there.' He'd then summoned up a rueful smile and answered my question. 'Yeah, of course the other people at the table spotted the thing at the same time I did, and once they started shouting with excitement, virtually everyone in the pub, including the bar staff legged it over to gather at the windows. As you'd expect, there were loads of theories flyin' round amongst the crowd as to what the object could possibly be. Some feller, who reckoned he used to work for the weather bureau, reckoned it was some type of meteorological device, and yer know what, he was probably right.

'But it *was* very eerie, just the same.

'It remained hanging there for at least five minutes. And then, amazingly, it began slowly descending towards the centre of the marsh and we could see then that it was definitely a solid sphere, about six feet in circumference. It disappeared into the rushes at the edge of the pool, and several people began to head for the exits to try and see if they could get a closer look.

'Before anyone actually stepped outside though, a Royal Navy helicopter suddenly appeared, heading towards us from a westerly direction. The chopper flew straight over to the spot where we'd seen the weird black object land and it hovered there at a height of about fifty feet or so for a couple of minutes, and then one of our bar staff, who'd been to grab a pair of binoculars, passed them on to me for a second. Through the lens, I could clearly see the helmeted co-pilot peering from the cockpit, very obviously searching for something below him. After a while, they appeared to give up, and the helicopter sped off towards the Point of Ayr.

'Afterwards, many people assumed it must have been some sort of unsuccessful military manoeuvre, or search and rescue training mission, and that certainly makes a great deal of sense to me. 'But just the same, there was something, I dunno, *unnatural* about the whole thing. Something that didn't quite sit right, and honest to God, that pair of somethings have haunted me ever since.

'Several of the locals decided to go out onto the marsh, to see what they could see, but like the helicopter guys, they couldn't find a single trace of the object either. They told me later that there hadn't been any unusual marks or indentations anywhere in the soft mud nor any sign of broken reeds or crushed grass. It was as though the black sphere, whatever the hell it had been, had simply winked out of existence.

'Of course, people who weren't there have since speculated that perhaps the thing had simply disappeared into the water, but along with most, if not all of the other people gathered here that day, I would be willing to swear on a stack of bibles, that it had definitely landed on the banks, a good twenty feet or so away from the edge of the pool. But then again, I suppose it's possible we could have been mistaken about the landing site. I mean, we *must* have been.

'There's no doubt that it was a solid, tremendously weighty-looking object. I'm certain it would have left clear, discernible traces of evidence of where it had come down, no matter how gently it landed.'

'Did anyone manage to take any photos or videos?' I asked hopefully. 'On their mobiles, or whatever?'

'Yeah, most probably, but I'm afraid *I* didn't,' Dave replied, looking sheepish. 'I can't believe it never even crossed my mind to use my video phone to film the thing floating motionlessly in that perfect winter sky, despite the fact that I had me phone in me hands at the time. And before you ask, no, I don't know of anyone who actually has any photos or obtained any footage, though I have asked around. The whole thing was really, really strange, I'm tellin' yer!'

'So, there's no evidence that the incident took place, aside from anecdotal testimony?' Gill asked in her most annoyingly patronising voice. 'Bit of a bummer, that!'

My ex-girlfriend's tone irritated the hell out of *me,* but to his credit, Dave never gave any sign that he'd taken offence.

'Well, I suppose that's a fair and honest assessment, hun,' he replied. 'To be honest, I would have had a great deal of trouble believing any of this story if I hadn't experienced the events for meself. And now of course, we've only just met, so I don't expect you to take me at my word.

'But I'll quickly tell you something else that's bothered me since the incident, if I may?'

'Yeah, go 'ead,' I said, 'I'm interested, even if my ever-charming other half isn't.'

Again, Dave had the good grace to pretend not to notice the abruptness of my remark.

'Well, it's probably not that important. A quirky coincidence and nothing more. But, it was only later that afternoon that the people who had witnessed the incident, began to remark upon the fact that during the time that silent object was suspended in mid-air, and for that matter, a good few hours after it had "landed", there were very few, if any, birds about.

'Not even the usually, ever-present, squadrons of scavenging seagulls.'

Dave shook his head at the week-old memory. 'The marsh is, as I'm sure you know, normally a wildlife lover's paradise, teeming with God knows how many different species of sea and marsh-birds, but during "The Sighting", and that's what everyone round here is calling it, by the way, and for a good while afterwards, the entire area was strangely silent and deserted-looking. Having lived here in Parkgate for the past five years or so, I can assure you that would have been more than just a little bit strange on a perfectly ordinary, non-UFO day. But on the day the "Black Sun" came, it just added to the sense of unreality. Like I say, it creeped me out, lad, and I don't mind admitting it.'

'I'm not surprised,' I said, and I meant it. 'Has anything else happened since then,' I added, 'And did the local press publish anything about the incident?'

'No,' Dave replied, and cocked his head to consider this. 'I suppose that's a little odd, too. What with there being at least three dozen or so witnesses, plus any number of passers-by out on the Promenade, you'd have thought that at least *one* of them would have written in to *The Wirral Globe*, *The Wirral News*, or *The Liverpool Echo*, but either no one did so, or else the papers, for some reason, didn't think it was worth reporting.'

'Yeah, who needs stories about crappy old UFOs, when you've got the latest Stevie Gerrard transfer rumour to spread,' Gill, the "light of my life",' drawled sarcastically. 'Or an exclusive on Parkgate's latest super-duper, wine sensation!'

'Right,' Dave had said, his face visibly reddening, as he made a show of inclining his head towards the bar where he doubtless imagined his wife would soon be standing, glaring balefully across at him. 'Sorry, I'd best be getting back to work. Nice to have met you both. See you again, soon, I hope.'

'You can count on it,' I said, and reached out to shake his hand. He wiped his palm on his apron, gripped my hand firmly, shook it once, twice, a third time, and then with a brief nod towards Gill, took his leave.

There was a long, drawn out moment of terse silence in the wake of his departure. Then, when we couldn't avoid catching each other's eye any longer, and as if awaiting the firing of a starting pistol, we were off and charging headlong into "The Blasted Land of Apocalyptic Disagreements", a truly wretched terrain, chock full of bitter resentments, festering malcontent and towering heap of frequently gnawed, "Bones Of Contention".

Oh, and guess what?

We never *did* get to try the house wine.

Above: The Boathouse. *A wonderfully traditional alehouse, situated on the edge of the Dee marshes in Parkgate. The reputed site of a particularly strange UFO experience during in the autumn of 2004.*

Photo Credit: Stevie Gee

CHAPTER TEN
WHEN AUTUMN'S CRYSTAL EYE TURNED COLD

'It looks like somebody here is dreaming,
Funny things hanging in the air
Some have names, some have numbers, some are empty,
And it's hard not to stare...'
***More* - The Comsat Angels**

I had cause to recall Dave's curious story of strange aerial phenomena a couple of years later, when I myself witnessed something unusual hanging in the bright blue skies, not a million miles from Parkgate, but on the opposite side of the Wirral Peninsula.

In mid-November 2010, at a little before 11 o'clock in the morning, I was with another of my ex-girlfriend's, Angie (I know, I know, I sound like the Omar Sharif of Liverpool, but in my defence, I was undergoing an especially turbulent period of my life, and stability in terms of relationships was about as alien a concept as, well, the possibility that extraterrestrial/multi-dimensional craft are occasionally appearing in our skies) along with her ten-year-old daughter, Eleanor, and my close friend, Stevie Gee (he of the "new", 1975 "Spring-Heeled Jack" encounter, described elsewhere in this book) along with a couple of neighbours, outside my parent's home on Bolton Road East, New Ferry.

We'd just returned from Cammell Laird's Social Club, where Steve and I had been DJ-ing at my niece's engagement party the night before. It was a sun-blessed, pleasantly warm day, and the visibility was excellent.

As we were standing alongside Steve's car, having unloaded the last of the disco gear, we decided, on an admittedly childish impulse, to release a couple of helium-filled party balloons we'd brought back from the club, just for the sheer "what-the-hell?" fun of it, and this turned out to prompt one of those weird coincidences that sometimes presage instances of apparently anomalous phenomena.

A few minutes after watching the balloons rise high into the virtually cloudless skies to drift off at a leisurely pace towards the River Mersey, Steve suddenly drew my attention to what appeared to be a triangular formation of eight, white spherical objects, hanging motionless at a great height above the rows of houses on the corner of Eccleshall Road, directly opposite where we were stood.

The obvious assumption was that the objects must have been more balloons, released by guests at somebody else's overnight party after we'd let our own two inflatables go. It was a little strange (coincidental?) that they'd chosen that precise moment to do so, but it was perfect balloon-flying weather after all. There was only a light, scarcely-there breeze that carried with it the evocative autumn smells of wood smoke and decaying leaves, and something about those flawless skies just kind of *compelled* you somehow to want to launch something high into its deep blue midst; a kite, maybe, or a Frisbee, a model airplane ... a *balloon.*

Just the same, I couldn't shake the feeling that there was something vaguely dream-like about the sight of those eight stationary globes, hovering in a perfect V-pattern, almost as though some surrealist painter, René Magritte, say, had added them due to an inspirational impulse to an otherwise ordinary landscape, entitled something like:

One November Morning....There's Worse Things Waiting

Then things had got even stranger when the objects suddenly began moving slowly across the sky to a point directly above our heads. They changed formation on several occasions, and it crossed my mind that they might be pale laser projections beamed from The Liverpool Echo Arena, which was literally just over the water from my parents' house. I'd frequently seen these laser projections in the past on both sides of the river, although previously it had always been long after dark, and certainly not relatively early on a Sunday morning. This time, however, there was no trace of any tell-tale ray of light emanating from the ground, and besides, you could just tell by the simple act of looking that these objects, whatever they were, were definitely real, animate objects, not the result of any types of laser beams.

For a wonder, in this day and age, no-one in our group had a camera phone or video recorder to hand, or at least, no-one had the wherewithal to pluck one out of their pockets or the depths of their handbags, and actually film the damned things.

Eventually, the objects, now gathered in a circular formation, slowly drifted into a fleecy white cloud bank that had suddenly bubbled up from out of nowhere, over to the east, and were thereafter quickly lost to sight.

Angie and her daughter remained totally convinced throughout the "sighting", and indeed long afterwards, that the UFOs were nothing of the sort, seeing as how, in their eyes at least, they were perfectly identifiable as ordinary balloons, and that if we'd only been able to lay our hands on a pair of binoculars, or a telescope, we would have been able to discern clearly decipherable writing on the sides of the objects. Not some exotic extraterrestrial inscription, most likely, but something as disappointingly mundane as **"Happy 21st Birthday, John!"** or **"Congratulations To Mike and Christina On Their Engagement!"** or whatever.

And the reason the objects remained in close formation on that virtually windless morning?

With a visual aid we'd easily be able to make out the white string that neatly tied the bunch together! You know what?

So yeah, the two girls were very probably, not to say wholly irritatingly, correct (their giggling incomprehension at the amazed reactions of the males present during the "encounter" had me grinding my teeth in annoyance). The helium balloon explanation, after all, makes total sense, whichever way you happen to slice it.

But, and please don't take this as being another glaring example of the arl Fox Mulder "*I Want To Believe!*" syndrome, I would still contend that there was something indefinably unsettling about those floating, silent, shiny, silver globes.

A sense of *wrongness*.

A certainty that they simply didn't *belong* there in that otherwise sane and normal autumn sky.

It haunted me then, and it continues to haunt me now.

I know it similarly affected Steve, too.

A few days later, he sent me a text message that sent a cold chill running up and down my spine. In response, I texted back in what I hoped would be perceived as an off-handed, casual reference about what we'd seen on that silent Sunday morning. Steve had immediately replied (and in my mind's eye, I had a vivid image of him at his place of work, a printing firm in Runcorn, perhaps taking a ten minute coffee break, out in the yard, shaking his head before casting a furtive glance towards the heavens).

As though he more than half-expected to see something hovering up there, all silent stealth and inscrutable alien intelligence.

Floating....

Waiting...

"Yer know what, lid! That was defo weird that!" his simple message read.

"And do **you** *know what, lid,"* I felt like replying, *"though it flies in the face of accepted logic, I find I couldn't agree more!"*

*****

Nine months later, and yet another of those curious coincidences came capering down the local news wires like a mischievous hobgoblin.

Probably clutching a balloon.

A silvery-white party one, with indecipherable lettering etched in black.

In early August 2011, the New Brighton lifeboat crew were scrambled by the Liverpool coastguard to investigate a report of a mysterious silver object falling from the sky into the Irish Sea.

The Atlantic 85 class inshore lifeboat *Dibdin* was sent to the scene, and Cliff Downing, lifeboat operations manager, told *The Wirral News* (probably with a great big condescending grin on his face): "Our volunteer crew were very excited at the possibility of being the first RNLI unit to make contact with extraterrestrial life, and accordingly launched the boat in record time.

"When they reached the scene, the object seemed to have several components to it so that it resembled a huge silver jellyfish.

"Sadly, closer examination *revealed a series of balloons tied together, presumably from a wedding or a birthday celebration.*" (and yep, the italics are most assuredly mine).

"We recovered the item as it would have been a hazard to shipping had it wrapped itself around a ship's propeller."

I read this mini-article in the living room one warm sun-kissed summer evening, with the smells of barbecues and the perfumed fragrance of freshly-mown lawns wafting through the half-open windows.

And the sound of children's laughter floating, dream-like on the sweetly scented air.

Taunting.

Mocking.

CHAPTER ELEVEN
SUNDAY MORNING, COMING DOWN
Hangovers, Irate Girlfriends And Chemtrail Conspiracy Theorists

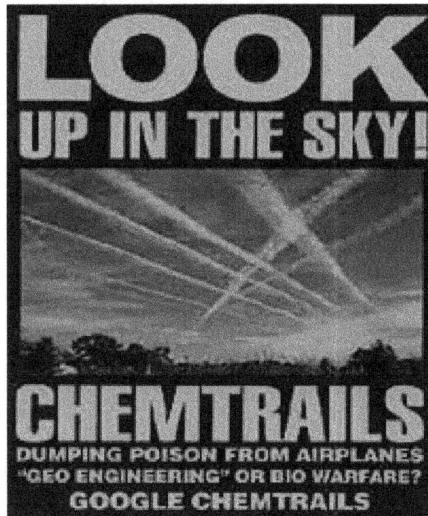

A t a little after 7:30, one gorgeous, sun-bright Sunday morning in late July 2013, I was awoken from the depths of a king-size hangover, roughly the size of Loch Ness, by the shrill, insistent ringing of my mobile phone. In the midst of the previous evening's alcoholic fug, I'd forgotten to switch the "highly amusing", shrill-as-a-screeching-harpy ringtone, to the slightly-less weekend-lie-in-bothering silent mode, much to the "delight" of my fiancée, Yvey, though I'd like to think her swift, unerringly accurate kick to my naked buttocks as I sat up to see who was calling at this ungodly hour was doubtless an involuntary, reflexive reaction, having been shaken from her own, Bailey's induced, slumber.

As I gingerly rubbed my arse cheeks, and wondered whether I'd be requiring a pain-numbing cushion or two to be able to sit comfortably in our little oasis of green at the far end of Falkner Square, for our planned picnic later that day, I stared, bleary-eyed at the display screen, and almost launched the phone across the room, when I saw the caller ID.

It was Brian Smart, a man of indeterminate age who I'd never actually met, and who I only knew from the weird and wonderful realm of social media. I remembered he'd sent me a friend request a few months earlier, during a Facebook debate I'd somehow gotten myself involved in concerning the warped motivations of "The Boston Bombers", and, much to my subsequent regret, I'd accepted the request.

Well, in my defence, many of us do that, right?

We might pause, if we're not too busy, or otherwise engaged, to briefly check out the potential "friend's" personal details, their likes, what type of music they're into, which football team they follow, whether we have any mutual acquaintances, that type of thing. But all too often, so long as they don't come across like potential serial killers, perverted sex maniacs or hate-filled, racist bigots, then more often than not, I click the "accept" button.

In this particular case however, I had cause to regret my complacency because it eventually turned out Brian Smart was a virtual nuisance, in every sense of the term. An over-enthusiastic student of "conspiracy-fying" as Brian termed it, he took to sending me long, incredibly convoluted messages about the New World Order, and the latest breaking news concerning government cover-ups, the "truth about 9/11", the faked Apollo moon landings, and back-engineered alien technology, whether I wanted to read it or not.

At first, I have to admit, I found his daily up-dates mildly entertaining in a good-for-a-giggle kind of way, and I used to share them with Yvey most nights when we were cuddled up on the sofa, with The National or Frank Turner's latest albums playing on the CD, and a glass of rosé or an ice-cold beer close to hand.

I learned that Brian lived just over the water in central Birkenhead, and at some point, probably after I'd sunk one too many ales, he persuaded me that he had "some terrifying true-life ghost stories" he wanted to share with me, "if I cared to exchange phone numbers", and foolishly I agreed.

After a month or so had gone by, and I'd started receiving thirty-odd (with the emphasis on "odd") posts and phone calls a day from Brian, the novelty had decidedly begun to wear off. This was annoying enough during the day, especially when I was working on various writing projects, or spending some leisure time with Yvey, but when we were awoken in the early hours by my phone vibrating under the pillow announcing I had new notifications from my "Lone Gunmen"-esque Facebook friend, I decided enough was enough.

The very next day I'd politely asked him if he could lay off calling or messaging me, unless I specifically requested him to do so. Otherwise, I'd have to consider deleting him from my friend's list. To be fair to him, Brian had readily agreed, and promised that unless he had something of "world-shaking importance" to tell me, the only time he'd make contact would be to add a "like" to one of my own, ahem, "deeply insightful status updates", or to wish me Happy Birthday or Merry Christmas, or whatever.

To be even fairer to him, he'd kept to his word, and I hadn't heard from him until this moment. And whilst it couldn't really have been a more inopportune time than if he'd decided to call me whilst I was lurking in the bushes, having been caught short on the way home from the pub, I answered the phone.

'Lee, sorry to bother yer this early on a Sunday, lad,' Brian began, sounding not remotely sorry at all. 'But you've really gotta see this. Take a look out yer window! And tell me what yer think!'

'For Christ's sake, Brian, this had better be good,' I said. I stumbled from the bed, not daring to open the blinds, less Yvey completely lost her temper, and she resorted to throwing something at me; the heavy glass water jug she always kept on the bedside cabinet was disconcertingly close to hand. And so without another word, I closed the bedroom door softly behind me and stumbled into the living room to make my way to the large bay window.

Still wiping sticky-yellow lumps of sleep out of my eye, I took in the view from our South Liverpool apartment; the familiar rows of grand Georgian houses converted into flats, their high-bricked walled gardens and driveways, bordered with lines of trees in glorious full leaf, the residential car-park, 'Garfield', our next-door neighbour's fat ginger moggy, eyeing up the pigeons feeding on scraps near to the unsightly collection of blue and purple plastic bins, and the mostly cloudless pale blue skies

'And just what is it that I'm supposed to be looking at?' I mumbled down the phone, my voice sounding muffled, my mouth seemingly stuffed with wads of cotton wool.

'Can't yer see them chemtrails, Lee?' Brian yelled excitedly. 'The skies are absolutely full of them! It's not normal! Something's going on! Mark my words!'

A great lover of exclamation marks, was old Mr Smart. His epic Facebook messages always contained at least a dozen of the things, at the end of every supposedly meaningful sentence he deemed to be of vital importance, which was pretty much every single one of them. I could sometimes see them in my mind's eye when he spoke, too, stretching away like a black-painted picket fence glimpsed though some wavering, shimmering, heat-haze.

'Chemtrails, in conspiracy-speak,' he continued, 'are a hugely imaginative combination of the words "chem." (for chemical) and "trail" (for er, trails).

'It's a bit like what H.G. Well's, wrote in *The War Of The Worlds,* don't you think? *"A beautiful, but somehow disturbing sight!"* Okay Mr Well's wasn't referring to Chemtrails back then, of course, but yer get the general idea.'

'Oh aye,' I said, thinking no such thing. The only beautiful and disturbing image in my mind at that moment, was that of my fiancée, and the deadly-looking water jug.

'Listen Brian, this is all very interesting and that,' I said, 'but I'm gonna have to get off now. I promised Yvey brekky in bed. And I was on a bit of a promise, if yer know what I mean?'

I'd seen "chemtrails", as Brian called them, hundreds of times, of course. Probably thousands, in fact, and that's hardly surprising. The skies above Liverpool 8, indeed across the whole of the county, especially this close to the river, are frequently traversed by all manner of aircraft, from the everyday Easyjets and other passenger planes taking off and landing at John Lennon Airport, to RAF military jet fighters streaking down the Mersey with a deafening roar, on routine training flights (I've even seen a low-flying AWAC, on one memorable, and somewhat ominous occasion, a few weeks after 9/11).

And I could clearly see on this largely cloudless Sunday morning, a portion of the sky was indeed criss-crossed with a mesh of white, gossamer-like trails, conjuring up images of a giant-size potato waffle.

'Oh, I bet most people staring out the window this morning will just dismiss it, if they even truly see it at all,' Brian announced portentously. 'They'll be too busy stuffing bacon butties drowned in sauce down their cavernous pie-holes, or watching some inane cookery programme on the arl goggle box, to notice. And even if they do happen to look up, and pause to wonder for a couple of seconds, they'll reassure themselves that the aviation experts with their raft of plausible explanations for chemtrails, are perfectly correct, and there's absolutely nothing to worry about.'

Brian harrumphed, like he was in on the biggest joke in the universe.

'The authorities, of course, reckon the trails are just the lingering traces of exhaust fumes emitted by jet planes flying at extremely high altitudes, where the temperatures are on average -40 Fahrenheit. And yeah, it makes perfect sense. Any jet engine's vapour trails are gonna be instantly transformed into ice crystals. But here's something for yer, Lee, so best pin yer lugholes right the fuck back. Whilst I totally accept that explanation, I've been doing a spot of research of my own these past few years, and I've found out a fact that even the aviation authorities make no attempt to deny.'

'And what's that, Brian?' I said, rolling my eyes. 'The chemtrails are really caused by aliens in environment-unfriendly, vapour-spewing UFOs?'

'Not quite,' replied Brian, wilfully ignorant, or plain past caring about the element of sarcasm in my voice.

'It's worse than that, if you can imagine a worse, and infinitely more worrying scenario.'

'Well, I honestly can't,' I said, trying and failing to stifle a yawn.

'This might keep you awake lad. Surely you've noticed, unless you've been walking around with yer head down, intently studying the laces of yer brand new trainers, there's been a considerable increase in the sheer number of chemtrails, the consistency and thickness of the damn things, and the fact that they seem to be hanging around for far longer periods of time than they used to.

"*I know something that's consistently thick and has been hanging round for far too long, this morning,*" I thought, but didn't say.

'Er, yeah, I suppose so,' I replied, with all the enthusiasm of someone who'd just learned they'd won a two week holiday in Yakutsk, Siberia, the coldest city on earth. 'I can't think why, like, or particularly care, to be honest, but I'm sure you're gonna enlighten me, anyway...'

'Oh, I certainly am!' Brian replied. 'Like I said before, it's vitally important that I get this across and alert the world to the imminent apocalyptic crisis. Before it's too late!'

The slightly stilted quality of his voice dredged up images of him reading from a stack of prepared notes, probably copied verbatim from some highly dubious website, his piggy eyes narrowed in concentration, a deadly serious newsreader expression on his face.

'It's my honest opinion, that I have finally succeeded in discerning the reasons for the multiplicity and longevity of present-day chemtrails!' (I swear he used those exact words). 'I believe there are those in power; a cabal of shadowy individuals, who are conducting a top-secret, black ops-type programme, using crystallised vapour trails as a literal, and highly convenient, smokescreen.'

'A smokescreen for what, exactly?' I asked, before sighing loudly enough to announce to the world the birth of a new martyr.

'Oh, I'm so glad you asked, mate!' Brian said. 'I'm convinced that the perpetrators of this global conspiracy, The Illuminati maybe, are using high-altitude aircraft, commercial or otherwise, to deposit *other,* far more sinister substances in the skies above our major towns and cities.'

'Like what?'

'Well, this might put yer off yer Sunday morning cooked breakfast, like, but that doesn't make it any less feasible. I think there are those who have a nefarious plan to add certain types of harmful chemicals in a bid to control the population.'

'Right..and how are they doing this, if you don't mind me asking?'

'Again, Lee, I'm so glad I've got your attention, and that you haven't hung up and dived back under the covers to be with your good lady. These horrible, cold-hearted bastards, who we foolishly entrust with looking after our well-being, are actually adding invisible strains of God only knows what kind of deadly chemicals and lethal types of diseases, hidden amongst those supposedly harmless "contrails".'

'I see,' I said, not really seeing at all. Save for a vivid, and entirely unwanted mental image of a fat, bearded, middle-aged slob, standing at the grime-encrusted window of some pokey bedsit, dressed in a three-sizes too small *X Files* T-shirt, idly scratching his sweaty balls, whilst his voluminous ale-gut wobbled jelly-like over a pair of multi-stained boxies.

A gorge rose in my throat, and I knew I'd be skipping breakfast. Most probably lunch, too. 'Listen, Brian, this is all very interesting, but I think I just heard Yvey calling me. I'm gonna have to go, sorry.'

'Okay, I get it, but, before yer get off, don't you wanna know *why* it is these power-crazy scum-bags are spraying poison into the skies?'

'Er, no, not really,' I mumbled. 'Like I say, I er...

'Well, let me tell yer!' Brian all-but yelled, 'cos, believe me, this is something you *need* to hear!'

'Brian. Mate. *Lad,* I'm gonna hang up now, and...'

'They want to eradicate the weakest members of society, Lee! The elderly. The sick. The infirm. This stuff has no odour, it has no taste. Its like the advanced variant of the 'flu bug, or maybe pneumonia, but a billion times more lethal.'

'And not only are THEY busy dispersing these deadly diseases into the air, THEY are also engaged in various forms of weather manipulation and utilising it as a unbelievably powerful military weapon! And yep, you guessed it, these new type of "contrails" provide the perfect foil for secretively carrying out their villainous experiments.

'It's like the '80s video for that boss Kate Bush track, *Cloud-busting*. The one with the sinister Men In Black carting off poor old Donald Sutherland, whose invented a Wilhelm Reich-like Orgone. Imagine the devastation *THEY* could cause Droughts and floods. Cyclones and unimaginable, killer heat-waves. There's really no limit to the meteorological horrors they're capable of inflicting upon us.'

Brian paused for a second, either to catch his breath, or more likely, for dramatic effect, before adding, 'In fact, yer know that 3.5 earthquake felt across North Wales and here on Merseyside, the other week. The one the media claimed was entirely natural, and nothing to worry about whatsoever. Well, who do you think was truly responsible for that? Oh, I could go on an on...'

'Or rather yer could, lad, if I could be arsed listening to any more of your paranoid delusions,' I suddenly blurted out, cutting him off mid-rant. 'I'd better get off, before that super-flu or whatever rains down from the skies like a full-on plague, or the Heavens fall, or even worse, the sun goes and disappears behind those criss-crossing, blue sky-bothering, "Bird's Eye Potato Waffle" style contrails! *Goodbye* Brian!' I said, and promptly hung up.

And switched off my phone.

*****

It may sound a trifle hypocritical of me, but a few minutes after taking Brian's call, I have to admit I was just a little bit intrigued by our mostly one-sided conversation. And after tip-toeing across the hallway, and daring to peek my head around the bedroom door to check Yvey had gone back to sleep, I decided to do some intensive research of my own...

Well, okay, I made the gargantuan effort it took for me to drag out the laptop from its place on the shelf, unzip its garish, flowery, plastic casing, plug it in, and type "Chemtrail Conspiracies" in the Google search box. I was slightly surprised when a couple of things pretty much leaped out and struck me straight away. One was the huge amount of photographs and apparently genuine video footage of what the late Charlie Fort, would doubtless have termed "the damned things".

And secondly, it appeared the government/military weather manipulation theory does have at least some degree of credence.

According to an article published in the 30th August 2001, edition of *The Guardian*, a batch of declassified documents made public under The Freedom of Information Act revealed that back in the August of 1952, a team of international scientists had collaborated with the RAF to carry out an experiment they called "Operation Cumulus". The aim of this top secret joint venture was supposedly to create thick layers of cloud cover, that would in turn produce artificial rainfall.

The article, printed in one of Britain's more credible newspapers, stated that, coincidentally or not, on 15th August 1952, *'one of the worst flash floods ever to have occurred in Britain swept through the Devon village of Lynmouth. 35 people died as a torrent of water and thousands of tons of rock poured off saturated Exmoor and into the village destroying homes, bridges, shops and hotels.*

'The disaster was officially termed "the hand of God," *but new evidence suggests another possible explanation.*

Squadron leader Len Otley, who was working on "Operation Cumulus", told a BBC Radio 4 documentary called The Day They Made It Rain *, the RAF jokingly called the rain-making exercise "Operation Witch Doctor".*

'His navigator, Group Captain John Hart, remembers the success of these early experiments:'We flew straight through the top of the cloud, poured dry ice down into it. We flew down to see if any rain came out of the cloud. And it did about 30 minutes later, and we all cheered.'

'The Meteorological Office has in the past denied that there were any rain-making experiments conducted before 1955, but investigators from the BBC, have unearthed documents recently released at the Public Record Office showing that they were on-going from 1949 to 1955. RAF logbooks and personnel corroborate the evidence.

'The scientists were based at Cranfield School of Aeronautics and worked in collaboration with the RAF and the MoD's meteorological research flight, based at Farnborough. The chemicals were provided by ICI in Billingham.

'Met Office reports from these dates describe flights undertaken to collect data on cumulus cloud temperature, water content, icing rate, vertical motions and turbulence, and water droplet and ice crystal formation. There is no mention of cloud seeding.

'But a (then) 50-year old radio broadcast unearthed by Radio 4 describes an aeronautical engineer and glider pilot. Alan Yates, working with "Operation Cumulus" at the time and flying over Bedfordshire, spraying quantities of salt. He was elated when the scientists told him this had led to a heavy downpour 50 miles away over in Staines, Middlesex.

'I was told that the rain had been the heaviest for several years -and all out of a sky which looked summery...there was no disguising the fact that the seedsman had said he'd make it rain, and he did. Toasts were drunk to meteorology and it was not until the BBC news bulletin about Lynmouth, was read later on, that a stony silence fell on the company,' said Mr Yates, at the time.

'Operation Cumulus was put on hold indefinitely after the tragedy.'

Declassified minutes from an air ministry meeting, held in the War Office on November 3rd, 1953, show why the military were interested in creating rain and snow by artificial means. The list of possible uses included '"bogging down enemy movement, incrementing the water flow in rivers and streams to hinder or stop enemy crossings."

'UK weather modification experiments at the time presaged current practice in the US. The idea was to target "super cool clouds", and to increase the volume of freezing water vapour particles

Most methods involved firing particles of salt, dry ice, or silver iodide, into clouds, either from an aeroplane or from burners on the ground. The clouds would then precipitate, pulled down by the extra weight of dense particles, thus making it rain sooner and heavier than it might otherwise have done. Significantly, it was claimed that silver iodide could cause a downpour up to 300 miles away.

Not surprisingly, several of the people whose property or business suffered damage as a result of the devastating floods, as well as the family members of the deceased sought compensation for their tragic losses, but, and here's something that sounds dreadfully familiar, the authorities denied all knowledge of the experiments, and that the whole thing was a terrible act of nature, thereby making it impossible for anyone to make a successful claim.

Actually, did I just write that two things immediately jumped out at me, and caused me to question my previous outright scepticism?

Perhaps we'd better make that *three*.

Even the briefest of trawls along the highways and by-ways of the Internet, revealed that it was all but common knowledge that '*Many countries, these days, use the technology, which has considerably improved during the past 50- odd years.*'

If that assertion really is true, then God alone knows what scientists are capable of in the second decade of the 21st century.

Of course, I tried to reassure myself that in all likelihood, these conspiracy theories might have about as much basis in reality as a Tory, pre-election Party Political Broadcast, but nevertheless....

Sometimes stories, regardless of whether they're true or not, are like fishing lines caught on some immovable underwater object. Once spun out, they can never be reeled back in.

And another thing:

The day had started out bright and mostly blue-skied, and I'd been looking forward to a picnic lunch in The Square. But the gradual increase in both the number and the sheer thickness of the "chemtrails" covering the skies above Liverpool, as early-morning slid into mid-afternoon, had me losing my temper, and shaking my fist at the heavens....

'Thank you so bloody much Cameron and Clegg', I shouted. 'If my overly paranoid 'friend, Brian,' has got it even *half* right, with his Government/military weather manipulation hypotheses, yous two have both been complicit in cutting back our quota of all-too infrequent summer sunshine.

'Yer heartless shitehawks!'

CHAPTER TWELVE
WHEN HOPE SPRINGS FROM
WHERE THE DARKEST SHADOWS FALL

'I laughed, until, it got too dark,
Somewhere else, a voice will bark
Someone else will be involved, Someone stronger still'
Lost Outside The Tunnel - Aztec Camera

ONE

I've known Annie Calland for a good-sized portion of my adult life. Since my long-ago college days, indulging in the myriad joys of the laughingly-entitled 'Horticulture & Gardening Made Easy Course', based in Rock Ferry, to be precise, and we even had a mini-fling, a sort of three-consecutive-drunken-Sunday-night stands, (if that makes any kind of coherent sense), at some half-remembered point of 2009, that chaotic period I've come to regard as "The Crazy Space Between The Ex's."

*So whilst I couldn't honestly claim that Annie was what you'd term a particularly close acquaintance (and never mind the groups of assembled sniggerers and their snide, 'Well, I don't know about you, but **I'd** call being shacked up together beneath the silky-sequined quilts of a double bed to be **pretty** physically close!' - type remarks), I'm fairly certain she's not the sort of girl who'd simply tell outright lies for no good reason.*

And even if it turns out Annie did make the whole thing up, invented the story of what she claimed happened to her best friend, Linda Dawson, one moonlit evening, a few weeks prior to my bumping into Annie for the first time in ages (and no, that's not intended to be a euphemism) I'd still maintain that its recounting here has some degree of merit, not least because hearing it for the first time left me feeling sort of warm and fuzzy inside, like I'd just downed a single malt whilst sat before a roaring log fire, as snow flurries pattered at the windows and a chilled wind howled mournfully in the eaves....

TWO

'You've most probably seen Linda, around town, Lee. She lives in Rock Ferry, like, but she spends most of her time in Liverpool City Centre, or maybe a little further out-of-town, particularly around Hope Street and The Georgian Quarter, the area where she was born. You'd defo notice her if you did set eyes on her. No doubt about that. 'She stands out the proverbial mile. An attractive, late thirty-something, with a stunningly pale-white complexion, even at the height of what passes for a Liverpool summer, and she's got one of those Louise Brooke's, 1920's style, jet black, bob haircuts. She always dresses in these kinda floaty, chiffon gowns, retro Hippy '60s chic, I'd suppose you'd call it. Mamas & The Papas, Peter, Paul & Mary, Bob Dylan, before he went all eleccy on everyone's arses, in Newport, in July 1965, yer know what I mean?

'Anyway, Linda's probably me best mate, and I can assure you right now, she confides *everything* in me. And I do mean, *everything.*

'The day Linda experienced what she once described as being the most romantic moment of her life, lying amongst the sand-hills at Crosby Beach, one glorious bank holiday afternoon, whilst her lover gently caressed her bare shoulder with a thin, wiry piece of marram grass and the only sounds were the crash of the surf, the laughter of children floating on the warm, salty air and the lazy drone of an airplane flying high overhead.

'The bitter aftermath of the subsequent break-up from her fiancé, one bleak mid-winter evening the following year, presaged by an argument, the sort that begins with some relatively trivial nonsense, then escalates rapidly, like a rapacious killer disease, greedily eating its way through all that's good and true and healthy in a relationship, and brings to mind vivid cartoon images of that "Pac Man" character, madly chomping on the dots and dodging the ghosts, in that old computer game we were all addicted to back in the day.

'The time she'd flirted madly with the driving instructor to ensure she passed her test first time. The frequent occasions when she was little more than a child she'd stolen large bars of Galaxy or Bourneville, from "Woolie's", and hid them beneath piles of neatly-folded underwear and training bras, only ever searching them out and tearing open their shiny, crinkly wrappers, whenever she was feeling down or particularly stressed out, and in desperate need of an instant sugar hit.

'I'm telling you all this because I think it's important that you understand, that Linda has never kept anything from me, so far as I know at least, and I certainly don't think she's the sort of woman to deliberately make things up. To invent stories merely as a way of getting attention. "As honest as the day is long" is an old and much-used saying, but I don't think it makes it any less true. Not in Linda's case, anyway.

'So when she rang me, a couple of weeks ago, a little after one in the morning and virtually begged me to meet her at her flat on Rock Ferry's Esplanade, I readily agreed.

'Even when she told me she'd just seen the ghost, or to be more accurate the *shade*, of her

ROCK FERRY ESPLANADE

(Above): The Rock Ferry Espalande: The pedestrian walkway that stretches along a half-mile or so of the Wirral side of the Mersey river-front, forming a boundary between the chilly, predominantly slate-coloured waters and the Victorian splendour of the magnificent mansions that make up Rock Park.

Photo Credit: Grant Walker

recently-dead father, I didn't doubt or hesitate for a single second. I believed her.

'And here I am now, relating Linda's story. You with yer kecks half-way down yer ankles, a drunken gleam in yer eye and saliva drooling from yer gob like a sex-starved blood-hound with two dicks!

'Do me a favour, Mr Lover-man. Can you hang fire for just a few more minutes?

'It might sound mad, but I really need you to hear her story.

'Like you, it won't take long to reach a hopefully satisfying climax, I promise...'

THREE

'Linda was born and raised in Liverpool, but she moved over the water with her dad when she was still in her early teens, and for all the years I've known her, she has lived alone in the top-floor flat of one of those grand, five-storey mansions, over-looking the Mersey. You know the ones. The sort that look as though they haven't changed a jot in the last hundred years or more, and most probably haven't. Well, aside from the odd smashed window, the mostly over-grown gardens and the white-paint sprayed graffiti adorning the walls that line the park, anyway.

'My best friend's apartment even has one of those delightful, ornamental balconies, the kind where you can sit out on warm summer evenings and gaze out across the river and watch the ferries shunt back and forth, and the giant oil tankers and merchant cargo ships set sail from the docks bound for far-off lands. I've always loved them buildings, had in fact dreamed of living in one, though I don't suppose it will ever happen. Not on my wages.

'Anyhow, it was no surprise to me then that's precisely where I found Linda, not long after she rang me, that night. Sat out on the balcony, in one of those metal lawn chairs at a candle-lit table, a three-quarters empty bottle of rosé at her side, and a small white, battery operated electric fan in her lap, fighting a losing battle against the humid, late summer air.

'She'd left the communal front door unlocked, and I'd climbed the five flights of winding stairs, my heels echoing loudly in the hollow silence, though for all the notice Linda took, I may as well have ascended barefoot.

'She didn't even see me at first, standing in the open bay window doors, with the net curtains draped across my shoulders like a lacy shroud. In truth, I don't think she saw much of anything. Her eyes were glazed and swimming with what appeared to be un-shed tears. And you only had to look at her to know she'd undergone some sort of at once traumatic, but ultimately life-affirming experience, one that had left her wearing a distant, dreamy smile, like someone who'd awoken from a dream in which they'd walked arm in arm in the fresh, dew-soaked fields of springtime with a loved one.

'The night beyond the flickering candlelight was blue-black, illuminated only briefly by the scarlet winking lights of the buoys out on the river, and it seemed to me at that moment the only thing missing was the melodic chirrup of summer crickets, and we could have been transported wholesale to the American Deep South, gathered on the veranda of some vast colonial everglades mansion.

'Hi, Linda,' I said, in a hushed, almost reverential voice. 'I came as quick as I could. How are you feeling?'

'I silently cursed myself for the inanity of the question, knowing as I did that she had lost her dearly beloved father, just a couple of months earlier. How the hell did I think she was feeling? Hadn't I seen first hand, the way her arl fella's passing had all but shattered her dangerously brittle heart into tiny, irreparable fragments? I remember hugging her at the funeral, and being frightened of holding her too tightly in case I heard the sound of those broken pieces rolling around inside her pitifully skinny body, like loose ball bearings in a sack.

'Her dad, Tommy, a huge, six foot eight, giant of a man, and built like the proverbial brick khazi, had been a solid rock of support ever since his wife had left him when Linda, an only child, had been just 13 years of age. And Christ, don't I know from shitty, personal experience, that is the *one* time in a young girl's life when a daughter needs her mother most. All of those painful changes, both physical and emotional, coming at you thick and fast, like a Biblical blood-red rain blown by a shrieking gale.

'Tommy had been there for her through it all, though; the floods of bitter tears, the hurt and confusion, the wild, unaccountable mood-swings, the desperate, pitiful cries for her ma in the small hours, or when Linda lay curled, foetal-like on top of the bedspread, a crumpled photograph of some handsome schoolboy clutched in her hands like a rosary, while a series of primal sobs racked her young body. Even on the occasions she'd sworn at him, told him she hated him, blamed him entirely for failing to do everything in his power to keep their family together (even though Linda knew this wasn't remotely true) still he'd held her and cradled her in his powerful, comforting arms, smelling of Castella cigars and Old Spice aftershave, as he whispered over and over that he loved her with all his heart, and that everything was going to be all right in the end.

"I will always be there for you, sweetheart. No matter what. I will never run out and leave you, the way your mother did. I loved her with all my heart, just as you did, but for some reason, one day, she simply stopped loving us both back, and all I can do now is promise you faithfully that whenever you need me, at the times when all hope seems to have seeped away like teardrops into sun-parched earth, I will be there."

'A real poet, was old Tommy, always coming out with these madly eloquent lines, and saying all the right things at the right time. If yer ask me, he could have had a future as the writer of greetings card messages, rather than working as he did as a freelance electrician. He was a boss 'spark', though, by all accounts, and he was always in demand, travelling all over Merseyside and the North West, and certainly, Linda had never wanted for anything growing up. When she left school and got a job as a typist for a Wirral-based firm of solicitors, Tommy had "loaned" her the deposit for her very own flat in Rock Park. She'd decided long ago that when she got her own place she would always remain in close proximity to her dad, who lived alone just down the road in New Ferry.

'There's no doubt Linda has been happy there, and aside from the bitter aftermath of the break-up of her one and only long-term relationship, things were good and there had been no sign of any black clouds looming on the horizon.

'But yer never know what's just around the corner, do yer?

'On a rain-soaked, misted evening last June, Tommy had been driving back along the M62, after having completed a wiring job at a hotel in Manchester, when a lorry suddenly jack-knifed directly in front of his car, causing a multiple pile-up.

'Tommy had been killed instantly.

'People say that's kind of a blessing, but I'm not so sure that's the case. I mean, it sounds good, as platitudes go, but certainly Linda didn't consider it to be any kind of consolation for her sudden and tragic loss. A couple of weeks after the funeral, she'd told me she'd had real trouble eating or sleeping and in a bid to ward off the recurrent bouts of insomnia, she'd fallen into the habit of going for late night, solitary walks along the length of the Esplanade.

'And that's precisely what she'd done earlier that evening. Took a walk alone, I mean. How desperately sad those words sound, especially when weighed against the lyrics of that world famous, Liverpool anthem.

'But anyway, this is what Linda told me had happened:'

FOUR

"I set off at a little after ten this evening, an hour or so after full dark had fallen," Linda began. "I've lived in the Park since I was 13 years old, two years after mum left, and my Dad had decided to sell the large apartment in Liverpool 8, and move over to the Wirral. So, I felt perfectly safe amongst the reassuringly familiar, even long after sun-down.

"Besides, for the first time in what seemed like ages, I felt strangely elated, as though a part of me, the tiniest portion perhaps, but noticeable for all that, had hinted I was finally beginning to come to terms with my father's passing, as heart-breaking as it undeniably was. Maybe it was due to the fact that the night skies tonight above us are almost impossibly star-sparklingly clear, and it's so warm; the August air so pungently sweet-smelling. Or maybe it was due entirely to the curative powers of alcohol. Whatever. I suppose it doesn't really matter much why I suddenly felt this sense of renewed optimism. I was just heartily glad of it and suddenly eager to get out of the house and take my usual evening stroll, but with an extra spring in my step this time around.

"I turned left at the end of the tree-lined driveway taking my familiar route through the Rock Park estate and out onto the Esplanade itself. The quiet, humid air was heady with those late-summer aromas of freshly cut grass, hyacinths, dahlias and late blooming roses.

"There were very few people about at that hour. One or two dog-walkers who smiled politely as they passed me by and a middle-aged couple taking a stroll, arm in arm, and blissfully unaware of everything and everyone save themselves.

"It was no surprise to me the roads were quiet, though. Since *The Admiral* pub closed down a year or so ago, the entire area's gone into seemingly terminal decline. The only visitors attracted to the place these days are bird-watchers, amateur photographers or those with an interest in local history, and even they were gradually decreasing in numbers with each passing month.

"I walked a little faster as I passed the subway that ran beneath the modern New Ferry by-pass, though. The sight of the garish yellow light pouring from the entrance never failed to unnerve me. I can't stand that concrete tunnel, and not just because it appeared to be hideously out of place amongst such grand Victorian splendour. I had on occasion seen gangs of probably harmless enough teenagers gathered there, and rumours abounded that a couple of local women had been accosted during the last few months, although as far as I'm aware if they had, no one had ever come forwards to make a complaint to the police.

"There was another reason to dislike the underpass, too.

"The former home of the novelist and former US consul to Liverpool, Nathaniel Hawthorne, one of my all-time favourite writers, had once stood on this very site. Not any more, though. The residence had been razed to the ground to make way for the access road and that eyesore of a subway running beneath the A41 by-pass, back in the early 1970s, and I shook my head, as I always did when I reached this point, at the thoughtlessness of the county council and the ignorance of the town planners.

"Thankfully, it wasn't too far from there to The Park entrance gates, and as I made my way down the small hill that led on to the front of The Esplanade, my spirits soared once more at the spectacular sight of the Liverpool waterfront, its brightly-lit magnificence reflected on the still, mirror-like Mersey. Though of course, I saw this view every time I glanced out of the windows of my flat or sat out on the veranda, still it never failed to move me, and make my heart swell with pride and a real sense of belonging. I've always found it therapeutic to walk along this stretch of the river, especially on warm, windless, late-summer evenings like this one. It was so incredibly peaceful. The promenade was deserted and the only sounds were the crunch of gravel beneath my feet and the gentle lapping of the river at the edge of the stony shore. The tide had been in earlier that day, leaving the litter-strewn stretch of sand and the accompanying mud-flats filled with little rock pools. It looked perfectly safe to walk across and explore, but I knew from experience it could be treacherous.

"I felt perfectly safe walking amongst the reassuringly familiar, and for the first time in what seemed like forever, my memories of my dad didn't piercingly sting my heart. And if I were shedding tears, they were neither bitter nor borne of intolerable grief.

"I remembered the stories my dad used to love to regale me with when I walked here with him when we first moved to The Wirral, I was still little more than a child. Tales based on the genuinely rich history of the area. Of pirates and smugglers and the ghosts of lovelorn women, endlessly weeping for some "dastardly cad with a heart of stone". And when at last I found myself three-quarters of the way along The Esplanade, I recalled him telling me about the sad remnants of the Rock Ferry Pier, the sight of which I always came to regard as being a sort of marker that I was nearing the end of my journey, especially on cold winter evenings, when the jetty foretold the promise of a hot bath and a cosy evening curled up on the sofa before a roaring fire.

"Apparently the pier had been so badly damaged after a ship had accidentally collided with it in the midst of what the old-timers called "a thick pea-souper", during the early hours of the 30th of January, 1922, that it was decided by the authorities that it was too much trouble to rebuild and re-open the Pier, and nowadays its redundant skeletal remains jut out into the river, sadly obsolete

"And they have the nerve to call it "progress," I muttered to myself as I paused to gaze across at the pier, lost in fond recollection of days long-passed. 'Not all change is for the best, some things are worth keeping exactly as they.....

"I snapped my mouth shut, and my entire body froze in place.

"I was suddenly filled with a dreadful certainty that someone was standing directly behind me.

"I tried to tell myself I was being stupid. I'd walked this path countless times before, and I'd never had any cause to feel afraid. Not even on the occasions when the insomnia had been so bad I'd climbed out of bed and gone walking down here on the wrong side of midnight.

"But nevertheless, I was afraid to turn around and check just the same, applying the same childish logic that dictated that when you awoke in the wee small hours, convinced "The Nightmare Man" was standing at the edge of your bed, so long as you didn't let it know you were awake and were aware of its presence, it couldn't harm you.

"Face the bedroom wall. Keep quiet. Try not to breathe or swallow too loudly. And most of all, never risk turning to gaze upon its terrifying countenance."

'But I wasn't a child any more, and I knew eventually I had no other option other than to check whether there was truly anyone there.

"When I did, I saw something startlingly ordinary, though it still caused fear to slither into every inch of my skin.

"Standing in a line, just fifty feet away at most, were three still and silent figures.

"They appeared to be three young men, late-teenagers, by the looks of them, though of course, most of their features were obscured by the uniform of choice for the majority of male youths these days: jet-black hoodies.

"It might sound paradoxical, but despite the fact that their shapes were little more than vague silhouettes, still they looked instantly, and chillingly familiar, and it was all I could do not to give in to panic and run screaming along the remainder of The Esplanade. But something stopped me. Call it pride. Call it a stubbornness to back down from potential danger, inherited from my dad. Call it sheer pig-headedness. Rather than take flight, instead I listened to the calm, logical inner voice of reason that told me I was very likely getting all worked up over nothing. These lads were very probably on their way to a house party or something and in a few moments they'd march right past me without giving me so much as a second glance. After all, I was very likely old enough to be their mother, and I've long come to realise, that once you hit the wrong side of thirty-five, you become all-but invisible to teenagers.

"I went to turn away, to continue my casual walk along the river-front as though I hadn't a care in the world, when a brief, but graphically intense memory struck me with stomach-sickening force:

"*I'd been ten years old, a magical age, when life seemed fresh and good and all my best days lay ahead of me. I was with my mum and dad and my best friend, Becky, walking back from a May Day Bank Holiday funfair held in Sefton Park, in the South End of Liverpool.*

"*We two girls had had our faces expertly painted. Becky was a fierce-looking tiger. I was the proudest of lions. My parents, still happily married and with not the slightest hint of the tumultuous times ahead, had stopped on the corner of Prince's Avenue, and as we'd neared our home on Sandon Street, adjacent to the wonderfully green park of Falkner Square, the madly nattering adults had allowed us to race a short distance ahead, so long as we promised to wait for them outside our house and kept well clear of the busy roads.*

"*The two of us went pounding across the baking hot pavement as though it were the vast open plains of the African savannah, our painted nostrils wrinkling pleasurably in the bright-white summer heat. A heat that somehow felt like the carefree spirit of absolute freedom and childish wonder.*

"*We'd almost reached my parents' house, when I'd suddenly felt something warm and acrid-smelling splat into the back of my head, and I'd heard Becky scream, and whirled around to see three lads, a year or so older than us, gathered on the other side of the road, creased up with laughter and pointing in our direction.*

"*How do yer like that, yer pair of friggin' piss heads!" the tallest of the boys had yelled, and his mates had slapped him on the back as if he'd cracked a joke of unparalleled comedic genius.*

"*They'd filled party balloons with their own urine and launched them at us and they'd scored a direct hit as they instantly burst open drenching our hair and faces.*

"I glanced at Becky, and I saw some of the pee had splashed onto her perfect tiger make-up and it was already running down her cheeks in thick, greasy rivulets.

"Seeing her like that, and feeling my own face paint begin sliding away in a similar fashion, along with all the perfect goodness of that previously idyllic day filled me with a burning rage and without a word I ran over and kicked the lad I assumed to be the ring-leader as hard as I could. I caught him squarely in the balls. He'd crumpled to the floor clutching his groin like he'd been shot and his mates had backed off, expressions of shock and dismay clear on their faces. As he rolled around groaning in a high, reedy voice, I stood over him wanting so much to tell him that he'd got what he deserved for bullying two little girls and ruining our day, but I was so angry I couldn't do anything other than roar at him, like, well an infuriated lion, until I felt Becky tugging at me begging me to come away and I heard my mum and dad shouting and the lad had struggled to his feet, and run as best he could, doubled-over and with balls that had likely swollen to the size of overripe watermelons.

"I'll get you for that, yer little skank!" he'd yelled as he'd disappeared around the corner, his voice still high and girly. "Yer'd better watch yer back. Me and me mates are gonna get yer. No matter how long it takes. You remember that!"

"And now, here they were again. The three of them had finally come to get me, as they'd promised they would. This was apparently, how long it had took. They were a good few years older, true, but still…

"I mean it *wasn't* them. Not really. But as they began to slowly approach me, and pulled back their face-obscuring hoodies, I could see they wore the same petulant expressions, the same arrogant sneers as the cruel tormentors of my youth, and when they were only a few feet away, the tallest of the three, shouted amiably enough, 'Excuse me, girl, 'ave you got the right time on yer?'

"Trembling, I glanced at my watch, and in a dead mechanical voice I hardly recognised as being my own, I told him it was getting on for twenty to twelve.

"Nice one for that," he said, with a thumbs up. "Sound as, girl." He nodded to his two mates, and went to move past me. "In a bit, eh?" He dropped me a wink, and for a single moment, I dared to hope I'd completely misjudged them, my instincts had been hopelessly wrong, and that just a few minutes from now I'd be safely at home, chuckling to myself over yet another chilled glass of rosé at my *Daily Mail*- inspired sense of paranoia.

"But then, the lad who, just as so many years earlier, I'd come to regard as being the ringleader, suddenly turned and flashed a smile at me, revealing a set of impossibly white teeth that glistened all wet and slick.

"And then he shook his head, and slapped his two companions on the back in a horribly familiar fashion, and three things immediately became apparent to me, and I felt my heart sink like a stone. Firstly; though his two mates might have been somewhat the worse for drink, Mr Pearly Grin-dee Grinner, appeared to be sober and in control of his faculties. Secondly, there wasn't a pick on him.

He looked like he worked out regularly at the gym, and I felt sure he would be very hard to out-run should the need arise.

"And thirdly, and perhaps worst of all, his eyes may have been devoid of emotion, but there was the unmistakable spark of intelligence there, too. That, and something else. Something dark and dangerous.

"There's something puzzling me here though, yer know," he said, glancing sideways at me, so that I caught a whiff of his aftershave. Something not too expensive, but not exactly cheap either. "Yer might think it's a bit rude to ask yer this like, seeing as how we've only just met and that." He made a big show of stroking his hairless chin, as though he were a scientist faced with some perplexing, yet hugely intriguing mystery. "But what's a nice girl like you doing down here, all alone, at this time of night?"

"Oh, nothing," I said, trying to keep my voice steady, and just about succeeding. "I'm just out trying to get some fresh air." My explanation sounded so empty I felt compelled to quickly add: "Well, it's just so oppressively hot in my apartment, even with all the windows open."

"I see," he said, and now his smile grew tight-lipped and knowing. "So you live in one of them big massive posh houses in Rock Park, then? It's alright for some, eh, boys? He glanced at his two companions who continued to stand there stock still and with their mouths wide open, so drunk they were virtually slobbering. "You must be friggin' minted, girl!"

"Nuh-nuh not really," I replied, hating the involuntary stammer now apparent in my voice. "My husband inherited the place from his parents, years before he even met me."

"Is that right?" Mr Grinner said with a sigh, making a big show of looking crestfallen before lifting his face to the star-filled skies. "I knew it!" he mock raged. "Why are all the beautiful birds in this world either happily married or up the duff? It's always the bastard same. It's enough to drive a hot-blooded, horny as fuck, male completely insane!"

"I've got to be honest, I had to quickly throw my hand over my mouth to keep from giggling hysterically at that moment. The sight of this graphic display of late-teenage angst was too over the top to be remotely credible. I kept it stifled though, because I knew instinctively, laughing out loud at him would be a terrible mistake.

"Instead, the second he took his eyes off me, I blurted out; "My hubby works as a bouncer at *O' Neill's Irish Bar,* over in Liverpool. Perhaps you've heard of the place? I'd best get going, actually. He'll be wondering where I've gotten to, and he's got a terrible temper on him at times."

"So saying, I went to turn and walk away, but I before I could take more than a couple of steps, I felt a hand drop heavily on my shoulder, and I was spun round so roughly I felt momentarily dizzy. But I soon came to my senses when I saw the expression on the face of Mr Grinner. It was he who'd grabbed me of course. He who'd sent me spinning like a roulette wheel. He who was now glaring at me with eyes that burned fiercely like glowing embers, and I could see that all traces of humour, real or otherwise, were gone. It had all been an act. That apparent loss of control. He'd been toying with me from the moment I'd become aware of his presence. He and his two seemingly imbecilic cronies, standing on the edge of the otherwise deserted riverbank like a trio of scally sentinels.

"He knew I'd been lying about my being married to anyone, let alone a hard-as-nails scouse bouncer. "Because somehow, as crazy as it sounds, he knew *me*....

"Yer know, it must be great to be married to someone who doesn't mind yer wandering round on their own late at night," Mr Grinner said, and now up close, kissing close, you might say, those pearly white teeth looked to have somehow elongated, become filed sharp and wolfish. And his breath on my cheeks was furnace hot. "But you've got me all puzzled again." He glanced down at the fingers of my left hand. How come, if yer so happily, *betrothed,* yer not wearing the arl traditional band of gold?"

"The audacity of the question, and the surreal nature of being forced into a position where I somehow felt obliged to come up with an answer, when all I'd done was to take a solitary walk along the water-front, finally saw anger replace my fear.

"You know what," I said, "I've had enough of this. I'm going home. If you really want an explanation, why don't you come round to my flat, and ask me fella, who's a bouncer, remember, why I'm not wearing a ring? I'm sure he'll be absolutely made up to make your acquaintance!"

"Now, that sounds like a boss idea," Mr Grinner whooped. "What 'd yer reckon, boys. Shall we escort the young lady back to her blissful marital home?"

"His two silent, salivating comrades suddenly awoke to some kind of zombie half-life, grunted their approval, and edged closer to me on either side, and I felt like an unwilling sacrificial victim being borne to the altar in some corny old *RKO* horror film.

"Only this wasn't a film. This was real. And when I saw Mr Grinner produce a knife, a six-inch blade that shone and glittered like a dreadful promise, I held up my hands and felt all hope quickly drain away.

"Now, let's play nice,2 he said, waving the knife a few inches from my face, so I could hear the swish and displacement of air. "No one has to get hurt if you just play nice."

"What the Hell do you want with me?" I said, my voice now little more than a whisper. "I haven't done anything to you. Please, why don't you just leave me alone?"

"Oh no, we can't do that," he chuckled, as though we were all good friends together, and I'd suggested we take a naked midnight dip or something. "No, like I said, we just wanna walk you home. See you get there safely. Hubby will be waiting. He'll be getting worried. We can't have that. Come on, love, let's get moving." He thrust the point of the blade towards me, and feeling sick with fear, I knew I had no choice but to do as he said.

"We must have looked like a decidedly odd crew, three teenaged lads and a plainly terrified thirty-something woman, marching along The Esplanade beneath a fat August moon, but of course, there wasn't anyone around to see us, and I knew that even if anyone had been looking out of their windows, the path was hidden from view by the thick screen of trees and various types of shrubs. And so we walked in silence towards the pier and the end The Esplanade, and God only knew what was going to happen to me then. We'd just reached the edge of a small, overgrown wooded area when Mr Grinner, who was just a foot or so behind me, suddenly told us all to stop.

"I think that's far enough, for now," he said, and worryingly for me, that chuckle was back "We don't wanna tire her out too quickly, now do we?"

"This odd remark inspired a ripple of sardonic laughter from his two cronies, and when they began ushering me towards the pungent smelling darkness beneath the trees, I realised with horror exactly what their intentions were. And any doubts I may have had, were soon dispelled, when Mr Grinner's companions drew blades of their own and spoke for the first time.

"Tell you what, girl," one of them said. "Why don't we sit off here for a bit. It looks nice and snug and *secret* under those leafy branches, where no one can see us." He paused, and they slapped each other on the back before adding: "Yer know, love, my friend's right. This is deffo a nice place. The type of place where we could definitely do, ahh....*things.*"

"I knew then that they meant to kill me. The sound of those emotionless, almost robotic voices. There was no arguing with them. No reasoning. I knew that if I didn't at least try to somehow make a break for it now, there would never be any hope of escape. And so, even though my limbs felt like jelly and I was on the verge of throwing up, I offered up a silent prayer and as we stood at the very edge of the copse, the air filled with the heady aromas of summer flowers and tangled undergrowth, I resorted to the oldest trick in the book: I pretended to stumble and nearly lose my footing....

"Amazingly, it worked a treat.

"As Mr Grinner went to grab me, momentarily lowering the knife, and his two friends stood there like gormless statues, I lashed out with my elbow in what I hoped was the direction of his face and I heard a satisfying crunch as I made direct contact with his nose, and before anyone could react, I pushed my way past him and tore down the pathway. In a blind panic, I ran straight ahead towards the end of the Esplanade, despite the inner voice that screamed I was going in the wrong direction, lost as I was to the metallic-tasting, brain-scrambling instincts of pure terror. Too late, I saw, looming before me, the darkened, boarded-up shell of the closed down pub, and the equally redundant surroundings of the former Vesta Oil Terminal.

"I was charging headlong into the thick darkness of a literal dead end.

"All I could do was offer up a silent prayer to a God I no longer truly believed in that there would be one of those jagged holes torn in the wire mesh fencing by local kids or that the factory gates would be miraculously ajar, but the moment I stepped into the gap between the pub and the skeletal remains of the industrial plant, I could see the fence was entirely intact and the gates firmly padlocked, though I reached out and shook them with all my strength just the same, whilst emitting small hitching cries of fear and frustration, dredged up from some deep, primal part of my being.

"I looked up and saw the bright, shining rows of razor-sharp barbed wire lining the top of the fence, and I knew I was trapped. There was nowhere left to go.

"I spun round, my eyes blurred with brink of falling tears, and attempted to run forwards, hoping against hope that I could somehow burst past my pursuers, catching them by surprise, but I'd only taken a few steps when I slipped in an oily puddle and went pinwheeling towards the unforgiving concrete. I threw my arms out trying to protect my face. I felt bright pain shoot up my arms with the force of the impact and the palm of my left hand was sliced open by a sliver of broken glass. I quickly struggled to my feet and with grim inevitability I saw my three tormentors standing silent in a line, exactly as I'd seen them when I'd paused to glance across at the old pier, an impossibly long time ago, it seemed.

"Equally predictable, it was Mr Grinner, who spoke first, streaks of blood that appeared coal-black in the moonlight, dripping from his obviously broken nose.

"Okay, girl," he said, his voice sounding muffled, as though he had a scarf wrapped round his mouth. "Let's all just be reasonable here. Let's just play nice, and before you know it, you'll be walkin' away laughin' about this." He'd grinned, wider than ever, if that were possible before adding; "Just think, love, in next to no time, you'll be going to sleep beneath your comfortable clean, white cotton sheets, laying yer head on the pillow, telling yerself that this whole thing was nothing more than a bad dream." He sniggered to himself. "Or one hell of a *good* one, if you'd prefer."

"I stood there, feeling increasingly helpless, and with all the fight draining from me like the rivulets of blood streaking from my upraised hands, a universal gesture of utter defeat.

"Please don't hurt me!" I whimpered. "I haven't got any money, not even a mobile phone, and I'm old enough to be your mother, and I don't think...."

"You just be quiet, now and you'll be alright, girl," Mr Grinner said, his voice unnervingly calm and calculated. "If you scream or shout for help, though, me and me mates here..." he shrugged regretfully . "Well, we are gonna have to cut yer!"

"So saying, the three of them began walking slowly towards me, the glint in their eyes as steely as the knife blades they each held before them, their obvious phallic symbolism all too plain to see..

"Oh, Dad," I cried so softly, it's doubtful any of those approaching heard me. "I wish to God you were here with me now. I know you'd protect me. *Oh, Dad...* "

"Something truly incredible happened then.

"The moment those semi-whispered words fell from my lips, the leers on Mr Grinner, and his companions faces faltered and then fell dead away, like cheap plastic masks slipping from a gang of drunken revellers at the end of a fancy dress party.

"Gone in an instant were the expressions of maniacal lust. Instead, as they stood dead in their tracks, almost within touching distance of me, their jaws dropped impossibly wide open, their eyes bulged from their sockets, and I swear their faces turned a full-moon shade of white.

"What the fuck...?" Mr (now decidedly *non*) Grinner mouthed, pointing at something a good few feet above my head, "What in Christ's name is that?"

"His two friends could only moan something unintelligible by way of an answer, and I noticed with amazement they'd both begun slowly backing away, as though they'd been confronted by some form of snarling, teeth-bared wild animal. The ringleader didn't move, though. In truth, I don't think he could. He was frozen to the spot with sheer terror, and whilst his all-too-obvious fear should have transmitted itself to me, I felt instead, strangely uplifted. As if the source of the horror, looming behind me, whatever it might be, could never, to my mind at least, be any greater than that which I'd been about to be subjected.

"And then I felt something shift, the sense of a huge presence, unseen, but undeniably there all the same, raising itself to its full height.

"Mr Grinner made a sound then. Though it was more like the mewling of an abandoned kitten, stuck in some terrible place, than the coherent speech of anything remotely human. It was enough to break his fear-induced paralysis, though. His knife dropped from his hand and landed with a dead splash in the centre of a viscous-looking puddle. He then nodded his head once, and without a single word, turned and fled back along The Esplanade, just as a thin, salty-smelling mist began drifting in from the river, shrouding the path in wispy tendrils, gradually enveloping his suddenly tiny and insignificant form....

"I sobbed. My body hitching with little spasms of relief.

"Then I turned around.

"At first, it was difficult to make anything out, it was so pitch-dark, but when my eyesight slowly adjusted, I saw something that was so plainly impossible, my mind struggled to acknowledge the reality of its presence. Even now, telling you this, a good hour or so after the event, I'm finding it hard to accept what it was I witnessed, so God alone knows what you and anyone else who gets to hear my story, will make of it. Question my sanity, no doubt, and who can blame them? But consider this: *Something* had terrified my three would-be attackers and likely rapists, and caused them to run off screaming into the night, and that corroborative fact helps to convince me I haven't completely lost my mind.

"I saw...I *know* I saw, looming before me in the darkness of the gap between the shuttered pub and the closed-down factory, a huge, hulking *shape*. That's the only word I can use to describe it. An immensely powerful-looking form, that appeared vaguely human, but with no facial features whatsoever, towering well over twenty feet above me as it roiled in the blackness that enshrouded it. And though it writhed and contorted in a constant state of flux, it remained eerily silent. Though undeniably real, for all that.

"For a few endless moments, I could only stand and stare, though strangely, it wasn't fear that held me in place.

"It was *awe*.

"There were other, over-riding emotions too.

"As insane as it sounds, I felt somehow comforted and at peace, convinced that this thing, this gargantuan apparition, meant me no harm. On the contrary, I was sure it had materialised from who knew where, to protect me, to act as some form of, oh I don't know, guardian angel, I suppose. I watched in amazement as the shape began, without warning, to rapidly diminish in size, like the smoky form of a fairy tale genie, siphoning down toward the tiny spout of its magic lamp. In less than a minute, it had disappeared completely, returned to whatever plane, realm or dimension it had emerged from, leaving behind not the slightest trace that it had ever truly been there.

"Except that is for a warm breeze that suddenly sprung up from out of nowhere, carrying with it a heady combination of aromas so powerful, I was almost overcome with the array of sensations.

"And memories.

"So many memories.....

"There was the unmistakeable smell of Old Spice after-shave. The hint of Bourneville dark chocolate, and Castella cigars. The sweet odour of sweat, embedded in the fabric of a much-loved jumper or T-shirt inhaled when my father held me in his arms either in joyful celebration, or when I was lost to the dark depths of despair...

"I distinctly heard the sound of his voice then too, though whether it was only in my head or the words were actually spoken out loud, I honestly couldn't say. And does it really matter much, anyway? Surely, the significance of the message conveyed to me is all that that truly counts, in the end.

"*I will always be there for you, sweetheart, no matter what. I will never run out and leave you, the way your mother did. All I can do is promise you faithfully that whenever you need me, at the times when all hope seems to have seeped away like teardrops into sun-parched earth, I will be there.*"

"*Oh, Dad,*" I whispered into the fragrant darkness. "*I love you so very much...*"

POSTSCRIPT:

Whatever the truth of Annie's moving story concerning her best friend, what is beyond doubting is that The Esplanade, a once-grand Victorian vista, is slowly and tragically being allowed to crumble and fade like an old, sepia-toned photograph tucked away in an attic-bound trunk, buried amongst the stacks of old party invitations, concert tickets and those faintly-perfumed love letters:

The ones you meant to throw out decades ago, but still kept, perhaps to provide some form of scant consolation on those cold January evenings, or on some desperately lonely Sunday afternoon,

Rock Ferry Mansion
Photo Credit: Lee Walker

when it seemed like all the world was asleep and bathed in a sickly shade of monochrome. It still retains more than a modicum of its former grandeur, however, as the photograph I snapped, during the winter of 2013, more than attests.

Should you ever get the opportunity to visit the area, and take a stroll along the mile-long stretch of Mersey riverbank, you can't help but be impressed by the sight of the row of splendid houses lining the water-front, imbued with a sense of history, of lives lived and of a faded, but still existent grandeur, it's easy to imagine the buildings in their heyday.

The brightly-lit ballrooms filled with swirling dancers, the men dressed in formal dinner suits, the women in flowing evening gowns, tiaras and long white, satin gloves. Endless garden parties held on the lush summer-dappled lawns or picnics laid out upon the golden sands of the small beach just beyond the high stone walls.

Afternoon tea on the verandas, watching the steam-ships and ferry boats traverse the mighty river. The welcoming light, pouring from the large bay windows, drawing the work-weary home on cold winter evenings...

As it was, and as it shall ever be.

In the mind's eye, at least.

CHAPTER THIRTEEN
THE NIGHT OF CAPED SHADOWS
'A New' Spring-Heeled Jack Sighting
Comes To Light From 1975

One of the most terrifying entities in the annals of Fortean phenomena is the fire-breathing, bizarrely-costumed figure of Spring-Heeled Jack. Frustratingly for researchers, although there exists a fair amount of anecdotal testimony from eyewitnesses across Britain, including London, the Midlands, Lincoln, Sheffield, Scotland and Liverpool, in the years between 1837 and 1904, there is a distinct lack of any hard evidence that the character was actually anything other than a vivid example of mass hysteria, elaborate hoaxes and contemporary media manipulation. There does however remain a wealth of eyewitness testimony from across Britain, including London, the Midlands, Lincoln, Sheffield, Scotland and Liverpool, in the years between 1837 and 1904.

Anyone remotely interested in the mysterious entity, a figure that has long since passed into the misty realms of "Bogeyman" legend, would do well to read Dr Mike Dash's hugely authoritative and pretty much conclusive essay published in the excellent Fortean Studies Volume 3 (1996).

It's always interesting when 'new,' modern-day accounts of 'Jack' emerge, however, and I sincerely hope the following, which has only ever been published in the e-zine version of Dead Of Night (Vol 2, Issue 1, January, 2011), *proves to be of interest to both scholars and anyone else remotely interested in the subject, and I look forward to hearing his opinions about an incident that took place 36 years ago, in fittingly enough (considering the county was, according to legend, the location of the final 'confirmed' sighting of Jack, in Everton, 1904 on) here on Merseyside...*

> *'One cold, damp evening, the world stood still,*
> *I watched as I held my breath,*
> *A silhouette, I thought I knew...*
> *Came through...'*
> **Second Skin - The Chameleons**

A very close friend of mine, by the name of Stevie Gee (the very same excellent guitarist and bass player who accompanied me and our Grant along the sodden sands of West Kirkby, on a foolhardy band video expedition to the island of Hilbre – see Chapter Eight) once told me of a frightening childhood encounter with a strange humanoid figure near to his former home on Bromborough Road in Bebington, on the Wirral side of the Mersey.

It's an incident which occurred over a quarter of a century ago now, but he still recalls with near-perfect clarity...

'One bitterly cold winter's evening, back in 1975, when I was 11 years-old, I had raced outside straight after tea in the company of my sister, Pam, who is two-years older than me. We were eager to meet up with a group of mutual friends at our usual hang-out, the line of garages situated just over the road from where I lived, and we weren't remotely bothered about the freezing weather. It seems to me that you don't feel the cold so much when you're a kid, do you.

'One of the friends we'd arranged to meet was also a near-neighbour, named Robbie Lyons, who was the same age as Pam, and who, I suppose it's fair to say, I regarded with something akin to admiration. This was due in part at least to the fact that he attended "The Big School", something that had always commanded wide-eyed respect amongst kids my age, because he'd successfully made the transition from the comparatively carefree, halcyon days of life at Church Drive Primary and Junior Schools, to spending five days a week at the towering, Dickensian monstrosity that was Bebington Secondary – where, according to local, pre-teen folklore, all manner of dreadful horrors lay in wait, ready to pounce the second you stepped through the wrought-iron gates.

'Robbie was, therefore, living proof that those brave enough to rise to life's challenges, could, like a knight in shining armour on a holy quest, not only survive the ordeal in one piece, but emerge all the stronger for having done so.

'The estimable Mr Lyons, also looked out for me and my friends whenever there was trouble brewing, and regularly intervened on our behalf whenever some difficulty arose, and it never crossed my mind back then that his motives may not have been entirely motivated by a noble sense of truth, justice and the Merseyside-ian way. In my naïveté, I really didn't pay much attention to the way he looked at my sister when he thought she wasn't looking. I just assumed he was regarding her with the contempt most kids my age reserved for the company of girls. Whenever the subject of the opposite sex was raised, our gang were in unanimous agreement with Bruce Cabot's hard as nails character in the original 1933 version of *King Kong,* when with a dismissive flick of his cigarette stub from the foredeck of the good ol' *Venture,* he proclaimed that all girls were a '*nuisance... They can't help it. They're just made that way, I guess.*'

'This chauvinistic display of misogyny did not of course extend to my sister, Pam. She *was* my sister, after all, and so we were all agreed we could make a somewhat grudging exception in her case.

'Anyway, on this particular bone-chilling evening, dressed in our duffel coats, gloves and thick, woolly hats and scarves, we'd sought to keep warm by engaging in various games and activities, the most popular of which proved to be that perennial favourite - hide-and-seek.

'I remember Pam and I chose to secrete ourselves behind the back of the garage where my Dad kept his pride and joy; a metallic-brown, Hillman Avenger. It's always struck me as being more than a little strange the things you recall clearly from ages past without the need to refer to old photographs, diary entries or crumpled letters lining the bottom of a chest of drawers.

'A case in point: I can still recall the number plate of my Dad's car: LHF 203K. I have no idea why this should be so, because I certainly couldn't tell you (should you, for some unfathomable reason, express a sudden desire to know) what letters and numbers make up my *own* current car registration plate. Perhaps it's because I knew, even at that tender age, how important that car was to my Dad. How much time and effort he had put into keeping its engine running smoothly and its chassis polished so frequently it appeared to be as shiny and new as the day it first rolled off the assembly line. Often, it seems to me now, that as children, the things that were precious to our parents: a much-loved record, an ornamental figurine, a well-kept bed of sweet-smelling roses, acquire a sort of semi-mythical status, like the "holy relics" exhibited in certain churches around the world, and we recollect everything about these cherished objects later as adults, because they serve as memory-inducers, an unbreakable attachment to the relatively simple days of childhood, and the people who loved us unconditionally back then.

'So anyway, there we were, my sister and I, crouched low behind the walls of the garage, trying desperately to keep our teeth from chattering, and cupping our hands to prevent the twin plumes of smoky breath from giving us away, when Pam suddenly whispered harshly, "Steve, what's that up there on the garage roof?"

'Angrily, I turned to her to tell her to keep quiet, but then I caught the expression of sheer terror on her face, and I snapped my mouth shut, and craned my neck to see what she was pointing at, and quickly forgot all about the game of hide-and-seek.

'A strange, dark figure was crouching on the roof of the garage immediately above us, and although I couldn't make out any facial features at first, the bright winter moon being directly behind it, rendering it little more than a cartoon silhouette, still I *knew* it was staring intently right back at us, and I felt what I can only describe as an overwhelming malevolence radiating from the form in near-visible waves. 'Then, as we watched, paralysed with fear, unable even to cry out for help, the terrible figure slowly rose to its full height, with its arms outstretched, as if in soundless supplication to the diamond-chipped void above.

'It stood there for a moment, as we continued to cower in the shadows, silently praying that the thing, whatever the hell it was, would just simply go away.

'Like many kids our age in the mid-1970s, I'd been brought up on a steady diet of American comic books and TV programmes, and I recall being struck by the figure's uncanny resemblance to *Batman*. I mean, it didn't have the famous bat insignia smack in the centre of its chest, nor as far as I can remember, was it wearing a face mask of any kind, but it most certainly *was* wearing a black cape and a pair of equally black, knee-length boots, and well, I *was* an eleven-year-old, and DC and Marvel comics were pretty much my sole frame of reference at that time...

'I want to make it abundantly clear however, that there was nothing remotely super, or indeed heroic, about this menacing costumed character. I remember thinking that this figure was most definitely *not* some eccentric individual playing a bizarre practical joke upon a couple of quite clearly terrified children. I was inexplicably certain that this was no mere drunken refugee from a local fancy dress party with a garage-climbing fixation. This was no drunken, hopelessly deluded individual on a one-man mission to save mankind from the nefarious shadow men of the criminal world.

'Sane and logical explanations all they may have been.

But two things I was convinced of then, and remain utterly convinced of now are: One, the sane and logical had temporarily taken leave of that dark plot of garage-land, where my sister and I chose to hide from our "seekers", that bitter winter evening.

'And second, as young and inexperienced in the ways of life as I inarguably was back then, still I was more than old enough to know, deep in the gut instinct core of my being that we'd encountered Evil personified.

'And I remain every bit as certain, thirty-five years or so along the path of my life, about the validity of those two things, right *now*.

'I really don't give a flying one about the inevitable ranks of shaking heads, exasperated expressions, raised eyebrows and knowing glances of cynics and hard-nosed sceptics.

'I'm not at all sure how we finally managed to break the trance-like spell, and summon up the courage to make a run for it. But at some point, that's just what we did. We ran, yelling and screaming away from the garages, not even daring to glance back once to check whether anything was running (or *leaping,* that was the image that somehow *sprang* to mind, if you'll forgive the pun) after us, and as we tore around the corner, back onto Bromborough Road proper, we literally bumped into Robbie Lyons, and in high, panic-stricken voices, we told him what we had just seen.

'Ever the brave, stoic defender of those in mortal danger (and the eternally horny protector of the archetypal damsel in distress, given Pam's presence) Robbie took us at our word and raced fearlessly towards the row of garages, whilst Pam and I waited anxiously for news in the warmth and safety of the roaring fire in our parent's living room.

'As it turned out, we didn't have to wait too long.

'A couple of minutes later, there was a frantic hammering at the front door, and I opened it to find Robbie standing there, his pale face and the look of wild fear apparent in his eyes, enough to confirm he had likely encountered the very same thing we had. We ushered him in, to get warm by the fire, but it was a minute or two before he could compose himself sufficiently to be able to tell us what had happened.

"He was right there, juh-juh-just like you said," he stammered (and whether it was due to the bone-freezing temperatures or wretched, unspeakable terror, I really couldn't say) "I saw him, all dressed in buh-buh black, standing on the friggin' garage roof!

"But that wasn't the worst of it,' he added quickly, swallowing a click in his throat. "As I got nearer to the figure, it suddenly swivelled its head, and it glared at me over its shoulder, and then, Christ almighty, it just *bounded* high into the sky and landed on another garage roof, about thirty feet further along. And then it did the same thing again. And again.

"And again.

"Until it cleared the entire row of garages and jumped onto the roof of one of the houses on Ellen's Lane, and I lost sight of him. I've never seen anything like it. And I really hope to God, it's the only time I ever do!

"As for myself, watching Robbie ('the Lyon-Hearted'), trembling with fear and rubbing his hands across his face as if he could eradicate the sheer impossibility of it all with a single sweaty palm, convinced me more than anything else that happened on that never-to-be-forgotten night that what we saw was undeniably, incontrovertibly, real.

"As for the answers to what the figure actually was?

"Do I think it was a practical joker?

"A drunk in a fancy dress costume?

"A mentally deranged individual?

"Or Spring-Heeled Jack, making another, typically capricious appearance on the back streets of Merseyside, one of his favourite haunts? I have my own suspicions as to the figure's true identity, but whilst it may sound like a king-size cop out, I leave it to you, the reader, to draw your own conclusions."

HIDE-AND-SEEK

NB: Incidentally, the recounting of Steve and his sister Pam's experience, taking place as it did whilst they were both hiding, hunched and cowering in a place of concealment, brought to the forefront of my mind a question that's been lurking somewhere deep within its darkest recesses for years beyond counting: Just what is it about children's games, especially that old perennial favourite; hide-and-seek, that seems on occasion to act as some sort of summoning ritual: A ceremony that, however unintentionally, provides a conduit for "otherworldly entities" to slip into our dimension....

I remember reading an article in The Observer, *(Sunday, August 3rd, 2008), regarding the changing attitudes of modern-day-parents towards their kids freedom to take part in seemingly innocent games...*

'A major study by "Play England", part of the National Children's Bureau, found that some parents are going to such extreme lengths to protect their children from danger that they have even said no to them playing **Hide and Seek.**'

It prompts me to ask whether our parents, with the wisdom borne of experience, are aware of something sinister associated with these supposedly "innocent activities," and the following account sent to me in 2013, concerning another, equally terrifying experience, said to have taken place in the Cheshire town of Ellesmere Port, during the winter of 1981, only serves to give weight to my suspicions that sometimes, only sometimes, mind, the games of children can have unforeseen consequences.

CHAPTER FOURTEEN
'BALEFUL ECHOES FROM THE BLIGHTED-WINTER EARTH'

'We're dredging up the past again. These twisted, sordid recollections of a life that's passed us by.
'An empty age without a name, just sad reminders, bitter landmarks we'd do well to leave behind...'
Now There Comes A Darker Day
- The Lids

The following account was related to me by way of an increasingly archaic mode of communication in this technologically-obsessed, social media-dominated age: An honest-to-God, hand-written letter. On paper, no less. If you can believe that?

Contrary to the cynical views of the majority of my family and friends, I am no latter-day techno-phobe. I've got a computer, a laptop, and a half-way decent mobile phone.

So what if the desktop is a cheap, second-hand model, with a screen that glows bright green, making me look like I've been bitten by one of the slimy giant maggots in an old episode of Dr Who, *or that the laptop only works if you use it in safe mode, and my mobile is so unreliable it can only pick up a signal if I climb into the airing cupboard and point the phone in what my mini-compass assures me is a vaguely north-westerly direction?*

All that matters, when you get right down to it, is that despite my embracing of contemporary news-relaying gadgets, I was nonetheless heartily glad to receive the details of one of those rare, allegedly true-life encounters with the unexplained that chill you to the bone, by way of an actual hand-written letter; 'the product of its author's body, a hand extended across an estranging distance,' *as someone, whose name escapes me, once wrote.*

The story, penned in neat, block capitals gave me a serious dose of the shivers the way those old "BBC Ghost Stories For Christmas" used to terrify me as a child (and indeed, continue to do so). Not because they were overly graphic or drenched in copious amounts of excessive gore, but rather because they relied purely on atmosphere, and subtly suggestive horror, based as they were on the classic works of M.R. James and Charles Dickens.

I first read this story alone on the wrong side of midnight, with the first snow-storm of winter howling at the window panes, and in truth it had unnerved me so much, I had cast the sheets of lined paper aside long before reaching the end, and raced to the bedroom to seek the comfort of my fiancée's arms.

I would contend though that it would still have sent shivers down my spine if I'd have read it whilst sat on a packed, sun-drenched beach on a perfect summer's day.

Some accounts of events, real or purely imagined, have that effect.

ONE

The letter had been written by Richie White, another very good friend of mine, and someone who we met a little earlier during the chapter featuring *The Silent Watchers.*

'Dear Lee,
'I want to tell you about something that supposedly happened to two of my childhood friends, the Wilkinson brothers, Bill, aged ten and Jim, who was a couple of years older, during the afternoon of the cold and frosty Christmas Eve of 1981.

'The two boys, dressed in thick sheep-skinned coats, blue and white scarves and then-trendy half-Everton/half-Celtic woollen bobble hats, had met up with me and a group of mutual friends, all of them lads of a similar age, at the edge of the bone-hard playing fields just off Overpool Road, in Ellesmere Port. The fields are slap in the middle of the council estate where most of our gang lived back then, and we'd gathered for a game of eight-a-side footy amongst ourselves.

After an hour or so, however, one of the boys present, a tall, gawky looking individual named Ricky Ross, badly twisted his ankle on the ice-encrusted surface after trying, and failing, to control the erratically bouncing Mitre Casey, and had limped off bawling his eyes out, clutching his football defiantly under his arm. As no one else had thought to bring a ball, or could be arsed volunteering to go and fetch one from their homes, we'd been forced to abandon the game and seek

NOTE TO READER: *I admit I have, with Richie's permission, rewritten and edited his account for inclusion in this book, for the pure and simple reason that as Mr White would readily attest, whilst he is a highly creative person, blessed with genuine artistic skills, 'I'm no writer...I'll tell you the bare bones. The facts that I know to be true. You tart it up a bit in your usual style...'*

some other form of entertainment in a way in which we could while away the few short hours until daylight seeped from the sky and we could trundle home, dive in a nice warm bath and then sit before the roaring fire to watch the Christmas films and various Yuletide TV specials.

'We were all equally anxious to kill time, so me and me mates stood around in a rough circle at the edge of one of the penalty areas and began shouting out the names of other games we could maybe play. And you need to remember, this was the early 1980s: "The Dim And Distant Pre-Technological, Social Media Age". We therefore had to resort to participating in games that required we utilise our largely uncorrupted childhood imaginations or (shudder) actual physical exercise.

'Somewhat knackered after the intense footy match, I decided to kick things off by suggesting that we all just simply sat off somewhere quiet to swap spine-chilling ghost stories, school-day anecdotes, and the legends of your first ever, full-on-the-lips kiss with the girl you've fancied for ages, but this was quickly dismissed by a chorus of objections which ran along the lines of , "Eh, lad, I am not parking me arse-cheeks *anywhere* outside today. It's friggin' freezin'. Do yer really wanna spend Christmas Day sufferin' from a bad case of piles?"

"Well, how about a game of Truth or Dare?" Gareth, a freckle-faced, ginger-haired boy, whose high, reedy voice had yet to truly break properly, piped up. "We don't have to sit down to play that."

'This was greeted by a few half-hearted murmurs of assent and just as many grumbles of protest, and I suspect the reason for this was that taking part in this supposedly "laugh a minute contest" often involved you revealing some hideously embarrassing secret, ie; the fact that you study, with immense forensic interest the contents of the slice of used tissue paper after you've pigged out on peanut butter sandwiches, or that you get a massive erection every time the cartoon version of Thelma from *Scooby Doo,* appears on the telly, and whilst none of these revelations applied to me, I hasten to add, I was heartily glad when Rob (the tallest, and officially the hardest member of our gang) raised his right arm and yelled, "Nah, how about we play Knick-Knock, instead?"

'The suggestion that we go round the far-flung reaches of our estate frantically rapping on doors and ringing bells, then giving it toes the moment we heard the sound of the occupier striding down the hallway, did have several things to commend it, not least the fact that getting chased down the icy roads by an irate, middle-aged man in a string vest and a pair of carpet slippers or a woman with rollers in her hair, waving a spatula with deadly intent, never failed to set the pulse racing, and as an added bonus, legging it through the streets would certainly ensure we soon forgot about the below freezing temperatures.

'I did think it a little strange though that it had been Rob who had made the proposal, seeing as how the last time we'd played Knick-Knock, in early September, the person at whose door he was about to knock, a relatively young man in a trackie top and a pair of Real Madrid shorts must have seen Rob sneaking up the garden path, and had thrown the door wide open before he could even raise his hand. The man, who looked as if he worked out at the gym on a regular basis, lifted my terrified friend off his feet and virtually threw him over the other side of the five-foot high garden fence.

'Luckily for Rob, he had a soft landing.

'Unluckily for Rob, he'd landed splat in the middle of the largest pile of freshly laid, still-steaming dog shite I have ever seen in my life. It must have been dumped by the world's largest Great Dane, or some similar breed. And when my best mate had tried to get to his feet, he'd slipped, and landed headfirst in the mass of excrement, sending splatters of it flying in every direction.

'We'd all fallen about laughing hysterically till our stomachs ached and tears streamed down our faces, but poor old Rob had spent the next few days desperately trying to scrub the dog muck out of his pores and his thick, blonde, wedge-cut hair, but still, the smell of shit had hung around him like a vile-smelling cloud for the best part of a week, attracting the last of the summer's flies in madly buzzing, sky-darkening hordes.

'Despite the awful fate that had befallen our companion, however, I think we were pretty much all in agreement that it was high time we resumed our "door-bangin' shenanigans", and we began making our way to the edge of the playing fields in the general direction of the rows of identical-looking, council houses lining Pooltown Road. We'd just stepped through the gaps on either side of the barred metal gate and out onto the icy pavement, when David Williams, a usually shy, quietly spoken boy, suddenly shouted, "Hang on a sec, boys. I've got an even better idea!"

'It was the one the tip of my tongue to tell him to shut up, we'd already decided what game we were gonna play, and I was anxious to get on with it, when I noticed the excited gleam in David's eyes, the kind of barely concealed state of anticipation exclusive to pre-teenage lads, who are still more likely to be thrilled by the sight of a new *Spiderman* comic or the unveiling of the latest Liverpool/Everton kit than catching a glimpse of our class-mate, Jackie Goodchild's, rapidly expanding gazzoglas during P.E. lessons.

"Alright, lad, pipe it in, will yer!" Jim, the elder of the Wilkinson brothers, said with an air of impatience, though his tones were not unkindly. "What's yer big plan then?"

"Well," Dave replied, a great big beaming grin splitting his features. "Who reckons we have a game of hide-and-seek, instead?"

'Now as "big plans" go, this was one was hardly ever gonna feature high in the list of Life's True Eureka Moments, and doubtless anyone reading this account will, having reached this point, be rolling their eyes heavenwards or shaking their heads in befuddlement at the "Wow, Thrills-Ville City, la!" prospects of this most basic of games that, in later life, appears to have all the raw-edged excitement of watching a couple of pensioners pulling a cheap Christmas cracker in a smoke-filled corner of the Ellesmere Port Conservative Club.

'But the honest truth is, we'd always loved playing hide-and-seek, especially if you were lucky enough to be the ones doing the hiding. I suppose you can blame it on our over-active imaginations or the viewing of our favourite TV programmes, like *Tales Of The Unexpected,* or the scary films our parents sometimes let us stay up late to watch at weekends, but the prospect of being hunted by the seeker, desperately trying to remain silent and still, hardly daring to breathe as you heard the heavy thud of footsteps slowly approaching your hiding place, was still enough to release entire squadrons of butterflies from deep within the pit of your stomach.

'Perhaps you won't find it so surprising then that no sooner had David made his suggestion, than our entire gang, Cynical Jim included, had set into motion the process of selecting the position of Seeker. It was seldom that anyone volunteered their services, and so we usually had to draw lots or engage in a seemingly never-ending, knock-out contest of Paper, Scissors, Stone, but on this occasion, perhaps due to the ever-increasing coldness of the air and the aforementioned risk of contracting piles if you crouched in some frozen hiding place for too long, Rob had raised his hand to the increasingly snow-threatening skies as we'd lined up to begin the elimination rounds.

"There's no need for any of that today," he announced, in a voice that brooked no argument. "I'm gonna be the Seeker. Yous load set about pairing up and then get on with finding somewhere to hide, anywhere yer like within a quarter of a mile of the Estate." He turned his back on us and placed his hands over his eyes. "I'm gonna count to a hundred, and then I'm coming to find yer, ready or not!"

'It was an unspoken rule amongst the members of our gang that it was forbidden for anyone to ever choose to hide anywhere on their own, not even at the height of summer, and certainly not on an increasingly gloomy, late December afternoon. I chose to partner up with Gareth, and the rest of our gang formed into duos, before racing along the main road or turning right onto Princes Road, where I lived, as fast as we could, splitting off in several different directions at the first opportunity, and disappearing into the near-deserted cul-de-sacs and side-streets, the outbuildings and dead winter gardens like Fagin's band of pickpockets and ragamuffins scurrying for safety during a police raid.

'Me and Gareth headed directly for the tree-house my dad had built in our back garden a couple of summers ago. It was a somewhat obvious hiding place, but it would definitely be a good deal warmer tucked up in the thick blankets my friends and I always kept in there, and it beat the alternative of concealing ourselves anywhere out in the cold, and with heavy snow apparently on the way.

'The below-freezing temperatures didn't seem to concern Jim and Bill very much, however.

'I remember watching them, with vague feelings of unease, as they dived into the centre of the five-foot high privet hedge and the row of mostly leafless trees and thick bushes opposite the rows of council houses on Festival Road, silent and deserted in the semi-twilight, save for a middle-aged woman pushing a pram, its handles and undercarriage laden to tipping point with last-minute Christmas shopping.

'I paused for a second, gazing across at the two brothers, giggling and playfully punching each other in the arms as they clambered into the hedge, and I had time to notice the way their shadows, cast by the last rays of pale, watery sunlight seemed horribly thin and somehow uncertain looking, like figures glimpsed in a wispy morning fog.

'I turned to speak to Gareth, but he'd run on ahead a little, and by the time I'd caught his attention, Jim and Bill had been swallowed up by the sugared-frosted hedgerow, and with a shiver that had less to do with the cold than the fact that, for some reason, I'd never liked that hedged and heavily wooded side of Festival Road, and had always considered that bright, optimistic-seeming name: "Festival", to be entirely inappropriate.

'To me, half that road at least, always appeared too dark and somehow ominous-looking, even on the very brightest of summer days. It unnerved me greatly, and I would avoid walking alongside it, unless I absolutely had to. It reminded me of the all-but impenetrable fairy-tale thickets, the kind that spring up overnight as the result of some wicked witch's spell, complete with poison dispensing thorns and choking vines, created to keep sleep-enchanted princesses within, and noble knights without.

'It smelled funny too. Aside from the ordinary odours of dead leaves, wild growth, and decades-old rotting mulch, I sometimes caught a waft of what smelled like a lady's perfume, sickly-sweet and cloying and so pungent, I'd been sure that if I'd had cause to peer over the hedge into its wooded depths I'd have seen some lone, mad-eyed woman standing there silent and still, or crouched amongst the knotted tree branches, the bluebells of spring or late winter snowdrops, the fronds of ferns and clumps of high stinging nettles.

'For God only knew what purpose.

'To tempt and ensnare the unwary, perhaps? A couple of young, highly-impressionable boys playing hide-and-seek for example?

'It occurred to me that I should maybe run across the road and try to persuade the two brothers to pick somewhere, *anywhere* else to secrete themselves, and I'd actually taken a few hesitant steps off the kerb when Gareth had begun yelling at me to hurry up and get a move on.

"Rob's gotta have reached a hundred by now. He's gonna come lookin for us and find us standin here like a pair of blerts with their kecks down round their ankles, pissin ice crystals!"

'I turned away, shaking my head as I ran to catch up with my best friend just as the first snowflakes of what would quickly develop into a full-blown blizzard, landed on my cheeks.

'I expected I'd see the two brothers soon enough, emerging from the hedge with great big victory grins splitting their red raw faces, after Rob had conceded defeat, and we'd be forced to endure their smug smiles and highly-annoying bragging for the remainder of the afternoon.

'But it turned out I couldn't have been any more wrong about that if I'd tried.

TWO

'Gareth and I had been hiding inside our tree-house for precisely twenty minutes and thirty-three seconds when the screaming started.

'I know this for a fact, because I was the proud owner of an incredibly accurate Seiko wristwatch: a gift my parents had bought me the previous Christmas, back in the days when such devices actually told you the correct time as opposed to singing to you in a hideously tinny voice that, as if you didn't know, it was sheeting down with rain or blowing a bastard gale, yet again.

'I had just happened to glance at my watch to check the time at the exact same moment the eerie silence of Princes Road was shattered by the sound of a series of high-pitched wails that raised the hairs on the back of my neck and had me clapping my hand over my mouth to stifle a scream of my own.

'I'd been snuggled in the *Paddington Bear* duvet I'd had since I was a child, gazing out the single cracked window at the rapidly increasing snow flurries already blanketing the small section of Princes Road, visible from our vantage point, (ready to duck down if I caught sight of Rob the Seeker, walking past the driveway) and Gareth, who had been wrapped up in a tasselled tartan blanket, his head buried in a old tattered copy of *Football Monthly,* and who seldom swore shouted "What the fuck was that?" hastily casting aside his blanket and magazine before jumping quickly to his feet to join me at the window.

"I don't know," I said, struggling to keep my voice steady. "But it sounded like a couple of kids screaming, and I don't think they were just messin' about, lad. They sounded friggin petrified!"

'As if to confirm my suspicions, the snow-storm muffled air was rent by another set of unearthly shrieks that faded in and out of ear-shot like the broadcasts of a radio half-tuned to some distant foreign station, and I glanced at Gareth, and saw nerve-shredding fear coursing through every fibre of my being, reflected in his wide, staring eyes.

"I can't see a thing out there in this blizzard, Gareth," I said, before adding uncertainly, "Er, so I suppose we'd better climb down and go and find out what the hell's going on?"

"Yeah, I reckon yer right," my friend mumbled with even less enthusiasm. It's to my eternal shame though that neither of us made more than a tentative move towards the trap door and the retractable ladder that led down to the garden below, but instead continued to gaze out of the window at the swirling snow-flakes, as though we were both in a trance.

'In the end it was the hunched, but unmistakable figure of Rob, with little Davey Williams at his side, trudging purposefully through the snow along Princes Road, waving his arms about wildly and yelling something about the game being over, "we could all come out of our hidey-holes," that brought us to our senses. "Yer don't think he's having us on, do yer?" Gareth whispered without any real conviction. "I mean, maybe he just can't be arsed looking for us in this weather."

"Well, you could hardly blame him if he did decide to cheat," I replied. "But as much as I hate to say this, I wouldn't mind bettin' that was a couple of friends of ours we heard screaming just now." I looked Gareth in the eye. "And if that's true, lad, no wonder Rob's decided to cancel the game."

'Gareth didn't say anything in response to my remarks, and he didn't need to. We both knew I was right, and so in silence, we set about lifting up the trapdoor and making our way out into the swirling snow, the shock of the cold instantly numbing our hands and faces, and making us less eager than ever to learn the truth of what had taken place.

"Hey, Rob!" I shouted, raising a hand in greeting. "Me and Gareth are over here!" I tried on a grin as he and Davey approached us, a smile that felt horribly false. "What's happenin'?"

"It's Jimmy and his little brother, Bill," Rob said, and I noticed he was panting and struggling to catch his breath.

"What about them?" I urged when he failed to elaborate any further, even though a good sized part of me dreaded hearing his response. It's funny how many awful potentialities can go racing through your mind at such moments of tension, and I saw a succession of images, each more terrible than the last, spool before my eyes like a video tape on fast forward; the brothers being jumped by a gang of scallies from the estate, their suffering some dreadful accident, their being sexually assaulted by some vile child-molester, their being attacked by a homicidal escapee from a lunatic asylum...

'But when Rob finally spoke, I was left feeling even more mystified than I had before.

"This is probably gonna sound a bit mad, like," he said, sheepishly. "To be honest, it was hard to get much sense out of either brother, they were running that fast and wailin' like a pair of out of control meat-wagons, as I'm sure you heard."

'Gareth and I nodded in agreement. "I think the whole estate must have heard it," I said. "I'm surprised no one called the bizzys or ran out to see what was going on."

"Maybe they all thought it was just some kids messin' about, playing a game, or getting over-excited about it bein' Christmas Eve," Rob said with a shrug. "Who knows? All's I can say for defo is that just as we were approachin' the front gates of their mam and dad's house, I did clearly hear Jimmy say that the two of them had seen somethin' when they were hidin' in that line of hedges, half-way down Festival Road."

"Something?" Gareth asked impatiently. "Something like what?"

"Well, if yer shut yer grid for a minute, I'll tell yer, motor-gob," Rob snapped back, and I wasn't sure if the anger that clouded his face was directed at my best friend for interrupting him or whether it was sheer frustration at being confronted with a set of highly unusual circumstances. I suspect it was the latter, because he heaved a weary sigh before continuing; a solid, weighty sound in the blanketed winter silence.

"Of course, I asked Jim what the hell he was on about, what was it that had so obviously scared the livin' shite out of him and his brother. It's unbelievably hard though, lads I'm tellin' yer, tryin' to get a half-way sensible answer from someone when yer runnin' as fast as yer can just to keep up with them, and when they're clearly scared out of their wits and sobbin' like a couple of girls at the end of some cheesy arl weepie. No wonder I couldn't make much sense of what Jim was babblin', but it sounded like, and ahh, this is gonna sound nutty as a friggin fruitcake, too, but it *sounded* like:

"Oh, God, there's tiny grinning Doll People in the hedge, Rob!"

"Tiny grinning Doll People with pale-blue faces and dead, staring eyes!"

THREE

'Well, it will hardly surprise you to learn that none of us knew quite what to make of any of that. Jim's garbled, panic-stricken comments to Rob, chilling as they undoubtedly were, had made about as much sense to me as the algebra lessons my sadistic maths teacher had begun inflicting upon me and my uniformly blank-faced classmates during the previous autumn term.

'Over the ensuing days, there was much talk between the members of our little gang as to whether the brothers' experience, whatever it was, had been purely imaginary, whether they'd been the victims of some of bizarre kind of practical joke, or, well, whether they really had seen something supernatural in the middle of the hedge, but it was hard to form any opinion given the scarcity of information we had to sift through.

'It turned out that my friends and I had to wait until the day before New Year's Eve to hear the full story of what Jimmy and Bill insisted had taken place during that ill-fated game of hide-and-seek. This was due to the fact that the brothers were too afraid to venture outdoors, save for trips in the car with their parents to visit various relatives during the Christmas holidays, and so therefore, none of us got the chance to speak to either of them directly until a little after midday on the penultimate day of the year.

'In truth, I wouldn't learn the *entire* story for the best part of another twenty years, when, like you, Lee, I'd started producing a small-press publication dealing with the paranormal, and I got to interview Mr Jon Wilkinson, Jimmy and Bill's father, for that "esteemed periodical".

'But if I can crave your patience for just a short while longer, I'd like to deal with events chronologically, if I may:

'This is what the brothers swore took place, (placing their hands on the leather-bound cover of their mum's somewhat battered copy of the Holy Bible as they did so) on that surreal, dream-like Christmas Eve afternoon, when the adult world had seemed lulled to sleep, with no one but us kids walking the empty streets in barely suppressed excitement, and staring in wide-eyed wonder at the scenes of glacial beauty surrounding us. It had been unnaturally silent.

Breathlessly still.

'And truly, anything had seemed possible.'

FOUR

'The brothers thought they'd found the perfect hiding place. One that Rob would be unlikely to overlook entirely, but might well be tempted leaving till last, seeing as though searching the length and breadth of the half-mile length of hedge and its accompanying strip of woodland, could take the best part of half an hour or so to search.

'They weren't even unduly bothered about the fact that it was so bone-freezingly cold amongst the virtually leafless, densely-packed branches, despite having to huddle up together for warmth, their teeth chattering like manic castanets. They were too pumped up, too giddy with anticipation at the prospects of the wondrous night of Christmas Eve that lay before them.

"All we've gotta remember, Bill," Jim assured his younger brother, "is that we've only got to hold out for 30 minutes or so, at most, and then we'll have won the game. Imagine the look on all our mate's faces when they give up looking for us. What a sound way to start the Chrimbo festivities, that'll be!"

"Yeah, and don't forget, we're on *Festival* Road!" Bill sniggered, his breath puffing to clouds so greyly-thick they resembled emissions from the pollution-belching pipes of the nearby Shell Oil Refinery. "Festival Road, do yer gerrit?"

'Bill made a double-fisted salute as though he'd just made a joke of Wildes-ian genius, and though normally Jim would have issued some witheringly sarcastic put-down whilst painfully grinding his knuckles on his brother's forehead, he had been so deliriously happy he'd simply cackled, "Good one, kidder! You are defo the undisputed Comedy King of Elly Port!"

"Whoo hoo!" Billy had yelled, and Jim had mock admonished him by hissing "Aye, aye, keep it down, soft-lad. You'll give us both away," and they'd thrown their hands across their mouths in a cartoonish attempt to keep the betraying fits of giggles at bay, and all had seemed magically right at that moment.

'The reason for their high spirits and low temperature-defying excitement might seem hopelessly trite to us adults, looking back with the supposed benefit of grown-up hindsight, but nevertheless, the boys, bursting with anticipation at this time of year, were particularly looking forward to this particular Christmas Eve, because they had both been granted the rare opportunity to stay up without a babysitter until their parents came home from their annual odyssey to *The Strawberry,* for the very first time. And that meant they had the run of the entire house from seven till midnight.

'They'd already drawn up an itinerary for the evening, which included gorging on chocolate and lemonade, playing a slow motion game of "Headers And Volleys" with a Santa-decorated balloon doubling as a football, dancing to their favourite tunes on their dad's record player, and finishing up with a late-night search for their hidden Christmas presents, all the while keeping an ear out for the dreaded sound of the key in the front door, announcing their parents were home, smelling of beer and whisky and the mouth-watering aromas of their Chinese carry-outs.

'Yeah, they told themselves, it was going to be the very grandest of times. And just to add to the fun, this final hour or so, before sundown, would likely see them bathed in the rosy glow of victory, over their sure to be envious friends.

'Jim and Bill had only been in the hedge for a few minutes, when the air turned dead-still and their view of the houses, glimpsed through the branches, was further obscured by feather-like flakes drifting slowly from the sullen skies.

"Look, Billy, it's started snowing!" Jim whispered excitedly, placing his arm around his brother's shoulders. "If that starts sticking, and God knows it's cold enough, we're gonna wake up tomorrer to a real White Christmas."

"Wow, that would be fantastic," Billy said, struggling hard to keep his voice low. "It'd make a change from the usual pissin' down rain and howlin' wind and the misery-arse gloo...."

'His flow was interrupted just then by a rustling sound coming from somewhere deep within the bushes directly behind them.

"What was that, Jim?" his brother asked, suddenly wide-eyed and fearful.

"Oh, it's nothin' to worry about," Jim replied, in what he hoped were reassuring tones. "Probably just a bird or a wood mouse, or somethin'." He considered for a moment, and then added. "Hey, yer know wha,' it might even have been a hedgehog."

'Bill visibly relaxed and smiled widely at this latter possibility. He was thinking back to the fifth of the November the previous year, when the family, their neighbours, and several of their school-friends had been gathered in their back garden for a mini-firework display, and his dad had found a small creature curled up into a spiky ball in the centre of the pile of combustible refuse and deadwood they'd helped stack for burning on the bonfire. He'd gently picked it up and showed it to the group of assembled children, and the kids had cried delightedly as the hedgehog had slowly unfurled, revealing a shiny black nose that quivered in the flickering glow of the firelight.

"Ahhh, he's dead cute. Can we keep him as a pet?" Bill had pleaded, but his dad had shook his head as he'd placed the animal gently down upon the lawn, well away from the fire and the large rubbish heap in which it had obviously been sheltering. "He belongs out there in the wild, son. We just need to like, sort of nudge him in the general direction of safety, and he can rejoin his family and friends."

'The kids had whooped and cheered and waved their newly-lit sparklers in a bright white sizzling farewell as the hedgehog, shuffling like an old man weighed down with all the cares and troubles of a lifetime, crossed the swathe of wiry grass before slowly disappearing into the clumps of bushes at the bottom of the garden.

'Bill considered this to be one of the most heart-warming of recent memories and it calmed his fears, and he turned to Jim and gasped: "Do you think, if that noise just now really was a hedgehog, it might even have been the same one our dad rescued last Guy Fawkes Night?"

'Jim had smiled, despite himself, and turned to tell Bill, that yeah, it very likely was the very same one, when the rustling in the branches came again, only this time it had been a great deal louder and sounded far more substantial.

'Unnervingly closer, too.

"Aww, shite!" Jim exclaimed, "It must be Rob, looking for us. He's sussed out that we're hiding somewhere in this hedge." He roughly pushed his brother away from him, so forcefully, Bill went sprawling on his hands and knees on the frozen earth in the gaps between the mostly-bare and twisted branches.

"I told you to keep yer gob shut and stay quiet. Yer a useless waste of space, Lad!"

'Bill had looked as though he were about to burst into tears, and very likely would have done if just then, the blade-sharp winter air hadn't have been rent with the sound of twigs snapping like firecrackers. A startling sound that emanated from the thick, densely packed forest of dead-fall and evergreens, just beyond the hedge.

'A powerful smell began drifting from the frozen undergrowth, too. It wasn't unpleasant exactly. On the contrary, it was cloyingly sweet, like the odour of their regular babysitter's perfume when she was all dolled up and waiting for her boyfriend to call round on the sly after she'd none-too-gently ushered the boys up to bed, but out here, in the depths of the winter-wild, there was nothing and no one to account for the aroma. And that was worrying.

'Bill turned to Jim to ask him what he thought the origin of the smell was, but the question died on his lips as the sound of children's high-pitched laughter echoed from somewhere off to their right, and they swivelled their heads in that direction, half-expecting to see a couple of five-year-old kids standing amongst the trees, pointing and giggling at the brother's very obvious fear.

'But the sniggering stopped the moment the boys turned to look, and they could see straight away there was absolutely no one there.

'And then suddenly, the laughter, shrill and teasing, was directly behind them, and they spun around quickly, and this time there was something there.

'Slumped face down in a cleft between the snow-coated branches of the opposite side of the hedge, just a few short feet from where Jim and Bill were crouched, were two, tiny, identically-dressed figures, no more than twelve inches in height, looking for all the world like a pair of hastily discarded toy dolls.

'And quite naturally, that was just what the boys assumed them to be: A couple of unwanted playthings deposited in the hedge by kids, (the same ones currently hiding and laughing at them now, no doubt) attempting to creep them out still further.

"Now how the hell did they sneak up behind us and lob those dolls in the hedge without us seeing or hearing them?" Jim said, more to himself than to his brother. "And what was the point, exactly?"

"Cos they're trying to wind us up?" Billy shrugged. "Or scare us?"

"Huh," Jim snorted, "Well, if that's the case, it defo hasn't worked." He leaned forwards to peer closer at the figures, both of which were clothed head to foot in green, their pants and tunics, their scarves and buckled belts, their low-heeled shoes and pointy caps. "I mean," he spoke loud enough for anyone lurking nearby to hear. "What's so frightenin' about a pair of plazzy dolls?"

"Yeah!" Billy said, curling his lip in an a fair approximation of an Elvis Presley sneer (he'd been secretly practising it in the mirror after seeing a photo of The King in one of his dad's old music magazines). "They must think we're a right pair of fannys. We'll teach them they shouldn't try messin' with us." He winked at Jim and without another word quickly shuffled over to the figures and reached out his hand to grab the one nearest to him. Billy placed his gloved fingers around the doll's mid-riff and went to remove it from the branch but the second he did so jerked his hand back as though he'd suffered an electric shock before spinning around, white-faced and with his eyes very nearly bulging out of their sockets.

"What is it, Bill?" Jimmy yelled, shocked by the look of sheer terror on his brother's face. "What is it? What's wrong?"

'But his brother didn't reply straight away. He just continued to crouch on his haunches with his back to the figures, as though frozen in place, making these tiny, little mewling sounds as he desperately struggled to form words. Jim, who was more unnerved by Bill's behaviour than he cared to admit, scuffled over to him and shook him roughly by the shoulders. "Fer Christ's sake, Bill, what's wrong with yer? What the hell are yer so scared of?"

'When Billy still didn't (or couldn't) answer, Jim all but lost his patience. "Tell me, Bill," he said, removing his thick woollen gloves. "Tell me, or I'll slap yer grid so hard it'll be stingin' till Boxing Day!"

'The threat of receiving one of Jimmy's "Smartin'-Bastard Go-Longer's", as he called them, proved effective, and Billy suddenly threw his arms around his brothers neck and buried his head deep in the folds of Jim's quilted coat.

"Oh, God, Oh, God, Oh, God, Jimmy," he sobbed. "Those things aren't dolls. Those things aren't friggin' dolls!"

"Don't be soft, lad," Jim snapped, though not unkindly. "Of course they're dolls. What else could they be? "I don't know," Billy replied, his voice muffled, his grip on Jim's neck so tight it was painful. "But I do know when I touched one of them just now, it felt warm. Even through my gloves, it felt warm. Like it was alive. Like it was *really* alive."

'He slowly withdrew his face from the coat's padding to look Jim fully in the face: "Jim, I swear on our mam and dad's life, I felt it *breathing*!"

"Right!" Jim exclaimed through gritted teeth. "Okay. Living, breathing, warm-blooded dollies, is it! What a load of arl bollocks!" He chuckled humourlessly. "It's obviously some sort of trick aimed at scaring the livin' crap out of us, and yer can bet yer last few measly pence our gang of so-called mates are behind it all, somehow."

"Buh, but, Jim," Billy stammered, "it's not a tuh-trick. Puh-please, let's just get out of here!"

"Gerrout the way, empty head, and let me at 'em," Jim replied, shoving his brother aside. "Forget hide-and-seek. I'm gonna grab those two little dolly fuckers and volley 'em right down the middle of Festival Road." He stopped to consider for a moment and then half-smiled. "Hey, who knows, maybe if me luck's in the dolls will hit Rob and his merry band of laughin' boys smack in the fuckin' pie hole. That'll teach em!"

'Jim turned back round, and with a defiant yell, stretched out his hands and went to grab the still-slumped figures.

'But the cry caught in his throat when, with shocking suddenness, the two child-like figures, one male and one female, he now saw, suddenly sprang bolt upright, entirely of their own accord.

'Jim took a single step back, and made a tiny, inarticulate noise, that may have been a strangled scream. A breathless gasp of denial. He wanted nothing more at that horribly surreal, nightmarish moment than to turn and grab hold of Bill and charge headlong back through the hedge, but instead he found himself being compelled to stare, transfixed, in silent, wide-eyed horror as the "dolls" eyes flickered open, obsidian black and undeniably dead and yet somehow radiating an inherently evil petulance. Their lips parted too, revealing rows of glistening, yellowed teeth, and they'd both grinned slyly before exchanging glances with each other and bursting into gales of bitter laughter, a cruel and terrible sound that filled the late December air like the voice of soul-destroying desperation, of hopes brutally dashed and the slow and painful death of everything you'd ever held dear.

'And God knows, no one could possibly lend their ears to that dreadful cackling for long and hope to remain even half-way sane....

'But it was only when the two "dolls" leapt with lightning speed from their perch, hit the bone-hard earth with an audible thud, and began quickly shuffling towards the two brothers, that Jim and Bill snapped out of their fear-induced trance. They made no attempt to locate the gap in the hedge through which they'd entered, but instead tore blindly through the densely-packed tangle of thorny branches that clawed and whipped at their faces, somehow managing to avoid tripping over the exposed roots that snaked across the frozen earth, emerged, screaming at the top of their lungs, onto the snow-coated pavements of Festival Road.

'They ran as best and as fast as they could given the adverse weather conditions, towards home, and aside from pausing for the briefest of moments to gabble some nonsensical gibberish to Rob the Seeker, they refused to stop running until they'd reached the assumed safety of their parents' nondescript semi-detached house.

'Once inside, Jim and Bill poured our their story to their mum and dad of how they'd witnessed something terrifying whilst playing hide-and-seek, just down the road, and course, their tale was dismissed with an understandable degree of scepticism if not outright disbelief. When it turned out however, that no amount of reasoned argument or calm words of reassurance could dispel the boys' state of hysteria, the boys' father, Jon, a big burly man with the proverbial heart of gold, offered to accompany his sons back to the hedge so they could point out exactly where it was they had been hiding at the time of their "encounter." He told the pair of frantically head-shaking brothers that he planned to enter the bushes in order to prove to them there was nothing to be afraid of and through all their Dad's powers of persuasion, they eventually agreed to go return with him, on the strict understanding that they would do nothing other than point out the gap between the branches from a distance of at least ten feet away.

"No problem," their dad had said as he threw on his coat and scarf. "I'll go in there alone and let you know if I see anything remotely unusual." He'd clapped them both on the shoulder then before asking, in all sincerity: "What do yer reckon, boys? Does that sound like a fair deal?"

'Jim and Bill had reluctantly agreed that it did, and the trio, each of them wearing their snow boots, and with wildly varying degrees of enthusiasm, determinedly crunched their way back towards Festival Road.

FIVE
'Less than twenty minutes later, the boys' father emerged from the hedge with a double thumbs-up and wearing what he doubtless hoped was his most reassuring smile, and if there had been something slightly hesitant or mildly uncertain about it, surely that was doubtless due to the increasing cold and the rapid onset of twilight.

SIX
"See, what did I tell yer?" he called across to his sons, standing with their arms around each other on the opposite side of the road. "There was absolutely nothing there. No demonic dolls. No invisible, madly giggling children. Nothing."

"Now come on. It's Christmas Eve. Let's go and have some fun!"

'During the short walk home, the brothers tried to tell themselves that the vaguely forced quality of their Dad's cheery tones, was very likely due to the fact that the slowly melting snowflakes crowning his hair were trickling in tiny icy rivulets down the back of his neck, and that's never the most pleasant of sensations.

'And certainly they must have succeeded in convincing themselves that thus was indeed the case, because by the time the Christmas holidays were over, and my friends and I faced the dreaded return to normality that came with the start of the bleak January school term, Jim and Bill had appeared, on the face of it at least, to have entirely accepted they must have somehow imagined the things they'd once sworn on the Good Book they'd seen. When my friends and I queried this sudden change of attitude they grew visibly angry and stormed off, mumbling words to the effect that they didn't want to discuss the matter any further.

'But it's true to say, neither Jim nor Bill were ever quite the same following the events, real or illusory, of that strange day.

'You know it might sound paradoxical but I'd always considered those frequently bickering brothers to be amongst the most constantly cheerful boys I'd ever met. Nothing, not the most seemingly endless spells of crappy weather, the droning diatribes of the boring as hell teachers at secondary school, not even Everton getting beat in a Merseyside Derby, something that seemed to happen with depressing regularity back in the early '80s, ever seemed to get either of them down for very long.

'But following that ill-fated game of hide-and-seek, the two brothers became increasingly surly and withdrawn and pessimistic in their outlook, and as the weeks and months passed by, so the pair of them gradually drifted away from our circle of friends. By the time the following spring rolled round, we were seeing less and less of them, and when the heat of high summer had all but melted away the memories of the previous winter, Jim and Bill had become vaguely recognisable semi-strangers, the kind you favour with the briefest of nods should you happen to pass them by on the street, or in the corridors between classes at school.

'But this wasn't the end of the story.

'Not quite.

'As I stated at the outset, when writing for a small press publication, two whole decades later, I discovered that the boys father, Jon Wilkinson, hadn't been entirely truthful when he'd emerged from the centre of the hedge on that brink-of-twilight Christmas Eve, at the dawn of the 1980s…

SEVEN

'I got to interview Mr Wilkinson, thanks to a mutual friend, who'd told him I was researching an article on paranormal phenomena in and around the Ellesmere Port area, and as he remembered me from the days when I'd been good friends with his two sons, he'd readily agreed to meet me over a drink or two in a local pub called *The Woodland,* (or "The Woody", as some if its more hugely imaginative patrons had long-ago christened it).

'I'd walked into the bar on a glorious summer's evening, at a little after eight, and with the slabs of golden sunlight slanting between the window posters for *Sky Sports* and forthcoming events and food menus, and conversations about ghosts, elemental spirits, or indeed anything remotely supernatural had seemed faintly ridiculous. But I'd ordered a drink, a soft one, because I'd been in the midst of one of my notoriously short-lived get fit campaigns, and glanced around the half-empty bar-room.

'I'd spotted Jon, straight away. He really hadn't changed that much, aside from the fact that his formerly jet-black hair was now streaked with silver-grey, and the moment he'd caught my eye, he'd smiled thinly and gestured towards the empty seat directly opposite him. With a thumbs-up, I'd approached the table and placed my pint of horribly watery looking blackcurrant juice topped with tiny brittle slivers of ice that were already melting and adding to the general, well...wateriness of the less-than-refreshing-looking drink, onto a soggy beer mat and sat myself down.

'Like I say, I could hardly claim to know Mr Wilkinson that well. I hadn't seen him for a good few years, and I'd feared our initial conversation would be a little awkward and filled with the sort of trivial small talk most of us use to fill in the gaps between embarrassing silences. I needn't have worried, though. No sooner had I taken my seat, and reached into my pocket for my Dictaphone, than Jon had taken a huge gulp of his pint of lager, threw back a single malt whisky chaser and immediately launched into the story he'd only ever previously shared with one of his closest friends, and then, only when he'd been (as he'd appeared to be on this occasion) three sheets to the wind.

'Having heard what he had to say, I found I could scarcely blame him for getting in that state: all glassy-eyed and slightly slurred of speech…

"Yer wanna hear somethin' *really* strange, lad?" he began, leaning towards me so that I could almost physically *see,* never mind smell, the alcohol fumes on his breath. "I mean, somethin' even stranger than the impossible things me two boys swore they'd seen on that colder-than-a-witch's arse cheeks afternoon?"

'I'd nodded, though I'd guessed the question was entirely rhetorical, and subtly switched on my tape machine.

"The very second Jim and Bill came chargin' along the hallway like the Devil Himself was at their heels, before they'd even begun babblin' on about "invisible kids" and what they called "evil, grinning Doll People," I knew exactly whereabouts they'd been playin', and that whatever had so obviously scared the hell out of them was very likely *real,* in some sense." He'd sighed, and drained the last of his pint, before adding. "The most relevant sense. The only one that really counts, anyway."

"How do you mean?" I prompted as he'd reached for one of the three frothing, full-to-the-brim lagers gathered on the table before him. "How could you possibly have known that?"

'Jon didn't answer straight away. Instead his eyes took an even more glassy sheen, his jaw fell slack, and though he'd been sat right there directly opposite me, at that precise moment, he may as well have been about a billion light years removed from the bright, sun-lit confines of that dusty, summer evening bar-room. I may have been barely thirty years old, back then, and I had thankfully lived a life shorn of the personal tragedies and awful experiences that had sadly befallen so many of my friends and associates, but I had often witnessed the soul-wrenching pain in others caused by the dredging up of bitter recollections, or of things they are plainly at a loss to explain. I might have told Jon, Mr Wilkinson, that is, to forget discussing a subject that had so obviously upset him to the point where he felt compelled to drink himself half-insensible before he could even bear to make reference to it, but just then, he'd suddenly shook his head and I'd seen awareness slide back into his features like seawater surging into a scooped-out sand-trench when the tide comes rolling in.

"Sorry," he said, smiling ruefully, "I lost meself there for a minute. What was I saying?"

'I opened my mouth to answer, but before I could speak, Jon sighed and said; "Ahh, yeah. I was, I believe, just about to give voice to my opinion that there are places out there, certain places, *haunted* places, for want of a better term, where a subtle sense of the-not-quite-right exists. Something off-kilter. Something plain *wrong....*"

'He let the words hang in the stale bar-room air whilst peering at me, his eyes narrowed to slits, as if daring me to contradict him.

"What'd yer reckon, lad? Does that sound to you like I've had one too many bevvies, or that I'm suffering from a late mid-life crisis and me marble collection's gone rolling half-way down the road to full-blown senility?"

"No, I don't,' I said, leaning forwards excitedly, "On the contrary, Mr Wilkinson, I think you're defo onto something there, and I....."

"Never mind," he said, dismissing me as if I hadn't spoken. "I don't give a flyin' fuck what you think, to be honest." He raised his glass as if toasting his fellow drinkers (most of whom were clustered round the tiny TV screen watching the England cricket team getting snotted by the Aussies, yet again) with the stating of some great and immutable truth.

"They're like borderlands, these places," Jon had all but yelled. "Borderlands, between our world and some other, darker realm, a ragged rent where the veil is thinnest, through which all manner of awful things can, on occasion, slip through into our world.

"I know it sounds mad like, but I've come across these gaps, these portals, several times on me travels around this country, and abroad, too. Not on a regular basis, like, but often enough to convince me of their existence. That they are real. And I learned something else, too. They're not always in what might be considered obvious locations. The type of spot dripping with dollops of eerie atmosphere like an old shuttered mansion on some blasted heath, a stretch of lonely-lookin' moorland, or the dark waters of some remote, Scottish loch." He paused for a moment to consider. "I mean, *sometimes* they are, but maybe not as often as you might expect."

"I think I know what you mean," I said nodding vigorously, "I've felt the same about   certain places...."

"Kindly shut yer gob, lad!" Jon snapped, clearly unimpressed with my attempts to empathise with him. "This isn't easy for me to talk about, yer know. If you interrupt me one more time, I'm gonna get up and leave, but before I do, I'll be sure to ram that tape machine yer holdin' so far up yer fudge tunnels you'll be shittin' mini cassette reels for weeks! Have I made myself clear?"

'I clamped my mouth shut, gulped loudly, and not trusting myself to speak, gave a rather shaky thumbs-up to indicate he'd made himself *perfectly* clear.

"Good," said Jon. "I can get on with me story. I just need to wet me whistle first." So saying, he downed the remainder of his pint, and slammed the empty glass on the table.

"Me arl fella knew about these type of places, too, these "Borderlands". Only he had a far more fancy term for 'em: "Sites redolent with baleful echoes". How poetic is that?" Jon chuckled . "I've often thought the local council should post up a sign with those very words written in letters twenty feet high at either end of the thin stretch of woodland that lines one side of Festival Road. Yer know the place I'm talking about? Don't bother answerin.' The question's purely rhetorical. Of course, yer know. It's right by where you and yer mates used to have kick-a-bouts and proper, eleven-aside footy matches. Just around the corner from where you and yer mam and dad lived on Princes Road. Yeah, you know it well. The hedge and the woods where Jim and Billy were playing a traditional kids game on Christmas Eve, twenty-odd years ago, and......"

'Jon had suddenly paused, and once more he'd leaned towards me, but this time an unmistakable look of pure astonishment had lit up his face. "Dear God!" he exclaimed. "You really *do* know it well. Know it for what it truly is, I mean." He'd rubbed his eyes as though he might be dreaming. "Christ, and all this time I thought I was the only one to sense the place's aura of wrongness. Well, aside from my two sons, that is. No one, not my friends, not my neighbours, not even the residents who live in the houses on the opposite side of that damned road, not a single one of 'em has ever mentioned they've felt anything remotely strange or unusual about the place."

'He chuckled again, a deep and throaty sound that spoke of too many days and nights spent drinking in smoky pubs and bars, and added, "Maybe it was fate that brought me here this evening to talk to you and share my story, short and frustratingly inconclusive though it is. I wasn't gonna come at one point. I almost cancelled at the last minute. But I'm so glad now that I didn't."

'Jon had shocked me by reaching across the table to shake my free hand, almost causing me to drop my Dictaphone. "You have no idea how relieved I am to meet someone who can see these places for what they are: Sly. Sneaky. Cunning. *Evil*, if that's not too strong a word, for an old atheist like me"

'He finally released my hand, and I had to resist the temptation to gently massage my fingers, so firm had been his grip.

"Well, at least now I don't feel quite so reluctant to tell you about my own experience. I know you won't take the piss when we're done here, or dismiss me as being an out-and-out bladdered gob-a-loon." He laughed, and now there was some trace of genuine humour there, I was heartened to see. "Well, okay, I admit the bladdered part may still be applicable."

'I laughed along too, feeling at ease for the first time since I'd sat down to interview this unusual man, part bad-tempered drunkard, part highly articulate individual, and I actually summoned up the courage to speak. "Well, it's no wonder to me now that you knew straight away where your sons had been playing when they ran screaming, terrified out of their wits," I said. "But didn't it ever cross your mind to warn them to stay away from The Hedge and the wooded area?"

"A fair question," Jon replied, "and one I've asked meself *countless times.* I suppose I should have had a word with them. But would they have listened or taken any notice? You know how kids are. Tell em to stay away from somewhere; the iced-over pond, the old, closed-down factory yard, the local rubbish tip, you may as well tell them to head off down there, straight away. Oh, you'll love it. It's a veritable kids' wonderland."

'I smiled and nodded, remembering the many occasions my friends and I would solemnly promise our parents that we'd steer well clear of the places they declared were strictly off-limits, and genuinely *mean* it ... at least as long as the time it took for us to take a break from whatever game it was we were playing, wolf down our packed lunches and discuss how we should spend the remainder of the day. And inevitably, and with minimal discussion, we'd head directly for one of "The Forbidden Sites", peering guiltily over our shoulders but with shame-faced hyena grins splitting our faces.

"So, no I didn't warn them," Jon shrugged. "But I'd be willing to bet the last time they ever went within half a mile of that perfectly ordinary, but nonetheless terrible place, was the time they accompanied me on the return journey in the snowy, twilit dusk of that-long-ago Christmas Eve."

EIGHT

"Something else I've asked meself many times over the years is why it was I'd been so insistent that the three of us should head back out to the hedge straight away, in the midst of a virtual blizzard, and with the last dregs of daylight rapidly fading. It's fair to say as mature and considered adult responses to resolving a child's trauma go, my genius brain-wave wasn't ever gonna feature highly in any Parental Guidance Manual.

"I think perhaps the most plausible answer though, and certainly the one that I've come to accept as making the most sense to me, is that I desperately wanted to be utterly wrong about the sinister nature of the locale, for me suspicions to be hopelessly off the mark, for me wife's assertion that our sons had been made the victims of a cruel, but ultimately harmless prank to be proved one hundred per cent right.

"But more than anything, I'd wanted to help convince Jim and Bill that there was absolutely nothing to be afraid of, not least so's I could get to see the terror fall from their faces like an ugly mask, and see the wide, full-of-the-joys-of-the-season smiles they'd both been wearing when they'd left the house that morning.

"So it was then that I wound up stumbling my way through that thorny thicket, whilst me sons stood huddled, arm in arm, on the opposite side of the silent, deserted road, their dark forms silhouetted by the glow of multicoloured strings of fairy lights and Christmas trees flashing in the windows of the rows of red-bricked council houses.

"Although my sons had only pointed in the general direction of where they'd been hiding, I'd been able to tell straight away where they'd made their panic-stricken exit from the hedge. It was abundantly clear from the amount of broken stems and splintered branches, and I'd stood there for a second, with my gloved hands in my pockets, peering into the gloom.

I didn't feel remotely afraid. Not then. I'd only hesitated for a moment precisely because of this distinct lack of foreboding. It wasn't at all what I'd expected, and it had thrown me a little.

"Are you okay, Dad?" Jim had shouted, his voice trembling with concern. "Yer really don't have to go in there if yer don't want to, yer know."

"I'd turned and smiled reassuringly, though it's doubtful they could see it given their distance from me and the gathering murk. "No worries, boys, I'm sound," I shouted back. "I'll be in and out before yer know it. See yer in a bit!"

"I raised my arm and waved, turned my back on my boys and the neat and orderly terraced houses stretched out behind them, and entered the wildness of the hedgerow and the thin strip of woodland beyond...

NINE

"When I parted the ice-cold branches and began making my way inside, the logical part of me assumed that if I were to find anything at all, it would probably be nothing other than a couple of plastic-toy, *Ken* and *Barbie* dolls, all dressed up in plain green faerie, or elven-type outfits, tied with all-but invisible strands of wire to the branches of a tree or a bush, by a gang of kids determined to scare my two sons half to death.

"This was the sane explanation for what had happened, anyway, and if such proved to be the case, I'd dared to hope there was a chance the dolls might still be tied there. If so, I'd planned to drag them from their perch and show them to Jim and Bill, and I'd afforded myself a smile at the prospect of their heroic Dad, single-handedly dispelling their fears in one fell swoop, and of being sat gathered around the dinner table the following day, laughing good-naturedly about the "Terror of the Doll People" as we tucked into our Christmas dinner.

"But just then, a very odd thing happened.

"I'd made my way through the hedge and was stooping under the branches of a silver birch, when a pale-white wispy cloud that carried with it the unmistakeable aroma of pipe tobacco, had begun drifting towards me from somewhere amongst the tangled mass of undergrowth, no more than couple of feet in front of me. It was a poignantly nostalgic aroma, hugely evocative of my childhood, but I want you to understand that the memories that old, familiar fragrance brought to mind were not remotely pleasant ones. On the contrary, the moment I'd become aware of the scent, tendrils of sheer terror had slithered into my veins, and rendered me immobile, quite literally frozen in place, unable to take a single step in any direction. All that I was able to do was to narrow my suddenly streaming eyes and squint towards the origin of that pungent odour as trails of smoke, curled snake-like from the icy thickets.

"All the while, dreading what I might be forced to see.

'"How long I remained crouched there, shivering in the biting cold, I'm not entirely sure, but it could only have been minutes, at most, because when I heard the noise of a branch snapping, shockingly loud in the silence, I could see there were still remnants of daylight slanting down through the gaps in the trees marching along the edge of the playing fields.

"The noise had been so sudden and unexpected, but strangely familiar, too, and I'd stumbled backwards a little, emitting the tiniest of screams. An awful recollection surfaced with the snapping of the bough. A vile memory of something I'd long ago buried deep within the darkest wells of my subconscious…

"My old secondary school…

"The Victorian monstrosity, encircled by thick, red-bricked walls and a spike-topped metal fence, it had been my misfortune to attend during my teenage years. The uniformly wooden desks, equipped with long-obsolete inkwell holes, and with dried up husks of apple cores, stale bread crusts and the obligatory rolled-up ball of pink chewing gum keeping the wallpaper-backed exercise books company beneath their squeaky lids.

"The toilets that smelled of discarded ciggie stubs, soggy paper towels and cheap, rock-hard bars of odourless soap. The huge, grime-encrusted, plate-glass windows and the ever-present motes of chalk dust spinning lazily in pools of grey-light.

"And presiding over all, the cruelly sadistic headmaster, who's real name I won't reveal here, for reasons that will soon become clear, but who the pupils, and indeed, most of the teachers called (behind his back at least) "Stooky Bill".

"This was due to the uncanny resemblance the headmaster bore to the creepy-looking ventriloquist's dummy christened with that name, featured on a poster adorning the walls of our science and technology class. With its coal-black eyes, bushy eyebrows, mirthless smile and greasy-looking, slug-like lips, the puppet doll was certainly a dead-ringer for the terrifying bane of our miserable school-days.

"And on a drizzly, windswept day in Mid-November.....

"*Stooky Bill is standing centre stage upon his pedestal, holding court during morning assembly. I'm thirteen years of age, and I am paying him not the slightest degree of attention. I have my head buried in a* Whizzer & Chips *comic book and am so engrossed in the antics of "Shiner" and "Sid's Snake," that I'm not aware I've been spotted by old Stooky, even when he pauses mid-way through a 'rousing speech' about the importance of Church, School and State, and an expectant hush descends upon the packed assembly hall.*

"*I only look up when one of my friends elbows me in the ribs and I glance up and I see the headmaster pointing a single bony finger in my direction. 'You there, boy!' he says, in deceptively pleasant tones.*

'*Who, sir, me sir?' I mumble, hoping against hope, he is indicating some other luckless soul sat amongst the silent crowd of first to fifth-year pupils.*

'*Yes sir, you, sir,' he replies, an almost merry chuckle underlying the subtle threat in his voice. 'Could you please stand up, young man.'*

"*On legs that have turned to jelly, and suddenly desperate for the toilet I do as he asks, and struggle slowly to my feet.*

'*Now,' he says, holding his hand over his mouth as if to restrain an errant giggle. 'I wonder whether you could possibly hold aloft the doubtless esteemed publication I saw you perusing just now, for all those present here to see?'*

"*My face burning with embarrassment, I hold up the comic, and after narrowing his owlish eyes to coal-black slits, Mr Stooky peers at the formerly bright and cheerful cartoon cover, that now seems somehow crumpled and dreary-looking.*

"'*Mr Stooky' doesn't seem to mind, though. He chortles long and hard, and waves his arms to encourage the assembled pupils to laugh along with him; though even I can tell, young as I am, that it's a laughter born of heartfelt relief that it's not one of them stood there alone in the centre of that cavernous hall.*

"When at last he holds up his hands for silence, the assembly falls quiet, as though someone had switched off the telly or lowered the volume on a radio.

'Oh my word,' Mr Stooky says, wiping tears from his eyes. 'You are truly precious, young man. Truly, truly precious.

'Tell me, what is your name?'

'Jon Wilkinson, sir.'

'Is it, indeed?' he says, and pauses, as if considering some slice of philosophical wisdom, before nodding to himself as if he'd reached a definite decision. 'Well now, Mr Wilkinson, I think it best that you pass that work of literary genius to your form teacher for safekeeping. And having performed that task, you may sit down and remain seated for the remainder of this assembly.'

"I do as I am told, not daring for a second to believe that I have escaped punishment, and been let off so lightly. It soon turns out I haven't, of course.

"No sooner have I handed the comic to Mr Williams, a kindly faced man in his mid-20s who teaches music and is a halfway decent acoustic guitarist, and sat myself down beside my class-mates, than Mr Stooky's voice booms out from the stage and echoes round the hall.

'Oh, and Mr Wilkinson,' the headmaster yells (and there's still humour there, but it's increasingly forced). 'Would you do me the very great honour of reporting to my study at the chiming of the home-time bell. There are a few things you and I need to discuss, prior to your embarking upon the long trek homewards in the company of your school chums.'

'Yuh, yuh, yes, sir,' I mumble. 'Very good,' he says, smiling slyly. 'Yes, yes, very good. I look forwards to it, immensely.'

"I soon find he isn't exaggerating. Not remotely...

"Now the images come thick and fast, a kaleidoscope spun at whirlwind speed.

"The plain oaken door of Mr Stooky's study at the final peal of the hometime bell.

"I knock twice and he bids me to enter, and the moment I step into the room the headmaster, his features all but obscured by the thick fug of smoke swirling from his pipe, rises slowly from his desk and beckons me towards the empty, plush leather chair directly opposite him. I assume he wants me to sit down, but before I can do so, he steps towards me and places an arm across my chest.

''That chair is not for sitting on!' he declares, and there is no trace of humour, real or affected in his voice. His tones are brisk and business-like and he clearly considers time to be of the essence.

201

'It's a reclining chair,' he says pointing to it. 'Do you know what that means, Mr Wilkinson?'

'It means it leans right back so yer can lie flat on it,' I reply.

'Very good, boy.' He gestures towards the chair. 'So, let's get on it with it, shall we?'

"*I don't move. I feel hot saliva leap into my mouth, and when I swallow it tastes bitter and metallic, and I find myself staring at the book-lined walls, the shelves crammed with hard-backed volumes stretching all the way up to the ceiling.*

"*I find my eyes drawn to the framed pictures on the walls, too. The reproductions of madly complicated scenes, with titles like* The Garden of Earthly Delights *by Hieronymus Bosch and* Night Hag Visiting The Lapland Witches *by Henry Fuseli.*

'Come on, come on,' Mr Stooky urges impatiently. 'We haven't got all evening. I have things to do. Important things. Things that really can't wait. Take your trousers down, young man, and then lie face down across the chair, if you'd be so very kind.'

"*I wanted to turn and run from that smoke-filled room, but you have to remember that this was the late 1960s. Not so very long ago, relatively speaking, but a billion light years distant from today in terms of secondary education. Back then, corporal punishment was rife, and was administered for the slightest of misdemeanours. Such things were simply accepted. Deemed to be as much a part of school-day ritual as detention classes, musty-smelling lost property boxes and being forced to run across the rain-sodden playing fields in the depths of midwinter in flimsy PE kits.*

'So I find myself doing exactly as I am told. Shamefaced and terrified. But wholly compliant for all that.

'And whilst I prepare myself as best I can, anxious to get this over with, I glance over my shoulder as Mr Stooky reaches into a desk drawer, withdraws something, and strides purposefully towards me. When he is just a foot or so behind, I see he has produced a whip-thin bamboo cane which he holds in his right hand and swishes through the air, slicing through the bluish pipe-smoke that swirls around the room. His other hand meanwhile is almost casually rubbing the area around his groin, and there is a highly visible bulge forming beneath the fabric of his suddenly too-tight trousers, whilst flecks of foamy slobber drool at the corners of those fat, greasy, slug-like lips. I am filled with the awful knowledge that Mr Stooky is visibly aroused by the pain and humiliation he is about to inflict .

"*I hastily avert my gaze and instead find myself staring once more to the paintings on the walls, the hugely detailed depictions of angelic beings and demonic entities, and they seem to me to provide the perfect backdrop to the sound of my screams as the cane makes contact with my bare flesh; a noise like branches snapping in a wildwood*

"*And then at last it's over.*

"*Mr Stooky, sweating and panting and struggling for breath after his exertions, makes his way to his desk and slumps in his seat, whilst I painfully pull up my trousers with tears streaming down my face.*

"Very well, Mr Wilkinson," the headmaster wheezes, *"that will be all."*

"I sob, and unable to look him in the face, I slowly limp towards the door. As I reach for the brass handle however, I hear a sound behind me like hot, bubbling mud, and I feel compelled to crane my neck to detect its source. And when I do I see Mr Stooky gazing at me, his eyes wild with lust and desire, his teeth clenched in a feral grin, and I realise the sound I'd heard was his low, throaty chuckle.

"Yes, that most certainly will *be all, boy."* he says.

"I open the door and step outside with my hands clamped firmly over my ears, but still his final two words follow me out into the corridor, and reverberate along the path of the dreadful, abuse-filled school years that still lay before me.

"For now, boy! **For Now!***"*

NINE

"And had I really thought that my finally leaving that Dickensian abomination of a school behind after three years of torment, both mental and physical, or that my attempts since at burying those very darkest of memories deep beyond recall, could ever hope to secure my freedom from Mr Stooky's malign influence?

"If so, I was to be sorely mistaken.

"For there, crouched in the rapidly falling dark of those mid-winter woods, amidst the all-too familiar tobacco scents, the sounds of wood snapping or striking naked flesh, I could have sworn I heard my former headmaster calling my name, beckoning me to his study, an ethereal whisper that drifted towards me like a voice in a dream…

"And if I doubted my other senses, the shocking sight of an impossibly tiny face, glistening and pale and somehow plastic looking, and with its mouth twisted into a sneer of pure contempt, suddenly looming up from the pitch-black centre of the wild and thorny shrubs, provided hideous proof that try as we might, we can never truly escape the ghosts of our past.

"It was a doll's face, of course.

"A long-dead face.

"Mr Stooky's face.

"A face that smiled and nodded confirmation as it continued to emerge more fully from amidst the frozen vegetation.

"My nerve snapped then. I somehow managed to scramble to my feet and I began wildly flailing my way back towards the gap in the hedge, all the while clamping my mouth firmly shut, determined not to frighten my two sons, who I hoped, were still waiting for me on the other side of the road, the pair of them praying for reassurance that all their fears were groundless.

"It seemed to take an inordinate amount of time to locate the ragged opening in the hedge, but that was doubtless due to the fact that I was disorientated by fear and the diminishing quality of light, and when at last I found it and staggered through the gap, I heaved a sigh of relief, and sought desperately to compose myself.

"I saw my two boys, still standing huddled together half-way along the opposite side of the road, bathed in the Yuletide glow; the false festive cheer of cruel, dead December.

"I raised my hands to wave and hoped, given the distance, they wouldn't notice how badly they were shaking, and began making my way towards them, the treacherous snow and ice thankfully masking the true reason for the unsteadiness of my progress.

"It was just as I was about to cross the road that I swear I heard what sounded like cold-hearted laughter, child-like, and yet incredibly ancient, emanating from somewhere high in the trees directly above me. It resembled the spiteful sniggering of those who derive pleasure from playing the cruellest of practical jokes on the unwary, and I felt compelled to crane my neck to glance upwards at the leafless, snow-encrusted branches…

"And saw nothing.

"Nothing…

"Save for a single bough, gently vibrating and with tiny particles of snow sifting from its newly-bare surface, as though a bird or some small animal had just vacated it.

"And I ran then, as best as I could, grinning like a loon from ear to ear, to meet my boys.

TEN

"The rest, of course, you know," Jon said, leaning back in his chair, yet still holding my gaze. "And for what it's worth, I want to thank yer for sitting there all quiet and patient and hearing me out."

"No worries, Jon, it was a pleasure," I said, and I meant it. "Thank *you* very much for sharing your experience. It must take a lot of courage to unburden yourself of something that's still so emotionally raw."

"Ha," he replied slapping the table so hard it caused several of the mostly empty pint glasses to rattle loudly on the shiny metal surface. "You bet it does, lad. It hurts deep down in what the old priest, the one who spent two years counselling me during me late teens, used to call *'the God part of your soul.'*"

"I didn't know quite what to say to that, to be honest, and it turned out it didn't matter much, because he suddenly rose, somewhat unsteadily to his feet, picked up the last of his single malts and downed it in one, burping so loudly several of the men that stood glued to the TV screen, spun round to glance in his direction. They soon looked away, though.

"I don't expect people to believe any of me story, like," he said, still gripping the whisky tumbler. "Even though, strangely enough, I strongly suspect at least a part of *you* does believe. Probably 'cos of what you yourself have seen in this life. What you've experienced. What you've *felt*."

"I went to answer, but he cut me short. "Nah, lad," he said. "I'm all talked-out now. I do feel sort of cleansed talking' to you, like a massive weight's been lifted, and all that, but at the same time, I can't help feeling sort of deflated, like a shaken-up, punctured beer can, with all the sparkle, all the vim and vigour spittin' and hissin' right out of me. I reckon my only option is to fill this table up with drinks once more and then line them up and count each one off like a rosary. It might help me to forget it all again. Those things we've dredged you, you and I. For tonight, anyway."

'He laid a large hand of my shoulder and gave it a gentle squeeze. "See yer around, lad," he said, and like a big ship cast upon stormy, turbulent seas, slowly swayed his way to the bar.

'I switched off my tape machine, pushed back my chair, and stepped outside into sweet summer twilight, and the breathless, still-trapped heat of the day gone by....'

BASED ON THE WRITTEN ACCOUNT OF RICHIE WHITE,
Ellesmere Port, Summer 2000.

A BRIEF SERIES OF AUTHORIAL WAFFLINGS
MASQUERADING AS FOOTNOTES

First off, I'd like to state that I am not a big fan of the 'expert-in-the-field' overviews, tagged on to the end of an account of a percipients 'supernatural'/hallucinatory/externalisation of unconscious archetypes/temporal lobe related event (delete where your views deem applicable, or indeed, feel free to add your own) as a kind of horribly self-opinionated, hopelessly biased, one-eye-on-the-word-count pile of space-filling drivel.

You usually find them attached, like a hideously bloated leech to the underside of a chapter dealing with the alleged experience of a witness, or located at the back of the book in the impressively official sounding *Appendices* section.

To coin a Scouse phrase: 'It does me swede raahh in, la!'

Having said all that, and at the risk of sounding like an er, horribly self-opinionated, hopelessly biased, one-eye-on-the-word-count pile of space-filling drivel, several things occurred to me when I first read about this fascinating, if highly unnerving experience.

First off, in yet another example of the sort of curious coincidences that seemingly plague writer's when collating supposedly true stories of the paranormal, I'd been busy proof-reading and editing the final draft of this chapter of the book, when during an hour's lunch break, I'd sat down with a piping hot veggie pasty, to read some more of Stuart Maconie's excellent book *Hope And Glory: A People's History of Britain.*

Whilst browsing through the pages, I came across a chapter dealing with the history of television, and there, almost leaping up out of the page at me, was a brief reference to none other than *Stooky Bill: "The First Ever TV star."*

I have to confess, I had never heard of this character prior to receiving Richie White's letter, but I soon discovered that

Stooky Bill was indeed the name given to a typically disturbing-looking ventriloquist's doll by John Logie Baird, the Scottish scientist who back in the mid- to late-1920s, had been carrying out experiments aimed at broadcasting recognisable images, ie human faces, via primitive TV transmissions from his laboratory in London, to other parts of the UK, and beyond.

Putting Stuart's book to one side for a second, I decided to Google the subject and sure enough, the 'font of all knowledge' that is Wikipedia stated that "Stooky" or "Stookie" is Scots for stucco or for a plaster cast used to immobilise bone fractures. The term is also used to describe someone who is slow-witted or awkward in his movements, which seeing as how it turns out the doll was little more than a garishly-painted head on a stick, seems a fairly accurate way of describing the pretty much sedentary "Mr Stooky B esq."

At the time of the experiments, the excessive heat involved in lighting the subjects of the transmissions was so great that the scientists were forced to use test dummies rather than live humans.

That was about it as far as Wikipedia was concerned, so I returned to Stuart Maconie's account of the transmitting of the first ever TV signals from the UK to continental Europe (more specifically, Berlin, Germany), in July, 1929. The author quotes Baird's chief engineer, Jay Barton-Chapple as saying: *'My heart pounded as we waited for our colleagues in Berlin to make contact. Heaven knows how Baird felt waiting at headquarters. Then came the familiar whirring sound through the ether. Our men in Berlin were coming through, and upon my soul, so was an image on the screen. It was blurred at first, then it became a crude face....'*

'The face of a gnome with a pointed beard and a peaked hat.' *(My highlights).*

Equally intriguing were Stuart Maconie's observations following the author's own 21st century visit to Kingsbury Veteran's Group (formerly used by Baird's team of scientists, back in the 1920s):

'I've seen that gnome before,' he writes. 'I was ushered through the downstairs rooms of a building, and I saw the doll. And it was creepy. I was shown it by some friendly techie history types whom I was put in touch with. They brought the doll down to Kingsbury Manor when they met me in an upstairs room. Baird and his posse seem to have enjoyed using ghoulish dolls for their researchers.

'The first ever TV star ever was a fellow called "Stooky Bill." Fellow's a bit of an exaggeration. Bill was actually just the painted head of a ventriloquist's dummy used by Baird in the very first TV pictures ever sent from room to room. "Stooky" was used (as the subject) his lurid doll's face with its mad smile melting and frying under the intense heat. The resulting images comprehensively creeped me out when I saw them. 'Nightmarish and flickering...'

I found myself returning to Richie White's account, and in particular, Bill and Jim's description of the entities they claim to have seen (and to a lesser, and rather more ambiguous extent, the account related by their father), in the midst of that small area of woodland on the edge of an ordinary housing estate.

As someone who has long been fascinated by alleged real life encounters with the inhabitants of "The Middle Kingdom", I considered Jim and Bill's experience to be of great interest, whilst their dad's story, unsettling as it undoubtedly is, reads more like some sort of subconscious memory of childhood terrors that had suddenly risen to the surface after decades of suppression, triggered by the eerie atmosphere of that wooded locale.

Leaving aside the possibility that the witnesses have deliberately fabricated their accounts for some unknown purpose, or that they simply misperceived or imagined the whole thing, there are some points I'd like to make, that may or may not have a bearing as to the potential "reality" of the phenomena described here.

To start with, let's consider the time of both alleged experiences. The twilight.

What the Scots, with a typical display of poetic lyricism call "The Gloaming". According to ancient tradition, that peculiar combination of semi-darkness and thin, diluted daylight is supposed to be one of the most propitious times to encounter all manner of otherworldly creatures, including Hobgoblins, Gnomes and Pixies and other dark inhabitants of The Realm of the Faerie.

Of course, I'm well aware that this last paragraph may well inspire a snorting fit of hysterical giggles amongst even the most open-minded of readers, and I can hardly blame them for doing so. After all, we live in an increasingly cynical age, and our perception of Faeries has long since been well and truly *Disney*fied, to such an extent that most people nowadays consider them to be about as threatening a prospect as a depressed Samurai warrior falling onto a cheap and brittle plastic sword with a pathetically hopeless sigh.

But it wasn't always that way.

As the author Roger Clarke points out in his *A Natural History of Ghosts (*Particular Books, 2012), "Curious though it may seem to the modern individual suffused with pop culture, Faeries and Elves were considered extraordinarily dangerous in the past. A film like *'Paranormal Activity'* is much closer to the lore of Faerie-folk than *'Lord of the Rings.'"*

Other students of the subject have also pointed out that for centuries, people across Europe, believed that the Twelve Days of Christmas, the darkest, bleakest part of winter, were up there with Halloween and Walpurgisnacht (May Eve), as being another of those times when, as the author Paul Hawkins, describes; "malevolent spirits, devils and witches were granted licence to wander the earth searching for doomed souls to feast upon. Goblins too, were said to venture above ground to spread strife and mischief amongst the population. They stole things, destroyed property and even abducted children in order to turn them into one of their own. (*Bad Santas* - Paul Hawkins (*Simon & Schuster, 2013).*

Not only that, but these evil entities possessed the power of "Glamour," the ability to take on wildly different forms, and Katherine Briggs, one of the foremost "experts" on all aspects of Faerie Lore has written of how this shape-shifting gift is a form of "mesmerism or enchantment cast over the senses, so that things were perceived or not perceived as the enchanter wished."

As I've already made reference to at the start of this chapter, the apparent connection between the children's game of hide-and-seek, and the sighting of mysterious entities, is not something I've ever heard mentioned anywhere amongst the works of paranormal researchers or the annals of Fortean literature, and perhaps that's because any connections are purely coincidental....

However, I can't help wondering...

Various authors when writing about the subject of Faeries and/or the Faerie-like creatures reportedly seen emerging from landed UFOs, have made reference to their propensity for acting in a manner that could be described as a form of ritualistic dancing or game playing, and though their behaviour appears curiously child-like to the witnesses, it may be of extreme significance to the entities. Consider these examples:

According to an account in Janet Bord's excellent book; *Fairies: Real Encounters With Little People,* (Michael O Mara, 1997), on October 25th, 1985, in Norway, a large number of 'Little People' were reportedly seen by a group of children, aged between seven and twelve, whilst they were outside watching a lunar eclipse. It was a freezing cold night, and as they huddled together for warmth, the children suddenly became aware of a strange oval light in the clear skies that gradually began to descend towards them. When eventually the source of the light touched the ground one of the more adventurous kids decided on a whim to shine their torch beam in the direction of the anomalous light and there, illuminated in the bright flash-light beam, the children claimed they were clearly able to discern "a hundred tiny beings less than two feet tall standing in the road. They all wore box-like structures on their heads, and were all different colours including white, brown and black. They ran away on seeing the children, but were seen repeatedly during he next three hours, *sometimes apparently playing a game like hide-and-seek'* (my italics).

And in his book *Fairies,* the renowned author Edward L.Gardner, included the following account related to him by a woman referred to as Miss Hall, who hailed from Bristol, England. 'My only sight of a fairy was in a large wood in West Sussex. He was a little creature about half a foot high, dressed in leaves.

'I was a child of six or seven years, and then, as now, passionately fond of all flowers. I was seated in the middle of some cornfields, playing with a group of poppies, and never shall I forget my utter astonishment at seeing a funny little man playing *hide-and-seek* (my italics, again), amongst these flowers to amuse me, as I thought. He was quick as a dart. I watched him for quite a long time, then he disappeared. He seemed a merry little fellow, but I cannot ever remember his face. In colour he was sage green, his limbs were round and had the appearance of geranium stalks. He did not seem to be clothed, and was about three inches high, and slender. I often looked for him again but without success.'

There are other similar instances on record too, enough evidence, as I say, to give me cause to ponder whether there's a connection between otherworldly beings and the games we played as children.

Although quite what that might be..... ?

To conclude this chapter, which has already stretched on for far longer than I'd intended, I'd like to make a brief reference to the notion that certain places, certain locations, are somehow inherently, if indefinably, 'wrong.'

It was something both Jon Wilkinson and Richie White felt worthy of mention, this sense of outwardly ordinary seeming vistas that nevertheless raise vague feelings of disquiet should you happen to pass them by.

"Sites Redolent With Baleful Echoes", Jon's dad had called them, and I think that's a more than apt description of these types of dread-inducing places.

Certainly it's on a par with the views expressed in an article I once read a couple of years back. It was featured in some paranormal periodical or other, (though I can't for the life of me remember what it was called or indeed, the name the author), concerning the subject of earth mysteries. The words have stuck firmly in my mind. 'It has long been my belief,' the writer stated, 'that certain places exist, dotted around the globe that are somehow spiritually blighted, and which act as beacons capable of transmitting malign radio waves.'

After reading about the bizarre experiences referred to above, it's a theory I have little trouble believing in myself.

.

CHAPTER FIFTEEN
A CITY BATHED IN THE GOLDEN GLOW OF VINDICATION

'When all the lights go out forever,
Somewhere near the end of time
The noise will pass and the dust will settle...
And you'll be on my mind...'

Heart As Big As Liverpool - **Pete Wylie**

Okay, before we go any further, a quick word or two of warning, Dear Readers....

The contents of this next section might well cause certain 'Paranormal Purists' to shake their heads contemptuously and quickly skip through these pages in search of the **real** *supernatural stuff. And if you choose to do so, I guess I can't really complain.*

It's the reader's prerogative, after all.

Having said that, I really do hope that I can crave your indulgence and ask that you bear with me for the duration of the piece. I would contend that there are at least some *Fortean elements present herein, especially for anyone interested in vast, scarcely believable Conspiracy Theories, and I would further suggest there are also some deeply spiritual aspects present, too.*

Even if you should happen to disagree with this assertion, and accuse me of stretching things to the very brink of tenuousness (and hey, it wouldn't be the first, or very likely the last time someone's made that particular allegation!) I sincerely hope you'll momentarily cast aside any prejudices you may have, and judge me only when you've read the chapter ...

I hope.

ONE

And as someone infinitely more famous than yours truly once wrote; 'Hope is the very best of things...'

Honestly, this has been by far the easiest thing I've ever had to write...

Honestly, this has been by far the *hardest* thing I've ever had to write...

Memory is a sometimes maddeningly capricious, downright tricksy thing.

It can conjure up bland images from our past and bathe them in a roseate, 'good arl days' glow.

It can mercifully black out that which no sane person would ever consciously *choose* to recall.

And sometimes it can cruelly project scenes from your worst waking nightmare directly into your mind's eye, in vividly stunning HD quality, (and as an added, unasked for bonus, there's often the special 3D option, the sort that comes without the need for donning those red and green-lensed cardboard glasses, making you look like an Elton John wannabe during his great-big-mad-goggles-wearing phase).

And sometimes, these moments in time mark out the path of the years like huge, foreboding monuments indelibly engraved with dates and times, confronting us with their grim immutability, on an annual basis.

Here are two of the ones that mark out mine, and those especially close to me.

One from 26 long, long years ago.

And the other from the early autumn of 2012.

TWO
Saturday, April 15th, 1989
Hillsborough, 3:40pm

I'm sat slumped against the brick walls of that shit-hole of a stadium, not far from the peeling blue-doored turnstiles, like a marionette that's had its strings suddenly snapped by some cruel, uncaring puppeteer. I'm amidst the first dreadfully surreal stages of shock, although I don't know it then, of course. I don't know much of *anything*, in fact.

Only that I've just been led screaming from the unimaginable horrors of Pen 3, and dragged along that bone-numbingly cold, inner-city subway-type tunnel, by a big, fat police officer, who'd slapped his leather-gloved hand over my eyes, and kept yelling at me: *'Don't look! Don't look!' Don't look!'* over and over again like a religious mantra, and whether he'd said it for my benefit or for his own, it's impossible to say.

I'd tried to tell him it was too late.

Far, far too late.

I'd already *seen.*

And the mere *seeing,* wasn't the worst of it.

Though I wish to God, and all his attendant Angels, that it was.

But all that emerged was a rasping sob. A hideously primeval sound dredged up from the very core of my being; the coal-black place where all of our darkest fears lie, coiled like a mass of highly-venomous snakes, patiently awaiting their moment of awakening.

I'm clutching a cheap plastic cup of lukewarm water handed to me by a St John's Ambulanceman, and I try to lift it to my lips, but my hands are shaking so badly I drop it to the floor. I watch its contents ooze across the sun-splashed concrete, the trickles pooling around discarded ciggie stubs, and cheese-burger and hot dog wrappers, and what looks to be a wholly intact match ticket. The flimsy cup rolls from side to side for a second, and is then crumpled beneath the sole of an Adidas trainer (*'Boss trabs, lad!'* an undeniably Scouse voice pops up crazily in my head)*,* and I lift my gaze as vast crowds of people, police officers, yellow-jacketed stewards and my fellow Liverpool fans run around aimlessly; though their movements seem to me, in my traumatised state, to be slow and exaggerated, and curiously silent, like figures in an endless dream sequence.

For a blessed moment, a part of me tries to reassure me that none of this is real.

That I've somehow fallen asleep in the back of my mate, Stevie Madgin's car, en route to yet another FA Cup Semi Final, and that any minute now, our Grant will shake me awake and laugh incredulously: "Friggin' 'ell, yer tired, lazy, idle get! Yer missin' out on a boss view of the Pennines!'

But then, a tall, middle-aged man, with closely-cropped hair, lumbers into view, his shadow falling coldly across me and temporarily blocking out the sun.

'Are you all right, son?' he says kindly, and bends down so that his weathered, multi-scarred scally face is just inches from mine. I have never met him before, but I see his eyes are pooling with tears. His thin white lips are set in an anguished grimace, and the meaty hand he lays on my shoulder is trembling, like powerful volts of electricity are coursing through his veins. A policeman casually ambles over, the V-shaped stripes on his shoulder indicating he's a fully fledged, kiss-me-arse, sergeant, and says in a patronisingly officious tone: 'Can you and yer lad get movin', sir! As you may have noticed, we're in the midst of a rapidly developing situation, here!'

Things happen very quickly then.

The sorrowful expression falls from Mr Scall's face like a stone, and is quickly replaced with righteous, burning anger.

He rises to his feet and whirls on the startled sergeant with unnerving speed, and jabs a thick, calloused finger into the middle of the officer's chest.

'Let me tell *YOU* somethin', dickhead!' he half-shouts, half-sobs. 'I might not know much of anythin', but I know *this much!* This is all you and yer fuckin' cronies' fault!'

I see the suddenly pale-faced officer take a couple of involuntary steps backwards, reeling before this spit-flecked volley of unrestrained fury, and even in my distressed state, I see a flicker of guilt cross his features; a faint, but unmistakable trace of self-reproach.

And even then I *know.*

When all around is chaos, a nightmare scene of pure and utter bedlam, still I *know.*

Those terrible words had struck home with all the force of undeniable truth.

This police sergeant, for all his air of affected authority and self-control was scared shit-less because he knows he's been rumbled.

He splutters something about 'drunken Scousers,' but his voice lacks conviction and he continues backing away, shaking his head, and alternately casting glances left and right for some assistance, and it strikes me that at that moment he looks diminished somehow, the school bully, who turns out to be a total coward when he hasn't got his mates around to back him up.

'All your fault!' Mr Scall shouts again, and this time, the policeman turns tail and quickly merges with the milling crowds of fans, some angry, some stunned into shocked silence, others desperately searching for missing loved ones.

My own tears come streaming then, stinging my eyes and forming on my cheeks like tiny glass globes and the world mercifully swims out of focus, and almost without me being aware of it, I am hauled to my feet by a couple of uniformed paramedics and led to a waiting ambulance.

I try to form words as I'm sat unceremoniously on a stretcher.

I try to tell anyone who'll listen that I'm physically okay, and anyway, I can't leave yet. I haven't seen my brother since just after I entered Pen 3, seconds after Peter Beardsley's pile-driver struck the crossbar down the opposite end of the ground, and the crowd had surged forward like a massive tidal wave that hit the shore, but somehow never retreated back out to sea.

I've gotta go back and find him.

But nothing comes out. I feel numb, like I've been pumped full of some powerful, speech-immobilising drug. So I just sit there whilst the sun-kissed Sheffield air is filled with the constant wail of sirens, the crackle of police radios, a helicopter whirring insistently overhead.

But over-riding all, is that lone accusatory voice, repeatedly proclaiming that 'undeniable truth',

'This is all you and all yer fucking cronies, fault!'

THREE
Twenty Three Years Later......
96 Lanterns

'WHEN ALL THE RAINY PAVEMENTS LEAD TO YOU'

And here I am running, as best I can, along Hardman Street, in the midst of a torrential downpour.

Just to add to the fun, there's a bitter near gale-force wind that whips the cold rain directly into my eyes, and stings every exposed area of skin. Not only that, but it succeeds in blowing my supposedly all-weather brolly inside-out so frequently I end up losing me temper and sling it in the nearest available bin, all the while ranting and raving at the traitorous brolly like a Scouse version of John Cleese, hurling abuse at the 'defective' fire extinguisher in that classic episode of *Fawlty Towers*: (*"Right, that's it! I've had enough! Gerrin the bin, yer useless shower of shite!"*) much to the giggling amusement of a young Chinese couple standing at the bus stop opposite St Luke's ('bombed out') Church.

Another memorable line, uttered with unshakeable conviction by Jim Garrison, in Oliver Stone's appropriately conspiracy-laden *JFK*, suddenly pops into my mind as I turn the corner onto Renshaw Street:

'*Let Justice Be Done or The Heavens Fall!*'

Is right, Jimbo, lad. I'm on a mission. And it's going to take more than a spell of inclement weather to force me to turn back and admit defeat.

This is the day I've waited nearly a quarter of a century for.

A day that's surely, when the sheer enormity of what has occurred has begun to sink in, will be regarded as one of the most monumentally important in the blessed county of Merseyside's long and venerable history.

Not that you'd be aware anything of the remotest interest had taken place, as I wend my way, head down, amongst the lines of oblivious passers-by.

All around me, people are going about their normal, everyday business. Young mothers pushing prams, weighed down by finger-numbing plastic carrier bags filled to the brim with shopping. Older women impatiently ushering their kids along the rain-slicked city streets, anxious to be home and dry and out of the wind and rain. Groups of students seeking shelter in the doorway of *The Barcelona Bar*. Headphone-wearing teenagers, their smart phones held devoutly before them like priests armed with prayer-books warding off armies of viciously attacking demons.

It's hard to give credence to the possibility that every single one of these people are unaware, or are sniffly dismissive, of the events that had taken place a couple of hours earlier, but that's how it seems, and once more it feels like I'm in the midst of a dream: The surreal sort where you're for some inexplicable reason, standing stark naked in the middle of the dance-floor at some packed night-club, feeling horribly embarrassed and self-conscious, even though no one's paying you the slightest attention.

A passing bus sprays a jet of freezing rain-water from the over-flowing gutter, and I narrowly avoid getting even more drenched than I am already, but my evasive actions serve to shake me from my cheerless little reverie, and I hurriedly check my mobile and see that I've got about ten minutes to get from here to *The Head of Steam* alehouse, opposite St George's Hall, to meet up with our Grant, his wife and kids and our mutual friend, John McGlone, (who tragically lost his cousin, Alan McGlone, at Hillsborough).

It had just been announced on Radio City and the other local stations that at precisely 3:06pm, the church bells will ring out defiantly to announce the start of a minute's silence, on both sides of the Mersey. I am desperate to share that hugely poignant moment of remembrance and solidarity with a group of loved ones.

I glance across the road and see the grimy facade of the old Lewis's store-front, (still with its *'statue exceedingly bare'* waving from its plinth*)*, loom into view and I realise with relief that I'm gonna make it with time enough to spare. I switch off me phone and thrust it deep into me pocket.

And I try to steel myself for what I know will be a desperately longed-for, but hugely emotional occasion.

Three hours had passed since I'd received Peter Hooton's (editor of *The End* fanzine and lead singer of The Farm) heart-stirring post on Facebook, about the apparent conclusions of "The Hillsborough Independent Panel's Report", and of how *'the revelations were so momentous,'* they'd been greeted with loud applause by the families of the 96, present amidst the huge, echoing expanse of the Anglican cathedral, earlier that morning.

Two and a half hours since Prime Minister David Cameron had delivered his speech, making public "the real truth about Hillsborough" in the House of Commons. 150 minutes since the scenes playing out on the 42 inch plasma TV screen had suddenly begun to blur as I'd felt tears well, and my body to start shaking like an alky with a bad case of the DT's.

I find myself replaying the sounds and images in my mind's eye, as I near the far end of Renshaw Street, and prepare to turn the corner to catch my first glimpse of old St George's Hall, grey and suitably sombre in the late afternoon stormlight.

Labour Leader Ed Miliband's Justice Flame badge pinned proudly to the lapel of his suit jacket.

The highly audible gasps around the packed house as the 'awful revelations' fell from Cameron's lips like black, poison-soaked confetti.

The expressions of shocked disbelief on the faces of experienced senior politicians, as the sheer levels of the media/police conspiracy to cover-up the truth, the unforgivable degrees of negligence, and of the despicable actions of irredeemably evil men, were finally laid bare, like a set of bloodied bones uncovered by the rough turn of a farmer's spade in the blighted corner of some winter-dead, January field.

Steve Rotheram (Labour MP for Walton, Liverpool), looking visibly strained and not a little melancholy (though inside he must have felt a huge sense of exultation) as he asked Cameron whether he would now be writing personal apologies to each of the bereaved families...

There was so much to take in, to try and get my head around that I'd suddenly found my thoughts ceaselessly wandering, my mind becoming somehow detached from my physical self in the way described by those people who claim to have undergone a Near Death Experience.

And here they come.

The sorry collection of ex-workmates, casual acquaintances and fair-weather friends; a shame-faced assembly, struggling, but unable to meet each other's eyes, in the manner of those who are always so quick to judge and condemn from a distance.

Here, too, are the only-really-interested-in-the-gruesome-details ranks of hangers-on, a fresh pint of fizzy lager or an expensive cocktail close to hand, who listen raptly to all I that I have to tell them about my experiences at Hillsborough, shaking their perfectly coiffured hairstyles in mock sympathy, right up to the point where I make reference to the equally dreadful aftermath, and the massive conspiracy aimed at covering up The Truth. That had always been the signal for them to start either glancing at their watches or else to roll their eyes heavenward, as though I were some mad-arse conspiracy theorist, the kind who believes wholeheartedly in crashed flying saucers, September 11th being an inside US Government job, and that the total wash-out of a summer just gone was down to some kind of military experiment aimed at controlling the weather.

Or worse, that I was simply in denial. Another thuggish, scally footy fan of a club already tainted with the indelible horrors and deep-rooted shame of Heysel.

Oh, and here at the very last, they also come, of course. My personal *bête noire*.....

In the late autumn of 1989, seated side by side in the plush leather chairs at the far end of the waiting room of the Corn Exchange Barristers Chambers on Fenwick Street, are two men in their late 50's, cackling like the pair of endlessly sarcastic, scrunchy-faced theatre critics from *The Muppet Show,* as they share a copy of *The Liverpool Echo.*

I'd been working for a local firm of solicitors back then as a criminal law clerk, and had attended the imposingly ornate building for a conference. As I was waiting for our client and Mr Aubrey QC, to return from Liverpool Crown Court, I'd heard one of the men, dressed in an expensive-looking three-piece suit, turn to the other and say, "Oh please, do me a favour. Have you seen this, Charles?"

Something in his voice made me glance over, and I saw he was pointing to the inside front page of that day's edition of the paper, though I couldn't quite make out the words of the article's headline. "It says here that there's a whole mob of cynical money-grabbers out there who are seeking financial compensation for having been, and I quote: *"confronted with scenes of unimaginable horror at Hillsborough?"*

"My God, that's absolutely scandalous!" his companion stated with a derisive snort. "I mean to say, it's common knowledge those Liverpool supporters are all mindless, violence-loving hooligans to a man!" He paused, and shook his head, before adding: "Do you know Charles, I heard from a good friend of mine, a senior police officer no less, that gangs of ticketless yobs crashed open the gates, and charged like a crowd of inebriated maniacs into the stadium!"

"Yes, Andrew, that's what I heard too. I don't believe the police would lie about something like that. And neither would the authorities. I mean, it's obvious the so-called fans were entirely responsible. Have they no shame?"

"Apparently not. But one day, God willing, the truth will out, and no amount of pitiful, whiny, pleas of denial will deflect the blame from falling upon the sub-human scum we know to be truly responsible. *"His judgement cometh, and that right soon"*, eh, Charles?"

"Oh, yes, I think I can have faith in that. I *know* it, in fact." He clapped his friend on the shoulder in a gesture of irrefutable certainty. "In the very depths of my soul, I *know* it!"

It was easy to imagine now, all these years later, the two sad, bitterly deluded old men (assuming they were still alive, of course) watching this morning's news, perhaps sat alone in their cheerless, empty houses, with a plaid blanket covering their legs, an empty tobacco pipe lying atop a stack of junk mail piled on the arm of their favourite chair, and with nothing but gilt-framed photographs and a welter of rapidly fading memories for company. Or maybe sat in the communal room of a residential home, staring at the TV screen with a growing sense of incredulity, their jaws hanging slackly, their rheumy eyes wide open, their hearts fluttering in their chests like trapped birds, panicky and desperate for flight.

And as for their immortal souls. I hope for their sakes, their God is as all-forgiving as they'd always believed Him to be.

FOUR

The moment I reach Lime Street, the incessant downpour stops as suddenly as it had begun.

The skies above are still a gun-metal-coloured ceiling of dark foreboding, but the wind has dropped considerably, gently billowing the proud banners proclaiming *'We Never Walked Alone'* and *'Justice For The 96'* tied to the pillars of St George's Hall.

A group of what look to be suited dignitaries, their features impossible to discern from this distance, are gathered at the entrance way, and as I prepare to walk into the alehouse, the unmistakable strains of Pete Wylie's *Heart As Big As Liverpool,* drifts in the chilly air, its anthemic chorus hugely appropriate to the occasion, and again, I feel the tears begin to well. I remind myself that this is only a rehearsal for "the real thing" later this evening, and that I need to steel myself as best I can, or else I'll be a quivering, mental wreck long before sundown. A bevvy or two should help, and I dive into *The Head Of Steam.*

The huge bar is all but deserted, save for those who'd I'd arranged to meet, and as it turns out, there's not even time to shout in a swift half.

It's 3:04.

We walk back outside, and that feeling of detachment from the normality of the every day grows as we join a small crowd of perhaps seventy odd people, gathered alongside the memorial to the fallen of two world wars situated at the edge of The Plateau.

There's a moment to take in the surroundings. The towering Victorian edifice with its statues of Wellington and Disraeli, and Prince Albert astride his horse. The majestic stone lions. The Union Jack flying at half-mast, and most poignantly of all, the sculptures lining the walls, one of which is called, appropriately enough:, "The Attributes And Results of Justice".

The request for silence is hardly necessary. No one is engaged in conversation, anyway.

The minute passes.

Life goes on all around us.

The ceaseless rumble of City Centre traffic: the screech of brakes, the impatient honking of car horns, the squeals of double-deckers as they pull up at the bus stops on Commutation Row.

But amidst the huddle of people grouped together here, the silence is so immaculately observed, it seems as though somehow, the sounds of the outside world have been muted, like God suddenly dug out his remote control from where it had slipped between the cushions on his Heavenly sofa, and angrily pressed the mute button.

And there's another thing, too.

It might sound unbearably corny, and the more cynical amongst you could be forgiven for thinking I am guilty of employing artistic licence (I've been accused of worse, and doubtless will be in the future) but you know what, I was there, and I'll go to me grave stating the truth of a weird "coincidence" that took place on that magical, heart-rending afternoon.

At the very start of the minute's silence. The very moment the church bells ring out across the City and beyond, announcing the commencement of the reverent hush, I swear a single ray of autumnal sunlight suddenly emerged from a tiny, ragged gap in the clouds. A solitary golden lance that speared the greyness.

Looking for all the world like the blessed light of vindication.

FIVE

Of course, the Vigil proper, which took place later that evening, was extremely emotional too. Not least the late, great Anne Williams' speech and her absolution of we survivors of any blame for that god-awful disaster, which, needless to say, reduced me and my brother to floods of grateful tears.

But really, in a strange way, I think the day's earlier, sparsely-attended ceremony, for me personally at least, more than typified the indomitable spirit of this magnificent City. It's stubborn and bravely determined refusal to surrender, even when faced with seemingly insurmountable odds.

Like a small band of people, braving the cold and wet of a mid-September afternoon.

Simply to pause for a moment's silence.

And to somehow succeed in temporarily blocking out the overbearing din of an entire county's hustling, bustling life.

CHAPTER SIXTEEN
THE SOFT WHISPERS OF THE DEAD:
OUIJA BOARDS: 1

'Ouija board, ouija board,
Would you help me?
Because I do still feel
So horribly lonely...'
Ouija Board, Ouija Board - Morrissey

ONE

The Ouija board, that notorious and still-popular board game (and yes, it is, first and foremost classified as a *game,* despite the often hysterical assertions to the contrary) is considered by many people to act as some kind of psychic hotline to the spirits of the dear, and not-so-dear, departed. And I'm willing to bet most people reading this book will have been unable to resist having a sneaky go on one of them at some point in their lives.

It might have been at Halloween, when despite your grave misgivings, you felt compelled to take part in a séance as the result of a seasonal dare by the person you've secretly fancied for ages. Perhaps it was when, at the fag-end of a drunken house party, the sort where everyone's totally danced-out and in various states of drunken collapse, but not quite ready to phone a taxi to take them home just yet, the host had gone to the cupboard under the stairs and dragged out a battered-looking cardboard box before announcing with a flourish, "Right, who fancies a chat with the disembodied dead, then?"

Or, as in my case, as a way of killing time during a particularly boring, rain-lashed lunch hour in the staff canteen at work.

For the record, all that I can recall of my first and so far last experience with Ouija boards, is my being seated together with a group of friends and like-minded colleagues at a dining table over in the far corner of the room, its plastic surface cleared of the usual plates and coffee mugs and assorted lunch-boxes and replaced with the letters of the alphabet, neatly-cut and arranged in a crude circle, and with the words "Yes" and "No" placed in the centre.

In an atmosphere that could best be described as "mock seriousness" (though to tell the truth, most of us were giggling like school-kids when faced with a set of explicitly detailed diagrams during our first lesson on sex education), we'd decided to attempt to contact any resident ghosts daft enough to want to haunt a decrepit government training youth scheme workshop like this one. We'd placed our fingers on an upside down glass tumbler, and after a suitable pause for dramatic effect, the glass had begun jerkily moving across the table towards the various letters, provoking the odd gasp of astonishment and at least one nervous chuckle, all but drowned out by a stream of vehement denials along the lines of: "Well, I'm not pushing the friggin' thing, I swear to God!"

One of the lads present, a gawky, bookish-looking individual named Phil Grundy (although everyone called him by his nickname "Grundig") had the job of making written notes of any message that came through from the 'OTHER SIDE', and if I remember rightly, he stuck diligently to this task right up until the moment he'd suddenly thrown down his pencil with a startled yell, jumped up from his seat, knocking his chair backwards, and stomped out of the room without a word.

We'd stared at each other in astonishment for few seconds, and then Billy Welch, a veritable man-mountain, feared for his fiery temper, had reached over and snatched up the A4-size legal pad in which Phil had been recording the "messages", glanced briefly at what was written there, and with a solemn expression lifted it up for all of us to see, as a late summer storm raged outside.

Printed neatly in black Biro, in large block capitals, had been that crucial communication delivered from beyond the grave.

It had said simply this:

'GRUNDIG GRUNDY WEARS GAY UNDIES.'

TWO

Not surprisingly then, following that less-than rewarding experience (unless you had an unhealthy interest in your male colleagues preferred choice of underwear, at least) I never again displayed much interest in taking part in any further Ouija board sessions, or indeed in any other forms of alleged contact with "the other side", including planchettes, tablerapping, automatic writing or even full-blown séances.

That's not to say I wasn't intrigued by some of the stories I subsequently heard doing the rounds in later years concerning Ouija boards, however. In fact, one supposedly true account related to me by Paul Williams, a friend with a more than passing interest in the paranormal, has been a source of morbid fascination to me ever since first heard it back in the summer of 1994.

Paul is a highly-experienced solicitor who specialises in criminal law, and I spent many an afternoon during my time working as a law clerk at the same firm based on The Wirral, engaged in conversation with him about a wide variety of subjects, including Fortean phenomena.

I remember meeting up with Paul during the luncheon adjournment of a hugely complicated fraud trial (a case that was to drag on for the best part of six long months, and was so excruciatingly tedious I swear I saw a couple of barristers nodding off behind huge piles of strategically placed files and legal statute books on more than one occasion when court was in session). We were sat in Derby Square, directly opposite Liverpool Crown Court. It was a baking hot late-summer afternoon, and we'd sought the shade of the stone steps of the Queen Victoria Monument – that sombre memorial to a sour-faced monarch, that had somehow survived the Liverpool Blitz, when all around her was reduced to rubble.

The Square had been packed with the usual assortment of bag-laden shoppers, sweaty office workers, court staff, and gangs of teenage skateboarders in black Metallica T-shirts, and baggy, knee-length shorts, showing off to impress the groups of young girls who affected an air of cool indifference, whilst the heady aromas of August's "dog days" drifted on the light whisper of a breeze; coconut oil and under-arm spray, burgers and hot dogs and vanilla ice cream.

It was a day more conducive to talking about holidays and summer music festivals, or the start of the new footy season, than for sharing tales of the supernatural, but after we'd polished off our packed lunches, Paul had turned to me and said right out of the proverbial blue, "Yer know what, Lee, me ma's priest said the strangest thing to me last night."

"Sounds intriguing," I said, fanning myself with a copy of *The Echo*. "But can yer make it quick, lad, I'm melting here like a discarded ice pop."

Paul, who had an uncanny ability to remain perspiration-free no matter how hot or humid it was, had merely grinned, and then seeing that I was sweating so profusely it looked like my skin was leaking, he launched into his tale. Except really, it wasn't his story to tell. That dubious honour fell to "Father Bun–Loaf," (as Paul, a lapsed Catholic who'd lost his faith at around about the time he stopped believing in Santa Claus and the Tooth Fairy, constantly referred to his parish priest, though not, I noticed, without a degree of affection).

"Okey dokes, lad," Paul said handing me a Wet Wipe from a packet he kept in his briefcase. "Use this to freshen up a bit while I quickly tell yer what happened. I'm sure yer'll find it worth braving the scorching elements for."

Mopping my brow I leaned further back into the blessed shade of the Queen Victoria statue, glum-faced as ever as she peered down imperiously at the assembled throng below.

THREE

"Last night, at a little after eight, the good Father came round to me mum's to dish out his usual well-meaning dollops of spiritual guidance. That's something he does on a regular basis, of course. I reckon it's more than a coincidence though that every time I decide to pay me arl girl a visit, he just happens to be there. I'm not sure if it's cos he enjoys me ma's company, her piping hot brews and stacked-high plates of chocky bickies, or the opportunity to engage in some deep theological debates with yours truly. Maybe it's all three. Who can say?

"All I am certain of is that last night, while me ma was busy in the kitchen putting the kettle on, rattling the crockery and raiding the battered arl bicky tin, Father Bunloaf and I wound up sitting opposite each other in the living room, and he and I got talking. But rather than the usual discussions about religion, the church, and the evidence, or distinct lack of it, for the existence of some benign, omnipotent God, sat on His Heavenly Throne surrounded by beatific hosts of Cherubim and Seraphim, he asked me whether I'd ever used, or was thinking of using at some unspecified point in the future, a Ouija board or any other form of spirit communication.

"Well, at first I thought he was joking or winding me up. I mean, it was just so out of character for him to mention anything to do with ghosts or the supernatural. Aside from all that metaphorical stuff in the Bible about miracles and angels and witches and demons, of course, and Father B knows better than to get involved in an argument with me about any of that nonsense.

"He wasn't taking the Mick, though. Not a bit of it. One glance at his stern, unsmiling features, a deadly serious expression that I'd long ago come to regard as being his "Father Karras-Having-a-Major-Crisis-of-Faith Face", was enough to convince me of that.

"So I came right out and told him the truth. Of course I'd messed about with Ouija boards during my time at uni. What pot-headed, well-oiled student hadn't? I didn't for one second believe they could be used to genuinely contact the dead, like. But then nor did I think there was any harm in them. They were just glorified toys. After all, hadn't the Parker Brothers company begun manufacturing them back in the mid-1960s, and selling them as board games alongside Cluedo and Monopoly and the like? They did a roaring trade, as I recall, and I certainly never heard of anyone complaining to trading standards about evil spirits sending them terrifying messages from beyond the grave.

"Father B had shook his head angrily at my cynical attitude before suddenly leaning forwards in his chair and I'd instinctively backed away, filled with a horrible certainty that he was gonna reach across and painfully grip my shoulders to try and draw, to *exorcise*, if yer will, the ingrained scepticism from "deep within the innermost core of my being".

"Instead, as if coming to his senses, he sat back and relaxed a little, and even summoned up a tired-looking smile, though there remained this aura of tension in the room and I found myself willing me ma to hurry up and get a move on with the tea and biscuits. Actually, it had dawned on me then that she must have known Father Bunloaf was intending to have a private chat with me about something he considered to be important, because she never normally took any longer than five minutes to brew up a cuppa.

I decided if that was the case, I'd sooner get the conversation over with, for both our sakes.

"Why are asking me about this sort of stuff, Father? I mean, I enjoy our theological chinwags as much you obviously do. But really, Ouija boards, and ghoulies and ghosties and things that go bump in the night?"

The priest sighed loudly. "Look, Paul, I'm well aware you are a confirmed atheist. I'm not here to deliver a sermon aimed at persuading you to see the error of your ways. I'm not being a big fan of that overly dramatic "Road to Damascus", conversion technique."

"I'm glad to hear it," I'd replied, relaxing a little. Father B might be a devoutly passionate, God-fearing man, rapidly approaching late middle age, but it always cheered me to see he'd never lost his quirky sense of humour. "So, come 'ead then, Father," I said. "What is it you actually *do* you want to discuss?"

"I'm not here to discuss anything," he said. "I'm here to issue a friendly warning that you should never let your distinct lack of belief in the forces of darkness, of evil incarnate, to trick you into meddling with things that man would do well to leave alone."

"Nice one, Father," I'd spluttered between bursts of laughter. "I've seen that arl 1930s *Invisible Man* film too, yer know. And sorry to tell yer like, but yer concluding line there sounded a lot less corny when Claude Raines spouted it out, laced with bitter regret and heartfelt remorse."

Father B smiled and said, "For once, Paul, we find ourselves in total agreement. Sad to say, the Good Lord never saw fit to bestow upon the me the gift of that wonderful actor's velvety tones, much to the disappointment of my long-suffering congregation."

"But still," he'd added with a shrug, "I've found that on occasion, quoting dialogue from classic Universal monster movies is sometimes the most effective way of making a point."

"Yeah," I said. "And some might say that's because those types of films feature characters every bit as mythical as the ones starring in that large black book you're always referring to."

"You know something?" the priest replied. "You're far too young to be so cynical. I can just imagine you at midnight every January 31st, phoning all your family and friends to tell them, "Happy New Year! Everything you believe is a lie. Faith is an illusion. And one day you're going to die. Alone!"

"No, Father. I'll be far too busy sharing a tongue sarnie with the slapper in a sexy nun's habit at *The*

Krazy House Fancy Dress Party in town."

Father B had shaken his head, and smiled. "Oh, there's a certain section of Dante's Hellish Inferno reserved just for the likes of you, Paul. It's called "The Rhett Butler Suite For Cold-Hearted Misanthropes".

"Catchy," I said with a grin of my own, but before I could come up with something half-way amusing, the priest had held up his hands and I'd watched the smile slide from his face.

"All joking aside though, I want you to know that I *am* being deadly serious about my warnings regarding playing around with planchettes, Ouija boards and the like. If I had any doubts about that, they were thoroughly dispelled by something that happened to me just a few short days ago. Please, Paul, do me a favour. Just hear me out...."

"I see you've got that intense, Damian Karras look goin' on again," I said. "Go ed, then, Father, I'm all ears. Spill it."

And without waiting for any further encouragement, he immediately did just that.

FOUR

"Like most people with even the most fleeting of interests in occult matters, I'd long ago heard that any form of supposed spirit communication was fraught with all kinds of potential danger, and not least because someone with acute emotional or psychological problems might be adversely affected by dabbling in such matters. For example, let's say some highly suggestible person at a séance is seated together with a medium and a group of likeminded individuals, all of them desperate to speak to the spirits of their deceased loved ones. They touch the tips of their splayed fingers around a bare wooden table top, whilst the medium utters some dreadfully corny cliché along the lines of that all-time classic: 'Is there anybody there?'

"And after a while, as the tension in the room rises to the point where it becomes just about the right side of bearable, a voice emanating from some invisible point on "The Other Side", distant and maybe a little echoey-sounding like it's emanating from the bottom of a well or a mineshaft, fills the ears of the gathering and raises goose-flesh on their arms, and hope in their hearts.

"Initially, it spouts incoherent gibberish, almost baby-like in nature. But then gradually the vocalizations become louder and ever clearer, to the point where eventually, individual words and the occasional sentence can be made out, and at some point, someone, usually the most sensitive person present in the room, claims to recognise the "suddenly familiar tones" of a much-missed relative or a close personal friend.

"It tells them things then, this Oz-like "Voice From Beyond". More often than not, they are simple platitudes about how they, or their immortal souls at least, are in a far better place and that there is no longer any need for anyone to grieve for their passing because the "separation is only temporary. They'd be reunited with them again one day, when at last their own time came to cross the threshold."

"Well there's no real harm in that, you might say, even if you consider the whole spirit communication thing to be nought but an elaborate hoax, and you'd doubtless be right. We live in a world where faith in anything we can't pick out and order from the laminated pages of an Argos catalogue or order from Ebay, is an increasingly hard thing to come by these days, so what's wrong with generating a tiny spark of hope, false or otherwise, when the paths of life so often seem draped with the dark shadows of despair?

"Nothing.

"Nothing at all.

"But on occasion, rarely perhaps, but often enough to concern a far-too easily-troubled old priest like me, that great and terrible "Voice From Beyond" conveys a darker, far more sinister message. It might be a vague warning of imminent danger from an enemy who wishes them harm. A serious form of illness that's about to afflict them. An accident that results in a life-changing injury, or worse.

"And it really doesn't matter whether these communications are emitted by a *bona fide*, otherworldly source or are every bit are as fake as those old fortune telling slot machines I remember from the seaside amusement arcades of my childhood. What most decidedly *does* matter is that the warnings can have a hugely damaging effect upon a person who is convinced beyond doubting they are in direct contact with the well-meaning spirit of a departed loved one.

"Now, I'm no student of psychology, Paul, but even I know that the power of suggestion can be an incredibly potent thing. We've all heard stories, and not *all* of them published as "truth" in some thoroughly disreputable tabloid rag, or posted up on the internet, of how so-called witch doctors, faith healers, leaders of dodgy religious cults, and the like have succeeded in convincing people of all sorts of things, for all sorts of reasons, not all of them good or well-intentioned.

"In extreme cases, such unquestioning belief in the source of the communication can result in acute trauma, high levels of hysteria or even permanent psychological damage to the recipient. And little wonder. As history has shown, time and again, people can be convinced of just about anything, no matter how irrational, if their faith in the source of the information is strong enough.

"But forgive my rambling. Like I say, I'm no latter-day Jung or Sigmund Freud. I'm just a humble priest who still believes, however unfashionable it may seem in this day and age, to believe in the possibility of Evil as a literal, supernatural force, capable of manifesting in an vast array of forms, including, on occasion, the supposed "spirits of the dead". What's more, I think it's....

"Oh, I see you're growing increasingly uncomfortable now, Paul. And there's that all-too-familiar smirk starting to crinkle the corners of your mouth. I wondered how long it would take. In all honesty, I'm surprised you let me get this far. But I haven't even touched upon the important bit yet. The Big Picture, so to speak. I know you think my views are perfectly medieval in nature and as obsolete as *The Malleus Maleficarum,* but please remain seated for just a little while longer, if you'd be so kind. I want to tell you about something extremely strange that occurred recently. Something that's since haunted my dreams and plagued my every waking hour, to the point where

I fear for my sanity.

"Please listen.

"And consider it a well-intentioned warning, if nothing else.

FIVE

"During the early hours of Sunday last, I was awakened by the shrill ringing of the bedside telephone. I glanced at the luminous dials of the alarm clock and saw it was precisely 3am: "The Devil's Hour", according to some students of Biblical lore. I'm not convinced there's any evidence of that myself, but my stomach roiled with a sick feeling of dread just the same. No one ever calls with good news at that hour, and I had to resist the temptation to snatch the phone off the hook and cut the caller off. I almost wish I had now, though I would have been remiss in my duties as a priest had I done so.

"It was one of my most devoted parishioners, you see. Theresa Collins, a widowed, late-middle-aged mother of three, who seldom, if ever, missed mass, and to whom I'd offered spiritual guidance in the wake of her husband, Patrick's, sudden death, a few years earlier.

"I'm ever so sorry to trouble you, Father, at this ungodly hour," she'd said, sounding tired and desperate, and not a little afraid. "But it's my eldest, Mary. She's in a terrible state. She was supposed to be staying at her friend's house for a sleep-over, but she came home alone in a taxi cab a couple of hours ago, and she's been having a fit bordering on hysterics ever since."

'She'd paused to swallow an audible click in her throat. "It crossed me mind I that I should phone for an ambulance, but given the nature of some of the thing's Mary's been shrieking, I thought it best to call you first, Father." Theresa lapsed into silence again, and I'd known that as a fiercely independent woman, it must have hurt her pride to have to resort to begging me for help. "Please Father, I know it's very late. But can you possibly come over right away. I honestly don't know who else to turn to."

"I'll be there as soon as I can," I'd assured her, and Theresa had all but sobbed her thanks, and I'd told her she was perfectly welcome. "Just before I put the phone down, I'd plainly heard her two younger daughter's, Molly and Ellie, crying quietly in the background, and I'd silently berated myself for even contemplating not taking the call.

"And then the earpiece had been filled with screams so piercingly loud they'd sounded like the tortured cries of a badly wounded animal caught in the cruel and jagged jaws of a steel hunter's trap. I'd flung the receiver to the floor as though it were a burning hot ember, and clapped my hands over my ears to drown out that awful, awful sound.

"I tell you, Paul. I've never heard anything like it in my life. And I pray to all that's Holy that I never will again.

SIX

"It took me just over a quarter of an hour to drive to the address in the centre of Woolton Village, and I honestly hadn't known quite what to expect when I arrived at the unremarkable semi-detached house, the lights blazing from each and every window. But it's fair to say I was shocked by my first sight of Mary, dressed in a plain white silk dressing gown, and curled up in a foetal position on the edge of her bed, frantically rocking back and forth, mumbling what sounded like incoherent gibberish to herself. The room was in a state of mild disarray: Photographs of friends and various family members had been swept from the shelves, along with several Penguin Classic paperbacks and a row of CD albums whilst the bedside light was lying on its side minus its lampshade, its naked glow casting starkly outlined shadows on the walls and ceiling.

"For a moment, I'd found myself unable to speak, and it had been Theresa, who had accompanied me up to Mary's bedroom whilst a next-door neighbour looked after her other two daughters in the living room downstairs, who announced my arrival.

"The moment her mother spoke my name, Mary had suddenly snapped out of her trance, leaped off the mattress, and raced across the carpet bare-footed to throw herself into my arms, gripping me so tightly I could feel her heart thudding in her chest like a mini jack-hammer. Not knowing what else to do, I held her and stroked her damp, jet-black hair, murmuring what I prayed were soothing platitudes, whilst a feverish heat came off her skinny, almost child-like frame, in near-visible waves.

"It seemed to take an inordinate length of time, but eventually Mary had calmed sufficiently for me to able to prise her fingers from my neck and push her away slightly so I could take a look at her face. Immediately I did so I felt myself reeling from yet another shock: I've known Mary since her birth, and she'd always struck me as being bright, well-mannered and vibrantly full of life, who seldom if ever, missed Sunday Mass, but in truth I'd scarcely recognised the plainly terrified young lady stood before me. Mary had only turned nineteen a few weeks earlier but at that moment, bathed in the unforgiving glare of that shadeless light-bulb, it'd seemed like Mary had aged by at least as twenty years. Her hair, normally immaculately styled and healthy-looking had hung in greasy strands over her too-pale face and red-rimmed eyes. She also appeared to have lost an unhealthy amount of weight, and her cheeks were so sunken you could almost see the bones poking against skin that resembled ancient parchment. Mary had been dripping with sweat, too although her entire body had shivered spasm-like as she wrapped her arms around herself.

"Trying not to appear overly concerned, I asked her what was troubling her, what had happened to her at her friend's house to reduce her to this state, and Mary, the sweetly devout young woman, who I'd always considered (perhaps a little naively) to be the epitome of young adult innocence, raised her eyes to mine and said very calmly, and very clearly; "You priests haven't got a fuckin' clue as what truly awaits us after death, Father! Not a *FUCKIN'* clue!"

"Mary, how dare you speak to the Father like that!" Theresa had yelled, grabbing her daughter by the shoulders. "You apologise to him. Right now!"

"Get off me, you stupid bitch!" Mary screamed. "He wants to know what happened. What I saw. What Ko Ron's son made me see. Let me tell him."

"Theresa drew back her hand and without a word, slapped Mary's left cheek so hard, I was half-afraid that pitifully thin skin would tear apart, revealing the skull beneath. She may as well have gently caressed her face with a mother's boundless love for all the effect it had, though. Mary didn't even acknowledge she'd been struck, though it must have stung terribly.

"You do want to know, don't you Father?" She'd continued, now in cheerfully sat-by-the-fireside, conversational voice. "You do want to know what I saw during the Ouija board session we had at my friend, Karen's flat, earlier tonight? Of course you do. It was Ko Ron's son who made me look. Ko Ron's son who made me see. I didn't want to. God help me, I didn't want to. But he showed me anyway. What truly happens to us after death. And now I see it all the time." She laughed harshly, a crone-like cackle. *"Even with my fucking eyes tightly closed!"*

"Who is this Ko Ron's son? Some boy at the party, staying over at your friend's house?" I said, struggling to keep my composure as Mary threw her hands over her eyes, and began shrieking once more, that blood-curdling wailing I'd heard over the phone a little earlier. It was a maddening sound, like having a swarm of wasps buzzing manically round your ears whilst your hands were tied behind your back, and my temper had snapped to the point where I'd grabbed hold of her with more force than I'd intended, "Who is Ko Ron's son? What did he make you see? Answer me, child!"

"But she either couldn't or wouldn't answer and instead had backed away to slump back down on the bed, before curling up into a ball once more, all the while making those terrible wild animal cries, and though it shames me to admit it, I felt compelled to make my excuses and leave right then. I couldn't take, it Paul. I swear, being forced to listen to that incessant screeching for longer than a few minutes would test anyone's sanity. I wanted so much to shut her up that I was afraid if I stayed any longer I wouldn't have been responsible for my actions.

"So, staring intently at the creased leather surface of my shoes, as though there was something of immense scientific interest crawling across their surface, I'd advised Theresa that there was really nothing I could do for her daughter given her current mental state, and it would be best to call for immediate medical assistance.

"Feeling like a complete failure, I'd turned away and had to resist the temptation to race back down the stairs and straight out the front door, and it had took an even greater effort of will to stick around long enough for the paramedics, two big men and a well-built woman, to arrive.

"It was as well that the hospital had seen fit to send this trio of physically powerful individuals though, because although Mary was only a slight young lady, who couldn't have weighed any more than a mere eight stone in sopping wet clothes, still the three paramedics had had to use all of their combined strength to transport her from her bedroom to the waiting ambulance. Mary had kicked and screamed like a woman possessed every inch of the way, her body writhing and contorting like an electric eel's, and no amount of pleading with her to calm down, to reassure her that the nurses were only here to help her made the slightest difference.

"I don't think I'll ever forget the sight of Theresa, her eyes wild and rolling, her hands tearing frantically at her thick blonde hair as the three paramedics finally managed to sedate her daughter, and managed to get her to lie down on the trolley bed, although whatever sedative they'd administered hadn't been nearly powerful enough to render her mute. And as Theresa climbed aboard, the door slammed shut, and the ambulance sped away in the direction of the hospital, I swear you could still hear Mary's terrible wailing, a jarring, discordant harmony with the emergency vehicle's blaring siren.

SEVEN

"I called Theresa to check on Mary's condition that afternoon. The news wasn't good. In low, despair-ridden tones, barely discernible above the unmistakeable sounds of the constantly busy hospital, she informed me her daughter was still under heavy sedation and as the doctors were at a complete loss as to how to account for Mary's "sudden bout of acute psychological trauma", she was currently being assessed for a possible transfer to a specialist mental health unit over at Clatterbridge, on the Wirral.

"I passed on my sincere best wishes for her daughter's full recovery, and told her she could rest assured I would most certainly be praying for her well-being and would invite my congregation to do the same at the forthcoming Sunday Mass. I've got to admit though, the words sounded unconvincing, hollow almost, even to myself, and it was a blessed relief when she finally hung up, and I could attempt to focus on other things, *anything* other than the disturbing case of Mary Collins and her overnight slide into seeming insanity.

"But I knew, even then, that any respite would be merely temporary. And so it proved. Though I've pretty much told you all I can at this stage, Paul, there is still one more thing I need to add. A kind of postscript, if you will. I promise I won't keep you much longer…

EIGHT

"Late the following afternoon, I made my way on foot to my church, St Bernadette's, in the pouring rain. The weather may have been awful, but I'd needed some fresh air to clear my head, and so I'd left the car at home. When at last I'd arrived at the church, dripping wet, but perversely, feeling all the better for having immersed myself in the teeming rain, a young girl, about Mary's age, wearing a black leather jacket and a pair of ripped jeans, had been stood beneath the shelter of the stone-arched entrance. The moment she saw me walking towards her (although maybe *sloshing* would have been more accurate) she'd smiled and in a soft, gently lilting Scouse accent had introduced herself as Karen Hastings.

"I'm Mary's best friend," she'd said shaking my soaking wet hand. "Or at least I *was*, anyway. Now though? Now I'm not so sure." Karen had sighed and her smile had faltered just a little. "Hey, I'm sorry. I didn't mean to just turn up at your church unannounced like this." She shook her head and her cheeks flushed as red as her lipstick. "As you've probably guessed from the way I dress, I'm not a particularly religious person. I'm an avowed agnostic, if I'm anything, but the thing is, Mary told me all about you. She said you're not like most other priests, that you're dead approachable and that you always seem to listen and offer advice in a non-patronising way, and the truth is, I am so worried about her, Father, and I feel terribly guilty about what happened to her at me birthday party the other night. It was my big idea to drag the old Ouija board out, after all. An ex-boyfriend of mine had left it at me flat last Halloween, and I'd pretty much forgotten it was even there, shoved behind a pile of old shoes, me two-man camping tent and a selection of photie albums I haven't looked at in years, and I think I...."

"Miss Hastings," I said, raising my hands to interrupt this verbal equivalent of a force ten gale. "I appreciate your coming here today, I really do. But perhaps we'd both be a lot more comfortable continuing this conversation inside where it's warm and dry." I reached for the brass door handle and gently ushered her in out of the teeming rain.

"I'm sure we can rustle up some piping hot tea and a decent selection of biscuits, too."

"Sounds like a plan," Karen agreed, and followed me into the church without another word.

"Five minutes later, we were sat in a pew, a few feet from the altar, bathed in the orange glow of a three-bar portable heater and with clouds of steam rising lazily from our plain white mugs.

"Mary had been looking forwards to the party and the sleepover for months," Karen began. "It was all she ever seemed to talk about at college, especially in the last few days leading up to it. What she was gonna wear. What alcoholic drinks she should bring. Which compilation CDs? That type of stuff. It got so over-the-top at times, I began to worry that my humble little house party couldn't possibly live up to her mad expectations. I suppose that's why I was so determined to make sure it proved to be a memorable do, that it wouldn't just be the usual stereotypical mix of spewing up all over the hugely expensive shag-pile carpet, having sex with someone you'd normally not be remotely attracted too, or passing out in a drunken heap in the middle of an empty bath.

"I mean those things were very likely gonna happen, too, of course. We are teenagers, after all. We have a reputation to live up to. But just the same, I had a few ideas for livening up proceedings if things did start going down the pan, and one of them was to wait until that 'three-quarters bladdered' point of the night, the part where the remaining vaguely conscious guests are sat off talking about everything and nothing, before asking the loaded question: 'Who reckons we have a go at contacting the spirits of the dead?

"Sure enough, no sooner had I made that slightly-slurred suggestion than the eight or nine of us, including Mary, still at the party and capable of physical movement, dimmed the lights, switched off the music, and gathered round the dining table, while I went and fetched the Ouija board.

"I placed it in the centre of the table, and after lighting a single red candle, we placed our fingers on the top of an upside-down whisky glass before, and trying not to giggle, I called out 'Are there any spirits present who would like to speak to us?'

"For a while, a good ten minutes or so, nothing happened. Well, that's not entirely true. One of the girls with their fingers on the glass, Anna Wilson, a friend of a friend with a great big gob and an even bigger ego, let out a high-pitched squeal when she swore blind she'd felt an invisible hand caress the back of her neck, though the grin on Davey Fleming's face suggested a far more down-to-earth explanation than any ghostly contact. And when it got really quiet, an enormous fat lad by the name of Karl Watson, broke wind so loudly we all felt the floor vibrate beneath our feet. The truth is, aside from these mildly amusing, (though you-really-had-to-be-there) moments, outright boredom had quickly set in, and when the estimable Mr Watson raised himself a foot off his chair;

a sure sign he was about to unleash another, please excuse me Father, tectonic plate-shifting fart, I'd just about decided to give the whole thing up as a bad idea when Mary had suddenly shouted; 'God, I feel really cold!'

"There were a few nervous titters, and someone muttered, 'yeah, right!' but the thing was it really did seem as though the temperature had suddenly dropped several degrees, and I was about to excuse myself and go and check the central heating was still working when Mary piped up again: 'I think something is here. Something really is here...With us... *Now!*'

"I wanted tell her to stop messing about. That no one thought she was remotely funny. But then I saw the white fog of her breath emerging from her mouth and I realised I could see my own breath too, and before I could even remark on how it strange that was, the upside down whisky glass suddenly started shooting across the board at an impossible speed, and with our fingers still attached, like they'd been stuck to its surface with super glue. There were no accusations of anyone pushing the glass, now. No one said anything, in fact. There was only this bewildered, awe-struck silence as the tumbler sped towards the different letters of the alphabet, the 'YES' and 'NO,' and the various numbers, although if there was an actual message being spelled out, it was being relayed far too quickly for any of us to understand so much as a single word.

"Except for Mary, that is.

"My best friend seemed to understand what was being communicated all too well.

"Without warning she'd leapt to her feet, knocking over the chair on which she'd been sat, and began screaming 'Oh, no-no-no-no, God help me! Oh, no-no-no-no, God help me! over and over, before sweeping the glass from the table with such force it smashed to pieces against the far wall.

"Everyone jumped up then, and began babbling excitedly, icy clouds still puffing like steam from our wide open mouths. Everyone turned to Mary, still screaming those exact same words, her face a mask of uncomprehending horror, her palms upturned and held our before her like she was begging for deliverance from something only she could see.

"Davey Fleming, who was stood nearest to her, reached out and touched Mary gently on the shoulder, trying to reassure her and get her to calm down, but his actions had the opposite effect. Mary pushed him away and raced from the room and charged out the front door of my first floor apartment, in absolute hysterics. We stood there for a few seconds, exchanging 'what-the-hell-just-happened?' glances before three of us, me, Davey, and a girl I knew only as Anna, chased after Mary, 'cos we were worried that there was no telling what might happen if she were left alone for long when she was so obviously terrified out of her wits.

"We found her, frantically hugging herself and sobbing quietly on the kerb-side, just outside the block of flats. She'd finally stopped that terrifying screeching, though, and that was a mercy, believe me. I asked Davey and Anna to remain where they were while I tentatively made my way over to the side of the road, thankfully all but free of traffic at that time of night.

"I sat down beside my friend, gently placed my arm around her and in a hushed voice that was little more than a whisper I told her that everything was going to be okay. There was nothing to be afraid of any more. Her friends were here for her, there'd be no more messing around with Ouija boards or the like. We could take the damn thing out to the patch of waste-ground where the kids built their bonfires every November the fifth, douse the wooden board in petrol and burn it to ashes if that would help ease her mind.

"Mary was quiet for a moment, and I started to think she was gonna be okay, but the second I asked her whether she wanted to come back inside, she lifted her head and fixed me with the saddest eyes, eyes, brimming with tears.

"But none of you know," she'd said. "What I've been told. What I've been *shown*. Death is not the end. There are worse things waiting. *Far* worse. I know this for a fact, Karen, because He made me see."

"Who made you see?" I asked, my mouth suddenly so painfully dry it hurt to swallow.

"The one who appeared to me," Mary replied. "The Dark One. Ko Ron's son." She ran her trembling fingers through her hair and then added; "And if you knew what lies in wait for us. For all of us.. Dear God, if you only knew!"

"Mary had grinned, then, and I'd felt the world sway around me, and I'd known true terror then. Not the vicarious thrill we get when we're watching a scary film with the lights off or about to board the "Nemesis" at Alton Towers.

"This was pure primal terror, and I couldn't bear to face it for long.

"I somehow got to my feet and backed away across the lawn, shouting over my shoulder to Davey and Anna, asking, *begging* them to please phone for a cab, that Mary needed to go home right now. She was very obviously unwell. Davey fished out his mobile and rang a local taxi firm. I kept on backing away, and Mary kept on grinning, the leer of someone who knows a vile and dirty secret.

"I swear, Father, the five minutes or so that we stood, my friends and I, waiting for the taxi to arrive, none of us speaking, none of us even exchanging glances, were the longest five minutes of my life.

"Part of me was dreading the prospect of having to drag Mary into the cab. I felt sure she wouldn't go willingly, but I was wrong about that. The moment the taxi pulled up, some inane dance anthem blasting from the bass-heavy speakers, Mary had simply got to her feet unaided and got in the back seat without a single word of protest.

"The last I saw of her, she was staring out the back window, her face illuminated for a moment in the green glow of the dashboard lights.

"And I will never forget the expression on Mary's face, if I live to be a hundred. The grin had gone. A pleading look of desperation had replaced it. "As though someone had nudged the doors of Hell ajar, and compelled her to take a peek inside…

NINE

"Well now, that's quite a story, Miss Hastings," I said, hating the condescending tone that had crept into my voice, but unable to help myself. "If even half of what you say is true, or perhaps more importantly, if Mary herself believes it, I suppose that goes some way towards explaining why she's so, to use modern parlance, totally stressed out.

"I stared at Karen intently, and one look at her visibly earnest expression was enough to convince me that she hadn't come here on this miserable, rain-soaked afternoon, merely to play some puerile, not to say entirely tasteless, practical joke.

"Okay," I said, touching her arm gently. "What about you? Did you yourself see or hear anything strange that night? Aside from the sudden, drastic drop in temperature, I mean?"

"No," Karen conceded with a shrug of the shoulders. "A part of me wishes I could say that I did, like." She looked me squarely in the eye and then she shivered, like someone had suddenly walked over her grave.

"But a huge chunk of me is massively relieved that I didn't get to share Mary's experience. Jesus Christ, and please excuse me again, Father, but who would honestly want to?"

"No one, I guess," I replied, and I meant it. "But let me ask you something else. Something that's been nagging away at me like an overly persistent parishioner ever since I first heard mention of the name: Who is Ko Ron's son? You and Mary both mentioned his name on frequent occasions. I mean, was he the son of an Asian friend of yours, or something?"

"Karen did a cartoonish double-take, the kind of thing that Wile E Coyote does as he realises that the stick of dynamite he's just lit has become stuck to his hand, and it's about to explode.

"Oh, Father," she exclaimed, "What are you talking about? "Ko Ron's son" isn't a *person*. I honestly thought you, as a Roman Catholic priest, would have known that."

"I'm sorry to disappoint you, Karen," I said, honestly perplexed. "I really haven't got a clue what you're talking about. Tell you what, it's been a tough couple of days. Why don't you do us both a favour and just spell it out to me?"

"Fair enough, Father," Karen said. "The thing is, when Mary started spouting all that stuff about how "He made me see" and "How death wasn't the end, and that there are far worse things awaiting us after we pass", I decided to try to find out who or what she was referring to. I assumed it would be something to do with religion, and specifically the afterlife, given that Mary is a fairly pious person, so I went on Google and typed in "Koron's Son" and "evil entities" and directly below the search engine box came the question; 'Did you mean *Choronzon*?' I corrected the spelling and I knew straight away that this is what Mary had been referring to during that Ouija board session. The thing that had sent her screaming out into the street. She believed she'd witnessed a manifestation of *Choronzon,* ** "The Dweller In The Abyss", one of the major Demons who stands guard at the entrance to Hell."

"Karen reached into the pocket of her leather jacket and pulled out a sheaf of crinkled papers. "Here," she said. "I've printed off some stuff about *Choronzon* from the sites I Googled. I think it tells you all you need to know or forgotten about that particular Demon." She smiled grimly. "It's not a particularly cheery read."

"Goodbye, Father," Karen said as she rose slowly to her feet. "I'm not sure if my discovery will be of any use to either you or Mary. But at least now you know what you might be dealing with. For what it's worth."

"She looked at me then, and her eyes spoke of a determination to persuade me, a priest, to consider the existence of a world I had long ago dismissed as being purely allegorical.

"So saying she walked towards the heavy oaken door and closed it behind her with a reverberating thud. I suddenly felt a great sense of melancholy wash over me. My eyes were drawn to the high altar and the tabernacle and not the for the first time I found myself wishing that everything in life could be as simple and straightforward as the plain white cloth and the silver, unadorned crucifix that crowned it...."

FOOTNOTE:

* Frustratingly and in common with the majority of the stories in this book, frustratingly, I have no way of verifying its authenticity. I only have Paul Williams's, (a former friend I have sadly long since lost contact with) word to rely on, and, by extension, you only have mine. As I never made a note of the names of the characters involved, I have, not for the first time, had to employ pseudonyms, so there is no way of tracing the people involved, especially not the priest, who may or may not have once have performed mass on a weekly basis at St Bernadette's back in the mid-1990s, (the only church I can find of that name in Liverpool, is in the Allerton district of the city, and of course, "Father Bunloaf" is a common and widely used Scouse term for all Roman Catholic priests .

** Thankfully however, as the intrepid 'Karen' quickly discovered, the name "Ko Ron's Son"/Choronzon, can easily be located without spending hours with your head buried in big thick leather-bound theological volumes at Liverpool Central Library. Instead, with a simple click of the computer keys, you can discover all you need to know about the Demon from the Internet. According to "Thelemapedia," an Aleister Crowley-inspired site, for example, Choronzon first appeared in the writings of the infamous occultist John Dee, back in the 16th century, "where he was synonymous with the Serpent in The Garden of Eden. Crowley paraphrased Dee's description of the demon as "the first and deadliest of all the powers of evil," and also referred to Choronzon as the Dweller in the Abyss, *"that great spiritual wilderness which must be crossed by the adept to attain mastery. The Demon is there as the final obstruction. If he is met by the proper preparation, then he is there to destroy the ego, which allows the adept to move beyond the Abyss. If unprepared, then the unfortunate traveller will be utterly dispersed into annihilation."*

At the risk of sounding a little callous, that last line seems to pretty much sum up the fate that befell poor unprepared Mary Collins during an ill-fated Ouija board session...

CHAPTER SEVENTEEN
THE WELL FROM WHICH ALL HOPE
SPRINGS: OUIJA BOARDS: 2
(Or, on the other, slightly more optimistic hand...)

'I try to believe, but you know it's no good,
This is something that just can't be understood.'
After-Image - Rush

Dave Shirley, a good friend, fellow-Fortean and all-round sound individual (and whose acquaintance you've already made in these pages) submitted the following account to me a couple of years back, and is proof, as the title suggests, that despite the ominous warnings of priests and well-meaning, but quite possibly bullshit-spouting, long-absent friends, about the dangers of trying to contact the spirits of the dead that sometimes, only sometimes, mind, such attempts at ghostly communication can bring a renewed sense of faith and hope to those previously bereft of either.

ONE
As the hustle and bustle of the Liverpool night-life began to transform itself into a cacophony of taxi horns, the sirens of the emergency services and after-midnight buses transporting the hordes of revellers out of the City Centre, our Friday evening in the darkened *Head of Steam* pub continued unabated in the now closed, and almost deserted surroundings.

This was no ordinary out of hours lock-in, mind you. This was something altogether more surreal than simply quaffing a few cheeky ales outside of licensed hours. I had joined the Liverpool-based paranormal research team called "Night Vision Investigations", to personally experience and explore the dark, seldom-travelled nooks and crannies beneath Lime Street Station, and hopefully to capture evidence of a rumoured afterlife that still permeates the fabric of our everyday surroundings.

The night had begun below the alehouse, in the empty service tunnels that lie beneath the feet of the young and eternally optimistic students and boozed up-party goers above.

Their dark expanse used to house the workers and servants of the former hotel that had once stood on this site. The tunnels also acted as store-houses for all manner of food and drink. Now almost silent, and with the air, thick with a smell of putridity, this place appeared to be the perfect venue for a good, old-fashioned ghost hunt.

Disappointingly, this search for evidence of any resident ghosts proved to be entirely unproductive, but as the chiming of the pub's clock announced the advent of the "Witching Hour", we emerged from the dark depths, blinking in the relative brightness of the pub's electric lighting, and prepared for the next stage of the investigation. This was very much an ideal evening for the paranormal 'tourist,' the semi-initiated, who simply wanted to experience an inexplicable chill in the air that they were convinced could only be induced by the presence of the spirits of the deceased. But for me, as the smug and overly logical sceptic, I was there to simply see if I could figure out what these so-called 'hauntings' were really all about.

The night had begun, as expected, with me noting every pipe, duct, vent, bunched up electrical cables and the distant sounds of humming air conditioners and coolers, along with the rumble of the trains of the Merseyrail Underground directly beneath our feet. All of these things could quite easily play a part in convincing the average Joe that this place was indeed home to more spirits than the ones suspended over the bar (*sorry, I know it's an old one, but I simply couldn't resist*).

My initial sense of aloofness however, soon took a deflating knock as our group of twenty or so, which included the presence of my far more open-minded mother, was broken down into smaller teams, and together with two close acquaintances and my mother, I was assigned one of five experiments set out for us by the event organisers; we were instructed to embark on a spell of Table Top Glass Divination. An old favourite of mine. To be honest, much as I enjoy these type of sessions, I wasn't expecting an awful lot to happen, but within minutes, the glass began, seemingly, to respond to our careful touch and verbal questioning, but rather than share the uniform expressions of wide-eyed wonderment on my colleagues' faces, a voice in my sceptical, rational mind instantly screamed out "Ideomotor Effect". In simple terms, this entirely natural phenomenon consists of a series of involuntary motor movements made by humans without them being aware of it, often influenced as it is by unconscious desire and latent expectation.

So, that was it as far as I was concerned. The case was closed before it even got a chance to be prised open. Slap me heartily on the back for having so easily solved another of life's great mysteries. I'll take my tea and medals now, please.

Or rather, put them both on hold and forgive my presumptive dismissal. Because no sooner had I reached this logical conclusion, than things promptly began to take a decidedly intriguing turn. The answers to the questions posed by our group suddenly seemed to be leading to a highly unexpected conclusion. One that was painfully poignant to those gathered around the table. I watched the eyes of my fellow diviners as one by one they began to well up with tears as we appeared to have made "contact" with something far more enigmatic than mere "ideomotor effects".

It appeared we were communicating with the daughter of one of our group, a girl who had sadly passed on some seventeen years prior to our current séance.

My mind struggled to rationally assert what was really happening right in front of me, and my inner sceptic was still clinging stubbornly to the prosaic explanations proffered by "unconscious desire", but the voice of my heart was at distinct loggerheads with cold logic.

Was this for real?

Were we really in communication with the spirit of a dead girl?

I hoped so. I truly did. But I couldn't shake the idea that the combined will of all those seated around the table, who had been close to my friend's daughter in life, could have wanted this so much that it affected how we operated that upturned half-pint glass.

We had intended to try and "communicate" with the spirits from the tunnels below or within the wonderful old building we were in. Instead, we were all compelled to stare intently at this glass as answer after familiar answer to questions of poignant significance "came through" from someone who had been connected personally with my mother and our friends.

And I guess the final question was possibly the most important of all. "Are you happy?" asked my friend to what he fervently believed to be the spirit of his daughter.

We held our breath as the glass slid across the smooth melamine surface of the round table. In a beam of torchlight it settled. "Yes." We all of us smiled at this most simple and yet most beautiful of answers.

As did I, the avowed sceptic, too.

TWO

Afterwards, my mother, knowing of my life-long passion for all things supernatural, along with my inherent scepticism about its reality, asked me, in a voice cracking with emotion, "Could we really unconsciously will something like that to happen?"

That was the difficult, bombshell of a question, right there.

In my experience, the answer had to be a hugely disappointing, "more than likely."

The indisputable fact was that everyone gathered around that table knew our friend's daughter in life, and it was also an indisputable fact that we all would have loved more than anything for the communications to be genuine messages from her summoned spirit. But part of me knew that this willingness to believe was more than enough for us to collectively, albeit unconsciously, manipulate the glass to form the answers we all desperately wanted to be true.

I nodded, and gave voice to my suspicions, leaving just enough hint of a sense of vagueness in my answer to soften the blow.

And this is the fine line that a sceptic should walk when considering how a cool and logical mind derives prosaic possibilities from the seemingly impossible. When casually pulling apart a belief system, be it a ghost story or a séance, there is always the distinct probability that someone out there will be deeply hurt or otherwise affected.

During the early hours of that summer morning, I was compelled to open an inner dialogue between the metaphorical Devil and Angel on my shoulder. My desire to shout out "I know how it's done," was fortunately countered by my compassion for those who had quite possibly made contact with a passed-on loved one, and who have certainly derived much comfort from the "messages" imparted by an upturned glass on a table.

My inner sceptic was momentarily silenced, and I realised there was more to that session than simply a bit of fun, which I could easily rationalise with a disparagingly cynical term and a brief explanation, like the archetypal party-pooper.

There was a connection there with which I had no right to meddle; a simple acknowledgement that filled people's hearts with a combination of sadness and joy. Something spectacular *did* occur that night. What that was, on this occasion, it is not my place to say.

As a former co-organiser of the "Wirral Psychic & Paranormal Workshop", it is perhaps a pertinent question as to why I, as a self-avowed sceptic, would wish to be so heavily involved with such an organisation? After all, our group used to put on everything from Mind, Body & Spirit Fairs to Psychic Nights.

My carefully considered answer though is always the same.

Just because I am a sceptic, it doesn't mean that I'm not interested in finding out as much as I possibly can about the subject. If I was not remotely interested in this type of Fortean phenomena, then what kind of sceptic would I truly be?

Yes, I do enjoy the challenge of working out "how it's done", and I do enjoy being stumped from time to time. But I am constantly aware that sometimes the sceptic is faced with a stark choice as to whether to keep their pie hole shut, or to keep their personal theories to themselves. My advice is to glance around the faces of those who are receiving "messages" in whatever form, and if their countenance is lit up with a shining smile, and it appears that the weary weight of the world has been lifted from their shoulders, then it really is time to serve that sceptic within a healthy dose of diplomatic humanity.

Dave Shirley

CHAPTER EIGHTEEN:
'A MASS OF SWIRLING SHADOWS'

BASTET

During the late autumn of 2002, in response to yet another of my increasingly desperate requests on Radio Merseyside for local accounts of Fortean phenomena, I received a phone call from a well-spoken, seemingly level-headed middle-aged woman by the name of Abigail Joynson.

Abigail was extremely anxious to tell me her story (though really, it mostly belonged to a terminally ill patient at the former Isolation Hospital, an infirmary that was built to house patients afflicted with tropical diseases, which once stood on the banks of the River Mersey, until it burned down in the early 1960s, but we'll get to that in due course). She asked if we could arrange a meeting at her home address, whenever I was free, as she didn't feel she could do the tale any kind of justice relating it over the phone.

I've got to be honest, I wasn't too keen on the idea of calling round to a complete stranger's house just to record her account, no matter how intriguing it might prove to be. I mean, for all I knew, (and never mind the pleasant, rational phone demeanour, God knows, I've been fooled often enough by *that* before) she might prove to be a sexually frustrated, stark raving mad woman, with a penchant for preying upon gullible, wannabe writers, blindly wandering into her trap armed with nothing more than a pen, a writing pad and a notoriously defective dictating machine.

Besides, Ms Joynson, had told me she lived in the centre of Moreton, a good forty minute journey from my home at the time, not exactly on a par with Franklin's doomed Antarctic expedition in search of the North West Passage, granted, but far enough away to add to its low placing in the "can-I-really-be-arsed" enthusiasm stakes.

In the end, I think the only thing that finally persuaded me to go and speak to her was the pure and simple fact that I'd secured a brief DJ residency at *The Coach & Horses*, an alehouse situated on, of all places Moreton Cross, no more than a short, five minute walk from Ms Joynson's home address.

So, on the afternoon prior to my first gig at the pub, I called round to find a pleasant enough, semi-detached house, with a well-tended garden in the centre of which was a small pond surrounded by bulrushes from the midst of which peered the serenely grinning faces of a couple of plastic gnomes. I strode up the concrete path, and was greeted by a kindly-smiling, conservatively-dressed woman, I judged to be in her late sixties, with her grey hair tied up in a bun, and the sight of this grandmotherly-type figure instantly dispelled any fears I might have had about her being a homicidal sex fiend. She greeted me with a friendly smile that revealed a perfect set of pearly whites, and invited me to take a seat in the living room while she went to brew a cup of tea and I sat in one of the plush, leather armchairs, glancing around at the unremarkable, typically suburban furnishings.

Oh, and wonder of wonders, the dictating machine actually managed to function long enough for me to get the entire story down.

ONE

It turned out that Abigail ("Please, call me, Abby. Everybody does") wanted to tell me about the time she spent working at a place that was virtually on my doorstep, but may just as well have been situated deep in the still unexplored regions of the Congo, for all the relevance it held for me. Which just goes to show how pig ignorant you can be concerning the history of the county where you live, and how often you really don't have to dig that deep to uncover the secrets of its past. Sometimes, the most fascinating stories lie so close to the surface, the veneer proves thinner than the shiny, silver paint of a Lucky Dip.

Certainly, that had proven to be the case with the tale Abby Joynson told about her time as a nurse at The Liverpool Port Authority Isolation Hospital, during the 1950s, starting out when she'd been

NEW FERRY ISOLATION HOSPITAL

*(Above): The doctors', nurses' and medical staff's quarters at the Liverpool Port
Authority Isolation Hospital circa 1902 – built on the shores of the Mersey near the
small town of New Ferry, to accommodate those afflicted with contagious, incurable
diseases, a place of misery, despair and unimaginable suffering, burned to the ground
by a controlled fire in 1963.*

little more than 20-years-old.

'You won't remember the place, of course, Lee,' she said. 'It was destroyed a little before your time, burned to the ground by a controlled fire back in 1963. I was no longer working there by then. In fact I hadn't been anywhere near the hospital since the day I'd handed in my notice, five years earlier, but still I felt moved when I'd gazed at the pictures in the local papers of the flickering flames shooting high into the skies above the Mersey. I remember reading that you could see the flames as far away as Runcorn, and that these days, there's nothing left of the infirmary but a few broken bricks and the sad, crumbling remnants of one of the outer walls.

'Not much of a memorial for those who died and those who spent nigh on a century caring for the victims of contagious, incurable, and in many cases, fatal diseases. I hear they've built a modern, Wimpy-style housing estate there now, and that it looks for all the world as though it's been modelled on "Brookside Close". What's that saying? "From the sublime to the ridiculous." Ah, well, I suppose that's progress, for you.

'But anyway, I'm sure you didn't come here to listen to an old lady gripe about the relentless march of change. Let's get to it before you either nod off or the batteries drain on your little recorder thingy, there.

'I worked at the Isolation Hospital from 1952, right up to the day in 1958, when I spoke, for what proved to be the one and only occasion, to a terminally ill patient named Francis Stanley.

TWO

'I can still vividly remember the day Francis was first admitted to the hospital. It was January 6th, old Christmas Day, 1958, and Dear God, he was in such a terrible state. I later learned that the poor man was only 26-years-old, but every inch of his skin was covered with so many huge, disfiguring blisters and lesions, he'd looked impossibly ancient, and you simply couldn't help but stop whatever it was you were doing for a moment, to stare open-mouthed as he made his less than grand entrance.

'That's saying something, you know, when you consider the hundreds of patients that I'd seen brought in through the gates prior to Francis' arrival. Of course, you never quite get used to the sight of dreadfully sick people, eyes bulging with a mixture of hopelessness and outright terror, as they're led to the wards by orderlies in white face masks, but something about this case was different right from the off. Francis had to be wheeled in, for a start, strapped firmly to one of those metal trolleys, presumably for his own protection, and whilst even that wasn't entirely unusual, what I *did* find deeply disturbing was the manner in which, even under heavy sedation, he was screaming and raving nonsensically in a voice that at times, scarcely sounded human.

'That got to me. It plainly affected the rest of the hospital staff, too, judging by the shocked expressions I saw on their faces.

'I recall I was suddenly struck by a memory of when I was a little girl, aged around eight or nine. I'd been walking back from the shops with my father, holding his hand and feeling safe and loved, when a black and white cat, little more than a kitten, really, had suddenly emerged from behind a shop's sandwich board and dashed across the busy high street. I'd watched in horror as the cat was struck by a passing car and sent flying into the gutter. It didn't die straight away, but the sound of its awful agonised mewling haunted my dreams for weeks afterwards. I'm telling you, Lee, the noises Francis Stanley made as the orderlies wheeled him along the corridors, were eerily similar to the high-pitched squealing of that mortally-wounded cat.

'It unnerved me so much that I instinctively found myself backing away, and because I wasn't looking where I was going, I accidentally sent a pile of bed-pans crashing to the floor, their unbearably tinny clanging only adding to the sense of utter bedlam. It did give me something to focus on, though, and as I set about gathering up the scattered pans, the sound of that agonised screaming was mercifully cut off as the trolley was pushed through the swinging doors that led directly to the quarantine ward, and I offered up a muttered prayer for the comparative silence that descended in his absence.

'I was also grateful too, that I didn't have any personal dealings with Mr Stanley. Not at first, anyway. For one reason or another, he was never included on any of what I called my "tours of duty", although I heard enough about him from some of the nurses who had the misfortune to make his acquaintance.

"I know it's cruel to say it, like, but he gives me the 'orrors," Nurse Mary Wilson, a red-haired, freckle-faced Scouser from Tuebrook, once confided during a lunch break. "I hate goin' in that vile-smellin' room, even though he's nearly always out for the count due to his medication, and he seldom if ever mumbles anythin' I can make out, even when he is half-way conscious. It's not just the way he looks either, Abby, though Christ knows, that's stomach churnin' enough.

"It's somethin' else I can't quite put me finger on. Somethin about him reeks of, oh, I dunno, *Evil,* I suppose the Catholic in me would say. Sounds mad that though, dunnit? I mean, he's just a terribly sick man, who's last few days on Earth are gonna be spent coughing his guts up and turnin into the friggin *Creature From The Black Lagoon!*"

Mary had giggled then, and I'd forced myself to join her. But in truth our laughter had sounded forced and there was precious little humour in it, as it echoed along the plain-white corridors.

THREE

'One sun-bright, late February afternoon, a month and a half or so after Francis had been admitted, my luck in successfully avoiding his presence finally ran out.

'One of the nurses who had been caring for the patient, had herself fallen ill with a severe bout of the flu, and the ward sister had asked me to take over her roster until she was well enough to return. Actually, it wasn't a request. It was more of an order, and although I would much rather have whiled away the hours gathering the other multi-soiled bed-sheets and hand washing them with nothing but a bar of Lever's hand soap and a used Brillo Pad, than be forced to endure the presence of the awful Mr Stanley, it was clear I had no real choice in the matter.

'I'd tried to console myself with the knowledge that in all likelihood, Francis would be rendered unconscious by the drugs he'd been administered, but as it turned out, those hopes were dashed the moment I'd set foot in the room. An all but silent room that smelled of disinfectant and sickness and the coppery aroma of pus-weeping sores.

'I paused for a second, steeling myself before taking my first hesitant step across the squeaky linoleum floor.

"Please, nurse," a voice had cried out then. A surprisingly clear voice that came from the direction of the shape in the bed opposite, and I'd uttered a tiny scream and very nearly dropped yet another collection of tinny-clanging bed pans along with freshly-washed sheets and towels.

"Please, nurse," it repeated. "Please, I'm terribly sorry if I startled you. That honestly wasn't my intention, I assure you." There was a moment of silence, and then I heard a hollow click in Mr Stanley's throat and I realised that however clear and concise his tones, it must have been very painful for him to speak, and I felt a stab of guilt mixed with sympathy.

"That's perfectly okay, Mr Stanley," I said, mentally blocking out the grotesque sight that now befell my eyes, and the sickening smell of him, and forced myself to lean closer so that he wouldn't have to strain his voice unnecessarily.

"That's very sweet of you to say," he said, now in a half-whisper. "Ordinarily, I wouldn't seek to distract you from your daily duties. But circumstances dictate I must crave your indulgence for what I promise will only be a very short while."

'I told him there was no need to rush, even though part of me wanted to flee the room at the earliest opportunity.'

"Again, I am in your debt," Mr Stanley said, and I think, though I can't be sure, that he tried to crack a smile. "There is something I need to tell you, you see, Nurse, erm...?"

"Nurse Joynson," I said, pointing to my name tag. "But please, call me Abby."

'He nodded gently.' "Abby it is, then. I have something I need to tell you, Abby. Something I desperately need to get off my chest, before it is too late. I do not think I am long for this world, now."

'Of course, I tried to tell him not to lose faith. That I was sure he was going to make a full and complete recovery, but he slowly raised his left hand, causing several of the fluid-filled boils gathered there to burst open, and a thick, opaque liquid oozed slowly across the reptilian skin, as he weakly waved away my platitudes.'

"Please, Abby. We both know I am correct in my diagnosis. It is perfectly all right. I am not remotely scared of dying. I used to be, of course. But that was before...well..." He paused and I was startled to see a single tear go sliding down the ruined flesh of his cheek.

"Now, I promise you, death will be a blessing. A welcome respite from the constant pain, the sickness, the suffering."

'He looked straight at me, his bright blue eyes burning with a frenzied intensity. "But first, and although I'm painfully aware I have no right to request anything of you, I wonder whether you could possibly find it in your heart to do me a very great favour." He attempted a smile for certain this time, and his swollen lips made a hideous cracking noise as they tore and split. "Call it a dying man's last wish, if you like."

"Well, I really duh-duh-don't.." I stammered, feeling the heat rise in my cheeks.

"Oh please, don't misunderstand me," he said quickly. "I did not mean to suggest that you might perform a task that could in any way be deemed to be of an "improper" nature. Dear Lord, no. I merely want you to return something, a possession of mine, back to its country of origin. It is the sole item you will find contained within the bag, which I believe is currently being stored in the bottom drawer of my bedside cabinet."

'With a sigh of relief, I turned and opened the draw, and there was indeed a large black leather bag, and as Francis nodded encouragingly, I placed the large leather bag on a chair, before carefully unzipping the fastener, and somewhat tentatively reached inside.

'I withdrew an eight-inch tall statuette of a jet-black cat, with blank, pupil-less eyes and a pair of hugely prominent and pointed ears, in truth more like a jackal's than any feline I'd ever seen. It had a golden band draped around its neck, with what looked like an ancient Egyptian amulet dangling from its centre.

'It was handsome.

'And yet at the same time, it was indescribably ugly.

'Even worse, it felt unaccountably warm to the touch. Almost as though it were alive, as insane as that sounds.

'I quickly dropped it back into the bag, repelled by the loathsome, impossible furriness of its sleek-as-an-oil-slick form, and then suddenly Francis was beckoning me closer still to his bedside, and the stench of the infection caused me to gag, whilst the heat of his fever was akin to standing before an open oven door the way I had at my parent's house on occasion, helping my mother remove the basted chicken and the spuds for our Sunday afternoon roast, and when he coughed fitfully into a hankie, I noticed the speckles of blood blossoming on the material like a bunch of bright red roses.

'I had a face mask on, of course, and I really didn't want to get too close, for obvious reasons, but nevertheless, I found I was more than a little curious to hear what it was he had to say.

FOUR

"I have led an extremely lonely life, Abby," he began.

"I blame no one but myself for that bitter fact. I seek no sympathy. I have conspired, whether by accident or design, to drive away everyone I have ever cared for. Family, friends, and most latterly, my beloved fiancée. When Marianne told me she was expecting our first child, late last year, I cowardly succumbed to panic and elected to run away from my responsibilities, in both a literal and figurative sense. I decided on a whim, to travel abroad, to foreign parts, to escape the trap into which I foolishly believed I'd fallen.

"I'd inherited a fairly large sum of money when my father had died suddenly, a year or so earlier, and I withdrew a sizeable portion of the money so that I could embark on a solitary trip to Egypt. I sailed via Cyprus, to Port Said, and upon my upon my arrival in the ancient city, I decided to hire a car for the long drive to Cairo. I have to be frank, I found the city, once the exalted cradle of civilisation, to be disappointingly run-down and hideously dilapidated. The soul-deadening sight of grubbily-dressed citizens ransacking the road-side refuse bins caused me to avert my gaze and put my foot down as I headed towards the Sphinx and the majestic pyramids of Giza.

"But even that much anticipated experience turned out to be hugely anti-climatic. The very moment I alighted from the car, I was assailed by swarms of fast-talking, cheap tat-bearing vendors, and I was forced to head away from the Pyramids to escape their attentions and traipse instead across the baking hot sands towards a series of obviously new excavation sites. I walked slowly, oppressed by the incessant, head-bowing heat, staring at the sun-bleached, fine as silk white sand, my mind beset by a series of dark and my mind beset by a series of dark, depressing thoughts of the hopeless days that likely lay ahead.

"And then suddenly, my attention was drawn to a sparkling flash of light spearing like a golden lance through the otherwise featureless landscape. I knelt down and gently brushed a thin layer of sand to one side, and there revealed under the harsh glare of that merciless sunlight was a well-preserved effigy of some sort. A black cat-headed entity. An Egyptian Goddess, most likely. And I was struck by the fact that it was just lying there, glinting in the scorching glare, almost as though it wanted to be found.

"I bent down to take a closer look and after a moment's hesitation, I picked it up.

"It sounds strange. Irrational, even. But I honestly didn't like the way it felt in my hands. It was warm and pulsing in a way that had nothing to do with the intense heat of the desert. It felt more like a heartbeat. Of fervent life beating through every fibre of its being.

"But that was completely ridiculous of course.

"Every bit as ridiculous as my instinctively knowing beyond doubt that the statuette, though it could quite easily have been some cheap and nasty imitation, a cast-side trinket, was a genuine, ancient Egyptian artefact, and if such were indeed the case, I wondered how much it might be worth. I glanced furtively around me, and saw nothing other than the ever-present merchants waylaying groups of hapless tourists, too caught up in parading their wares to pay any attention to me. Otherwise, there was nothing but endless miles of empty desert, and so I got to my feet and went to place the statuette in the buttoned up pocket of my knee-length shorts. However, I didn't care for the prospect of having its throbbing warmness so close to my skin and so I chose instead to place it inside my travel bag.

"And then suddenly, a long, dark shadow fell over me.

"I spun around and found myself confronted by a huge black man, who had appeared it seemed, from out of nowhere. He must have been at least seven-foot tall and he was wearing nothing but a leopard-skin loin cloth and a gold necklace with a single pendant depicting the image of a cat, identical to the one I'd uncovered beneath that flimsy layer of sand.

"He was well muscled and had the appearance of a fierce warrior, as though he could easily, if he chose, crush my skull as easily as an egg shell. He raised his arm and pointed at my bag.

"You had best return that which you have taken," he said in perfect English. "I suggest you re-bury it. Perhaps much deeper beneath the surface of the desert than the shallow depths from which you retrieved it."

"I'm sorry, but I don't have the slightest idea what you're talking about," I replied, struggling to keep the tremor out of my voice. "I think perhaps you have misconstrued my actions just now. I was merely watching a dung beetle pushing a ball of camel excreta many times its size up to the top of a sand dune. It is a sight that never fails to fascinate me."

"The giant of a man slightly raised his eyebrows and smiled, and his perfect set of white teeth appeared disconcertingly sharp and incisor-like.

"I will tell you once more, for your own good. You had best put that revered item back beneath the sand. Where it belongs. No good will come of you removing it, I assure you."

"His grin, if possible, appeared to grow wider still. It was hard to ignore the impression that as intimidating as he undoubtedly was, he was merely going through the motions. That all this was some sort of well-rehearsed act he felt obligated to perform. Certainly, he could have taken the statuette away from me by force, if he'd wanted to, and there wouldn't have been a thing I could have done about it. But he made no such attempt. Instead he simply stood there, as if he were waiting for me to make a move.

"In the end, unsure of what else I should do, I shrugged my shoulders and without another word, went to walk away, half-expecting the grinning giant to reach out and grab hold of me. But he just remained standing there watching me, his white-toothed smile and the dead glimmer of his eyes wavering like a mirage in the midst of that impossibly arid heat.

"I considered it a mercy that he made no attempt to follow me. The last I saw of him, he was stood there, as fixed and immobile as the great Pyramids themselves, a monument to a revered but long-faded glory.

"If I am being honest, and why spin out this confessional tale if I am to resort to patent untruths, the drive back though central Cairo was fraught with the baleful glances of passers-by, be they ordinary members of the public, be-suited office workers, or uniformed policemen. Each of them seemed to eye me with suspicion or outright hatred as I sweated, even with the car windows wound all the way down, in the dead heat of an Egyptian afternoon.

"It was a relief to check out of my hotel three days early and to drive back to Port Said as fast as was humanly possible and when I gratefully boarded the ship to sail back to Cyprus, and from there for the long journey back to Liverpool, I felt relief to be homeward-bound, and once we were in mid-ocean I unzipped my bag and checked that my cat figurine (and I truly felt it *was* mine, now) remained safely nestled amongst the assembled piles of sweat-stained clothing, tubes of sun tan lotion, insect repellent and dog-eared books and magazines.

"It was there, of course. It's weighty (and throbbingly warm), presence as reassuring as an old and trusted companion.

"Except it wasn't. Reassuring, I mean. Not really. But it was valuable, and like the tragic creature Gollum, in Tolkien's classic novels, obsessed with The Ring he called his "precious," I loved it and loathed it at the same time. And I had to keep it near me, refusing to let it out of my sight, even when, during the latter stages of the voyage, I was plagued by terrifying nightmares and I began to fall increasingly ill.

"At first I thought it was merely a combination of heat exhaustion, sea sickness, and maybe a stomach bug caused by something I'd eaten whilst in Egypt. But the closer I got to home, the worse I felt. I couldn't eat a thing, my muscles ached abominably, and all of my energy had been completely sapped, as though a vampire had drained it away in the space of a single night.

"Then, a series of rashes, livid and oozing began to break out all over my face and body, and when I vomited, as I did frequently, though I hadn't eaten in days, it was bloody and contained small fleshy lumps that resembled pieces of undigested meat. I remained confined to my cabin, too frightened even to seek medical assistance, but when eventually we reached Liverpool, and I was too weak even to rise from my bed, a member of the crew found me lying semi-conscious on the bed in my cabin and immediately went to fetch the ship's doctor.

"I don't remember much of what happened after that. Just the expressions of revulsion on the other three crew member's faces when they'd been summoned to assist in placing me upon a stretcher, and the doctor's near-panicked reaction when asked to diagnose my condition.

"Oh, and the perhaps not incidental fact that when they transferred me from the ship to a smaller boat that later deposited me on the New Ferry dockside and the flight of steps that lead to this hospital, I was clutching the bag that contained that damned ancient cat figurine close to my chest. Though in my fever-induced delirium, I had no conscious recollection of my having placed it there."

"Nor could I explain how it was that though my entire body had been burning up with sickness, the cat figurine had appeared to be somehow, warmer still.

FIVE

"The rest, of course, you know, Abby.

"I have vague recollections of my arrival here, of being wheeled along what seemed to be an endless series of corridors, of faces peering down at me in the manner of mourners gathered at a graveside, of the sting of injections and tranquillisers and bitter-tasting medication.

"That, and the many frustrating and often painful attempts at trying to speak, or at least to communicate somehow with the succession of nurses who have flitted in and out of this room like waiters at some hugely popular restaurant. To convey to them something of the utmost importance. Always I have singularly failed. The words constantly catching in my throat like tiny fish bones, or falling from my cracked and blistered lips in a string of nonsensical gibberish. So, in truth, I'd all but given up hope of ever succeeding in making myself understood, before at last I slipped gratefully from this life into merciful death.

"Until this morning. When you walked in the room, and I awoke, and I opened my mouth and my voice had miraculously returned, and I felt it were as though God had given me one last chance to allow me to plead with someone, *anyone*, to do the right thing.

"Now of course, we come to it, at last. The great favour I would ask of you. Perhaps, you have already guessed as to its nature. If not, then I must spell it out plainly. I need you, Abby, to return that accursed figurine back to Egypt, for me. To send it back to its country of origin. Back where it belongs. I was foolish enough to ignore the warnings, my sense of dark foreboding, and now I am paying the ultimate price for my self-centred greed and dismissive arrogance. It is too late for me. Far too late. But it would, I believe, salve my conscience and doubtless ease my passing to know that if the statuette is transported home then perhaps the evil it has wrought, the harm it has inflicted, will be restricted purely to the rotting, stinking form you see before you.

"I have a fairly large amount of money secreted in the hidden side pocket of my bag. Please take it. Take all of it. Contact the Egyptology department at Liverpool museum, and acquire from them the address for Cairo Museum.

"Package the artefact with a covering letter and send it by air-mail, first class. Please, if I have to resort to the less-than honourable tactic of resorting to emotional blackmail, then I will. As I believe I stated at the outset; Consider it the granting of a dying man's last wish.

"Truly, this evil must end. And soon."

SIX

'The remainder of that's days "tour of duty" seemed to drag by with unnatural slowness, but perhaps that's hardly surprising given the disconcerting, not to say, surreal nature of the conversation I'd had earlier with Francis Stanley, weighing heavy on my mind even as I set about trying to focus on caring for the many other patients resident at the hospital.

'It wasn't that I believed for a second that Mr Stanley's terrible illness was due to some sort of supernatural curse involving a cat-headed statuette. I told myself time and again that the whole thing was nothing more than one of those bizarre coincidences that sometimes occur in life, leaving us feeling slightly woozy, like we've just awoken from a series of dreams that we can't quite remember. But just the same, Francis had made me promise I'd accede to his "last request", before I'd left his room, and perhaps not least because I was beginning to feel guilty for having previously regarded him with such utter revulsion due entirely to his appearance, I assured him I fully intended to honour my oath.

'I took what I imagined would be more than enough money to pay the cost of the air-mail from the thick wad of notes contained in the hold-all, and then wrapped the figurine in one of the fluffy white towels so no one would see it and ask awkward questions (but also, to be honest, because I didn't want the thing touching my bare skin any more than was absolutely necessary). I then smiled, nodded my head, and assured him I'd see him in the morning, when the deed was done.

SEVEN

'I drove straight home after my shift had ended, in the midst of a fairly heavy snow flurry, without even pausing to change out of my nurse's uniform. I felt incredibly tired, and wanted nothing more than to soak myself in a hot bath, have a bite to eat and slip beneath the fresh clean sheets of my double bed with a glass of wine and an Agatha Christie novel.

'But first, I had an important call to make.

'I arrived home at a little after seven, and made straight for the phone, anxious to get it over and done with so I could relax and enjoy the remainder of the evening. I have always lived alone, despite a succession of relationships over the years, some serious, other's scarcely more than one night stands, but the truth is, I don't think I'm cut out for marriage or even "living in sin" with a partner, simply because I prefer my own company to that of anyone else. I only mention this now, because it perhaps makes my subsequent actions later on that freezing cold February night, more understandable.

'I leafed through the directory to get the number for Liverpool Museum, and after speaking to a receptionist, I was put through to the head of the Ancient Egyptian Exhibition, a doctor something or other. His name escapes me, now, I'm afraid. I briefly introduced myself and then proceeded to tell him about the figurine and of how I'd come into possession of it, though of course I left out any mention of its supposedly being cursed, and after describing it in some detail, I asked him whether he could possibly identify the cat-headed figure.

"Oh, yes, indeed," he'd replied authoritatively. "It sounds very much like a representation of the ancient Egyptian Cat Goddess, Bastet. She was one of the most popular deities of that long-ago age, despite, or maybe because, of the fact that her name has been translated by some experts as meaning, "Devouring Lady".

"Cats, as perhaps you may well know, Miss Joynson, were highly venerated by the people of that great civilisation, to the extent that many cults dedicated to their worship were founded by disciples of other-worldly entities such as Bastet."

'He paused for a second and then added: "I would be extremely interested in taking a look at the artefact if that were at all possible, I would be able to tell you immediately whether or not it is of genuine antiquity."

'I replied that in ordinary circumstances I would have been happy to bring it over to the museum for him to examine to his heart's content, but that I had made a solemn promise to a terminally ill patient to send it back to Egypt, as soon as was humanly possible, and the doctor, whilst obviously disappointed, had the common decency to tell me he perfectly understood my position and passed on the address of the museum in Cairo, before bidding me a good evening.

'After writing the details down on a notepad, I'd tore off the sheet and placed it in the overnight bag I'd brought back from the hospital with me, alongside the statuette of the Goddess I now knew to be Bastet, still cocooned in its towel. I left the bag in the hall, planning to take it to the local post office during my mid-afternoon lunch break the following day. And I remember feeling a strange sense of relief, as I set about preparing dinner at the prospect of ridding myself of an object that though it may only have been in my possession for few short hours, had nevertheless filled me with a vague sense of apprehension. A cold feeling in the pit of my stomach.

'I ended up picking at my meal, forsaking the bath for a shower, and casting the Agatha Christie novel aside after constantly reading the same line over and over again.

'Then I turned out the light, and instantly fell asleep.

EIGHT

'I awoke bolt upright into pitch darkness, terror coursing through my veins.

'The house was completely silent.

'Nothing stirred.

'Nothing seemed to be amiss.

'And yet, I knew, with a dreadful sense of certainty, there was someone in the house. Downstairs. Standing in the dark and waiting. Just waiting.

'I didn't want to go downstairs and check. God, knows I didn't. But neither could I simply lie there, frozen in fear, fervently praying for first light. It took every ounce of will that I possessed for me to shake off the paralysis and quietly throw back the blankets and slide off the mattress. I switched on the bedside lamp, saw from the table clock it was only three in the morning, and trod carefully across the cold, carpet-less floor, wincing at every give-away creak of the floorboards. It was ice-cold in the bedroom. I could almost see my breath, and I reached for my thick dressing gown from its hook on the back of the door.

'After what seemed like an age, I reached the landing, and peered down into a dark, brightened only by a few slabs of mid-winter moonlight reflecting off the snow-covered rooftops of the houses opposite. I couldn't make out anything other than the slick and polished frame of the banisters, the framed photographs adorning the walls and the first of the upper stairs descending into the, what appeared to be a, mass of swirling shadows.

'I fumbled for the light switch, but the bulb must have gone because the stairs and hallway beyond remained cloaked in impenetrable blackness, and it was hard to resist the inner voice that pleaded with me to turn back and bury myself under the bedclothes till dawn. But I had to see who or what I was convinced had intruded into my home. As though I were in a dream-like trance, I made my way slowly down the stairs, again the inevitable creaks echoing in the stillness like pistol shots, and

I half-expected at any moment that something would suddenly reach out and drag me, kicking and screaming, down into the midst of those constantly roiling shadows. But I somehow made it to the foot of the stairs by spreading my arms out wide to feel my way into the hallway.

'The moment I did so, I knew that whatever awaited me, was standing on the other side of the oaken door that opened into the living room. It was standing ajar, and through the gap I could see pools of that silvery lunar light had formed beneath the large bay window. Once more I fumbled for the light switch, and once more there was no comforting electric light. *"Perhaps a fuse has blown or there's been a power cut,"* I told myself. *"Whatever the case, I've got two choices here: Either I can turn around and as quietly-as-possible sneak back up the stairs, climb back into bed, and mentally count down the hours to dawn. Or else I can push the door fully open and confront the source of my fear."*

'I want you to be clear that I was absolutely terrified at that point, and that inner voice, the voice of reason was beseeching me to take the first option. It made infinitely more sense. I mean, I hadn't even thought to pick up something I could potentially use a weapon.

'So, I made to turn away. I honestly did. But then instead placed the palms of my hands on the door frame and shoved it all the way open.

'And stepped inside.

'A figure, over six feet tall, and dressed in what appeared to a plain black-hooded cowl, was standing with its back to me, facing the far wall, seemingly oblivious to my presence.

'My first assumption of course was that it must be a male burglar who'd disguised their features, and who was either drunk or high on drugs, or both, and that their senses were so numbed they hadn't even heard me enter the room. I opened my mouth to challenge him. God only knows what I planned to say, but before a single word could leave my lips, the giant, virtually silhouetted figure turned to face me, the cowl falling back from its head and upper torso as it did, revealing its features in the glare of that cruel, February moon.

'The body at least, was human enough, though from the unmistakable swell of its breasts and its half-naked hourglass figure I immediately saw that I'd been completely wrong in surmising that the trespasser was male.

'The head, though…Dear God, *the head..*

'Thin and triangular in shape, black in colour and with slanted eyes that glowed red like twin furnaces. The large, sharply-pointed ears. The thick coating of silky fur rippling like a hot sirocco wind blowing across the surface of a bank of desert sand dunes.

'I stared, unable to believe what it was I was seeing, and I might have been able to dismiss the obscene thing that stood in the middle of my modern, suburban living room as being nothing other than an hallucination brought about by a combination of a rushed late night supper, and that strange conversation with the terminally ill Mr Stanley.

'But then, the lower jaw of the cat-headed apparition suddenly snapped open like a loose hinge, revealing a set of jagged, saliva-glistened fangs, and an ulcerated tongue that flickered in out, quivering wildly like a snake's.

'And then it opened its mouth wider still, and *hissssssed* at me.

'That vile sound, filled with spiteful malice was the crowning insanity.

'The room seemed to spin at a quickening speed and I fainted dead away.

NINE

'When I came too, I found I was lying safely tucked up in my bed.

'It took me a minute or so to realise I must have dreamed the whole thing, and a minute or two after that for the first wave of intense relief to begin to wash over me. A smile had just begun to form at the corners of my mouth, but then I became aware of a dead weight lying on my chest.

'I couldn't move a single muscle. I've never experienced a case of the "Night Terrors" before, though I'd heard of it of course. I was a nurse, after all. But yet here I was displaying all the classic symptoms. As paralysed as an embalmed corpse. An ancient Egyptian mummy, perhaps.

'I struggled with all my might to will myself to move, and eventually I was able to raise my head from the pillow, and almost immediately I wished that I hadn't.

'The effigy of Bastet was lying between my breasts, face-down, almost as though it were a real domestic cat, seeking the warmth of human companionship.

'The sight of that ghastly figurine, the statuette I had purposefully left secured in the zipped-up hold-all in the living room downstairs, was enough to break my sleep paralysis, and I swept the figure off the bed and onto the floor with a grunt of disgust. I threw the covers aside and filled with an eerie sense of déjà vu, I switched on the bedside lamp, and glanced at the clock. I saw, with no surprise, it was a little after three am. Once again, I crossed the room and made for the stairs, pausing only to snatch my dressing gown from the back of the door, as I did so.

'It seemed to me that things happened very quickly from that point on:

'I threw on every available light in the house, (and they all work fine, thank God), illuminating every dark corner. Every suggestion of shadow.

'I glance at the overnight bag on the living room sofa and see it's unzipped and empty, save for the towel. I get dressed quickly into my nurse's uniform, throw a thick coat on over it and go through to the garage at the side of the house. I don a pair of gardening gloves and then select what I deem to be the sturdiest of the suitcases stacked beneath the rows of shelving filled with half-empty oil cans and tins of long-gone hard emulsion paint, open the case and place several of the metal containers inside.

'I return to the bedroom where the feline effigy is lying prone at the side of the bed, its eyes seemingly glinting with malevolence, though I tell myself that's surely my imagination working overtime. Regardless, I scoop up the artefact in my gloved hands, and hold it upside down and at arms length as I carry it out to the garage and then wedge it firmly in between the sealed tins. I then lock the case away in the boot of my car, open the garage door, and drive as fast as I dare along the deserted, snow and ice covered roads that lead to my destination.

'I arrive without mishap, and park the car at the edge of a sloping cliff that looms above the River Mersey shoreline. I step out of the vehicle. The air is brittle. The skies are clear now. The tide is out and the polluted surface of the mudflats, forty-feet below, are slick and shiny. The desolate expanse, with its scattered detritus, flocks of immobile sea-birds and temporarily stranded river boats, looks deceptively tranquil and un-threatening. Like you could easily walk across its surface, *slide*, if you'd prefer, to the water's edge, like skating on thick winter ice. But as any local will readily attest, anyone foolish enough to set foot on that heavily-polluted mixture of mud and sand would pretty soon find themselves stuck up to their waists and in danger of sinking further still before the coastguard could be alerted.

'Smiling grimly, I fetch a torch from the glove compartment of my car and then go round to open the boot to lift out the case. It feels reassuringly heavy. I walk to the cliff edge, the snow crunching under my feet, and with a grunt, I throw the case and its contents as far out onto the marsh as I can. It lands with a satisfying plopping sound and in the light of the torch beam I watch it quickly sink beneath the oozing filth.

'Soon, there is no trace of it.

'No sign it had ever existed.

'And that is just fine with me.

'I don't care whether the statuette is truly valuable or not, or whether my actions could be considered wholly irrational. Nor is my conscience troubled by my breaking a promise I'd made to a dying man. That thing was evil. Pure and simple. I wanted rid of it. Buried somewhere it could cause no further harm and where no one would ever likely find it. The mudflats seemed to me as good a place as any.

TEN

'I decide, given the lateness of the hour, not to return home, but to sleep in the car, with the heating full on. The Isolation Hospital is only a five minute drive away, and my next 'tour of duty' was due to start at eight am.

'I awake as the bright winter sun rises, bathing the sugar-frosted fields in its thin watery light. I am tired, my eyes gritty with lack of proper, restful sleep, and there are aches in my shoulders and lower back, but still I feel a wave of blessed relief wash over me. A sense of a weighty burden lifted.

'The comforting sense of release lasts until the moment I step through the hospital entrance and I am just about to hang my thick winter coat up and remove my gloves, when I quite literally bump into Nurse Mary Wilson.

"Oh, Abby," she exclaims, her eyes glinting with the excitement of someone who is positively bursting with news, and never mind if it was good or bad. It turns out it was, depending on your point of view, somewhere in between.

"You'll never guess who passed away in the early hours of this morning," she says, dragging me to the one side, and answering her own question before I can respond. "New Ferry's very own Creature From Lagoons Dark and Fearful: Mr Francis Stanley!"

'I clasp my hand to my mouth and Mary nods her head in agreement. "Yeah. That was pretty much my reaction, too, after I found him this morning when I was doin' me rounds, an hour or so ago." She looked around and lowered her voice to a whisper. "Yer should have seen him, Abby. Or then again, maybe yer shouldn't have. He looked even worse in death than he did when he was first wheeled in here, if yer can believe that!"

'I ask her what she means and Mary wrinkles her nose and twists her lips in disgust. "Well, for a start, his face was contorted into this *really* 'orrible grimace, like somethin' had scared the livin' shite out of him before he died. But that wasn't the worst thing." Mary pauses for dramatic effect, obviously enjoying being the bearer of gruesome tidings. "The worst thing. The thing that'll no doubt be givin' me nightmares for God only knows how long, was the way in which Mr Stanley had frantically torn chunks of skin from his rottin' flesh during his death throes. He'd ripped the buttons off his pyjama top and I could see there was these mad series of deep gouges in his neck and across his chest." She shakes her head wonderingly. "Yer know what, Abby" she says, "it never ceases to amaze me the truly incredible physical feats human bein's are capable of when they're driven either by madness, desperation or intolerable pain. And as we know, poor arl Mr Stanley was afflicted with a dreadful combination of all three."

'Mary pauses again, but this time there's nothing remotely manufactured about it. A look of genuine puzzlement clouds her features.

"There was somethin' else that struck me as bein' strange. Yer might think I'm going round the twist or maybe I've been swiggin' the alcoholic hand gel or somethin', but I swear there was this weird-looking shape, an imprint, really, in the sheets alongside him. It looked to me like the outline a smallish cat would make, yer know, if it'd have been lying flatout on its back. I mean, I could clearly see what appeared to be pointed ears and the curl of a tail, as mad as that sounds. And when I reached out and touched the middle of the shape, it felt warm, as if whatever had made it had only recently just moved off the bed."

"Perhaps just moments before I'd entered the room.

'Mary shakes her head, smiles wryly, and from somewhere along the corridor, the scratchy, tinny sound of an intercom message paging a "Doctor Reid to Ward 21", reverberates throughout the vast spaces of the hospital.

"How weird is that, eh?" she says, and it's not voiced as a question, which is just as well, because I'm too dumb-struck with terror to answer. "It gets even madder, though.

"After a little while, I went to fetch the doctor and the ward sister to inform them Mr Stanley had died, and when we all returned to the room a minute or so later, that cat-like shape had completely disappeared. There was no trace of any indentation whatsoever. The sheets were as smooth and unlined as though they'd just been freshly pressed and ironed, and yet I swear I saw a…"

'Suddenly, Mary seems to be speaking from a great distance, I feel bile rising in my throat, and for the second time in a matter of hours I feel myself on the verge of losing consciousness.

'I slump to the floor, and the world turns mercifully black.

ELEVEN

'I'd studied long and hard to acquire a position at The Isolation Hospital, and the day I'd finally heard my application had been successful had been the proudest moment of my life. The work was often difficult and frequently stressful. The shifts seemingly never-ending and the hours depressingly unsociable.

'But I absolutely loved working there, just the same. I want to be perfectly clear about that because it might give you some indication of how much of a wrench it proved to be when I tended my resignation two months after the death of Francis Stanley.

'In truth, I believe I would have made that decision far sooner, had I been well enough to do so. As it was, I'd spent the best part of eight weeks on paid sick leave, the vast majority of that time, confined to my bed stricken with a fever that left me in a state of delirium and plagued with horribly vivid nightmares of feral cats and grinning black pedlars, howling hot winds and swirling dust devils, and slimy stretches of mud-flats that spew out objects too vile even for their poisoned, heavily polluted depths.

'By the time I felt well enough to rise from my bed and to eat something more substantial than a bowl of watery soup I'd lost three stone in weight, there were streaks of grey in my hair and there were not so much a set of crow's feet under my red-rimmed eyes than an entire murder's worth of them. I felt weak as a kitten (Ha! No pun intended), and mentally shattered, but one bright thought shone through the swirling fog of confusion; I could never go back to work at that hospital again.

'And I never did.

'My superiors, whilst disappointed with my decision to resign, kindly provided me with excellent references and I quickly found work as a carer in various old people's residential homes across Merseyside, right up until the day I finally retired from work for good.

'As I told you earlier, I couldn't even face returning to personally witness the destruction of the Isolation Hospital on the day of the controlled fire, in 1963. I do remember however, staring long and hard at the newspaper photographs of the crowds of people gathered on the river-front to watch the flames quickly reduce the buildings to smouldering rubble. I'd silently cheered and punched the air when I'd read the accompanying article that stated that by the time the fire had burned itself out, all that was left to remind anyone it had ever existed were the gateposts that stood at the former entrance and the red-bricked perimeter walls.

'Now, even those crumbling remnants are all but hidden from sight by wild plants and a small area of woodland.

'Of course, the local authorities had decreed that the hospital should be destroyed by fire due to it being contaminated with highly infectious diseases. But perhaps, although they couldn't possibly have known it, they'd succeeded in purifying the area in a spiritual sense, too.

'I'd certainly love to think so.

'I am thankful that nothing remotely supernatural has occurred in my life in the years that have since slipped by, and to be honest, I'm still not sure the whole thing wasn't just a series of vivid delusions, hallucinations, and nasty coincidences instigated by Francis Stanley's no doubt sincere belief that that he was the victim of a deadly curse.

'But I tell you this. Some nights I wake up and find myself unwillingly running back the reel of memories to that first week of January, 1958. There in the darkness these recollections lie bare for me to pick over like the remains of a foul-tasting meal that you feel obligated to feast on regardless.

'And I wonder whatever happened to that damned effigy of Bastet.

'I wonder if it's still lying buried beneath the depth-less mud flats, these past forty-odd years.

'I wonder whether it's possible that it somehow emerged to appear in Francis Stanley's hospital bed on the night he passed away.

'I wonder where it is *now*...

'*Sometimes I wonder....*'

*****

EPILOGUE

I'm not sure how much of Abby Joynson's story I believed, but I can't deny it played constantly on my mind in the aftermath of its telling. It had an undeniably haunting quality, in every sense of the word, and on a warm and sunny September afternoon, a couple of years back, I decided to pay a visit to the former site of the old Liverpool Port Authority Isolation Hospital, to see for myself what, if anything, remained of the place.

It turned out Abby had been fully truthful about one thing at the very least. There was hardly any trace that a large, forbidding-looking infirmary with high-walled grounds had ever existed. The area was indeed dominated by that *Brookside*-like housing estate, Abby had mentioned: the thoroughly modern infringing upon any sense of history, and I found myself wondering how many of the residents were aware they were living on a site once rife with sickness, misery and death. I sincerely doubted any real estate agents would have been falling over themselves to inform any potential "house-hunters" of that less than palatable fact in their glossy brochures.

I walked to the far edge of the estate and spotted a stile adorned with sign that announced the start of "The Wirral Circular Trail". The foot-path wends its way through the centre of an expanse of thick woodland, and through the occasional gaps in the trees, I could see glimpses of a sloping cliff leading down to the shoreline, and the remains of the steps that once served as a disembarkation point for the afflicted and their carers. When at last I was clear of the woods, the sparkling surface of the River Mersey was revealed, and it was easy to imagine the quarantine ships anchored here, whilst their miserable cargo of diseased human beings were carried up the steep banks towards the gates of the hospital. A one way trip, for so many of them.

It had evidently become an unofficial kid's play area, now, though. There were one or two discarded toys lying in a clump of bushes, along with a crumpled copy of *The Dandy,* whilst a length of frayed rope had been tied to a branch of an ancient-looking oak tree, the ground beneath it worn smooth by the feet of children launching themselves out across the muddy banks. It was hard to reconcile such innocent, carefree enjoyment with the doom-laden expressions on the faces of those being transported up that very incline, not so very long ago.

And then, as I reached the end of the path that leads towards the open fields on the other side of the housing estate, I noticed a single, orange-bricked pillar with a silver plaque attached to it, and I stopped to read the words engraved there....

'Memorial'
Liverpool Port Authority Isolation Hospital
1875 To 1963

"In memory of the people, travellers, sailors, and foreigners, that passed through this gateway, never to return home to their loved ones."

Built to decongest the Mersey River, of the Isolation Ships that were moored off shore, containing traveller's with contagious diseases, this hospital treated over 1,200 cases of tropical disease during the 88 years it was open.

Eventually closing its doors it was razed to the ground by controlled fire in 1963, and all that remains is this pillar and the low stretches of the sand stone wall. Now a woodland tribute to the memory of those who worked and died within these walls.

I was greatly moved by the words, and considered them a fitting epitaph for those who had spent their final days here.

I stood there for a long moment, all alone, pondering the words I'd just read and the story told to me by Abby Joynson, back in 2002, and it crossed my mind that if I were to wander back into the woods armed with a pick and a shovel, and start digging amongst the thickets and the bushes with their scarlet berries and prickly thorns, what you might find buried there.

The charred remnants of a letter that was never sent by a terminally ill patient.

A clip-board or a stethoscope that had somehow escaped the ravages of the fire.

Perhaps a scalpel or some other type of surgical implement.

Or a jet-black effigy of an ancient Egyptian Cat Goddess.

Its mouth split wide open in a permanent feral grin. Its fangs dripping wet with moisture. Its eyes blazing like flaming coals.

EPILOGUE: 2

And how's this for a particularly weird coincidence?

As I was typing up this story, on November 3rd, 2012, at my parent's home, my eyes began stinging and growing watery, a common malady familiar to anyone whose job involves staring at a computer screen for multiple hours on end. I decided the only quick-fire cure was to take a break, and went downstairs for a cup of coffee a and a bite to eat. I sat down with a steaming mug of coffee and a plate of tuna sarnies, in front of the telly. My dad had been watching Pointless, *his favourite TV quiz show, and because my eyes were still hurting, I was only kind of half-watching the screen.*

As I tucked into my sandwich, the first, multi-choice question came up on the screen, and I almost choked on an especially thick chunk of dead fish and mayonnaise...

The contestants had been asked to name the most obscure breed of cat from a selection of ten different breeds, some of which were entirely fictitious or were the names of cat-related deities, just to make things more difficult.

And guess what one of the potential choices was:

Yep.

Right there at option number two, was none other than our old friend, **Bastet** *– the ancient Egyptian Cat Goddess.*

You know what...

Sometimes, just like Nurse Abby Joynson, there are times when I really do *wonder.*

THE SINKING OF THE LUSITANIA, AND THE MURDER OF OVER 1,000 NON-COMBATANTS OFF THE OLD HEAD OF KINSALE, MAY 7TH, 1915.

CHAPTER NINETEEN:
ON THE DAY YOU LOST YOUR LIGHT
Panama Jack & The Lusitania

'He won't go for the carrot
They beat him by the pole
Some sunny day confronted by his soul
He's out at sea, too far off, he can't go home.'
***This Is England* - The Clash**

ONE
I've spoken of 'Panama Jack', before....

Anyone who read my début book with an even half-way attentive eye, will hopefully recall this incredibly colourful character, and his propensity for parking his jean-clad arse cheeks either side of a black-metal quayside bollard, to regale groups of fascinated, if somewhat sceptical children with a series of, for want of a better term, "tall, sea-faring tales."

But, as another Jack (this one christened with the decidedly more prosaic surname, White) once opined, '*I know I've said it once, but it bears repeating now!*'

From the magical ages of ten to thirteen, one of my favourite hangouts was the seemingly endless miles of docklands that stretched across both sides of the River Mersey.

These days, of course, a large proportion of the water-front has been completely transformed for the twin purposes of tourism and trendy accommodation for the well-heeled and a mix of both the genuine and decidedly borderline celebrity; the brightly illuminated spokes of The Liverpool Wheel, The Echo Arena (a 12,000-seater stadium where sometimes excellent, but all-too frequently young-girl-oriented 'pop combos', perform for those 'lucky' enough to be able to afford the price of the tickets) swanky restaurants and theme bars, and rows of impossibly expensive, but nevertheless much-sought after, river-front apartments.

Back in the late 1970s, and early '80s however, a fairly large proportion of the docks were in use, though even then the unmistakable signs of decline were very much in evidence, the skeletal frames of long-redundant cranes, the occasional fisherman forlornly casting his line into the depths of a stretch of long-dead water, his face etched with the cruel and certain knowledge that all his best days are long behind him.

Still though, there always seemed to be a sizeable amount of oil tankers and merchant ships, their sterns emblazoned with foreign flags and the painted names of impossibly exotic ports of origin, along with the occasional Royal Navy frigate and luxurious, multiple-decked, ocean liner.

There were also innumerable, crate-filled warehouses and ugly, fenced off scrapyards, where various items of rusted equipment had been dumped over the course of many years. There were literally hundreds of old, hollow pipes, and abandoned goods containers, with clusters of white limpets and barnacles still attached to them, giant wooden wheels that brought to mind pictures I'd seen in history books of the huge battering rams used in the epic sieges of magnificent walled cities, and anchors and pulleys, and lengths of metal coil that smelled of ocean fog and long-dead fish, and bitter, salty brine.

These discarded nautical objects provided a veritable playground of secret dens and clubhouses, or places where you could sit off when you needed a couple of hours in order to set your world to rights.

Fortunately for us kids, the smartly-uniformed security guards who patrolled the quayside and the hard-working dockers remained fairly tolerant of our blatant trespassing, even if they never actively engaged us in conversation.

There was however, one particular docker, who was to prove something of an exception to the rule.

"Panama Jack" (we never did find out his *real* name) was an arc welder in his late thirties, who was supposed to be applying his skills to the various vessels that came into the docks for repairs. In truth though, he seemed to spend most of his time sat smoking a sailor's pipe, with a hip flask close to hand, and a far-off, dreamy look in his eyes. If you ever approached him, however, he'd gab away merrily to anyone willing to listen, as my friends and I quickly discovered not long after we first made his acquaintance. The spring of 1977, that would have been. The year of the Queen's Silver Jubilee, the wonderful Sex Pistol's rise to nationwide notoriety, and Liverpool FC's bid for a then unprecedented Treble.

We could tell straight away that "Jack" was something of a unique character. He constantly wore a thick, black overcoat, even on the very hottest of days, and a battered sailor's cap that was so cheap and tacky looking, he could well have bought it at any fancy dress store, or one of those cheap, seaside souvenir stalls. He had a tanned, and prematurely grizzled face, lined with grey stubble, but there was a noticeable twinkle in his eyes whenever he launched into one of his extraordinary sagas. He had the gift of telling tales with the intimate grace of a confidant, ensuring that each one resonated with the enduring power of an ancient fable.

He told us he'd sailed the Seven Seas many times over during the course of his life, and had experienced many adventures, some more believable than others. He claimed to have spent his early twenties working on whaling ships off the coast of Newfoundland, and on one memorable occasion, had found a cetacean of such leviathan-like proportions, it would have given Captain Ahab second thoughts about spending a lifetime hunting it down, and never mind if that particular limb-chomping whale had succeeded in chomping off *both* of his pantalooned legs.

He'd also been shipwrecked on an impossibly sun-drenched tropical island, had once sighted a long-necked sea monster off the Cape of Good Hope, and had his merchant navy vessel attacked by a "monstrous, Kraken-like giant squid", as well as narrowly escaping a tribe of poison-dart blowing head-hunters, whilst sailing along the Amazon, and being half-drowned by the death-dealing tentacles of a shoal of "intelligent seaweed" in the middle of the Sargasso Sea.

I mean, come on, even as hugely impressionable children, we knew that most of what he claimed to be true, was likely to be every bit as fantastical as *Crystal Tipps & Alastair* getting together with the kids from *The Double Deckers* for a let's all build a space rocket to fly us to the moon to meet up with *The Clangers* and "the soup dragon" .

None of us could deny that he told great stories, though.

The kind that held you enraptured, no matter what level of credence you chose to afford them.

Certainly, that was the case when, one gorgeous, sun-blessed afternoon, during the six weeks school summer holidays, Jack had related the following story about one of Britain's worst ever maritime disasters, a series of dark and dreadful premonitions, and of true enduring love from beyond the grave.

TWO

'Okay,' Jack began, sat on his favourite pedestal, like "The Lord of all He Surveyed", 'I'm sure even those day-dreaming empty-heads amongst yer, who spend more time dreaming of scoring last-minute FA Cup Final winners or having a proper snog with that girl you've fancied since you saw her struttin' her stuff at the school disco, last Christmas, or maybe examining, with scientific curiosity, the gooey contents of the enormous snot-gobbler you've just dragged out of yer nose, has heard of the terrible fate that befell the *Titanic*?

'All right, allright! Settle down!' Jack had shouted in a bid to drown the clamorous yells of "Oh, aye, of course-we haves!" that followed in the wake of his rhetorical question. 'Let me ask yous something else, though. How many of yous have heard of the equally tragic sinking of the *Lusitania*?

The query was greeted with a few mumbled 'erms' and a mass shrugging of shoulders, but I remember thinking I had at least a vague notion that I'd heard the name *Lusitania* somewhere before, and I went to raise my hand, but before I had a chance, Panama Jack was speaking again.

'I thought that might stump yer!' he announced with a satisfied grin. 'And if yous will all do me the very great honour of snappin' yer big gobs shut, quit standing round like a pack of slack-faced divvies from some living dead B-movie, and park yer arses down there for a bit, I'll fill yous in with what I know about that great ship.

'I promise you though that the story I'm about to relate is more mess with the head, mind boggling, than trying to prise open a can of Princes salmon with a rusty fish knife and one of me ma's arl Victorian tin openers!'

As analogies went, this one wasn't far off the mark.

THREE

Someone once wrote, '*the saddest words of tongue or pen, are these:*

'*IF ONLY.*'

'I have good cause to agree with that sentiment, entirely.

'I know yous are only young, like, but most probably you, have too.

'I sometimes lie awake all night, mentally compiling my own seemingly endless list of "If Onlys", until the first grey slants of dawn begin to seep through the gaps in the curtains, and I can finally rest my weary eyes.

'Always featured high in those personal regret-filled charts, are these less-than-shining examples:

'*If only* I hadn't chosen to take shore leave that particular week in mid-November, 1974, and headed down to the West Midlands.

'*If only* I hadn't decided to head down to the West Midlands, in a likely pointless search for an arl flame I hadn't seen in years beyond counting, and who had, in all likelihood, forgotten that I even existed.

'*If only* I hadn't sat drinking, drowning my sorrows, really, in some grubby hotel room, before walking in a half drunken stupor, into town, on a cold, dark, winter's night.

'*If only* I hadn't stopped to speak with an ex-merchant sailor friend of mine, a big black feller, who used to live on Upper Parly Street, no less, standing outside that nondescript, but busy for a Thursday night, alehouse in Birmingham City Centre, at a little after 8:15pm. A few short minutes or so before the first of those two massive IRA terrorist bombs went off, and I was sent flyin' through the air onto the other side of the road by the sheer, terrible, hot-breath force of its ear-shattering blast

'And what I saw, lyin' on me back, me bloodied face turned side on so that I was looking straight through the shattered, smoke-billowin' windows.

'Amidst the hellish carnage of that torn-apart bar-room.

'Oh, dear God.

'*If only* I wasn't cursed with a bad liver and a terminally broken heart for company, most days.

'*If only* I hadn't spent the last three years pondering the damp drizzly November's of my soul.

'*If only*

'*If only* ...

'But aahh, here I go again kids, veering off topic. Swerving like the absent-minded meanderings of that stubborn arl seadog, Captain Le Serrec, who I can still see in me mind's eye, standing on the frozen decks, determined to the point of near-insanity, to steer the *Rotunda,* through the treacherous ice-floes of the North West Passage, and to be perfectly honest, I think if you allow me to continue in this scatter-shot manner, we'll be here till sunset, and as much as I love the sight of that fiery orange ball slowly sinking below the pale-blue rim of the world, I don't think yer parents would approve if I kept yous here way past past tea-time.

'So, to get back to where I was...

'Oh aye. The story. The hour groweth late, as they say.

'Best get on with it, I reckon...

FOUR
'Several years ago, I can't remember how many now exactly, and does it really matter, I was home on shore leave and one of the first things I did was call in for a pint or several at *The Baltic Fleet*, that wonderful ship's-bow-shaped alehouse, that's stood opposite the row of towering warehouses on the Dock Road, since the 1850s, and some would have yer believe, at least 200 years before that. Yous must know it. I know yer only kids and that, but I'd lay good odds yer arl feller's taken some or all of yiz there for half a shandy or a glass of lemonade and a great big bowl of steaming Scouse at some point. And while yer were busy shovelling it down on a freezing cold winter afternoon, or maybe sat in the blessed shade of a dusty corner on a blisteringly hot summer's day, he's very likely regaled yer with tales of the pub's history and its legendary reputation. Even though yous had likely been far more interested in the stories of it being haunted by four different ghosts and its mysterious blocked up tunnels down in the cellars, than his tales of smugglers and press gangs and the city's shameful association with the slave trade and I don't suppose I can really blame yous for that.'

'Anyhow, on that long-ago mid-morning, I entered the bar on me own-some, knowing full well, if I chose, I wouldn't be alone for very long. *The Baltic Fleet* is perhaps the last of the genuinely traditional Port of Liverpool watering holes, the sort where old sailors like me gather to drink themselves senseless, the better to bury, or maybe *drown* is a better word, the desperate loneliness of a life spent largely at sea. At least for a little while.

'It's also the sort of place where, if you wanted company, it was pretty much a cast-iron guarantee that within ten seconds of crossing the threshold, you'd either be gabbing to an old acquaintance yer hadn't seen for ages, or else someone you've never met in yer life, but who treats you like a bezzy mate just the same.

'True to form, I'd made it barely half-way across the bar-room floor before I heard a familiar voice pipe up from somewhere directly behind me.

"Jesus Christ, if it isn't Panama Jack! Get the ale in will yer, lad."

'I spun round, and there was me "Uncle Spike", who was neither really my uncle nor was truly named Spike, grinning from ear to ear. His creased and permanently tanned face had the look of a split casey, one of them arl brown ones that were heavier than a medicine ball on a wet and muddy school footy pitch. He was sat upon one of the wooden benches beneath a window grimy with dust, and it gladdened my heart to see him.

'I waved and returned his smile, ordered up a couple of frothing pints of real ale and sat down beside him. And though I hadn't seen him in God alone knew how many years, the conversation flowed freely along with the beer, as though we'd never truly been separated by the inexorable passage of time and distance.

FIVE

'And speaking about time, that's something else about *The Baltic Fleet* I forgot to mention: The ticking of the clock soon ceases to have any real meaning once you've made yourself comfortable with a bevvy close to hand and with the sun beams slanting long into the haze of that blue-smoked bar-room. How else can yer logically explain the fact that one minute me and me "Uncle Spike" were busy catching up with all that had happened in our respective worlds since we'd last met, the next it was drawing down dark outside and those ever-present smoke plumes were swirling lazily in pools of electric light.

'It was inevitable that at some point, given our city's binding links to the *Lusitania,* and the awful tragedy that befell her, talk would eventually turn to an article that had been featured in that day's early edition of the *Liverpool Echo*. It was a fairly lengthy feature about another of those planned, and always controversial, diving expeditions to explore the sunken wreck of the great ocean liner lying broken on the seabed, roughly eleven miles off the Irish coastline.

'I'd raised my voice to argue that I thought the venture was completely immoral and on a par with some heartless gobshite surmising it was a jolly good wheeze to desecrate the rows of plain white graves lining the banks of the Somme, when me "Uncle" had cut me short by suddenly punching me on the upper arm, hard enough to leave a purple black bruise, visible for a week or so afterward.

"Oh my God, Jack," he yelled excitedly. "I've just remembered something me ma once told about the *Lusitania*! Something I'd long forgotten. A ghost story no less. You wanna hear it?''

'Do I really have any choice?' I said, rubbing my shoulder with a grimace.

"Nah, not really," Spike had replied. "Especially seein' as it's your round next. Yer might wanna shout them in before we get started."

'I stared regretfully at the cloudy dregs of my pint glass, as flat as the becalmed, seaweed-choked surface of that dreadful Sargasso Sea, and agreed that maybe I should.'

SIX

"Right," Spike said, "I'm what? Twenty-odd years yer senior, a very close friend of yer arl fella, God rest his soul, and I'll always be grateful to him for allowing me the opportunity to see you grow up to be someone I'm proud to call a friend. But of course, as yer well know, I'm not yer real uncle. I'm not even remotely related to yer. And the only reason anyone calls me "Spike", by the way, is due to the fact that me current fat, footy-shaped head used to be, like the rest of me, sad to say, a whole lot thinner, and everyone used to joke that the crown of me swede seemed to taper off to a Brylcreemed, Teddy Boy, spiky point.

"But never mind that. I'm telling yer, Jack, none of that phoniness changes the fact that the story I'm about to tell yer was treated as gospel by me mam after she'd heard it first-hand from her best friend, a woman I only ever knew as "Auntie Mary".

"I remember the first time me mam introduced her to me when I was a kid. This was back in 1925, the days when we used to live in the leafy green suburbs of Childwall. I might only have been aged nine or ten at the time, but Auntie Mary certainly made an instant impression on me. This conservatively dressed woman must have been pushing forty, if she was a day, but she was extremely well-preserved, if yer know what I mean. She had one of those strikingly beautiful faces, like she was a famous actress or a model or somethin', and she had these gorgeous green eyes that sparkled like emeralds, and when she leaned over and planted a gentle kiss on me cheek, I caught this sweet whiff of expensive perfume, the kind that comes in heart-shaped bottles, emblazoned with swirly-wavy fancy writing. French, more often than not.

"Something else struck me about her too. Though she had smiled constantly and her voice had been as light as a summer breeze, still there had been an indefinable sense of sorrow about her, as though she'd suffered some terrible loss and was trying her utmost to cover it up.

"It turned out that I was right about that, although it would be several years after she'd emigrated to Canada with her husband (my "Uncle Jimmy", who I never got to meet) that I'd find out the reasons for Auntie Mary's all-but-hidden sadness.

"Again, it was me mam who told me what had happened to her best friend when I was sat her bedside at the hospital, every evening, when she'd been terminally ill with cancer, and I'd held her hand whilst we shared stories and reminisced about the good arl days.

"And this is Mary's story, pretty much as I remember it.

SEVEN

"Mary had been married before. Back in the late spring of 1913, she had gotten hitched to her childhood sweet-heart, a local boy named Alfred, when they'd both been barely out of their teens. Mary's parents, not surprisingly, were dead set against the idea. Perhaps if Mary had announced her intentions to marry just a couple of years earlier, when despite the death of the Queen in 1901, Victorian values still very much held sway, women were still largely subservient and suffrage seemed as alien a concept as, well, the astronomer Percival Lowell's belief that there were a series of artificial canals on Mars, she would have simply swallowed her disappointment and quietly given up any thoughts of matrimony.

"But instead, inspired by the thoughts and deeds of the likes of Emmeline Pankhurst, whom she admired greatly, she chose to openly defy her ma and pa, and told them that unless they gave their full blessing to her marrying Alfred, she would never speak to either of them ever again, *"nor will you be afforded the opportunity to see in person, any issue of our union. You will both of you be grandparent's in name only."*

"Faced with this ultimatum, and the look of fierce determination in their only child's eyes, they attended the wedding, wearing the sour faces of the chastised, it's true, but saying all the right things, and acting with admirable decorum, given the circumstances.

"A few months after they were married, Alfred had secured a position as a third class waiter on board the pride of the Cunard Line (which like its rival, White Star, had its offices on the Mersey river-front) the RMS *Lusitania,* the legendary "Speed Queen of the High Seas", a ship that surpassed even the *Titanic* in just about everything except the subsequent world-wide fame stakes.

"Mary had been so proud of her husband, she'd thrown a party in his honour at the couple's humble red-bricked terraced home just off Smithdown Road in the South End of the city, to celebrate, and never mind that there were a number of down-sides to her husband's new job. Yes, it meant that due to the *Lusitania*'s frequent round trips from Liverpool to New York, Alfred would be away at sea for long periods, and his wages weren't exactly a king's ransom. But as Mary frequently stated to her family and friends, '*Alfred considers his appointment to be merely the first important step on the ladder towards bigger and better things. Working on board such a prestigious vessel can only greatly improve his future career prospects.*'

"Not even the outbreak of the First World War, in August, 1914, just over twelve months into their marriage, served to put a dent in Mary's eternal optimism. She was constantly reassured by her husband, whenever he was home on shore leave, and by the heads of both the Cunard and White Star Lines, that when the *Lusitania* was traversing the vast expanse of the North Atlantic, Kaiser Wilhelm II would never be foolish enough to give his blessing to a U-boat torpedoing a world famous, unarmed civilian passenger liner, especially not one carrying large numbers of neutral Americans for fear of provoking the United States to enter the war on the side of the Western Allies.

"To be fair, as any student of this period of maritime history will be happy to inform you, such optimism was not without foundation. Submarine warfare was, after all, still in its infancy and was therefore not regarded as being a truly serious threat to Allied shipping. In fact, even when Admiral Hugo von Pohl, commander of the German High Seas Fleet made a big show of announcing the implementation of a grand, not to say, ominous-sounding War Zone, which came into effect on February 18th 1915, and which would encompass the *"waters around Great Britain and Ireland, including the whole of the English Channel,"* the British reaction amounted to little more than a nonchalant, so-what, do yer-worst shrug of the shoulders. Few, if any, at the British Admiralty seriously believed the colossal-in-every-sense ocean liners, with their incredibly powerful engines, could ever be in any danger of being sunk by a German U-boat, not least because the primitive submarines could only attain a maximum speed of 13 knots, woefully short of the 21 knots or so of the cruising, leisurely lope of RMS *Lusitania* (she was capable of at least five knots more, if she felt like showing off and leaving the competition fuming in the frothy waters of her sea-churned wake!).

"Little wonder then that Mary spent the first twelve months of the war in a state of calm reassurance, and though she missed her husband greatly every time he was away, she never truly feared for his safe return.

"But all that changed a week or so prior to Alfred disembarking for what should have been just another routine voyage to New York and back, on April 17th, 1915.

"Mary always claimed in later years that she could never explain why it was exactly, still she began to suffer from a terrible sense of dark foreboding. I've often heard it said of course that certain people can somehow sense when bad things are approaching, the way dogs and certain other types of animals seem to somehow be aware that a violent thunderstorm is gathering, just over the cloudless, blue-skied horizon.

"At first, Mary had tried to tell herself that her fears were based purely on superstitious fears, due to the fact that the date Alfred was due to return to Liverpool, the 8th of May, happened to be their second wedding anniversary, and they were planning a romantic candle-lit meal to celebrate the occasion.

"But on the night before the *Lusitania* was due to set sail from its usual berth at Princes Dock Landing Stage, Mary had a vivid and terrifying nightmare. The sort of awful, sweat-inducing bad dream that has you waking screaming in the dead of night.

"Alfred had awoken with a start, and seeing his wife's distressed state had taken her in his arms and tried to soothe her as a furnace-like heat came off her in near-visible waves, and for one horrible moment he was scared she might be stricken with some incurable fever, the kind that might necessitate his wife being transported over the water to the dreaded, red-bricked walled port of Liverpool Isolation Hospital, from where, once admitted, she might never return.

"Mary, however, her breathless words hitched between sobs, insisted that she wasn't feeling ill, but was instead consumed with a grim certainty that something terrible was going to happen to the *Lusitania,* and she begged him not to board the great ship in the morning.

'Oh dear God, Alfred,' Mary wailed. 'I just had the most awful dream imaginable.' She rested her damp forehead on her husband's shoulder.

'I dreamed I was cast adrift at sea. I was wearing this white, flowing dress, and I was cold and water-soaked and swimming desperately towards a misted coastline that never seemed to get any nearer. It felt so incredibly real. I was floating in deep, deep water. Floating, but feeling increasingly as though I were losing my buoyancy, and I heard this maddeningly insistent voice yelling inside my head, *"I can't die here. I really can't die here. Not this close to the shoreline!"*

"Mary had paused to wipe away her tears. 'I mean, I could clearly see the white plumes of ocean waves crashing on the jagged rocks, well within swimming distance, and I could feel the weight of my soaked dress, my boots, my corset, dragging me down, as though I were swimming in molasses.

'And then, the icy waves began gently tickling my lips, like cold, passionless kisses. I opened my mouth to scream and then saltwater gushed down my throat, literally drowning out my cries. And as I descended into the inky depths I saw I wasn't alone. All around me there were countless other people. Men, women and children. All of them slowly sinking.

'All of them wide-eyed and white-faced. All of them dead. Oh, dear God, all of them *dead!*'

"Mary's voice had cracked at that point, and for a while, nothing Alfred could say could serve to calm her. Though that didn't stop him from trying."

'Come on now, love,' he'd said, hugging her fiercely. 'There's absolutely nothing to be afraid of. It was just a stupid dream. I mean, I don't want to tempt fate or anything, but I have every faith that the ship is not in any danger be it from storms or icebergs, or technical catastrophe. And as I've told you many times, I honestly don't believe there are any U-boat commanders out there inhumane enough to try and sink a passenger liner. All those stories you read in the press about the Germans raping Belgian nuns, and skewering babies on bayonets simply aren't true. They're just propaganda, newspaper talk aimed at whipping up patriotic fervour. The Huns may be our enemy, but they're not evil monsters.

"Alfred had continued in this vein until dawn and Mary had settled sufficiently for him to dare to gently break their embrace."

'Mary, please listen to me,' he'd said, gently stroking her face. 'I swear on all I hold dear that I will return safely from this voyage. Nothing, not the entire German submarine fleet combined, is going to prevent me from coming home to you.

'Three weeks from now, we'll be celebrating our anniversary in style and snapping our fingers at bad dreams and night terrors.'

'Do you promise?' Mary whispered hoarsely.

'With all my heart,' he replied. 'Now, how about a smile to brighten up my day and send my spirits soaring?'

"Mary did her best, and considering the circumstances, her best proved good enough."

EIGHT

"That mid-April day had started out dull with the threat of rain, but a cool breeze had sprung up soon scattering the cloud cover, and by late afternoon the river front had looked resplendent, bathed in bars of bright spring sunlight. The *Lusitania*, it's four orange funnels painted a greyish-black by order of the Admiralty, towered over the large crowds of cheering, waving people gathered on the

Princes Landing Stage, to give the ship its usual rousing send off. The mood was almost celebratory, as though those who had assembled in such numbers were honouring the departure of a Royal Navy vessel embarking upon some noble and glorious campaign, and ordinarily the festive atmosphere and senses stirring sights, would have quickly dispelled Mary's premonitory sense of 'dark foreboding'.

"But not on *this* occasion.

"Not on *this* day.

"You wouldn't have known she was worried sick to look at her though. She'd hid it very well, just as she'd managed to do so earlier that morning, for her husband's sake. Alfred had looked so smart, dressed in his best suit, and with his hair slicked back and whistling *My Wild Irish Rose,* as they'd left their house at a little after eleven, and made their way down to the dockside together, never once speaking of Mary's nightmare or her fears of imminent disaster.

"She'd succeeded in keeping up appearances, though, wearing a smile that made her face ache abominably, right up until the moment it came to kiss each other goodbye. Even then, she pretended the fresh bout of tears she cried were more the result of the briny wind blowing in from the Irish Sea, than any fears she might never see her beloved again.

"When they were done, he'd touched her cheek tenderly and told her with heartfelt conviction, 'I'll be home soon. I won't forget my promise.'

"Then he'd turned to climb the ship's gangway, pausing as he reached the entrance to Third Class, to turn and wave and mouth, 'I love you.'

"Mary had raised her own hand in return, and just then a beam of sunlight had caught the band of her golden wedding ring, causing it to glitter and sparkle, and for a moment she was nine-years old again, standing with her father in their back garden, not long after sunset on a warn May evening. They'd been gazing up at the clear, gradually darkening sky, her father pointing out the constellations. He'd known the names of all of them, it had seemed, and at one point he'd knelt down beside her and placed an arm on her shoulder. 'And the very brightest of the stars is Polaris, or as it's commonly known, The North Star,' he'd said. 'My own father, your Granddad Edwards, used to tell me that whenever you see it, especially on nights like this one, you should cross your fingers and make a silent wish. And if you believe in the magic strongly enough, your wish will surely be granted.'

"For years afterwards she had believed implicitly in her father's words, and the memory had served to lift her depression somewhat. She'd stared as if hypnotised by the twinkling rays of light emanating from her wedding ring and without feeling remotely foolish she'd prepared to make a wish for Alfred's safe return.

"Before the first words could even begin to form in her mind however, a dark cloud had suddenly blotted out the sun, the temperature seemed to drop several degrees, and she shivered and felt gooseflesh rise on her arms.

"She heard music coming from somewhere deep within the ship as it began to pull away from the dock-side, the striking up of the resident band welcoming the passengers aboard, no doubt, but to Mary's ears, it was a tuneless dirge. A drunken cacophony. The sound of decaying wedding bells.

NINE

"Now I need yer to pay attention here, Jack, 'cos here comes some historical facts and information that hopefully won't bore yer rigid. Yer might be aware of some it. But I guarantee you won't have heard it all.

"The *Lusitania* had an uneventful journey to New York. She docked at Pier 54 on the following Saturday, the 24th of April. I read somewhere or other that many of the passengers, especially those in First Class, considered sailing on the *Lusitania* to be an almost surreal experience, so far removed from the horrors of war that it was hard to conceive of the wholesale slaughter taking place daily on the Western Front, the shores of Gallipoli (that ill-fated campaign had begun the day after the great ship sailed) and elsewhere across the globe.

"I remember one feller, booked in First Class, and whose name escapes me right now, had written in his diary (later published in a book about the disaster), of how it was like '*being on board a giant, floating hotel. What with passengers lolling on deck chairs, or taking tea in the large salon. The tables laden with fragrant-smelling roses and carnations. Couples taking romantic moon-lit walks along the Promenade Deck. Music drifting from amidst the ornate splendor of the Dining Saloons.*'

"Just the same though, it seems Alfred's Mary wasn't the only one to have had bad feelings or a full-on premonition about the fate of the ship prior to its final voyage.

"The wife of one of the survivors of the sinking, Professor Ian Holbourn, who hailed from the Scottish Isle of Foula, had a bizarre experience she would later describe as 'a waking dream'. On the night of May 6th, the Professor's wife had retired to bed at about eleven o'clock. She claimed that whilst she was in that weird slightly unreal state between sleep and wakefulness she suddenly saw a vision of 'a large vessel sinking with a big list, from side to side and also from stem to stern. There was a crush of frightened people, some of them slipping and sliding down the sloping decks. I thought it strange that I could be seeing this while I was wide awake, and I stretched my arms out of bed and clenched and unclenched my fingers to make sure that I was not dreaming.'

"Interesting, don't you think, Jack?

"If so, you will doubtless find it equally intriguing that several members of the ship's crew had reportedly had similar experiences, and rumours that the *Lusitania* was doomed began to spread amongst the more superstitious amongst them. It's a fact that more than a few of the crew chose to give it toes the moment the gangways were lowered at Pier 54, rapidly disappearing amongst the urban sprawl of downtown Manhattan. Legend even has it that even the ship's mascot, a four-year-old black cat named Dowie, skedaddled from the ship the night before she was due to set sail for Liverpool, a terrible omen, if, as many people believe, animals, particularly domestic cats, have an in-bred supernatural ability to sense impending danger.

"Of course, the mood of the remaining original crew members and those boarding the ship on the morning of May 1st, wasn't exactly improved much by the appearance in the pages of *The New York Times* that same day of a black-bordered message from the Imperial German Embassy, Washington D.C., dated April 22nd, 1915.

"The notice stated that '*Vessels flying the flag of Great Britain, or any of her allies, were liable to destruction in those waters, and that anyone taking passage on those ships did so at their own risk.*'

"Cunard officials dismissed the notice as being nothing other than a typically under-handed display of German subterfuge aimed at dissuading passengers from boarding the ship, and it seemed to have been fairly successful as a deterrent because many who had booked passage on the *Lusitania* felt compelled to switch to other ships or else postpone travelling till a later date.

"Ironically, someone who had more reason than most to actually pay heed to the ominous pre-sailing warnings, was Alfred Gywnne Vanderbilt Sr, '*the elegant symbol of the sportsman in high society,*' and one of the wealthiest people in the world at that time. However, he pointedly chose to ignore both the printed notice in the press and the personal telegram that had been handed to him by a member of the crew not long after he'd boarded the ship. To be honest, some writers claim the millionaire never actually did receive the telegram, but according to at least one newspaper reporter, Vanderbilt had not long reached his luxury suite located on the starboard side, when the journalist, eager for an interview, had knocked at his cabin door and personally saw Vanderbilt standing there clutching the piece of paper in his hands. The message it contained was brief and to the point: '*The Lusitania is doomed. Do not sail on her.*'

It was signed simply, '*Morte*'.

"If this story is true, it's somewhat surprising that Mr Vanderbilt chose to disregard the note as being merely '*somebody trying to have a little fun at my expense*' as he was quoted as saying at the time, because he was a great believer in following his gut instincts, not least because he had only been prevented by a stroke of good fortune from sailing on the *Titanic*, on her ill-fated maiden voyage just three years earlier.

"In April 1912, he and his wife were booked to make the trip to New York aboard the infamous ship, but had changed his mind three days before she sailed due to vague feelings of unease, perhaps inspired by the words of a family friend who counselled that many things could go wrong on a ship's maiden voyage. This friend didn't specify the dangers of hull-tearing icebergs exactly, but you get the general idea.

"Perhaps some of those who did choose to sail had reason to regret their decision the moment they set foot on board. A melancholy atmosphere pervaded amongst both passengers and crew, and spirits were hardly lifted by the damp, grey, drizzly weather, nor by the fact that the sailing was delayed by nearly two and a half hours, from 10am until shortly before 12:30 in the afternoon. This was because a large amount of passengers from the *Cameronia,* a British ship requisitioned by the Admiralty at the last minute, had to transfer en masse to the *Lusitania* along with their luggage.

"When eventually the ship did manage to set sail, with 1,959 souls on board there were, the superstitious-minded might say, at least three more less-than-morale boosting portents to endure. Firstly, not long after setting sail, the ship's Master At Arms found three unidentified German men had sneaked on board, and upon being discovered, had immediately been arrested and placed in handcuffs in the cargo hold.

"Secondly, a film crew had turned up to record the *Lusitania's* leaving Pier 54 for the last time, causing many of the ship's passengers to brave the elements and engage in gallows humour. 'Yer know, it's almost as if someone's tipped off the cameramen that today's the last opportunity to grab some footage of the *Lusitania* afloat!'

"And thirdly, one of the passengers, Lucy Taylor, was shocked into amazed silence when, without warning, a sailor had suddenly leaned across, grabbed her hat off her head and hurled it into the leaden waters of New York Harbour. Lucy had stared open-mouthed as her favourite hat, the crown of which was adorned with lavish peacock feathers, gently floated out of sight. 'Why on earth did you do that?' she finally managed to ask. 'Are you completely mad?'

'Lady,' the sailor replied sternly, 'I had to do it. Haven't yer ever heard? Peacock feathers always bring bad luck!'

TEN

"Six days later, and the *Lusitania* entered the German-imposed War Zone.

"A thick fog descended like an enveloping shroud not long after dawn on May 7th dramatically reducing visibility and obscuring the hoped-for views of the Irish coastline. On Captain William Turner's orders, the ominous sound of the ship's foghorns filled the dead, windless air, every sixty seconds, causing the early risers among the passengers to remark nervously that 'For Christ's sake, it's like the Captain's blatantly trying to give away our position to any lurking U-Boats!'

"At around 10am though, the warm spring sun got busy burning off the fog, raising morale as it did so, and by mid-day the last of the misty tendrils had evaporated and the sun shone brightly from a sky so blue it looked ready to shatter into a million pieces. A light breeze had sprung up but the sea was virtually wave-less, and the sight of the south-east coast of Ireland, tantalisingly close, and bathed in glorious May sunshine, brought smiles of relief to many of the passengers and crew.

"Not everyone was filled with renewed optimism, however. Some of the more seasoned travellers on board were more than a little concerned about the continued slow pace of the *Lusitania*. More than a few of those who survived later complained that they couldn't understand why, at this most dangerous of junctures, Captain Turner didn't order full speed ahead. One witness stated at the inquest into the sinking; 'It was if, especially given the idyllic conditions, the Captain were saying 'Here we are. Come and get us!'

"Of course, none but the most cynical or gullible of conspiracy theorists honestly believes that the Captain was doing precisely that for some nefarious purpose. But, as things turned out he may as well have been working to a plan, given the tragic fate that was about to befall the *Lusitania.*

"All that morning, the gap between the ship and what would prove to be its nemesis, the U-20, commanded by Kapitanleutnant Walter Schweiger, had been closing steadily. And what was worse Captain Turner's decision to alter his ship's course as the familiar sight of the Old Head of Kinsale came into view, played straight into Schweiger's hands. So much so in fact, that he later stated incredulously to his superiors; 'She could not have steered a more perfect course if she had deliberately tried to give us a dead shot. A short fast run, and we waited.'

"And while the U-20 lurked with deadly patience beneath the surface of the mill-pond waters, many passengers were sat oblivious to the approaching danger in the First and Second class Dining Saloons, drinking tea or coffee at the end of their lunch, and watching the band play *It's A Long Way To Tipperary,* or, like the English architect, Oliver Bernard, were enjoying taking a leisurely stroll along the upper decks to take in the fresh sea air.

"At 2:09pm, Oliver paused for a moment, near to the ship's Veranda Café, to gaze out to sea, convinced by the inherently peaceful scene before him that nothing remotely terrible could possibly occur on so perfect a spring afternoon.

"Sixty seconds later, and that comforting delusion would be quite literally blown apart.

ELEVEN

"A few years back, more than I care to remember to be honest, I set eyes on this hugely evocative illustration published in some book or magazine or other.

"It was a fine, black and white pencil drawing of the moment U-Boat 20's torpedo was first sighted by some of the passengers. It shows the starboard Boat Deck of the *Lusitania* bathed in bright sunlight. Thick clouds of oily-looking smoke billow from one of the funnels, and seagulls make curving flights overhead.

"A mother sits in a deck chair, reading a book out loud to her young son and daughter, the girl clinging to her ribboned hat lest she lose it to the stiffening sea breeze.

"A teenaged woman, dressed in an overcoat and a swirling scarf, looks on in alarm as two men, one in his fifties, the other visibly younger, are pointing out to sea. It's immediately apparent what has grabbed their attention. A white streak of foam is speeding across the placid waters towards the *Lusitania* like the wake of some malign sea creature risen up from the abyssal depths.

"It's a true, frozen-in-time moment.

"The children oblivious to the impending danger, are caught up in the simple joys of story-telling.

"The shock and fear apparent on the faces of the two men as they realise there can be no hope of escape, that the torpedo is bang on target and about to hit.

"The long shadows cast by the six individuals etched upon the wooden planks of the Boat Deck.

"The clouds of sky-darkening funnel-smoke, a grim foretaste of the death and destruction to come.

"That picture and these words from Oliver Bernard, have served to give me nightmares in all the days that have since elapsed.

'I saw a sunlit expanse of perfectly smooth water. The sea was like an opaque sheet of polished indigo, absolutely still. Then I saw on the starboard what at first seemed to me to be the tail of a fish. I was convinced it was a submarine periscope. As I stared, fascinated, I saw the fast-lengthening track of a newly-launched torpedo, itself a streak of froth. I could hardly believe the evidence of my own eyes.

'An American woman ran up to me for reassurance, exclaiming 'That isn't a torpedo is it?'

'I felt spellbound and absolutely sick, and I simply couldn't answer. A broad-shouldered American I was never to see again said. By heavens, they've done it!'

'Then the torpedo hit.

'I felt a slight shock through the deck, and then a terrific explosion. A column of white water rose high in the air followed by an eruption of debris. A moment later came a sullen rumble in the bowels of the liner.'

"The U-20's torpedo hit the ship at something like forty-five miles an hour, and it crashed straight into the coal bunker for Boiler Room Number One, and detonated on impact with a sound that Captain Turner later described as being "like a large door banging shut on a windy day."

"The explosion ripped a jagged hole roughly twenty feet long and ten feet high, and almost immediately, a huge plume of seawater mixed with various types of debris shot up through four decks to at least sixty feet into the air, and hung there for a few moments as the stricken ship passed by.

"And from that moment on, the ship and all but 761 of its passengers and crew, were doomed.

"Captain Turner, in a last act of desperation, gave the order to try and steer the ship towards the not-too-distant shore, in a vain effort to try and run the ship aground, but the speed with which the water came rushing in was at such a phenomenal rate, there was never any chance of success.

"Mere seconds after being hit, the *Lusitania* began rolling over on her side, like some mortally wounded sea beast, and to those on her decks, clinging to each other or to the nearest available object, it must have seemed as though she was never going to stop rotating. About ten seconds after the explosion, the roll finally stopped, but it brought no relief. The ship remained stuck at a steep, disorienting angle, and a few seconds after attaining that position, she began to plunge into the water toward the bow.

"And as if that wasn't bad enough, there then came a second, much larger and louder explosion from deep within the ship's bowels, causing the entire vessel to shudder violently.

"There was a moment or two of stunned silence.

"It was broken at last by Captain Turner, who gave the order 'Boat Stations!'

"And total chaos ensued.

"This was nothing at all like the *Titanic* disaster, just three years before. On that equally dreadful occasion, the sinking had started quietly and without any sense of panic. So blasé were the passengers after the *Titanic* had struck the 'berg, they had to be actively convinced by the crew that the ship was really sinking.

"In the case of the *Lusitania*, of course, it was obvious straight away that the ship was damaged beyond repair and that time was dead set against them. There was very little opportunity to launch all of the collapsibles, never mind the lifeboats, and given the almost surreal list of the ship it was virtually impossible to lower them safely into the water without causing them to tip their occupants into the freezing waters of the Atlantic, where they couldn't possibly survive for long, even if they'd been fortunate enough to acquire a life-jacket. In some instances, the chains suspending the lifeboats snapped and the hulls of the heavy wooden craft landed directly on top of the people stranded in the sea.

"Equally horrific was the fate suffered by a large group of passengers who had crammed into a lift to take them to the upper decks, only to became trapped in the elevator when the electricity failed. They couldn't unlock the metal sliding doors and so drowned, packed together in what had quickly become a literal cage.

"Help, when it finally came, arrived far too late for so many, including Mary's beloved Alfred.

"In just eighteen minutes, the *Lusitania*, "The Speed Queen of the High Seas", and the enduring pride of the Cunard fleet, had been unceremoniously dethroned; an already rusting hulk of punctured wood and metal, lying at the bottom of the North Atlantic Ocean.

TWELVE

"In the early years of the 20th century, breaking news, be it good or bad, didn't so much hum down the wires as bumble along like a particularly nervous person afflicted with a stammer, and for this reason it wasn't until five in the evening that Cunard's Liverpool office were informed of the disaster that had befallen the *Lusitania*.

"Of course, once the awful tidings had been relayed to the shipping company, that ever-reliable method of communication; word of mouth, ensured that the news spread like wildfire throughout the city, and within an hour, anxious crowds had begun gathering outside the Cunard building, desperate to discover the fate of their loved ones.

"Mary, head bowed, her face a pale white mask of grief, was amongst the first to arrive, but whilst the eyes of others were yet bright with the stubborn spark of hope, Mary's were lifeless and dull with despair. She was all-but convinced that by making the short trek to the Pier Head she was merely seeking confirmation that Alfred was gone. She knew it in her heart. Had known the very moment Mrs McCulloch, her next door neighbour, had come hammering at her door, yelling breathlessly, 'Oh my God, Mary, have yer heard? They're saying the German's have sunk the

Lusitania!'

"Still, Mary had felt compelled to join the throng of hysterical men and women fighting their way towards the counters at the entrance hall of the offices manned by shocked and harassed-looking members of staff, the crowds bellowing the names of friends and family members into their faces, as if by shouting them incessantly over and over, like a religious mantra, might somehow ensure their omission from the list of the missing.

"The vast majority of the crowd slept within the confines of the building that night, curling up to sleep wherever they could, keeping vigil throughout the night lest they miss the latest developments regarding the sinking. But not Mary. She was granted one small mercy on an evening riven with heart-breaking tragedy. At a little before midnight, the distraught young woman was approached by a tall, middle-aged man with a handlebar moustache and a large greatcoat who slowly made his way across the packed room towards her. Mary had felt her heart stop as the man had introduced himself as a Cunard representative, and with a solemn expression enquired as to her name. And when she told him, he gently removed his hat and spoke kind words of condolence that nevertheless sounded empty when pitched against her dreadful sense of loss.

"Mary somehow held herself together long enough to thank the man for his courtesy, before turning away and heading for the exit in the company of many others, just like her, sobbing loudly or silent and blank-faced, shuffling along like demoralised soldiers returning from a hopeless front,

as they made their way out into the cold, dark night.

THIRTEEN

"Mary had somehow made it back to her empty house all alone, wilfully shunning any prospect of company, unable to bear being assailed by the sympathetic platitudes of even her closest friends, no matter how well-intentioned they might be. She couldn't face seeing her parents, either. She simply harboured an overwhelming desire to just curl up on her own, and attempt to shut out all feeling.

"It struck Mary that there was only one way of achieving this objective. She stepped through the front door, and without even pausing to turn on the lights, went immediately to the drinks cabinet and withdrew the full bottle of single malt she and Alfred had been saving for their anniversary. She grabbed a tumbler, and poured herself a treble, swallowing it in a single, chest burning gulp. Then she poured herself another and trudged somewhat unsteadily, upstairs to the bedroom. Again, she emptied the glass, swallowing the fiery liquid, and feeling its warmth spread to numb every nerve end. Or at least the ones that needed anaesthetizing. Which to tell the truth, was pretty much all of them.

"At last, Mary, too emotionally drained and physically exhausted to change out of her clothes, collapsed flat out on top of the soft mattress. The room soon started swirling like a madly spinning carousel and for a moment she thought she was going to be sick, but before Mary could even try to raise her head, and contrary to all her expectations, she fell immediately into a deep, deep sleep.

"And dreamed a dream so real, she could scarcely dismiss it as such. Perhaps with good reason.

"*Mary dreams she is somehow floating above herself, gazing down at the moon-lit shape of her whiskey-drunk, fully clothed body, from a point just below the bedroom ceiling. She marvels at the clarity of her vision, the forensic soberness of her thoughts, and is amazed to find she feels not a single trace of sadness or bitter heartache. Instead she finds her spirits soaring along with what she has quickly come to regard as being her "astral self", although she can't for the life of her figure out why on earth she should feel so exultant.*

"*Not at first, anyway.*

"*But then she smells (and is it even truly possible to actually smell in dreams? she wonders) the brackish odour of the sea, fresh layers of newly applied paint, thick choking clouds of oily smoke.*

"*And something else.*

"*Something tantalizingly familiar, but just beyond recall.*

"*Then suddenly she has it: It's the pungent smell of Brilliantine, Alfred's favourite hair tonic, and along with the recognition, Mary hears the plaintive cry of seagulls, the crash of waves and the low thrum of a ship's engines propelling some mighty vessel through seas both calm and brutally storm-tossed alike.*

"Wonderingly, she glances around the room, illuminated only by heavy slabs of skeletal light that filter in through the gaps in the drape curtains, until finally her eyes are drawn to the antique full-length mirror, the one she and Alfred had been given as a wedding present by her grandmother, standing over in the far corner of the room. Encased in dark brown mahogany, the surface of the highly polished glass appeared to be strangely misted, as though it hadn't been cleaned in months. Mary peers closer and sees the glass is actually obscured by a swirling fog, similar to a sea mist, roiling in from the Mersey on a cold November evening.

"She watches the mirror in fascination as an unmistakably human form begins to appear in the centre of that churning grey murk, and whilst at first, the mistiness obscures the figure, gradually, the hazy outline soon begins to take shape, and the dream-version of her heart soars as she recognises Alfred, her husband, dressed as she last saw him, standing near the top of the Lusitania*'s gangway, just three weeks earlier.*

"He's grim-faced, and unsmiling, true, and every inch of him dripping wet by the looks of it, but it seems to her at that moment she has never seen a more wonderful sight in all her life.

"Overcome with joy, Mary tries to call out his name, and move closer to the mirror, but it appears that in her "astral form" she is unable to do either. She mouths the words but no sound emerges, and her form remains stubbornly immobile, floating above her sleeping physical body.

"Mary is still desperately trying to will herself to do something, anything to make Alfred aware of her presence, when to her astonishment, the solid glass of the mirror begins rippling like the surface of a pond blown by a stiffening breeze, and Alfred steps out of the mirror and into the moon-lit bedroom, and she plainly hears the wet, squishing noise his black leather shoes make as he first stands for a long moment, as if lost in contemplation, and then decision apparently made, slowly strides across the carpeted floor towards the bed, where the 'real Mary' lies snoring softly.

"Alfred stoops and gazes down at her, and for a moment, the faintest traces of a smile appear at the corner of his lips. He leans towards her, and droplets of clear water land on the pillow, just a few inches from her face. Mary stirs slightly, and moans something indecipherable, but doesn't awaken, and then Alfred speaks, and though his voice is little more than the hint of a whisper, still both Marys, the floating and the sleeping, can make out every single word."

'Oh, Mary,' he begins. 'You are my one and only true love, and always will be. I want you to remember that for the rest of your life' He sighs, a mournful sound, full of regret, of chances spurned and roads not taken. 'I wish now more than anything I had hearkened to your warnings. I wish I hadn't been so arrogant as to simply dismiss your fears as being

nought but delusions dredged up from the dark well of nightmares. I wish I'd placed more faith in you. I wish I'd listened. I wish I'd....'

"*Alfred's voice cracks, and it's a few seconds before he can compose himself enough to continue. And when he does, his tone is noticeably brighter. 'I did keep my promise though, my love,' he says. 'I promised you I'd come back, and so I have, although sadly, fate has decreed it is to be only the most fleeting of returns.'*

"*At that point, Alfred lifts his left hand and slowly, and with obvious reluctance, slips off his golden wedding ring and places it gently on the bedside table. 'I have come to tell you two things, Mary, my darling,' he says as he does this, 'Two things I consider to be essential to ensure your future happiness.'*

'*Firstly, although ahead lie darker days, days for grieving, days of loss, please swear on the precious memory of our love that you will always cling to hope, no matter what cruel fates may befall you. That you will never lose faith even if it sometimes seems as though all grounds for optimism have withered like dying plants in a winter-blighted field. Remember, hope is the hardiest of weeds. It sprouts up in the most adverse of conditions. It survives against seemingly impossible odds. Never give up on it. Ever.'*

"*Alfred then turns and points at the wedding band, and adds, 'Secondly, and after you have mourned my passing for long enough, I want you to be free to meet someone else, someone with whom you can share the remainder of your days. Never forget, a life lived pining for a past that can never be reclaimed, is no life at all.'*

"*Alfred suddenly straightens up then, his head tilted to one side as if listening to a voice neither of the two Marys can hear. He nods once, and then smiles a real genuinely happy smile that lightens up his face like rays of sunlight suddenly emerging from a gap in the clouds.*

'*I have to go now, my love,' he says. 'Please remember all that I've said. Goodbye my darling, Mary.'*

"*And with that he turns and walks back across the room, his feet still squelching, until he reaches the mirror into which he steps and quickly disappears from sight amidst the depths of those constantly swirling clouds of fog.*

"*Then Mary's floating form shakes off its paralysis, is at last able to move, and slowly descends towards her sleeping self..."*

FOURTEEN

"Mary awoke just after dawn, with, amazingly enough, no trace of a hangover, and instead feeling strangely refreshed and invigorated, as though she'd been to a sauna or a masseur's or something, and had all the impurities, all of the toxins, either sweated or pummelled right out of her, and though a part of her felt guilty for not waking in the throes of inconsolable grief, a much larger part of her felt relieved that this sense of serenity, brief as it would doubtless prove to be, had replaced the soul-aching emptiness of the evening before.

"Mary had vague recollections of having dreamt about her husband at some point during the night, and having been somehow floating outside of herself, but she couldn't recall any of the details, the memory of it fading in the cold light of day, the way dreams, even vivid ones, are often wont to do. The only thing she was certain of was that it hadn't been any kind of frightening nightmare, another thing for which she was extremely grateful.

"She sat up, mentally chided herself for having fallen asleep in her clothes and swung her legs onto the floor.

"And instantly she saw the set of wet-shoe footprints leading to and from the old mahogany-framed, full-length mirror.

"Mary caught her reflection in the now flawless glass staring back at her, and suddenly all the memories of her dream came rushing back, her mind a-whirl with the images, the pungent aromas, the words her dead husband had spoken.

"She tried telling herself it was impossible. There couldn't really be two lines of sopping wet footprints marking the carpet.

"The air in the bedroom couldn't truly smell of brine and Brilliantine and thick clouds of funnel smoke.

"And the glittering golden object lying in a small pool of water on the bedside table, looking for all the world like Alfred's wedding ring, had to be some sort of optical illusion.

"Didn't it?"

A HEART-FELT POSTCRIPT:

I've got to admit, reading this back, all these years later, fills me with a kind of aching nostalgia; the sort that haunts your soul and leaves you feeling almost overcome with bitter-sweet melancholy: The way it sometimes is with me on late September afternoons, gazing out across the rooftops of the city, as the clouds gather on the distant horizon, the air turns chilled, and the onset of autumn is heralded by the plaintive cries of birds migrating; a lonely, haunting sound that calls to mind out of season fairgrounds, deserted beaches and closed down for the winter amusement arcades.

I miss the days I spent sat at Jack's feet as he spun out his yarns like reams of golden thread, filling our heads with wonderful images, of unforgettable characters and exotic locations, the kind that I had never seen, but had always dreamt existed.

I can't remember the very last time I saw him, sat on that ugly, rusted bollard, his weathered face split with a friendly grin and his eyes twinkling like mid-winter stars. I suppose that's often the way of things. We forget the precise details of the final time we took leave of many of the people we encounter in life. Even those who we later come to regard as having influenced our lives, for good or bad; the childhood friends, the former workmates, the teachers that plagued or blessed our

Mersey River
Photo Credit: Grant Walker

school or college days, the first loves, the old flames.

Certainly, that was the case with arl' "Panama Jack".

But his stories, now.

They remain with me to this day.

And sometimes, like on the grey, stormy October afternoon I began putting this book together, and bereft of inspiration, I went for a walk and found myself standing at the entrance to The Maritime Museum, in the Albert Dock, it's almost as though I can still hear those soft Scouse tones carried on the wind.

The voice of a born story-teller, urging me to snap me gob shut, pin back me "lug-oles" and listen. He had another tale to tell…

*** *Author's note: The Christian names of the main characters in the* Lusitania *story, "Mary" and "Alfred," are both pseudonyms. The real names Panama Jack gave to us back when we were kids are known to me, but I've decided not to use them here, not because, as some cynical smart-arse once tried to imply when I narrated this story on local radio, that it was nothing but a work of pure fiction (though that may ultimately well prove to be the case – like I said at the outset, I'm only here to relate the stories/urban legends as I heard them, not to try and convince anyone that they are one hundred per cent, true), but out of respect for the families of the people Panama Jack claimed were involved.*

As a survivor of a terrible disaster myself, on a similarly idyllic, blue-skied spring day, seventy four years after the sinking of the Lusitania, *the last thing I want to do is risk hurting anyone for the sake of a good tale. 'Panama Jack' might have possessed no such scruples. I however, most assuredly do.*

CHAPTER TWENTY:
THE DESOLATE BEAUTY OF ALL WE LEFT BEHIND

'Here are the young men, no weight on their shoulders,
Here are the young men, and where have they been?'
Decades - Joy Division

The following account is, I would suggest, some form of corroboration, (albeit of an entirely anecdotal nature) that the area surrounding Bidston Hill, the highest peak on the Wirral Peninsular, a place steeped in history and tradition, is, as certain researchers have suggested, a potential 'Window Area'.

In other words, it's a location that seems to attract all manner of unexplained phenomena (some particularly striking examples can be found in the chapter featuring "The Silent Watchers," elsewhere in these pages). So I include it here, not least because I happen to think it's a good story, and it has, in my humble opinion, the ring of truth about it.

Anyway, this story was related to me by yet another of those endlessly yarn-spinning taxi drivers during a late night journey back from a DJ gig I was doing over in Birkenhead, during the summer of 1998.

ONE
'We'd been travelling along the left-hand lane of the M56, close to Bidston Hill, and talk turned from the current music scene and England's prospects at the World Cup in France, to the alleged UFO sightings and ghostly encounters that were rumoured to have occurred either on the hill itself, or within its immediate environs. The teller of the tale readily agreed to commit the following to paper on the condition that I retain his anonymity, although for the sake of the recounting of the story, let's call him "Bill".

TWO
'I remember it was a freezing cold afternoon in late December 1980, during that peculiar dead period between Christmas and New Year's Eve, that I came up with my "Great Big Idea".

'I've always thought of that sort of sleepy, partied-out phase that exists between the two opposite ends of the holiday period as a being a "Slow-Motion Time" - the quiet, almost eerie, stillness that speaks of the nursing of collective hangovers, periods of wistful meditation with the ghosts of Christmas past , and the slow gearing up for the last massive celebration of the season.

'So, that year, finding myself thoroughly fed up with succumbing to a severe dose of them arl' post-Chrimbo blues, I decided I'd do something positive in a bid to revive my deflated spirits.

'I called up my three best friends; John, Nicky and Jason, and suggested we do what any group of fun-seeking, late twenty-something men would do given the less-than-cheery circumstances.

'That's right.

'We arranged to meet up at one of the local cemeteries.

'This wasn't just any arl graveyard, though, I'm telling yer that right now. This one had been officially "closed for business" back in the glam rock saturated year of 1975, and stands in a fenced off enclosure on the rural outskirts of Birkenhead town centre.

'You'll probably think us nuttier than me ma's home-made fruit-cake (a concoction so jam packed with different types of nuts at the expense of any hint of actual fruit, it may as well just be called, well, plain old *Nut* Cake) but please let me try and explain a little, if I can.

'As my life-long friends and I had all grown up in pretty much the same area of Birkenhead, it was inevitable that Bidston Hill (or "Biddy Hill" as we locals call it) would become our natural hang-out, what with its acres of lush, green fields and meadows, thick woodland and fabulous views from the flat, sandstone summit overlooking a vast, picturesque panorama; a mixture of urban sprawl and verdant green countryside.

'Strangely, though, and unlike the vast majority of kids our age, we much preferred the comparatively sedate surroundings of Flaybrick Cemetery, 26-acres of sprawling fields containing thousands of graves, monuments and tombstones, and a quaintly picturesque, faintly Gothic-style church. Established in 1864, Flaybrick Cemetery stands on the opposite side of the road to Biddy Hill itself, and back in the early 1960s, when the place was still in use, the church wardens never seemed to mind me and me mates sitting off there from the ages of seven, right up to our early teenage years, providing we didn't cause any trouble or desecrate any graves, or whatever. Jesus, that was thirty-odd years ago now, though it surely doesn't seem anywhere near that long until you pause to measure out the span of time that's passed.

'Of course, I'm more than aware that choosing a place as cheerless as a graveyard, even one as undeniably cool as we considered Flaybrick to be back then, might well have struck our parents or our teachers at school as being more than a little morbid. But the fact remains that when we were kids we loved nothing more than to play hide-and-seek amongst the gravestones, climbing the trees that lined the avenues and pathways that criss-crossed the burial ground, or build secret hideouts in the thick copse that stood at the eastern end of the graveyard. We'd watch other gangs of kids heading up Biddy Hill with their footballs, cricket bats or skipping ropes, or with their arms wrapped around each others shoulders as they chanted *"All play War, in 1964!"* over and over, armed with cap guns and plastic-dart firing rifles, whilst our gang would stand guard at the cemetery gates and make believe we were defending the Alamo, or Rorke's Drift, and on hot, sunny days, we'd strip down to our waists and take turns pretending to be *Tarzan of the Apes*, or Kirk Douglas in *Spartacus.*

'Best of all though, Flaybrick Cemetery had been the scene of my first ever "proper" kiss, courtesy of a girl named Gaynor Evans. She was the daughter of a couple of regular church-goers, and I'd developed a king-size crush on the bubbly, always smiling blonde during my early teenage years, and we'd shared a heavenly snogging session whilst we were both sat on the worn chapel steps, one glorious summer morning, just before the congregation poured from the entrance after Sunday worship.

'So, was I really *that* surprised that when I called up my friends, now fully-fledged adults to invite them to meet up at Flaybrick for old times sake, they all of them readily agreed, despite the freezing conditions and the fact that two of them were happily married and had probably been planning on doing nothing other than lying collapsed on the sofa watching the endless repeats and Christmas Specials that pretty much made up the sum total of "festive" British TV back at the dawn of the 1980s.

'Not really, no.

'I've since learned from experience that the landmarks of your childhood days can sometimes draw you back like a siren call, especially when your spirits are at a particularly low ebb. And judging by the enthusiasm plainly evident in all of me mates' voices at the other end of the telephone line, that certainly applied to them, too.

'After all, there's only so many times you can bear to watch *The Great Escape,* or blatantly obvious, syrup-wearing, game show hosts dangling a "Brucie Bonus", like a pathetically shrivelled, manky carrot, before you go completely mad! Plus, we were only *meeting* up at Flaybrick. The plan was to later head into town for a lad's night out and indulge in downing copious amounts of alcohol whilst having a proper (and decidedly warmer) reunion/catch up.

'And so it was, that a little after two on a snowy afternoon, and with the light already fading from the pitifully short December day, we gathered outside the grey-walled cemetery, the way we used to when we were children; a halcyon, care-free time when all seemed right with the world, and we each of us felt immortal, a belief secured by the bonds of unconditional, ever-lasting friendship.

THREE

'Some things had inevitably changed with the passing of the years, however.

'There, poking up between the leafless trees and seasonal-looking evergreens was Flaybrick's towering church spire, its former splendour ravaged by time and disuse. Its now glassless windows, multi-stained stonework and the ugly, worn and weathered gargoyles, silhouetted against a white winter sky, looked as despondent as an old man standing at the top of Biddy Hill, raging at the heavens because his limbs ached, his hair had fallen out, and his face was the pallor of age-old parchment.

'The familiar iron gates were still there, though, standing wide open at the head of the path that led into the graveyard before splitting off into tributaries around the various sections, all of them deserted at this time of day. At this time of year. That was no surprise whatsoever, given the sub-zero temperatures.

'What was a little unusual however, was that Boundary Road, running along the outskirts of Flaybrick, normally busy even during the Christmas period, was largely free of traffic, despite the best efforts of the gritters the night before. This meant that the only sounds disturbing the suitably reverential silence were the occasional harsh cawing of a crow from the woods below the hill, and the heavy crunch of snow underfoot as we traipsed along the frozen pavement.

'Oh, and the accompanying tunes blaring from the bass-heavy speakers of me mate, Jason's, top-notch ghetto blaster, an unfeasibly large radio/tape recorder that he'd brought with him. The BASF cassette contained within (ask yer Granddads kids) its label neatly hand-written by Jason in black marker pen, provided (when it wasn't busy attempting to twist itself into brown, slick, worm-like coils around the machine's multiple metal innards, at least) the perfect soundtrack to the white-laced vista laid out before us and the sombre atmosphere that pervaded all.

'It was the Manchester band Joy Division's second album, *Closer*. A truly glacial lament for the dying days of the old year, and it definitely set the mood for our reunion.

"Well, here we are again," John sighed wistfully, as we walked through the entrance. "Anyone else think it's like we've never grown up, or never actually been that long away from here?"

'No one answered, and in truth, no one was meant to. The question was entirely rhetorical. I could see from the identical dreamy expressions on the faces of my friends that they were all in total agreement, each of them lost in their own personal recollections of days that had long slipped-by.

'The times we'd spent scaring ourselves silly by telling each other horror stories on dark, chilly autumn evenings, gathered beneath the arched doorway of the church, playing our torch beams out along the tops of the magnificently ornate tombs.

'Sat beneath the verdant boughs seeking shelter from the heat of August's dog days, swapping copies of *The Dandy,* American comics and footy programmes.

'Gazing wonderingly at the impressive monuments erected to honour the passing of the great and the good, and inventing stories about those who were buried there, including a Liverpool-born astronomer named Issac Roberts, who we learned, was rewarded for his contributions to science by having an honest-to-God crater on the Moon named after him, something that had struck us as being just about the coolest thing ever, back when we were kids.

'These, and a thousand other recollections played on the silver screens of our mind's eye , but for me, the most vivid and abiding memory, aside from the magic of that sweet first kiss upon the chapel steps, courtesy of the delectable Ms Evans, was of something that had *maybe* occurred on a similarly bone-freezing afternoon, during what later became known across the whole of Great Britain, as "The Big Freeze of 1963".

'I say, maybe, because the incident was so strange, and dream-like, I'm still not at all sure that I didn't actually imagine the whole thing.

'But anyway, this is what I remember.

FOUR

'One January afternoon, in the midst of that seemingly endless winter, the four members of our little nameless gang had gathered at Flaybrick as usual, wrapped up snug against the biting cold in almost identical woollen scarves, bobble hats and fur-lined sheepskin coats.

'It was a Sunday, an hour or so after that morning's poorly-attended church service had ended, and we had the entire cemetery to ourselves. A thick blanket of snow covered everything, in places it had collected in drifts four or five feet deep, making it next to impossible for the sexton or the grave-diggers to carry out their work, but for us it was a ready-made adventure playground, and we counted the sub-zero temperatures as a blessing.

'It was inevitable that at some point we'd start up an every-kid-for-himself snowball fight, and that's exactly what happened, as the pale, watery sunlight dimmed still further, and the thin shadows lengthened. Jase had, as usual, brought along his cheap, plastic transistor radio, tuned as ever to the faint, but essential sounds of Radio Luxembourg. He'd firmly wedged the radio between the branches of an impossibly ancient-seeming oak tree, its tinny music providing the soundtrack to the fight.

'Although not for long, as it turned out.

'John, whose left cheek was already bright red and stinging from a direct hit by one of Nicky's unerringly accurate throws, had packed a hard-as-stone snowball and aimed it at his attacker, who fortunately for him had seen it coming. Nicky had ducked and instead it had struck the radio sending it spinning from its perch to land on the edge of a concrete headstone, where it smashed to pieces on impact.

"Aah, bollocks!" Jase groaned, as he picked up the plastic fragments. "There goes our fuckin' sounds!"

"No big deal, lad," I'd said cheerily. "It's gonna be gettin' dark soon, anyway. I'll lend yer my radio, tomorrow. It's ten times better than that totally bass-less pile of shite." I smiled and gave him a thumbs-up. "Yer can keep hold of it until yer save up for a new one if yer want."

'My words were wasted on Jase, however. He was, and still remains, a close friend of mine, and I hope he always will be, but like all of us, he has his faults. And Jase's worst was a tendency to over-react if he didn't get his own way or if misfortune, however slight, befell him. So I wasn't really surprised when he glowered at me, turned his back, and stormed off without a word, ignoring the pleas and apologies of all of his companions.

'After a spell of eye-rolling and much shaking of heads, Nicky and John decided to traipse after him, but I really couldn't be bothered. I'd seen Jase when he had a king-size cob on after suffering a far lesser fate than losing something he rather bizarrely regarded as being his pride and joy, and I knew he'd likely sulk incessantly for the remainder of the day.

'At the very least.

'I called out to my friends that I'd meet up with them later, and they'd waved in response before jogging after Jase, whilst I stood there alone for a few moments with my gloved hands shoved into the depths of my pockets, the fingertips still tingling from the snow I'd scooped up during the height of the battle.

'After a while, I decided to take a walk around to the opposite side of the cemetery, where there was a second entrance, to take the long way home. The day had started out well, but I really hated it whenever the members of our gang fell out with each other. You can call me hyper-sensitive if you want, but I always felt a sick feeling in the pit of me stomach when dealing with the aftermath of what we always called, with typical Scouse eloquence: "a total blert of a bell-end argument".

'Maybe it was because those hateful occasions tended to remind me far too much of me own ma and pa's seemingly eternal, soul-destroying rows, which more often than not resulted in my mum weeping quietly at the kitchen table or hunched at the sink, the gushing tap water drowning out her heart-broken sobs, whilst my dad stormed into the living room, angrily fishing in the pockets of his cardie for his pipe, which he'd light and puff loudly, a sound eerily reminiscent of a shunting steam train in one of those arl black and white movies, *Brief Encounter* most likely, that both me parents loved to watch on the rare occasions when they could bear to be in the same room.

'I was suddenly struck by an unsettling image of the latter years of their marriage, a more than apt metaphor; Jason's precious transistor radio, breaking irreparably into a thousand tiny pieces against the edge of the marble gravestone, a vision so vivid I had to literally shake it from my mind.

'I took my hands out of my pockets and buried my face in the warmth of the gloves me ma had hand-knitted for me the Christmas just gone, and I thought I caught a faint whiff of the perfume she sometimes wore on the increasingly rare occasions she got dressed up for a night out.

'And I found myself standing before a large stone statue of a grim-faced, dirty-white angel, its wings chipped and dented, perched atop an ornate slab, one hand pointing Heavenwards, whilst the other clutched an open, ice-encrusted Bible.

'The epitaph inscribed on the tomb below it was entirely unreadable, having long since been eroded by time, but I saw that someone had taken the trouble to clear the worst of the snow, and the ground was littered with the frozen, dried up petals of wilted flowers left by relatives who still cared enough to visit their departed loved ones, even if it was only on an occasional basis.

'I shivered, and noticed it really was getting late in the day. It was neither fully dark nor entirely light, but was instead that strange combination of both, and I'd suddenly felt - if you'll pardon the pun - dead tired.

'I went to turn away, to continue on my journey back home, when something caught the corner of my eye and I spun back round and saw what I first took to be another smaller statue standing to one side of the angel, near to where someone, the sexton most likely, had shovelled the snow into a three-foot-high drift. I was still trying to work out how it was I'd failed to notice the effigy before when I saw it move and I realised it was an actual person standing there so silent, so still, it was easy to see why I'd made the mistake of thinking the figure was inanimate.

'There stood before me was a pretty young girl, who looked to be about a year or so older than me. She had a pale white face and long, blonde hair that cascaded like a golden waterfall from beneath her out-of-season summer bonnet, and she was wearing a distinctly old-fashioned white dress, tied at the waist with a bright pink satin bow, and she had flat, black shoes on her feet, and it struck me immediately that this Victorian-looking outfit was far too thin and far too flimsy to afford much protection from the bitterly cold conditions.

'She was staring at me intently from just a few feet away, though not quite close enough so that I could make out the true colour of her eyes, which appeared from the distance to be disconcertingly black, in the fast descending twilight.

'Not quite knowing what else to do, and unnerved by her piercing stare, I instinctively raised my hand in greeting and mumbled awkwardly, "Hello. Are yer all right there, girl?

You must be freezing."

'She didn't reply. She simply went right on standing there, amongst the gravestones, her immobility eerily reminiscent of that damaged, sculpted angel, raising its chipped and broken finger in eternal supplication to a sky darkening by the second, and I felt almost hypnotised, rooted to the spot. as much by the young girl's innocent beauty, as by the slightly strange turn of events.

'For some reason, and without invitation or obvious cause, a kaleidoscope of visions, some dream-like and of indeterminate origin, others as vivid as the Polaroid snapshots contained in my parents' photo album, began spinning through my mind.

A raven flying in slow motion across a vile, poisoned stretch of shoreline.

A white-bearded man in a black top hat peering down the lens of a telescope trained on the clear, star-filled sky.

My mum and dad arguing angrily over a plain white work shirt, the pointed collars of which were visibly stained with traces of kiss-shaped, bright red lipstick.

My dog, Max, lying on a cold metal table at the local vet's, his tongue lolling from the side of his mouth, blood pouring from a dozen wounds, and his tail still wagging pathetically at the sight of me; reaching out a trembling hand to pat his head one last time and reassure him he's gonna be all right.

A lighthouse and a fatally stricken paddle-steamer running aground on calm, nocturnal seas.

'I'm not at all sure how much real time elapsed.

'Perhaps it had stood still entirely.

'For me and the mesmerising girl at least, if not for the rest of the outside world, still blithely going about its daily business, beyond the cemetery walls.

'Who can honestly say?

'What I do know for sure is that it was the sudden cracking of a branch, perhaps burdened to breaking point by the sheer weight of the ice and snow, the sound of it shockingly loud in the pervasive late winter stillness, that served to snap me out of the trance-like state.

'And even then, it took a huge effort of will for me to take even a single step backwards. I wasn't frightened, exactly. I was just cold and succumbing to tiredness and a desire to be home, so I continued backing away, each step a little easier than the last, and I was just beginning to think I'd soon be free of her spellbinding charm when she suddenly spoke, her voice little more than a whisper, though keening and desperate in its intensity:

"I can't find my brother," she said. "He was here just a little while ago." She glanced all about her and then added, "Please tell me, have you seen him?"

'It was my turn then to be rendered speechless. I simply hadn't expected to hear her speak, and strangely, though it seemed the most innocuous of queries, her asking after her brother sent a wave of fear and dread washing over me (and that's exactly what I saw in my mind's eye; *waves,* swelling and sweeping, another image that immediately popped into my mind unbidden).

"I'm suh-suh-sorry, I haven't seen anyone suh-since me mates got off," I stammered holding my hands up in an attempt to ward off any further questions, as if the mere fact of me hearing them would send me screaming madly into the gathering gloom.

"Please," she repeated, "I just want you to try to help me find him. He's always getting lost." She began stumbling towards me, arms outstretched imploringly. "He needs to be safely back home with me. He gets so frightened. Especially after dark."

'I turned and ran then.

'I ran, and I only looked back once when I reached the sanctuary of the wide open cemetery gates.

"I am so, so sorry," I yelled, half-afraid, half-consumed by guilt. "But *I* have to get home, too."

'I was convinced when I peered over my shoulder I'd see a vague, white shape floating towards me like an untethered balloon.

'There was absolutely no sign of her, though.

'She'd gone.

'As if she'd never truly been there.

FIVE

'When I got home later that evening, after tea, and the obligatory hot bath, I lay awake into the early hours, wrestling with the dilemma as to whether I should tell John, Nicky and Jason what had (maybe) happened after they'd left me alone in the graveyard. They were my closest friends, and we'd always sworn we would never keep secrets, good or bad from each other, but on the other hand, I wasn't even sure that anything had actually occurred. Not only that, but by telling them of my "experience", they might well think I was going soft in the head and in dire danger of being dragged to the nearest loony bin by the men in white coats.

'So, understandably, I decided to break our code of honour and said nothing about it either to them, or to anyone else.

'Till now.

SIX

'As things turned out, my friends and I didn't get to return to Flaybrick for the best part of a month after "The Wireless-Destroying Snowball Fight", and my likely entirely hallucinatory "Encounter With The Ghostly Cemetery Girl", as I came to (privately) refer to the two incidents.

'This was due in part to Jase's protracted sulk over his smashed radio (it lasted for a whopping seven days, a personal, never-to-be-beaten record - though it might have dragged on for a great deal longer if his dad, who'd decided a week was more than enough to have to put up with his son's "face like a wet Echo", hadn't promised to buy him a replacement) but mostly it was down to the increasingly terrible weather. It may seem hard to credit in these days of relatively mild winters, but The Big Freeze of '63 stretched from Boxing Day, 1962, to the mid-March of the following year, and whilst we loved the fact that most if not all of the local schools were closed for weeks on end, we grew increasingly frustrated at our parents' refusal to allow us to venture outside, unless it was absolutely necessary.

'It goes without saying, having fun with your mates did not feature highly in their "Entirely Essential Need To Step Out Outdoors Charts". And by the time the snow and ice began to thaw a little in early March, and we'd been granted permission to emerge from our enforced hibernation, I'd all but forgotten about "The Cemetery Girl", real or otherwise.

SIX

'But then, on the date of our gang's adult Christmas Reunion, in the late December of 1980, it all came flooding back with a dizzying intensity.

'Although not straight away.

'It didn't actually hit me until after we'd spent the best part of an hour or so traipsing together around Flaybrick, and we'd decided we'd just about had our fill of childhood nostalgia. Or at least me mates had. The three of them had stopped near to the church spire itself and started stamping their feet and exchanging less-than subtle hints that they were in serious need of copious amounts of alcoholic refreshment; a couple of pints and a brandy or whiskey chaser to ward off the winter chill, and to see in the new year.

'I'd been in agreement, not least because one look at the rapidly darkening skies was enough to convince me that a full-blown blizzard was on its way, and we were half-way along the path heading for the gates when Jase, who must have assumed his new ghetto blaster to be impervious to the vagaries of snowball warfare, pressed "play", and from the tape recorder drifted the doomy vocals of Ian Curtis:

'*No words could explain, no actions determine, just watching the trees and the leaves as they fall...*'

'Upon hearing those achingly poignant lyrics, a distant memory had suddenly begun fighting its way to the surface of my mind, slightly obscured so that I couldn't quite define the shape of it at first, but just the same, it was powerful enough to call out to me, from somewhere across the acres of frozen churchyard, and I knew at that moment that I couldn't leave just yet.

'Not until I'd confronted it. Whatever *IT* was.

'Sorry, lads,' I said. 'Yous go on ahead. There's something I've forgotten to do. I'll catch up with yer in a bit.

'Me mates exchanged glances and Nicky made a twirly motion with his forefinger in the general direction of his temporal lobe, but they didn't question why it was I couldn't leave with them straightaway, and I was relieved about that, because I doubt I could have provided much of an answer.

'I watched them walk away, struck by an immensely powerful sense of déjà vu, and when finally they were out of sight, I felt unutterably lonely, too.

'But I turned and walked back into the centre of the cemetery, just the same. I had no clear idea of where I was headed, and as I walked past the ruined church once more, I found myself wandering along the icy path that led over to the left-hand side of the graveyard. I trod carefully, but still almost lost me balance a couple of times on the slippery surface. I refused to stop, though. I felt compelled by some inner voice to carry on making my way towards a destination I didn't yet know, but would immediately recognise the moment I reached it.

'Two thirds of the way along the path and that's precisely what happened. Something made me halt dead in my tracks. I looked about me, and saw with no real surprise, that I was standing directly alongside the statue of my old friend, the stern-faced, Bible-clutching angel, still gesturing with a single, crumbling finger up towards a leaden sky from which the snow began to fall in fat, goose-feather flakes.

'I knew instantly, this was where my "inner voice" had intended to lead me, although at first I wasn't sure why.

'Puzzled, I reached into my coat pocket for one of the big fat cigars I only ever smoked at Christmas and New Year, and after struggling for a moment to light it in my gloved hands, I took a long drag and blew a single large smoke ring into the bitterly cold air and watched it float for a second amongst the gravestones.

'Something about its drifting, flimsy quality was achingly familiar.

'Then it all came back in a dizzying instant.

'"The Radio-Destroying Snowball Fight." Jase storming off towards the cemetery gates with my friends in his wake. My reluctance to join them, choosing instead to stand alone in this exact same spot. Flaybrick barely illuminated by a strange steely light as dusk closed in. The sculpture of the angel.

'And of course, the sudden appearance before me of that beautiful, pale-faced young girl, from seemingly out of nowhere.

'For the first time in nearly twenty years, I not only remembered her. I found I could recollect everything about her, almost as though she were once more standing before me at the edge of a snowdrift, oblivious to the sub-zero temperatures. I remembered her old-fashioned clothing. The pitifully thin, white cotton dress. The long blonde hair that tumbled from beneath a chin-strapped summer bonnet. The pleading tones of her voice as she begged me to help search for her missing brother, lost somewhere amongst the graves of thousands of dead people. The way she'd seemed as delicate as a paper silhouette. Or as fragile as a dissipating smoke ring.

'The vision was so clear and sudden, I felt a little giddy, and I had to lean against the trunk of a nearby yew tree until I was able to recover, the white flakes swirling in ever-thickening flurries all about me. "How the hell could I have forgotten that I might have seen a real-life ghost?" I wondered out loud, "Okay, it was years ago, like, but even so..."

"Son," said a voice in my ear, "I think you're asking entirely the wrong question."

'I spun around, my mouth open in a silent scream, the Cuban cigar landing on the path in a shower of briefly-flaring sparks.

'I saw there was a small, wrinkle-faced man in a thick donkey jacket and a flat cap standing on the path less than two feet away from me. He had a spade and a pickaxe hefted on his shoulder and was carrying a sack filled with dead flowers, crumpled leaves and soggy memorial cards he'd collected from some of the more well-tended graves in the cemetery. He looked harmless enough, and I assumed he must be employed by the church, but I'd never seen him around before, and there was just something about him that immediately gave me the creeps. I tried not to show it, though.

"Friggin' hell, mate," I spluttered, making a big show of patting me chest. "It's a good job I haven't got a weak heart. Do yer make a habit of sneakin' up on people?"

"Only those I happen to encounter talking out loud to themselves about seeing ghosts in the middle of old graveyards," he rejoined smartly. He laughed long and hard, a wheezy sound that put me in mind of the old bellows me mam regularly used to fan the flames of our coal fire every morning when I was a kid. Then he put down the large brown sack of rubbish and punched me playfully in the arm, though to be honest it had hurt, and it was all I could do not to wince in pain.

"Don't go takin' offence, young shaver, me lad," he said with a grin, and I saw his teeth were in terrible shape, all greyish and somehow slimy looking. "I was only joshin' with you." He took a couple of steps back, and briefly looked me up and down, as though he were appraising me, and then having done so, shook his head dismissively.

"That's the trouble with the world these days," he said. "People always ask the wrong questions. How can anyone ever expect to learn anything half-way useful, that way?"

"Cheers for the philosophy lesson, mister," I said, backing further away from this decidedly strange individual. "Anyone ever told yer, you're wasted as a simple graveyard attendant?"

"All the time. All the time," the man replied, smiling wistfully to himself, as if he hadn't noticed the sarcasm I'd imagined was literally dripping from my off-hand remark. "I like you, son. You've got manners. I'm gonna let you in on a secret. The query you should be making is not how you came to forget, but *why* it is you remembered seeing a spirit of the restless departed, at *this* particular moment.

"It's none of my business," he continued rubbing his unshaven chin as though he was pondering some great moral dilemma, "but maybe you'd like me to provide you with a solution to that most perplexing of mysteries?"

"Well, I don't know," I replied, trying to resist the temptation to massage my throbbing arm. "It won't give me nightmares will it? I've never been a big fan of scary horror stories."

'The man, who I noticed hadn't bothered to introduce himself, snorted, like he'd just been told an especially dirty joke, "Of course it's a little bit scary. The truth often is." He held up his hands, smiled thinly and it was relief not to have to look at those grey-as-dishwater teeth.'

"But come on," the man continued, "You want answers, don't you? Come with me. It'd be easier if I simply showed you. It's only a little up there a-ways."

'He pointed to a row of fairly elaborate headstones, sheltered from the worst of the snow by a thick clump of holly bushes, the dark green prickled leaves and red berries poking here and there through the blanket of white. It was a sight I found for some reason deeply unsettling, and suddenly I really didn't want to go down the path to the foot of those gravestones.'

"Actually, mate, I think I'll leave it for today," I said, trying desperately not to stammer. "I'd best be getting back. I'm meeting me friends for a bevvy." I went to turn away. "Thanks for the offer, though. See yer around sometime."

"Nonsense," the man said grabbing me by the arm. "You *have* to see. You owe it to yourself. It will only take the briefest of moments."

I saw with growing alarm that whilst he was still smiling, and he spoke pleasantly enough, he had cast aside the shovel but retained the pick axe. That item, he'd lowered from his shoulder and held in a manner that wasn't quite threatening, but which sent shivers down me spine, just the same.'

"Please," he said, and now I could feel the strength of his bony fingers, gripping me like the tightening of a vice even through the thickness of my sheepskin coat. "You lead the way. I'll be right behind to tell you when to stop. I promise your earlier curiosity will be more than satisfied."

'So I went with this complete stranger down that path, even though my every instinct was screaming at me not to, and every footstep seemed to drag heavier than the last. I was scared. Terrified even, but a part of me still itched to find out where was all this was leading, and it wasn't as if the man had actually threatened me as such. Or at least I tried desperately to reassure myself.

'We hadn't walked more than a couple of hundred yards before I felt a hand on my shoulder. "There you are," the man said. "Look to your left. There lies the answer to all your questions."

'I did as he said, and I saw there was a fairly large marble headstone, standing upright and enshrouded by the clusters of holly bushes I'd seen earlier, and at first there seemed to be nothing outwardly remarkable about it. Flecks of ice and frozen snow had obscured the names engraved there, and I peered closer to try to make out what, if any, words were still visible.'

"Oh, I forgot to mention," the man said mockingly, "You will have use this implement to enable you to read the words. You won't mind a little work. It will warm you up in no time."

'I spun around to ask him what he meant and my heart nearly leaped into my throat as I saw him reach into the inside pocket of his donkey jacket and whip out a blade-like object that flashed silver as he brandished it, even in the half light.'

"Come now," he chuckled. "It's only a chisel. I carry this with me for all kinds of purposes." He inclined his head towards the gravestone. "I think it will prove more than sufficient to carry out the task in hand, don't you?"

'He laughed to himself once more as he passed me the tool and then stood back to watch me get to work.

Weirdly, I did so without question, though why it didn't once occur to me to use the chisel as a weapon to ward off this total 'ead the ball, and get the hell away from there, is another mystery on a day packed with enigmas. I knelt down to scrape away the tiny glaciers, so firmly frozen in place they seemed to be super-glued to the headstone, and I was struck by an image of Ebenezer Scrooge, compelled to sweep the snow from his own tomb by the terrible spirit of "Christmas Yet To Come".

'It seemed to take forever to clear the ice to the extent that I could read the epitaph, and my arms and legs were soon aching with the effort. By the time I had finished, I was half-covered with snow and it had pretty much grown full dark. So gloomy was it in fact that I could hardly see my hand in front of my face, and then I remembered I had a small pencil-torch attached to the keyring in my pocket, and so I withdrew it and played the tiny beam across the words that had been inscribed there.

And I saw it marked the final resting place of

"Agnes Gladstone aged 12 years, daughter of Elizabeth Gladstone, who with her brother, Thomas Gladstone, aged 10 years was taken from this life at sea near Portpatrick, Scotland, in the wreck of the Orion 18 June 1850.

"Oh my God," I whispered to myself. "That young girl in the white dress. She looked as though she was about twelve years old. And she was looking for her *brother."*

'I raised my voice "They're the same children, aren't they? The ones buried here, I mean. This is their grave, but the girl doesn't know she's dead. That's why she's still looking for her brother. Why she appeared to me and probably others, like me, who are maybe sensitive enough to see ghosts. I'm right aren't I?"

'When the man who'd led me here didn't answer, I got to my feet and turned round to shine the torch in his face, fully expecting him to be grinning that tombstone-toothed grin. "I said, I'm right aren't I, fella..."

'But the man wasn't there any more. He'd disappeared.

'All that remained were a set of footprints, clearly visible in the snow, though even they were rapidly being covered by a fresh batch of densely falling flakes. I saw that the tracks continued for several yards along the path, before suddenly veering off towards a small wood of leafless silver birches.

'In the dark, beyond the reach of my hopelessly weak torch-light beam, I thought I could just make out a darker shadowed, vaguely human shape standing there amongst the winter-naked trees, and for an unhinged, lunatic moment, I wanted to walk closer. To go and check for sure it was the graveyard worker.

'A bird cried out then from the centre of the copse. The high-pitched keening of a gull perhaps, blown in from the Mersey and stranded by the blizzard-like conditions.

'But just for a moment, I could have sworn it sounded eerily akin to the desperate wailing of a pretty young girl, doomed to wander for eternity in search of a long-dead loved one.

'I turned and ran as fast as I could from Flaybrick, slipping and sliding all the way to the cemetery gates, in the frigid chill of T.S. Eliot's *"violet hour"*, as the snow blew sideways in silent, hungry streaks, and this time, I can promise yer truthfully, I didn't *once* look back.'

POSTCRIPT:

There is of course, as is the case with so many of the supposedly true stories contained in this book, absolutely no way of verifying the truth of Bill's highly detailed account of the events that he claims took place at Flaybrick Cemetery (or Flaybrick Memorial Gardens, as it's known these days), during the snowy New Year's Eve of 1980. Or indeed, the infamous winter of 1963.

It may be of some interest to readers however, that having personally visited Flaybrick on several occasions, I can confirm the existence of a grave commemorating the tragic passing of both Agnes Gladstone, and her brother Thomas aged twelve and ten respectively, and who did indeed lose their lives during the sinking of the *Orion,* near Portpatrick, Scotland, on June 18th, 1850.

I did some research regarding the disaster, and although information was hard to come by, I came across an article published in *The Liverpool Journal,* (June 22nd 1850), the salient points of which are as follows:

'The passenger ship, the *Orion,* an iron paddle steamer, that was renowned for *"her great repute and admirable accommodation,"* had set sail from Liverpool bound for Glasgow, on a gloriously sunny, June afternoon. There were a total of 200 souls on board, including 160 passengers, several of whom were children heading home to Scotland for the summer holidays. The journey was largely uneventful, and by one in the morning of the following day, the vessel was sailing in near idyllic conditions, near to the lighthouse at Portpatrick. The ship was just 150 yards offshore, and all seemed well, when suddenly, and quite without warning, she struck a submerged rock, tearing a jagged hole in the hull. Lifeboats were launched, but in the panic that ensued, many of the passengers never had the opportunity to clamber aboard them.

In less than a quarter of an hour all but the single funnel high above the decks of *''The Orion'* had slipped beneath the waves along with 41 of her passengers and crew, including, sadly, the children of Mr and Mrs Lawrence Gladstone, who, as we know, were brought home for burial in Flaybrick's grand, if perhaps ghost-haunted, surroundings.'

CHAPTER TWENTY-ONE:
'THE HOLLOW ECHO OF MIRTHLESS LAUGHTER'
Weird Tales From The Heart of Liverpool 8

'There's always something new to look at in Liverpool 8. You can bet your life you'll see something or someone out of the ordinary. To an artist or a writer the place is a gift. Can't think of anything to paint? Just glance out of the window. A blank page taunting you from the typewriter? Take a walk down the street. If you can't find anything to spark you off there, you're probably in the wrong business...'

(John Cornelius – *Liverpool 8* – Liverpool University Press 1982)

I count myself as being extremely fortunate to live as I do amidst the leafy green, well-preserved, Georgian splendour of Liverpool 8, and as such I find I couldn't agree more with the estimable Mr Cornelius' poignant words, filled to overflowing as they are with an immutable truth that I can readily attest to.

The entire district, perhaps the only area in the City of Liverpool, that's far more often referred to by its simple, straightforward postal code number, than by two of its actual place names; Toxteth and Dingle, has a distinctly bohemian quality, enhanced by its multicultural ascetic and its deserved reputation for long being associated with some of Liverpool's finest poets, authors, and musicians.

There's an indefinable air of surreality about the locale, too. It's hard to put your finger on why that should be exactly, but maybe it's the way the cobble-stoned streets and back jiggers lined with century-old houses, watering holes and public buildings are integrated with thoroughly modern apartment blocks, identikit council houses and overgrown, litter-strewn stretches of empty wasteland: that curious juxtaposition of the historical and the contemporary.

Maybe it's the way in which the towering sandstone edifice of the Anglican Cathedral looms above the highest rooftops, and the way its huge, black arched windows are eerily reminiscent of a baleful ogre's sleepy, but ever watchful eyes, that seem to follow you whichever way you turn.

Maybe it's the way in which sometimes, at the end of a perfect, cloudless day when the sun dips low over the fiery horizon at the top of Huskisson Street, the view is of a long and lonely road, seemingly stretching to the very edge of the known world.

Maybe it's the sight of the gas lanterns, illuminated by electric light these days, but adding to the Georgian ambience, jutting out from the walls of the back roads and alleyways like candelabras held aloft by black-armoured knights, the rows of empty, derelict houses on either side of Princes Road, sad symbols of a regeneration project that ran out of money long before the refurbishments could get under-way, the wandering packs of "ghost-hunting" tourists led by a tall, top-hatted, cadaverous looking individual dressed all in black.

Maybe.

But if you pressed me, I'd tell you that the air of off-kilter, not-quite-rightness has more to do with the often bizarre, borderline supernatural incidents that seem to occur in the district. Here are just three of my own personal experiences…

A DAYMARE ON HOPE STREET

A year or so ago, I was walking along the appropriately-named Hope Street, the famous road upon which this city's two iconic cathedrals stand as virtual bookends, on a glorious late-August afternoon as the limits of vision rippled in a shimmering heat haze.

I was lost deep in thought about something or other, most likely the dawn of the new footie season and all that entailed; my head in the proverbial, if non-existent clouds, when I heard the silvery tinkling of a bell from just up the road ahead of me. It was a pleasant, almost dreamy sound that seemed to swim gently on the sweet summer air, but it shook me from my reverie just the same, and I saw a little blonde-haired girl, her hair bunched in ribboned pigtails, propelling herself towards me on a tiny, squeaky-wheeled scooter.

She was dressed in a shiny, bright pink fairy outfit, complete with a set of diaphanous wings that fluttered butterfly-like in the gentle breeze, and as she drew nearer I could hear she was singing some sort of "Lah-Lah-Lah" nonsense song, its lyrics indecipherable, but still it spoke eloquently of a child's joy of freedom, when school's out for summer and the morning's chores are long since done.

I smiled to myself as the girl approached to within a few feet of me, and it crossed my mind to say something, or at least give her a cheerful thumbs up as she drew closer.

But then my jaw dropped open like a loft door on loose hinges when I saw her for what she truly was; a dwarfish, late middle-aged woman, dressed in a child's outfit, her multi-wrinkled face plastered in garish make-up that looked like greasepaint, skipping along on her scooter, still singing that sing-song gibberish, in an impossibly high voice. She winked at me as she drew up alongside, grinning madly, revealing a set of obviously false teeth, the upper palate of which suddenly dropped down like a knackered elevator ("Looks like she skimped on the arl Polygrip, this morning!" I thought to myself) but it didn't affect her insanely merry singing for an instant. She pushed her teeth back into place with a practised flick of her tongue, a somehow obscene gesture that raised goose-flesh on my bare arms and sent a cold chill juddering up and down my spine, like the sun had disappeared for an instant behind the blackest of clouds.

It occurred to me then that though I'd never seen the woman before in my life, still she seemed oddly familiar, though it was only when she'd virtually passed me by that I realised what it was that had sparked this vague sense of recognition.

The child's fairy costume, a well-preserved remnant of long-gone summers.

The way her eyes glinted in the sunlight, filled with a darkly feral form of intelligence, and the waxy, pale white facial make-up. The blood red lipstick and the hideous leer that was far closer to a grimace or a lunatic scream. The frantic pedalling of the scooter, a hopelessly futile attempt to ward off the ravages of time's relentless passing.

It all came to me, then.

The woman was eerily reminiscent of Bette Davies, the genius Hollywood film star, and one of me ma's all-time favourite actresses, as she'd appeared alongside Joan Crawford in the 1962 movie; *Whatever Happened To Baby Jane?* And what I'd at first taken to be her singing a lyric-less "Lah-Lah-Lah" song, was in fact, the haunting, for all the wrong reasons, vaudeville melody of *I'm Writing A Letter To Daddy.****

I shivered once more, and watched in horrid fascination as the (probably) harmless, if overly eccentric old woman rode off along Hope Street, bound for who knew where, attracting the bemused glances and astonished double takes of passers-by, and I wondered at the abnormalities inherent in all of us, but are more pronounced in certain individuals, and what terrible quirks of fate

FOOTNOTE
*** *Whatever Happened To Baby Jane?* is a black and white, semi-horror classic, directed by Robert Aldrich, back in 1962, and features wonderful, truly memorable performances by Bette Davies, as the titular "Baby" Jane Hudson, and Joan Crawford, as her wheel-chair bound sister, Blanche. They are a pair of ageing divas and life-long spinsters who find themselves growing old together in a decaying Hollywood mansion, amidst an atmosphere fraught with tension and long-held enmity.

In the movie, "Baby Jane", was a child film star, who once wowed audiences in the manner of the likes of Shirley Temple, but who soon found herself being outshone in the talent stakes by the far more gifted Blanche, much to Jane's ill-concealed resentment. The insanely jealous sister, who may or may not have been responsible for the car accident that resulted in Blanche's paralysis, and life spent in a wheel-chair, mentally and physically tortures her helpless victim, most notably by serving her rats on a silver platter for breakfast (and then chiding her afterwards for refusing to eat her "din-dins") and binding her hand and foot and dumping her in the closet.

As you do.

As a noir-ish example of a hellish descent into madness the film has seldom been bettered.

*** *I'm Writing A Letter To Daddy* ... In one excruciating, wince-inducing scene from *Whatever Happened To Baby Jane?* Bette Davies "sings" this cloyingly sentimental vaudeville song in full "Baby Jane" costume and make-up, whilst performing for a pianist/composer (played by Victor Buono) who comes to the house to hear her audition.

The film critic Roger Ebert was spot on when he described the actress as resembling a *'shrill gargoyle with white makeup pancaked all over her face...'*

Truly the stuff of nightmares.

drive them to such outlandish extremes.

And all the while, drifting on the Merseyside air, came the distant strains of a sickly-sentimental song, sung by a late middle-aged 'child' riding to beat the passing of the ages.

AS THE DAY CLOSES DOWN

ONE

I've always found the twilight of an autumn evening to be an especially evocative time, replete as it is, it seems to me, with a sense not just of aching nostalgia, the bitter-sweet kind that stings the heart like a needle-point dipped in rosehip syrup, but of an acute, hard-to-shake feeling that you're standing on the very edge of things, both the good and the bad.

The momentous and the seemingly trivial. The heart-stirring and the bone-chilling.

Here's a highly disturbing example of the latter.

Late one rain-swept Monday afternoon in mid-October 2013, I was home alone in our flat on Sandon Street, sat at the kitchen table nursing a beer and feeling thoroughly sorry for myself, not least because my fiancée was spending a long weekend with some old friends of hers at a cabin in The Lakes, and I was missing her like hell.

I'm normally perfectly content to spend time on my own, writing, listening to music, watching a film, and drowning any sense of enforced solitude in the numbing consolation of the arl three-for-a-tenner red wine offer courtesy of the ASDA store over on Smithdown.

On this occasion, however, and maybe it had been due entirely to the weather and the time of year, I'd craved human companionship, and I'd made a seemingly endless succession of phone calls to friends, most of whom, admittedly, I hadn't seen in a while, and every single one of the calls had gone straight through to voicemail. I sent a flurry of text messages too, but they may as well have been posted into the infinite electronic ether for all the response they elicited.

My self-pitying mood hadn't been improved much when I'd happened to catch sight of my reflection in the large mirror above the mantelpiece in the living room, and I saw staring back at me a semi-bearded man I hardly recognised. I remembered I hadn't bothered to shave for at least three days, and as I'd sprouted whiskers that made me look like I'd glued a couple of roughly-hewn strips of a second hand "Welcome" mat to my face, I decided it was high time I reacquainted my grizzled cheeks with some shaving foam and a Bic razor.

I headed for the bathroom, filled the sink with warm water, and had just begun dragging the blade across my face with a sound like sandpaper being scratched by a werewolf with a set of especially cracked and jagged talons, when I heard a strange, insistent tapping noise coming from somewhere outside, and curious, I drew aside the laced curtains to see what was causing it.

At first, I couldn't make out the source. From the second floor window I could see that Sandon

Street appeared deserted, and given the fact that the rain, that had arrived with the dawn, was still descending in cold, clear sheets, perhaps that wasn't surprising. It was a highly evocative scene, like something from a Raymond Chandler private eye novel. It struck me that all that was missing was a flashing pink and blue neon sign with several of its letters missing, advertising beer or vacancies in seedy hotel rooms, and hissing clouds of billowing steam rising from underground vents.

Despite the awful weather though, I had expected that at the very least, I'd catch a glimpse of the ubiquitous gangs of builders and decorators, or excited kids splashing in the deep puddles on their way home from school, but there was not a soul about, and for a few moments there, I was almost overwhelmed by a terrible sense of acute loneliness, and I was astonished to feel tears start to prickle at the corners of my eyes.

But then the tapping I'd heard a few moments earlier suddenly grew louder and I saw first a white cane, waving from side to side like an insect's antenna, and then a tall, skinny man, dressed in a thick black overcoat and a similarly-coloured hat and a pair of dark glasses, come into view. He was very obviously blind, wielding the stick as he trod carefully along the rain-slicked pavement, and I felt a surge of sympathy for him and idly wondered where he might be headed. I am often accused, quite rightly, of being a confirmed people-watcher. It's the writer's curse, I suppose, and I felt compelled to stare after this complete stranger until he'd disappeared out of sight round the corner of Sandon onto Upper Parly Street.

When he was gone, the street was once again, empty of people.

With a sigh, I turned away, and let the curtain gently fall back into place.

TWO

I'd finished shaving, and was drying my newly-smooth features with a towel, when the tap-tap-tapping noise returned.

Faintly at first, but growing louder by the second, and this time bringing with it with a childhood memory: lines from Poe's *The Raven,* a verse I hadn't read in years:

'While I nodded, nearly napping, suddenly there came a tapping,
As of someone gently rapping, rapping at my chamber door…'

I shivered, but still I felt drawn back to the window to peer outside, and the second I did so, the tapping stopped and I immediately saw the reason why.

The blind man was standing directly below our flat, his gloved hands splayed between the spikes of the black-painted metal fence, just to the right of the gate of the pebble-stoned garden, and I noticed how deathly-pale his face was and how his cheekbones were so sunken they protruded from his almost translucent skin like the blades of blunt-edged swords.

I saw too how the glasses he wore were so opaque, the closed window blinds of the ground floor flat were clearly reflected in the lenses, and I thought at first that the blind man must be waiting for someone to emerge from that apartment, though if that were the case, he'd picked a God-awful day to stand around without the slightest hint of shelter.

He must be soaked right through, I thought to myself, watching the rain-water pour from the brim of his Trilby and the sleeves of his overcoat. But he didn't seem to notice. He just went right on standing there, silent and sentinel-like, and it crossed my mind that I should perhaps open the window and ask him if he'd like me to press the buzzer to open the front door so he could come in and wait in the relative comfort of the communal hallway for his friend. For some reason however, I felt reluctant to do so, and it wasn't solely down to his undeniably grim appearance. The logical part of me suggested I was just being stupid, not to say more than a little heartless, the man was clearly blind, skinny as a rake, and no threat to anyone, but still ...

Five minutes or more must have passed in the midst of that unrelenting deluge. Still the stranger stood immobile. His blank-faced expression never-changing. His blind gaze fixed intensely on the downstairs flat.

"For Christ's sake, lad, get a grip!" I whispered to myself, the rational, compassionate side of me finally winning out. "He's gonna catch his death out there."

I'd released the catch of the window lock and had half-slid the wooden frame up by its hooked brass handles admitting cold needles of slanting rain in the process, when two things happened in quick succession.

The blind man's head suddenly jerked up in my direction, alerted no doubt by the groaning squeak of the window being raised.

I paused for a second, and then suddenly, he swept off his black glasses with a flourish, revealing a pair of pupil-less, milk-white eyes that stared unblinkingly. The dead, marble gaze of a sculptured figure, a fallen God of ancient Rome or Greece.

He grinned, then "The Blind Man" leered and raised one leather-gloved finger, and pointed it straight at me. "I *see* you!'' he said in a voice that gurgled like thick, sulphurous mud.

"I seeeee you!"

He did, too.

I was in no doubt about that.

He might well be blind, but he saw me, regardless, and I knew, somehow, that he wished me harm. A bitter metallic taste filled my mouth and I tried to scream but all that emerged was a kind of hitching whistle and I slammed down the window with such force that the glass panes rattled and threatened to crack.

And then I turned and raced for the sanctuary of the living room, with its views of the opposite side of Sandon Street; the backyard and the brightly-lit residents' car park. I saw briefly that there were

SANDON STREET, LIVERPOOL
(Above): Our flat on Sandon Street, Liverpool 8.
The (hopefully) temporary haunt of a mysterious, black clothed, "Blind Man".

Photo Credit: Lee Walker

people, *normal* everyday people, coming home from work, sheltering under brollies, anxious to be home and out of the rain. A perfectly ordinary evening in the south end of the city.

But still I quickly pulled the thick shades down all the way.

Just in case.

THREE

I sat on the sofa with all the lights on, and the TV blaring, gulping down wine as fast as I could pour it for the remainder of that evening. I didn't dare return to the bathroom until I'd fortified myself with copious amounts of Dutch courage, and when finally I had to go because my bladder felt like it was about to burst, I sneaked into the darkened room on my hands and knees and peered over the lip of the window-sill to check 'The Blind Man' wasn't still standing there.

He wasn't, of course. The rain had stopped and full darkness had long since fallen, but the street was no longer deserted. I saw several people out walking their dogs and a group of loudly giggling girls on their way to the bus stop to catch the bus into town but there wasn't the slightest trace of my phantom-like tormentor, whoever or *whatever* he was, and I've never set eyes on him since, and it's my fervent hope that I never do.

Of course, in the days following this bizarre incident I frequently asked myself just what the hell had actually taken place on that dark, wet autumn evening, and leaving aside the supernatural angle, the most rational explanation I was able to come up with was that 'The Blind Man' had been some kind of prankster; a man dressed in a two-week-early Halloween costume with his face all made-up, and who had gone to quite ridiculous lengths and in atrocious weather conditions, to play an admittedly terrifying practical joke.

As time has slipped by however, I think it may be more likely that I simply dreamed the whole thing. Certainly, the experience had an eerie, nightmarish quality about it, and given my melancholic state combined with the amount of alcohol I'd drunk that night, it would hardly be surprising if I'd been especially prone to vivid hallucinations.

Just the same, though.

There *are* occasions, usually on rain-swept late afternoons when I'm alone in the flat, and the streets outside seem deserted, I find myself peering fearfully through a gap in the curtains, checking for the presence of shadows, dark and unsettling, and gathered in all the wrong places.

And I strain my ears, my heart filled with dread, for a noise like the tapping of a 'Blind Man's' cane....

Tap-tap-tap-tap-tap.....

THE COSMIC JOKER'S POIGNANT LAMENT

Have you ever felt yourself being haunted by the capricious spirit of coincidence?

Do you sometimes find yourself casting your sun-narrowed eyes skywards, your lips pinched in a bloodless line as you imagine a group of white-robed entities, beings that shimmer in the golden light beyond the ceiling of fleecy clouds: a group of tricksy angels, or chuckling gods gathered around a giant chessboard, with hapless humans substituting for helpless pawns?

Or perhaps, given the frequently hard-hearted, if not downright maliciousness of the series of weird coincidences you've experienced, you've gazed mistrustfully at the ground beneath your feet, half-expecting it to suddenly crack open to reveal some hellish nether region, populated by hideously grinning imps and wildly cackling demons?

Or do you simply shrug your shoulders, whistle unconcernedly and dismiss the synchronous events as being purely explainable in terms of rational science and good old-fashioned logic. The kind which insists that such things are nothing more than mere random events that only seemingly defy the odds. Whatever your view, it's undeniable that coincidence takes many forms. Some are as trivial as that out-of-the-blue phone call from someone you haven't heard from for ages, when just a few moments earlier, a memory of them had suddenly popped into your head for no particular reason, or a song that comes on the radio the very second you turn to your loved one to say; "Do you remember that tune from that boss, magical summer, babe?"

This sort of incident might inspire raised eyebrows and funny, puzzled little half-smiles (and a titter or two from "The Cosmic Joker").

Other, more extreme examples though, aren't remotely amusing. Unless you're cursed with an especially cruel and sardonic sense of humour, of course.

Consider the following example that took place during the early spring of 2013.

ONE

On the afternoon of March 20th, I'd walked down to Toxteth Library, to return some books and then grab a seat in one of the cubicles on the second floor to work on various writing projects. It was a chilly, white-skied day, with a keening wind blowing along the length of Upper Parliament Street, and I'd honestly been in two minds as to whether I should bother making the trip, short as it is, until the very last minute. In the end, I'd decided I'd be far more able to get stuck into some writing if I got out of the flat for a few hours, and so I wrapped up warm and ventured outside to brave the elements.

Roughly four hours later, I was left in a state of stunned disbelief by the actions of the ever-cackling Cosmic Joker, prancing down the "Aisles of Mirthless Insanity", once more, like a demented circus clown.

TWO

Before we get to the "eerie coincidence" part though, it strikes me as being extremely relevant to make mention of my enduring admiration for the works of one of my all-time favourite horror authors. I assure you, it's extremely relevant.

I first read (although perhaps *devoured* would be a better word), James Herbert's first book, *The*

Rats, when I was about ten years old.

As I've stated many times, I am lucky enough as a child to have to have extremely liberal-minded parents, not least when it comes to their eldest son's obsession with what they always referred to as *'that scary-as-hell, horror-type stuff'.* The net result of this was that whilst most children my age had their heads buried in the latest issue of *Look-In,* the ever popular Ladybird books or the latest *Shoot* annual, I had my head buried in the works of Poe, Bradbury, Wyndham and the likes, kindly purchased for me by my family and friends as birthday presents or at Christmas time. I loved all of these writers, along with countless others, although people, elders and contemporaries alike, used to tease me that they were all essentially near-identical variations on a theme, or put more simply; *"I don't know why yer bother reading that crap. They're all the bleedin' same!"*

The Rats, though, was the exception to the rule. And not even the most cynical of sceptics, young or old, could disagree with that.

I had to actually buy a copy of the book with my own pocket money, and that was unusual for a start.

Well, to be honest, I had to get me dad to go into the old W.H. Smith store on Church Street, to pay for it at the counter, because the blue-rinsed woman with the set of horn-rimmed glasses perched on the end of her nose sat at the check-out desk refused to serve me on the grounds that the *"depraved publication was plainly unsuitable for such an impressionable young man."*

To be fair, the reasons for the woman's reluctance to allow me to buy the book were perhaps understandable given that all the literary reviews I'd read concerning Mr Herbert's luridly-covered paperback had treated the work with all the contempt later afforded to the so-called "video nasties" of the 1980s. I remember the exact words used by *The Observer*'s book reviewer,* back in the mid-1970s; a quite appropriately, blood-soaked hatchet job, that only made me want to purchase the book all the more, of course;

'By page 20 the rats are slurping up the sleeping baby after the brave bow-wow has fought to the death to protect its charge. Enough to make a rodent retch, undeniably and enough to make any human pitch the book aside.' (Incidentally, for the more cynical amongst you, I can still recall the whole review verbatim because I cut it out and kept in my horror scrapbook, which I still have, tucked away in the attic at my parents' house. So there!)

Of course, despite, or more likely *because* of this review, it only served to boost the sales of the book, so much so in fact, that it went on to sell millions, and when finally, I got to read it for myself, it's fair to say, I was blown away. Having grown up on a diet of largely Gothic or small-town American-based horror stories, I was immediately struck, even at my tender age, by the modern-day, working class setting of *The Rats,* and more specifically, the East End docks. Having grown up within a five minute walk of the docklands of Merseyside, I could more than relate to this type of bleak, but dangerously exciting (to a kid, any way) locale.

I re-read the book on countless occasions, and eagerly awaited the publication of the author's subsequent forays into horror, and I was seldom, if ever, disappointed, be they novels dealing with science-gone-wrong, *Quatermass*-style epics such as *The Fog,* and *The Dark,* the supernatural weirdness of *The Survivor,* or the heart-warming saga of *Fluke,* 'the dog with the soul of a man.'

It's fair to say, that James Herbert was a huge influence on me, and he inspired me to try my own hand at writing, something for which I'll be eternally grateful, and it was a long-held ambition of mine that I would one day get to meet the author and tell him so to his face.

It seemed that in the spring of 2013, I would finally get my first opportunity to do so. The "Echo" reported that on April 25th, James Herbert would be the guest of honour at a Liverpool Literary Festival, held, appropriately enough, at the entrance to the enigmatic Williamson Tunnels, hidden from plain view within the sandstone bedrock beneath the Edge Hill area of the city. Needless to say, I purchased tickets for the event on-line, seconds after reading the article. And having marked the date on the calendar, I began counting down the days to the Festival.

THREE

To return to the events of March 20th, 2013, an unremarkable, if unseasonably chilly day, which I spent hunkered over a laptop, typing as fast as my primitive two-finger technique would allow, whilst the wind howled in the eaves and sent pellets of sleet rattling at the glass windowpanes. I was dreading the walk home, and I put it off for as long as I possibly could, but the library shuts down early these days, another lamentable result of this government's obsession with cutbacks, and so by 5:45pm, I reluctantly packed away my stuff and made my way to the exits.

I was walking with my head down, shoulders hunched, instinctively preparing to brave the elements, and I barely glanced at the shelving promoting the library's new books and recommended reads near to the entrance. Whilst normally I would have paused for a good few moments to check out the brand new titles I was more interested in simply getting home as fast as possible. But just as I approached the anti-theft alarms, something made me look back in the direction of the array of books, their perfect plastic covers glinting in the gloomy grey light, and my gaze was immediately drawn to an author's name printed in an all-too familiar font: JAMES HERBERT.

It easily dominated the collection of assembled paperbacks like a clarion call, and although I couldn't at first see the book's title, I nevertheless immediately felt drawn towards it. In truth, I hadn't read anything produced by one of my literary heroes since the relatively underwhelming (from a personal point of view) *Others,* back in 1999, but it was hugely reassuring just to know he was still busy churning out works of superior horror fiction against the tide of highly derivative drivel that makes up a large proportion of the genre.

I saw it was called *Ash,* which was the name, if I remembered rightly, of the sceptical paranormal investigator from *Haunted,* one of James' previous novels, and I felt a surge of excitement, the kind I hadn't felt since those long-gone days of stepping inside holiday camp souvenir shops and stumbling upon the works of authors such as Eric Maple and Peter Underwood, and I knew I simply had to take this book out on loan there and then.

There was however, one small problem, and even as I began reaching for the glossy library lending card, I knew full well it wouldn't be there. Well, why the hell would it be? I had developed a quite terrible habit of losing the damn things. I'd gone through five in the space of single year, and not surprisingly, after the most recent misplacement, Yvey had insisted that she keep the card buried in the depths of her purse for safekeeping, and I was sure I'd seen it there when my fiancée had been rummaging for change for the bus into town, earlier that morning. Gulping with disappointment, I nevertheless sunk my fingers into the depths of my coat pockets in a futile search for that which couldn't possibly be there.

And yet it somehow was.

Wedged between a ten pound note and a week-old Mersey-Rail train ticket, there was the red and white library card, resplendent with the crest of the Liver Bird in its centre, and I had absolutely no idea how it had gotten there.

I must still have been smiling and shaking my head wonderingly when I was stood at the counter checking out Mr Herbert's new book, because the librarian, a middle-aged woman with her hair cut in an iron grey bob, peered at me from over the top of her glasses and favoured me with a strange look. She then sniffed and wrinkled her nose like she suspected me of having been sneakily smoking a joint or two in the library toilets, and I realised she reminded me a lot of the similarly disdainful-looking cashier who had refused to serve me with *The Rats,* at the old W.H. Smith store, all those years earlier. I threw my hand over my mouth to stifle a giggle, a gesture that probably only served to confirm her belief that she was dealing with a fully-fledged cannabis fiend. It was plain too that the scowling librarian considered my literary taste to be on a level with those who purchased the magazines featuring scantily-clad ladies, lining the top shelves of certain newsagents, judging from the way she stamped the book like she was trying to splat a particularly loathsome insect before sliding the volume towards me as though she couldn't wait to get it out of her sight.

I did laugh out loud, then. I couldn't help it. I could no more have kept from braying like a donkey with a red hot poker up its arse than the fusty arl librarian could have concealed her prejudice for all things horror or remotely supernatural, and I went right on laughing all the way home, and never mind the freezing weather conditions.

The grin only froze on my face five minutes after I'd arrived home, whacked the heating on full, made myself a steaming mug of coffee and curled up on the sofa to read the first chapter of *Ash.*

I'd no sooner opened the cover though when, much to my annoyance, my mobile phone ringtone announced that I'd received an e-mail. "Screw that, I'll look at it later," I said out loud to the empty flat. "It's probably nuthin' important." Even as I said the words though, I found myself automatically reaching for the damn thing in that depressing, almost zombie-like way we all seem to do these days.

I saw it was a message from Mike Playfair, a good friend of mine, who's as hard as nails but has a heart of the purest gold. The email only contained two paragraphs of text, but I had to read and re-read the words three or four times before they truly sunk in.

And even then....God, even *then*.

"RIP, James Herbert," the message said. *"A true icon of my childhood passed today. Although I never got the chance to meet him, he spoke to me across the ages. From the distant days of childhood, through the hormone-troubled era of my teenage years, to the supposed serenity of full adulthood.*

"I hope when I get to Heaven, or whatever passes for an afterlife, you're still busy spinning deliciously dark tales in the esteemed company of Stoker and Shelley. Dickens and Poe. M.R. James and H.P Lovecraft. Those, and the countless others who ignited a spark in the imaginations of us kids and who, like Peter Pan and The Lost Boys, never truly grew up."

I continued to stare disbelievingly at my phone, whilst dropping the book to the floor.

It landed with its back cover facing upwards, and the picture of a craggy-faced East End rocker, clad in black leather, and with long, still mostly jet-black hair, stared back at me, on today, of all days.

The tears, when at last they came, were for the loss, not only of James Herbert, immeasurably sad as that was, but for the regretful impermanence of things, all that we hold dear.

All of it passes, yet remains forever preserved within the precious well of memory.

And so it should.

Lord knows, it *always* should.

LEE WALKER
Toxteth, Liverpool 8
20th December 2012 - 4th August, 2014

THE WORLD'S WEIRDEST PUBLISHING COMPANY
ANIMALS & MEN
ISSUES 16-20
THE JOURNAL OF THE CENTRE FOR FORTEAN ZOOLOGY
NEW HORIZONS
Edited by Jon Downes
BIG CATS
LOOSE IN BRITAIN
PREDATOR DEATHMATCH
WITH ILLUSTRATIONS BY ANTHONY WALLIS
Jonathan Downes and Richard Freeman
FOREWORD BY Dr. KARL SHUKER
CARL PORTMAN
THE COLLECTED POEMS
Dr Karl P.N. Shuker
STRANGELYSTRANGE
an anthology of writings by
ANDY ROBERTS

HOW TO START A PUBLISHING EMPIRE

Unlike most mainstream publishers, we have a non-commercial remit, and our mission statement claims that "we publish books because they deserve to be published, not because we think that we can make money out of them". Our motto is the Latin Tag *Pro bona causa facimus* (we do it for good reason), a slogan taken from a children's book *The Case of the Silver Egg* by the late Desmond Skirrow.

WIKIPEDIA: "The first book published was in 1988. *Take this Brother may it Serve you Well* was a guide to Beatles bootlegs by Jonathan Downes. It sold quite well, but was hampered by very poor production values, being photocopied, and held together by a plastic clip binder. In 1988 A5 clip binders were hard to get hold of, so the publishers took A4 binders and cut them in half with a hacksaw. It now reaches surprisingly high prices second hand.

The production quality improved slightly over the years, and after 1999 all the books produced were ringbound with laminated colour covers. In 2004, however, they signed an agreement with Lightning Source, and all books are now produced perfect bound, with full colour covers."

Until 2010 all our books, the majority of which are/were on the subject of mystery animals and allied disciplines, were published by `CFZ Press`, the publishing arm of the Centre for Fortean Zoology (CFZ), and we urged our readers and followers to draw a discreet veil over the books that we published that were completely off topic to the CFZ.

However, in 2010 we decided that enough was enough and launched a second imprint, `Fortean Words` which aims to cover a wide range of non animal-related esoteric subjects. Other imprints will be launched as and when we feel like it, however the basic ethos of the company remains the same: Our job is to publish books and magazines that we feel are worth publishing, whether or not they are going to sell. Money is, after all - as my dear old Mama once told me - a rather vulgar subject, and she would be rolling in her grave if she thought that her eldest son was somehow in `trade`.

Luckily, so far our tastes have turned out not to be that rarified after all, and we have sold far more books than anyone ever thought that we would, so there is a moral in there somewhere...

Jon Downes,
Woolsery, North Devon
July 2010

Other Books in Print

Centre for Fortean Zoology Yearbook 2010 by Downes, Jonathan
Predator Deathmatch by Molloy, Nick
Star Steeds and other Dreams by Shuker, Karl
CHINA: A Yellow Peril? by Muirhead, Richard
Mystery Animals of the British Isles: The Western Isles by Vaudrey, Glen
Giant Snakes - Unravelling the coils of mystery by Newton, Michael
Mystery Animals of the British Isles: Kent by Arnold, Neil
Centre for Fortean Zoology Yearbook 2009 by Downes, Jonathan
CFZ EXPEDITION REPORT: Russia 2008 by Richard Freeman *et al*, Shuker, Karl (fwd)
Dinosaurs and other Prehistoric Animals on Stamps - A Worldwide catalogue
by Shuker, Karl P. N
Dr Shuker's Casebook by Shuker, Karl P.N
The Island of Paradise - chupacabra UFO crash retrievals,
and accelerated evolution on the island of Puerto Rico by Downes, Jonathan
The Mystery Animals of the British Isles: Northumberland and Tyneside by Hallowell, Michael J
Centre for Fortean Zoology Yearbook 1997 by Downes, Jonathan (Ed)
Centre for Fortean Zoology Yearbook 2002 by Downes, Jonathan (Ed)
Centre for Fortean Zoology Yearbook 2000/1 by Downes, Jonathan (Ed)
Centre for Fortean Zoology Yearbook 1998 by Downes, Jonathan (Ed)
Centre for Fortean Zoology Yearbook 2003 by Downes, Jonathan (Ed)
In the wake of Bernard Heuvelmans by Woodley, Michael A
CFZ EXPEDITION REPORT: Guyana 2007 by Richard Freeman *et al*, Shuker, Karl (fwd)
Centre for Fortean Zoology Yearbook 1999 by Downes, Jonathan (Ed)
Big Cats in Britain Yearbook 2008 by Fraser, Mark (Ed)
Centre for Fortean Zoology Yearbook 1996 by Downes, Jonathan (Ed)
THE CALL OF THE WILD - Animals & Men issues 11-15
Collected Editions Vol. 3 by Downes, Jonathan (ed)
Ethna's Journal by Downes, C N
Centre for Fortean Zoology Yearbook 2008 by Downes, J (Ed)
DARK DORSET -Calendar Custome by Newland, Robert J
Extraordinary Animals Revisited by Shuker, Karl
MAN-MONKEY - In Search of the British Bigfoot by Redfern, Nick
Dark Dorset Tales of Mystery, Wonder and Terror by Newland, Robert J and Mark North
Big Cats Loose in Britain by Matthews, Marcus
MONSTER! - The A-Z of Zooform Phenomena by Arnold, Neil
The Centre for Fortean Zoology 2004 Yearbook by Downes, Jonathan (Ed)
The Centre for Fortean Zoology 2007 Yearbook by Downes, Jonathan (Ed)
CAT FLAPS! Northern Mystery Cats by Roberts, Andy
Big Cats in Britain Yearbook 2007 by Fraser, Mark (Ed)
BIG BIRD! - Modern sightings of Flying Monsters by Gerhard, Ken
THE NUMBER OF THE BEAST - Animals & Men issues 6-10
Collected Editions Vol. 1 by Downes, Jonathan (Ed)
IN THE BEGINNING - Animals & Men issues 1-5 Collected Editions Vol. 1 by Downes, Jonathan
STRENGTH THROUGH KOI - They saved Hitler's Koi and other stories

by Downes, Jonathan
The Smaller Mystery Carnivores of the Westcountry by Downes, Jonathan
CFZ EXPEDITION REPORT: Gambia 2006 by Richard Freeman *et al*, Shuker, Karl (fwd)
The Owlman and Others by Jonathan Downes
The Blackdown Mystery by Downes, Jonathan
Big Cats in Britain Yearbook 2006 by Fraser, Mark (Ed)
Fragrant Harbours - Distant Rivers by Downes, John T
Only Fools and Goatsuckers by Downes, Jonathan
Monster of the Mere by Jonathan Downes
Dragons:More than a Myth by Freeman, Richard Alan
Granfer's Bible Stories by Downes, John Tweddell
Monster Hunter by Downes, Jonathan

CFZ Classics is a new venture for us. There are many seminal works that are either unavailable today, or not available with the production values which we would like to see. So, following the old adage that if you want to get something done do it yourself, this is exactly what we have done.

Desiderius Erasmus Roterodamus (b. October 18th 1466, d. July 2nd 1536) said: "When I have a little money, I buy books; and if I have any left, I buy food and clothes," and we are much the same. Only, we are in the lucky position of being able to share our books with the wider world. CFZ Classics is a conduit through which we cannot just re-issue titles which we feel still have much to offer the cryptozoological and Fortean research communities of the 21st Century, but we are adding footnotes, supplementary essays, and other material where we deem it appropriate.

Headhunters of The Amazon by Fritz W Up de Graff (1902)

Fortean Words

The Centre for Fortean Zoology has for several years led the field in Fortean publishing. CFZ Press is the only publishing company specialising in books on monsters and mystery animals. CFZ Press has published more books on this subject than any other company in history and has attracted such well known authors as Andy Roberts, Nick Redfern, Michael Newton, Dr Karl Shuker, Neil Arnold, Dr Darren Naish, Jon Downes, Ken Gerhard and Richard Freeman.

Now CFZ Press are launching a new imprint. Fortean Words is a new line of books dealing with Fortean subjects other than cryptozoology, which is - after all - the subject the CFZ are best known for. Fortean Words is being launched with a spectacular multi-volume series called *Haunted Skies* which covers British UFO sightings between 1940 and 2010. Former policeman John Hanson and his long-suffering partner Dawn Holloway have compiled a peerless library of sighting reports, many that have not been made public before.

Other books include a look at the Berwyn Mountains UFO case by renowned Fortean Andy Roberts and a series of forthcoming books by transatlantic researcher Nick Redfern. CFZ Press are dedicated to maintaining the fine quality of their works with Fortean Words. New authors tackling new subjects will always be encouraged, and we hope that our books will continue to be as ground-breaking and popular as ever.

Haunted Skies Volume One 1940-1959 by John Hanson and Dawn Holloway
Haunted Skies Volume Two 1960-1965 by John Hanson and Dawn Holloway
Haunted Skies Volume Three 1965-1967 by John Hanson and Dawn Holloway
Haunted Skies Volume Four 1968-1971 by John Hanson and Dawn Holloway
Haunted Skies Volume Five 1972-1974 by John Hanson and Dawn Holloway
Haunted Skies Volume Six 1975-1977 by John Hanson and Dawn Holloway
Grave Concerns by Kai Roberts

Police and the Paranormal by Andy Owens
Dead of Night by Lee Walker
Space Girl Dead on Spaghetti Junction - an anthology by Nick Redfern
I Fort the Lore - an anthology by Paul Screeton
UFO Down - the Berwyn Mountains UFO Crash by Andy Roberts
The Grail by Ronan Coghlan
UFO Warminster - Cradle of Contract by Kevin Goodman
Quest for the Hexham Heads by Paul Screeton

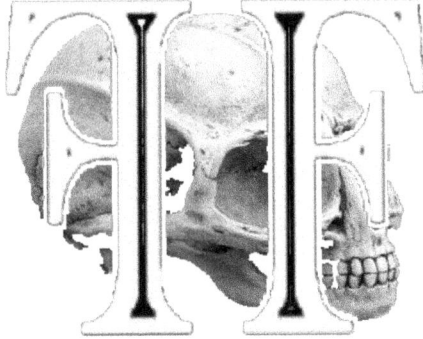

Fortean Fiction

J ust before Christmas 2011, we launched our third imprint, this time dedicated to - let's see if you guessed it from the title - fictional books with a Fortean or cryptozoological theme. We have published a few fictional books in the past, but now think that because of our rising reputation as publishers of quality Forteana, that a dedicated fiction imprint was the order of the day.

We launched with four titles:

Green Unpleasant Land by Richard Freeman
Left Behind by Harriet Wadham
Dark Ness by Tabitca Cope
Snap! By Steven Bredice
Death on Dartmoor by Di Francis
Dark Wear by Tabitca Cope
Hyakymonogatari Book 1 by Richard Freeman

www.ingramcontent.com/pod-product-compliance
Lightning Source LLC
Chambersburg PA
CBHW060003100426
42740CB00010B/1380